Operations Management

OPERATIONS MANAGEMENT
Policy, practice and performance improvement

Steve Brown, Kate Blackmon, Paul Cousins and Harvey Maylor

OXFORD   AUCKLAND   BOSTON   JOHANNESBURG   MELBOURNE   NEW DELHI

Butterworth-Heinemann
Linacre House, Jordan Hill, Oxford OX2 8DP
225 Wildwood Avenue, Woburn, MA 01801-2041
A division of Reed Educational and Professional Publishing Ltd

A member of the Reed Elsevier plc group

First published 2001

British Library Cataloguing in Publication Data
Operations management: policy, practice and performance
  improvement
  1. Production management
  I. Brown, Steve
  658.5

ISBN 0 7506 4995 X

For information on all Butterworth-Heinemann
publications visit our website at www.bh.com

Composition by Genesis Typesetting, Rochester, Kent
Printed and bound in Italy

FOR EVERY TITLE THAT WE PUBLISH, BUTTERWORTH-HEINEMANN
WILL PAY FOR BTCV TO PLANT AND CARE FOR A TREE.

Contents

Acknowledgements   vii

PART ONE   OVERVIEW

1   Operations management: content, history and current
    issues   3
2   Operations strategy: the strategic role of operations   38

PART TWO   POLICY

3   Innovation: developing new products and services   67
4   Operations processes: process choice and layout;
    developing new products and services   99
5   Managing supply   130

PART THREE   PRACTICE

6   Managing capacity: managing transforming resources   161
7   Managing throughput: improving material, customer and
    information flows   202
8   Project management: content, history and current issues   238

PART FOUR   PERFORMANCE IMPROVEMENT

9   Managing quality   265
10   Performance measurement and improvement   306
11   World-class operations   337
S1   Analysing manufacturing operations: quantitative methods   371
S2   Analysing service operations: service delivery, queuing,
     and shift scheduling   405

Index   429

Acknowledgements

Butterworth-Heinemann would like to thank the following international team of reviewers for their advice and help with developing this text:

Geoff Buxey, Deakin University, Australia
Professor Brian Carlisle, Glasgow Caledonian University
Jan Frick, Stavanger College, Norway
Frank Gertsen, University of Aalborg, Denmark
Adrian Mackay, Duncan Alexander and Wilmshurst Consultants, UK
Prof. Dr. Arnoud De Meyer, INSEAD, Singapore.
Birger Rapp, Linkoping Institute of Technology, Sweden
Dr F N de Silva, University of Aberdeen
Keith Smith, University of Northumbria at Newcastle
Frank Southall, Dudley College of Technology
Mike Terziovski, University of Melbourne
Dr Wenbin Wang, University of Salford

PART ONE
OVERVIEW

CHAPTER 1

Operations management: content, history and current issues

INTRODUCTION

Who comes to mind when you think of successful organizations? Perhaps Amazon.com for their level of customer service, Nokia or Sony for their innovative electronics, Toyota for their reliable automobiles, Dell for their ability to customize PCs to individual requirements, Andersen Consulting for their brand image, Sky TV for the variety of television programmes available, or McDonald's for sheer ubiquity, come to mind. These companies – or others you may have thought of – have come to dominate their market segments through offering the best goods or services, or have provided you with product or service that you think is excellent.

High-recognition firms like these are heavily marketed and constantly brought to our attention. Marketing hype alone isn't enough, however, to create excellence – organizations have to deliver on their promises or face disillusioned (and, increasingly, litigious) customers. In each case, the organization cannot be excellent without excellent operations. This is true for all organizations – those that help and protect us, such as hospitals, fire, police, ambulance and coastguard emergency services; those who provide general public services, such as schools, public utilities, transportation, and universities; and those who provide goods and services to customers and other organizations. Operations are at the forefront of service delivery in each case.

Successful operations management contributes substantially to organizational success or failure: operations is where, to use a metaphor, 'the rubber hits the road'. Imagine what would happen if Sega took too long to develop their next computer game – their old games would be made obsolete by new games from competitors and wouldn't sell, and the company would quickly cease to exist. Similarly, the pizzeria that takes twice as long to deliver your pizza as expected, or the accountant who makes mistakes with your taxes, will soon go out of business. Operations is vitally important because it links what the business does with the needs and desires of the organization's customers or clients, as shown in Figure 1.1.

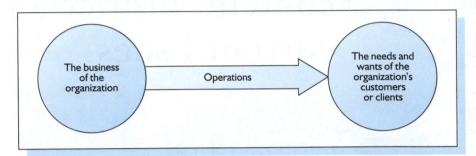

Figure 1.1 Linking the business of the organization with customers via operations.

The role of operations has become increasingly important in recent times, because the needs and wants of customers and clients have increased. This was described in a book called *Funky Business* (Ridderstrale and Nordstrom, 2000, p. 157):

> Let us tell you what all customers want. Any customer, in any industry, in any market wants stuff that is both cheaper and better, and they want it yesterday.

We'd probably all agree with that statement, but we tend to take it for granted how products are made better, cheaper and more quickly than before. The point is that all of these are achieved by operations capabilities, and that's why operations are so vitally important for businesses today.

 # Aims and objectives

Welcome to the world of operations management. Most of us probably think of operations management as having little to do with our lives and work, but each of us comes constantly into contact with aspects of operations management every day.

The purpose of this chapter is to explore the nature of operations and operations management today, and to:

- Define operations, operations management, and operations managers
- Explore the history and context today of operations management
- Introduce you to the key concepts and ideas that this book will cover.

After reading this chapter, you will be able to:

- Describe the role of operations in different sorts of organizations
- Show how operations management is relevant to organizations, managers and individuals
- Explain how operations managers bring together different contributions to satisfy customers.

The next section begins with a formal definition of operations, and then introduces some basic concepts for describing and analysing operations. Next, the roles and responsibilities of operations managers are described more fully. Succeeding sections consider the limits to operations management, its usefulness, and how operations management can help people manage complex organizations in highly competitive environments. The chapter closes with a brief overview of the important themes to be covered in this book, and presents a model for bringing all of these themes together.

WHAT IS OPERATIONS MANAGEMENT?

Every organization has an operations function, whether it is explicitly called operations or not. A traditional view of operations is that it is:

> Those activities concerned with the acquisition of raw materials, their conversion into finished product, and the supply of that finished product to the customer (Galloway, 1998, p. 2).

Another way to think about operations is that *operations is what the company does*. To identify the role of operations with an individual organization, ask the question, 'what do you do?' Amazon.com might answer that question with 'we sell books and other goods on-line'. Isn't selling different from operations? In this case no, because here selling involves the operations of transferring the ownership of products from the retailer to the buyer. Amazon.com's front-line sales process works so well that the company's customers come back over and over again. A hospital treats patients, and so we might ask: 'isn't that medicine?' It is, but if you look beyond the doctors and nurses who treat patients, a whole organization exists to supports their work – facilities management, staffing, catering and so on. All of this comes under the responsibility of operations management. So it's important to bear in mind that operations take place *throughout* an organization. It's often impossible to speak of operations taking place in just one specific area. Operations will take place in different ways in the entire organization and, as you'll see throughout the book, we will provide ways for you to understand the nature of the operations taking place in each case.

Within organizations, operations management describes the functional area responsible for managing the operations that produce the organization's goods and services for internal or external customers or clients. *Operations management* gives us a way of thinking about operations that helps us design, manage and improve the organization's operations in an orderly fashion. *Operations managers* are the people who design, manage and improve how organizations get work done.

A key aspect of operations management is that it focuses on *processes*. A definition of processes is, as Hewlett Packard describes, 'the way we work'. Due to the significant role that processes play in operations, operations managers frequently use tools and techniques developed for analysing processes, and we shall see a range of these in the book.

Operations management also describes the academic study of the different operations practices used by organizations. In this context, operations management draws lessons from organizational success and failures and makes those lessons available to students and managers. Studying operations management gives us the tools to analyse the operations of an individual organization or groups of organizations and to prepare them to compete in the future.

The study of operations management is highly relevant to whatever work you do or plan to do. Most managers are involved in some aspect of operations every day, but many never realize it. Familiarity with operations enables managers to manage their responsibility better, whether they are directly responsible for the organization's goods and service outputs or not.

Similarly, studying operations management is useful for all management students, because you can apply operations concepts to everyday aspects of your study and work activities. Also, because operations management is at the core of what any organization does, it has important connections with other functions including marketing, human resource management and finance

Policies, practices and performance: the four 'P's of operations management

Operations managers manage processes via the four 'P's of operations: Policies, Practices, Processes and Performance. Figure 1.2 defines each 'P' and shows the relationship between all of them. The four key elements and their relationships are described below.

Policies are the stated aims, objectives and strategies for the organization including operations. Policies are based on the desired state of affairs that an organization wants to achieve. The organization's mission statement has an important part in articulating the organization's policy. Strategy is concerned with *how* the organization will get there. Policies define the *practices* – the systems, procedures and technological capabilities – that need to be in place within the organization, and between the organization and its suppliers and customers. Policies cannot be realized without the support of appropriate practices. For example, the American department store Nordstrom's is famous for its policy of providing a high level of customer

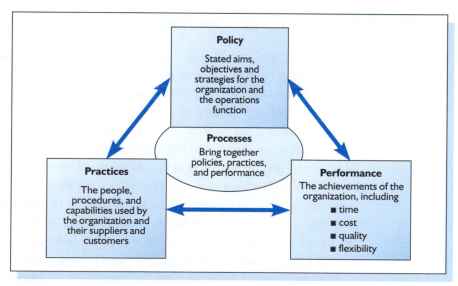

Figure 1.2 The four 'P's of operations management.

service at all times. This might require the store to employ additional staff to make sure that someone is always available to serve customers.

Policies also need to be aligned with *performance*. Performance describes how the organization does in terms of time, cost, quality and flexibility. Where there are gaps between policy and the desired level of performance, operations managers need to make improvements in order to close these gaps.

Performance is strongly linked to practices. For example, by adopting modern Japanese management practices such as just-in-time (described in Chapter 7), many organizations have improved their operations performance – including reducing space, lowering inventory levels and achieving faster throughput times – which, in turn, has lead to better financial results such as improved cash flows. Modern organizations continuously change their practices to improve their performance because, as we shall see in Chapters 2 and 11, the business environment is more competitive than ever before.

Both policies and practices determine what performance measures will be important. Key Performance Indicators (KPIs) such as customer service time, cost or quality provide feedback to the operations function and to the whole business as to how well operations is performing.

World-class, high-performing organizations explicitly link the four 'P's', making their effects clear. Only a few organizations can claim to be in this class – less than 2 per cent of all organizations (Voss *et al.*, 1997). On the other hand, most organizations only have weak links between the 'P's', as we will discuss further in Chapter 2.

Models of operations

Earlier, we mentioned how operations management includes transforming various inputs into outputs. These inputs and outputs will include tangible and intangible elements. In a factory, processing materials and stages of production are clearly evident; however, the transformation process from inputs into finished 'products' is not so obvious in many service operations. Even so, service organizations (including banks, hospitals, social services and universities) all transform inputs into outputs. Here we shall differentiate between the task that operations carry out in terms of the transformation process, and the task of an operations manager in bringing together all the necessary elements to enable the process to take place.

Operations are concerned with those activities that enable an organization to transform a range of inputs (materials, energy, customers' requirements, information, skills and other resources) into

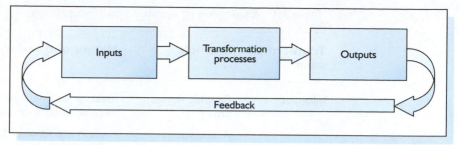

Figure 1.3 Basic transformation model.

outputs. These are different for manufacturing and for service organizations. A basic inputs/outputs model is shown in Figure 1.3.

As you can see from Figure 1.3, feedback plays an important role for operations managers. Such feedback enables managers to make improvements and to enhance the quality of goods and services provided for customers and clients. The feedback mechanism is an important one for operations managers, and can come from both internal and external sources. Internal sources will include testing, evaluating and continuously improving processes and products; external sources will include others involved in supplying to end customers as well as feedback from customers themselves. This basic model can be used in manufacturing and service environments, and in both private and public sectors.

The service transformation

Service operations generally transform information, people or animals, physical items or ownership. Examples of each of these transformations are given in Table 1.1.

The manufacturing transformation

For a manufacturing firm, the transformation process is more obvious. Materials are processed, changing their form. The materials may take a number of forms and determine the nature of the transformation process. Typically, an operation may be a raw material producer, a user of raw materials, combining or changing them into parts, which are then assembled by another operation into assemblies or finished goods. Examples of each of these are given in Table 1.2.

Table 1.1   Examples of service transformations

Transformed input	Example	Nature of transformation
Information	Graphic design firm	Ideas or outlines are transformed into detailed designs or layouts
	Accountant	Data in the form of financial records is ordered into the required form, calculations made and recommendations provided
People	Restaurants	A hungry person is transformed into someone who is fed
	Airline	The location of the person is transformed
Physical items	Car service	A car in need of work being performed on it has this carried out
	Logistics firm	Moves goods from one place to another
Ownership	B2B or wholesale operation	The ownership of goods is transferred from one party to another
	Car hire	The use of the vehicle is temporarily transferred from the hire company to the hirer

Table 1.2   Examples of manufacturing transformations

Transformed input	Example	Nature of transformation
Extracted products	Steel producer	Iron ore is the extracted product, and through a series of processes is converted into steel
Raw material	Silicon chip producer	Wafers of silicon are processed into chips
	Cloth printer	Rolls of cloth from the mills are transformed by the addition of dyes through the printing process
Parts	Washing machine assembly	All the parts from different suppliers (mechanical, electrical and electronic) are assembled into final products
	Drink bottling	The bottle, cap, label and liquid contents are all 'parts' of the finished product and are combined in the bottling process

The one-way flow in the transformation model is only one of the flows that occur around operations. Other flows include:

- Revenue – flowing from customers back down the supply chain to suppliers
- Information – passing both ways from product/service providers to customers and in feedback from customers to the providers.

Although this model is often used and can provide some basic insights into the nature of operations, we argue that operations management in the modern era is more complex than this suggests. This is because, as we shall see throughout this book, operations management is no longer limited to a narrow, organization-specific activity. One further problem of the transformation model is that it focuses on the ongoing nature of day-to-day operations. The reality is that operations usually take place in an environment in which little stays constant for long.

Having defined the function that operations perform in terms of the transformation process, it is now necessary to consider the role that operations managers play. They have a day-to-day management role, which consists of controlling the processes for which they have responsibility. This is simply maintaining the system in a state of acceptability. The real area where truly excellent operations managers make a difference is in their ability to design and continuously improve their processes. For this the transformation model is inappropriate, and so we propose the dynamic convergent model. Its main feature is that it represents the 'change' aspects of the operations managers' task, which take an increasing proportion of their time.

A dynamic convergent model of the role of operations managers

Now that we have looked at manufacturing and service operations, we can define in more detail the role of operations managers. Operations managers are responsible for managing the process of convergence that delivers goods and services to end customers or clients. Specifically, the operations manager brings together resources, knowledge and market opportunities. Resources are the people, physical resources and finances of the organization and its suppliers. The role of suppliers has become increasingly important recently, and the role of supply is therefore discussed in depth in Chapter 5. Knowledge comprises the experience of people within the organizations, their systems and processes, including the information technology infrastructure. Market opportunities are the customer needs, which are then translated into a set of deliverables by operations.

Operations managers perform three integrative key tasks in the convergence process (see Figure 1.4):

1 The *design* of the organization's products, the outputs of goods and services, and the processes by which they are created and delivered
2 The *management* of the day-to-day aspects of operations, making sure that work is performed, dealing with problems that arise, and liaising with other parties in order to make sure that operational objectives are achieved
3 The ongoing *improvement* of the operations process, through analysing existing ways of working, and developing and implementing improvements to particular performance aspects, in order to prevent problems from occurring or recurring.

The improvement aspect has been the centre of recent attention, particularly in globally competitive industries such as the automotive and electronics sectors. The best performing organizations today continuously improve their processes.

The stakeholders can potentially make any one of the contributions listed to the process.

The role of the operations manager is to select and integrate the contributions in order to design or develop the process. For example, during the expansion of their call-centre operations a leading

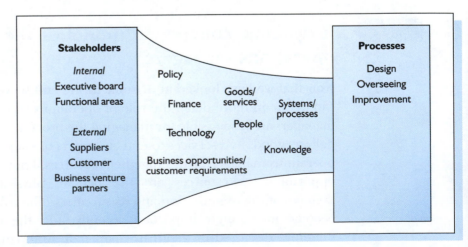

Figure 1.4 The convergent model of the role of operations managers.

telephone insurance brokerage needed to bring together a number of key stakeholders including:

- Suppliers of the technology to run their IT and telephone equipment
- The insurance companies whose products were being offered
- Financiers who would pay for the expansion
- Staff who would run the new expanded systems
- Customers, who through *focus groups* showed the firm their preferences for doing business over the telephone.

The operations manager united these requirements into a coherent system so that it would work not only on the first day of operation, but for several years to come.

A typology of operations

If you were asked to describe an operation with which you have come into contact, how would you do this? You might describe the operation in terms of your experience with it, or its size or reputation. A number of basic elements are helpful in describing operations. The first is whether it is a manufacturing or a service operation or, as will be seen in the following section, if there are elements of each in the organization.

Another aspect is the *nature* of the process taking place. Two characteristics describe this – volume and variety. High volume products such as cars, consumer electronic devices and fast food are typical examples of this. In order to achieve what economists describe as 'economies of scale', these are usually produced in low variety. The number of variations of a car may be significant when considering the different body styles, engine sizes and types, colours and options available, but the reality is that the variety is limited by the choices available, and so the variety is perceived rather than actual.

Similarly, low volume products and services are generally available in a higher variety.

The relationship between volume and variety is shown in Figure 1.5, and we shall explore this in more depth in Chapter 4.

As Figure 1.5 shows, the general position of operations is along the diagonal, where the higher the volume the lower the variety and *vice versa*.

Supermarkets offer a high variety of products and yet sell in high volumes. Doesn't this rather change the rule? Not in this case, although

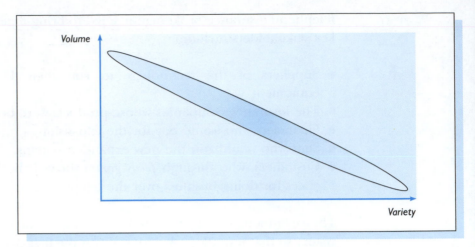

Figure 1.5 The relationship between volume and variety.

there may well be examples where both are offered. The point here is that the *process* is the same for all customers – it is standardized. Everyone is treated in the same way – it is not tailored for the individual. Therefore, from a process perspective, the variety is low, and the general finding still stands.

There are two other dimensions that provide insight into the nature of the operations environment in which the organization operates. The first is the degree of competition in the market for the organization's goods or services. Generally, high volume organizations operate in highly competitive markets, with many offerings competing for market share. The extreme is the mass-market for cars and computers, where *global hypercompetition* exists. This is not the case for all firms, as many operate in niche markets, often serving local customers. The second dimension is that of *position in the supply chain* or *supply network*. Regardless of whether an operation is manufacturing or service-based, it is part of a network or chain of activities. These may be serving end-users directly, or providing a contribution towards that directly or indirectly through their products.

In summary, the typology of operations is shown in Figure 1.6.

This classification is useful as it will tell us something about the general characteristics of the operations that we describe in this way. These are summarized in Table 1.3.

Considering the first element of this typology, manufacturing and service operations are different, yet both are important to the success of an organization. The following two sections consider the operations issues associated with each of these environments. As we have

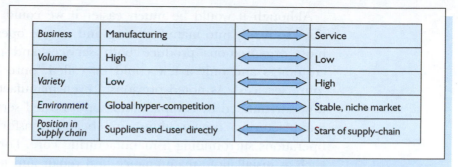

Figure 1.6 A typology of operations.

mentioned, operations management isn't just about managing manufacturing operations; service operations are equally important. We usually describe organizations that transform physical materials into tangible products (goods) as manufacturing. In contrast, organizations that *influence* materials, people or information without physically transforming them may be termed as service organizations.

Table 1.3   The general characteristics of operations

Task	*Manufacturing*: the creation of physical products	*Service*: all work not concerned with the creation of physical products
Volume : variety	*High volume – low variety*: high levels of capital investment, systemization, routinized work and flow through transformation system, resulting in low unit costs	*Low volume – high variety*: usually flexible technology, people and systems performing high value-adding work resulting in high unit costs
Environment	*Hyper-competition*: organizations are pursuing any possible avenue to create competitive advantage, or simply survive	*Niche*: organizations optimize existing systems to maximize return on their investment
Position in supply chain	*Supply end customer/user*: driven by needs of consumers, must integrate supply networks to deliver these needs	*Removed from final customer/ user*: driven by needs of intermediaries in the process, work as part of supply networks

Although it would be much easier if we could separate organizations so neatly into manufacturing and service operations, in real life most organizations produce both services and products for their customers and only a few could be called 'pure manufacturing' or 'pure services'. As noted previously, even manufactured products are now surrounded by complex and sophisticated service packages, and manufacturing organizations are being transformed into service operations surrounding a manufacturing core. For example, services such as installation, maintenance and repair and technical advice are usually provided with household appliances such as refrigerators and washing machines. Software applications such as word-processing or spreadsheet programs generally come on physical media such as floppy disks or CD-ROMs, accompanied by technical documentation manuals.

It is important to bear in mind two major differences between services and manufacturing, which are:

1 *Tangibility* – whether the output can be physically touched; services are usually intangible, whilst products are usually concrete
2 *Customer contact with the operation* – whether the customer has a low or high level of contact with the operation that produced the output.

These two factors – intangibility and customer contact – lead to other differences between manufacturing and service operations, as shown in the following list:

- *Storability* – whether the output can be physically stored
- *Transportability* – whether the output can be physically moved (rather than the means of producing the output)
- *Transferability* – ownership of products is transferred when they are sold, but ownership of services is not usually transferred
- *Simultaneity* of production and consumption – whether the output can be produced prior to customer receipt
- *Quality* – whether the output is judged on solely the output itself or on the means by which it was produced.

Although some aspects of the production of goods and services will differ, the operations function itself is becoming increasingly similar for goods and services. Recognizing this, Chase (1983) suggested that operations could be ranged along a continuum from pure manufacturing to pure services, with quasi-manufacturing in the middle, as shown in Figure 1.7.

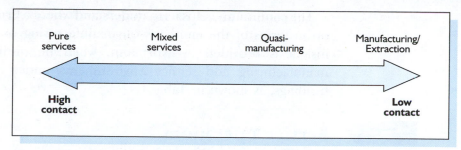

Figure 1.7 The service–manufacturing continuum

Table 1.4   Typical differences between manufacturing and services (Normann, 1991)

	Manufacturing	Service
Tangibility	Product is generally concrete	Service is intangible
Ownership	Transferred when sold	Not generally transferred
Resale	Can be resold	Cannot generally be resold
Demonstrability	Can be demonstrated	Does not exist before purchase
Storability	Can be stored by providers and customers	Cannot be stored
Simultaneity	Production precedes consumption	Generally coincide
Location	Production/selling/ consumption locally differentiable	Spatially united
Transportability	Can be transported	Generally not (but producers might be)
Production	Seller alone produces	Buyer/client takes part
Contact	Indirect contact possible between client and provider	Direct contact usually necessary
Internationalization	Can be exported	Service usually cannot (but delivery system often can)
Quality	Can be inspected *in situ*	Cannot be checked before being supplied

The continuum helps us to understand where a firm's operations line up in terms of the emphasis on manufacturing or services. Another insight is provided by Normann, when he distinguishes between manufacturing and service environments under a number of key headings, as shown in Table 1.4.

Service operations

Services experts haven't yet agreed on a definition of service operations. Some definitions of services use manufacturing operations as the norm – for example, Schroeder (1999, p. 75) gives the traditional perspective on services that they are 'manufacturing with "a few odd characteristics"', while Russell and Taylor (2000, p. 91) suggest that 'services and manufacturing companies have similar inputs but different processes and outputs'. Other definitions focus on the human aspects of services, such as Normann's (1991) definition of services as 'acts and interactions that are social contacts', and Zeithaml and Bitner's (2000, p. 2) description of services as 'deeds, processes, and performances'.

In this book we will define *service operations* as:

transformation processes in which there is a high degree of interaction between the customer and the organization, and in which the output may be primarily or partly intangible.

The importance of service operations

Service operations are an essential focus of modern operations management. Service organizations range from one-person small businesses to large, multinational corporations, including organizations in the following sectors:

- Business services – consulting, finance, banking
- Trade services – the distribution, installation and upkeep of physical objects, including retailing, maintenance, and repair services
- Infrastructure services – communications, transportation
- Social/personal services – restaurants, health care
- Public services – government and non-profit organizations, including education, health care, government.

In many developed countries, more people work in services than in previously dominant sectors such as agriculture and manufacturing.

Over time, employment in most developed economies has shifted, first from agriculture to manufacturing, and more recently from manufacturing to services. The proportion of people working in services in these economies has increased from about 1 in 20 in the 1880s to three in four today. This is partly due to the increase in the efficiency of other sectors. Agricultural, extractive and manufacturing industries have increased their productivity so much through the application of modern techniques that it is possible for relatively few people to produce large outputs. Consequently, in many highly developed nations the service sector accounts for most of the gross national product (GNP). As a result, the service sector contributes to economic well-being and productivity at the national and individual levels.

Even within organizations primarily engaged in agriculture, extraction or manufacturing there is a large 'hidden' service sector. A large part of the value created by manufacturing companies is created by service activities rather than manufacturing activities, including both internal services required to support the organization's ongoing activities and external services provided in association with products.

Responsibilities of operations managers

The operations manager often has to manage a range of responsibilities and these can be profoundly important to the competitive performance of an organization. Operations responsibilities include the management of human resources, various assets and costs. We shall look at each of these in turn.

Human resources

A motivated, trained and skilled workforce has to be in place for any manufacturing or service operations if an organization is to compete successfully. Human resources can be closely linked with the firm's *core competences*. This term was devised by Hamel and Prahalad (1994), who describe core competences as 'a bundle of skills and technologies rather than a single discrete skill or technology'. Although it is incorrect to limit core competences to human resources only, it is clear that human resource management must form at least part of the organization's core competence because 'skills' come from human capabilities.

Human resources are so important in the modern business arena because new ideas for innovation in all forms – including new products, new processes, continuous improvement initiatives and so on – come from harnessing this human creativity. Creative ideas do not come from machines or 'technology'.

There is already compelling evidence about the benefits of strategic human resource management, seeing people as part of the solution rather than as the problem for an organization. For example, in his research on companies in the USA, Pfeffer (1998) notes the strong correlation between pro-active people management practices and the subsequent performance of firms in a variety of sectors. It is strange, then, that human resources will often be the first target of cost reductions for firms. Such a 'quick-fix' approach will often rob an organization of one of its most important assets – human commitment and expertise. This is one of the tensions that operations managers have to face if they are excluded from corporate decisions: a corporate decision – for example, to downsize the workforce – can have a dramatic impact on operations capability, and often result in operations *incapability*.

Assets

These include fixed assets such as machinery and plant used in the transformation process, as well as liquid assets such as inventory. Both fixed and current assets are vitally important, and will either support the firm or cripple its capabilities in the market. As we shall see in Chapter 4, process technology is a key part of the firm's innovation capability. It enables the firm to provide a range of models and variations that modern business markets demand. Innovation is not restricted to the launch of new products (vitally important as this is); it also includes acquiring and managing new process technology. However, investment in new process or product technology is, by itself, not enough; an important part of the overall innovation process is in ensuring that there is sufficient and suitable *human* capacity – know-how and learning – in place to accompany and complement the investment in new process technology. This is a key interface between technology management and operations management.

Costs

Managing costs is a key responsibility for operations managers. Whether operations managers are involved in price sensitive or premium price markets, it will fall to operations managers to create margins between costs and price. In his book *Competitive Strategy*, Porter (1980) suggested that organizations needed, ideally, to compete *either* on low cost *or* by providing differentiated products in order to be profitable and to avoid being 'stuck in the middle'. However, this is now seen as overly simplistic, because an organization in the current era of market requirements may have to do both simultaneously. Even so, costs will always be an important responsibility for operations managers. In high volume production, where margins are usually very slim (for example, cars and PCs), costs and prices must be carefully controlled. The ability to do so does not necessarily mean a reduction in workforce numbers and other drastic measures. Instead, accumulated know-how and experience, appropriate use of technology and better process quality through continuous improvement will enable the organization to reduce costs.

A HISTORY OF OPERATIONS MANAGEMENT

Before we consider the topics that will be covered in this book, it is useful to understand how operations and the study of operations management have developed, and where they are today. Operations management has made many contributions to the development of modern management theory, beginning with scientific management and industrial engineering early in the twentieth century, through to the influence of Japanese management at the end of the century.

Over time, the set of operations practices used in organizations has become more complex. Figure 1.8 shows the three main types of operations practices that have evolved over time.

Operations, broadly defined, may be argued to have existed as long ago as the Pyramids and other great works projects, but the academic

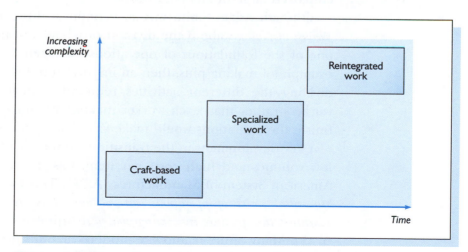

Figure 1.8 The evolution of operations practices.

study of operations management only took off after World War II. However, many influential managers and scholars who shaped the modern practice of management have been associated with either the practice of operations or the study of operations management.

On the other hand, as products or services and the organizations and processes required to produce them have changed, the way in which organizations and operations are organized has become larger and more complex. Most of the goods and services that we consume, as well as the goods and services used by the organizations that produce them, are routinely mass-produced.

Over time, operations have evolved from craft production, to mass production, to the systems in use today. In this section we will provide an overview of how the study of operations management has evolved, although over a much shorter time period.

Craft production to batch manufacturing

The earliest way of organizing the production of goods and services was *craft work*. This is where individuals (or small firms) develop and deliver goods and services. Most industries originated as craft-based work, and many are alive today – particularly when customers demand individual products or services, such as bespoke tailoring.

However, the Industrial Revolution signalled the change in methods of working and the replacement or extension of human and animal power with machines. Activities that had formerly taken place in homes or workshops were transferred to factories, which often employed large numbers of people.

Although Adam Smith was an economist, his observations in *The Wealth of Nations* about the division of labour are now recognized as one of the foundations of operations management. Smith used the example of making pins, then an important industry, to show that by dividing the different activities required to make a pin between workers rather than each worker making an entire pin from start to finish, the operations would make significantly more pins.

A key development in the transition from craft production, with its low volumes and high costs per item, was the development of the American System of Manufactures (ASM). This can be defined as *the sequential series of operations carried out on successive special purpose machines that produce interchangeable parts* (quoted in Hounshell, 1984, p. 15). Many of the features of modern manufacturing are associated with ASM, including an organized factory structure, specialized machines, precision manufacture, interchangeable parts, co-ordinated work sequences and materials flows, and quality techniques.

Key historical figures in developing the ASM were Eli Whitney, Samuel Colt (firearms), Oliver Evans, Isaac Singer (sewing machines) and Cyrus McCormick (agricultural machinery). The main promoter of the idea of interchangeable parts was Eli Whitney, probably better known as the inventor of the cotton gin, who contracted to build a large volume of small arms with uniform parts made by machines rather than by hand, although he never really achieved either. On the other hand, the other entrepreneurs listed above made considerable progress during the last half of the 1800s towards developing truly interchangeable parts, even though the goal wasn't achieved until the remaining problems were resolved during the early twentieth century.

From batch production to mass production

The transition away from craft production continued with the development of methods for analysing and improving the organization of work and the methods for getting work done: this became known as *scientific management*. 'Taylorism', as the system of the organization and management of production developed by F. W. Taylor became called, consisted mainly of setting rates for piecework and the practice of time study and the analysis of the elements of any task. He also proposed changes in the organization of supervision and management, as well as the workforce itself, including the development of planning departments for scheduling work.

The final ingredient in modern production systems was the development of the moving assembly lines at Ford in 1914, which created a new kind of production system. Ford had experimented widely in earlier automobile models with production techniques that had been developed for the new bicycle industry. Ford's system was highly effective for manufacturing a single product, in high volumes, on a continuous basis, to rigid standards. Producing in large batches, with tight inspection of products and machines (since workers weren't responsible for spotting errors), enabled Ford to use unskilled, often untrained workers, which compensated for the lack of skilled craftsmen. Ford's system for manufacturing the Model T at Highland Park (and later River Rouge) set the standard for production excellence until the 1930s, when the company abandoned its strategy of making only a single product and tried to produce varied products, for which the system was spectacularly unsuited. General Motors, under the leadership of Alfred Sloan, then took over the leadership of marketing and production in the automotive industry.

The term *mass production* itself came into popular use when the *Encyclopaedia Britannica* published an article about assembly line manufacturing at Ford. Henry Ford was the first person to see the potential for selling products cheaply to mass markets rather than to the wealthy: Peter Drucker has described this revolutionary strategy as achieving maximum profit by minimizing production costs whilst maximizing production volume. Between Ford's original Model T production system and the post-war mass production systems at Ford and many other manufacturers', mass production became associated with a degenerated emphasis on throughput to achieve high volume and low cost, but with low quality and low flexibility. In fact, the pre-1930s Ford mass production system is very similar to the post-war Japanese just-in-time (JIT) production systems pioneered at Toyota (although the post-war Ford system can be considered to be the complete opposite of JIT, as we shall see in Chapter 7).

From the discussion above, you might fairly conclude that most of the development of modern production systems took place in the USA. The Americans did make their workshops and factories open to inspection by competitors, and many British and other European engineers and managers visited them and came away with new ideas about both machines and methods. On the other hand, adoption of American-inspired practices was often limited because they did not fit with the different evolution of European production systems, and the different managerial ideas guiding this evolution. (For example, British trade journals were publishing stories about Taylor early on.) However, the specific conditions that encouraged the development of the mass production ideology, based on mass markets, existed only in the USA and not elsewhere, so that it was mainly American machines and technology, rather than American management techniques that found a broader audience. Despite its name and origins in the USA, the key ideas of the AMS, for example, had been brought to wider attention by the mid-nineteenth century, especially in Britain through the display of American products at the Crystal Palace Exhibition of 1851.

Beyond mass production

During the 1980s the economy of Japan expanded enormously, predominantly due to the competitive advantage that was being achieved by its automobile and electronics firms. It became clear that there were some fundamentally different methods being used by these firms in the design and production of their goods. Quality differences were noted – Japanese cars had gained a reputation for their quality and reliability in particular, but when this was measured objectively they contained less than one-hundredth of the defects of their western counterparts. In addition, productivity differences of 2 : 1 were found (Womack *et al.*, 1990) – the Japanese plants were twice as productive as their competitors. The quality difference was noted to be associated with an approach that became known as *Total Quality Management* (see Chapter 9). The firms were noted to hold very little stock and parts were delivered as they needed them – just-in-time (JIT – see chapter 7). Overall, these firms were noted to be *Lean* or *World Class* (see Chapters 2 and 11).

Part of the reason for these differences in performance was through a fundamentally different approach to organizing work. The mass production era promoted specialism, with firms being organized into a functional structure. This worked well for many years, but eventually each function began to concentrate on its own needs to grow and perform. An example of this is the marketing department of a leading brand of soft drinks, who decided to increase sales by announcing a cut-price promotion (12 cans for the price of 8) during a summer heat wave even though the bottling plant was already running 24 hours per day, 7 days per week to keep up with demand. When the promotion increased demand for soft drinks, the existing stocks were exhausted and revenues actually fell since the drinks being sold were being retailed for much less. The blame for lost revenues fell on operations, not marketing.

The focus on specialism neglected a key issue: *customers do not buy products from functions, they buy the output of processes.* Processes are

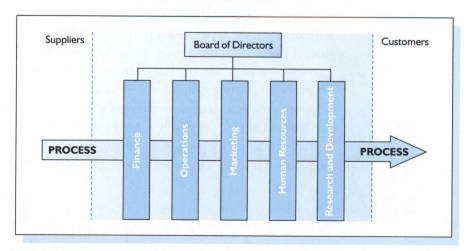

Figure 1.9 Functions and process.

typically cross-functional, rather than being based in a single function (Figure 1.9). For example, product quality depends not only on shop-floor workers, but also on the work of designers, purchasing, distribution and marketing. To meet customer expectations, different functions must be reintegrated around processes that create and deliver products that customers want to buy. Furthermore, with increasing proportions of the value of products and services being bought-in (or *outsourced*) rather than made in-house, the imperative to integrate suppliers into the process has become even stronger. Customers are also a part of this process, and much work has been carried out in operations management to enhance the means by which customers are integrated.

CURRENT ISSUES IN OPERATIONS MANAGEMENT

Some of the issues that operations managers must face include new pressures on operations management, the different operations management challenges of different types of organizations, and new imperatives for operations performance.

The new scope of operations management

Operations management has developed beyond its roots in the study of manufacturing, also known as factory management or production management. Although operations management is still concerned with manufacturing operations, organizations as varied as hospitals, overnight package delivery services and charities are all concerned with operations. Operations management is increasingly important in not-for-profit organizations such as government departments and agencies, and other organizations that provide services such as charities and other non-governmental organizations (NGOs). Instead of producing goods and services to make a profit, not-for-profits must use limited resources wisely – for example, through trying to provide services to as many people as possible, or as high a level of service as possible to a fixed customer base, at a given level of resources.

Operations as an open system

Despite the differences between manufacturing, service and not-for-profit organizations, all of these can be viewed as systems for acquiring inputs from the environment, transforming them, and exporting outputs to the environment.

The modern view of operations management treats operations as an open system, rather than a closed system. The old *closed-system* view treated operations as independent of its environment, suggesting that, in a stable and predictable environment, management's task was to design the optimum system to fit that environment and then to run things efficiently. This is very much the attitude of scientific management, operations research and industrial engineering. It was appropriate for the less competitive business environment of the past; it is wholly inappropriate for the modern business era.

By contrast, the *open-system* view of operations takes into account the need for operations to interact with the environment, including acquiring the resources that it consumes and exporting resources to the environment. As the environment is continuously changing, operations must change and adapt to environmental change, and thus the design of a static, unchanging operations function is not feasible.

During the 1990s, operations management became concerned with managing operations *across* organizational boundaries as well as *within* them. As the limits to improvement within particular plants or divisions began to be reached, operations had to look for new ways to create efficiencies. Instead of looking within the organizational boundaries the focus became external, with concentration on the management of supply into and through the organization. The ideas put forward in the early 1990s were concerned with creating efficiency both into and through the organization. The various terms for concepts, including World Class Manufacturing, Lean Manufacturing and Agile Production, all focused on one key issue; the alignment of internal and external process – the management of the supply chain.

Supply chain management is not only concerned with the purchasing of goods and materials but also with the development of strategies to manage the entire supply process – i.e. not just inputs but also throughputs. This strategic focus has led to the development of strategies such as Outsourcing, Partnership Sourcing and Supply Base Rationalization and Delegation strategies. All of these strategies have been designed to align with internal strategic initiatives such as just-in-time (JIT) and Total Quality Management (TQM) – i.e. working closer with fewer suppliers to add more value to the business.

The value adding principles of strategically focused supply strategies are well documented. If managed effectively these strategies can enhance value by improving time-to-market, sharing technologies to create new innovations, sharing risks to allow enhanced development of ideas, sharing costs and sharing benefits. In addition, the imposition of outsourcing strategies and supplier tiers can make the customer more flexible to global competition, as it can concentrate on its core competencies such as design without being bogged down with having to manage the assembly parts of the process. Furthermore, by working together suppliers and customers can identify cost drivers and find ways to reduce these jointly, instead of focusing purely on price. This *cost transparency* approach can yield significant benefits for both the customer and the supplier organization.

Strategic purchasing and supply covers the whole of operations. *Purchasing* acquires and manages the inputs – raw materials, sub-assemblies, and services – that the organization uses to create and deliver its outputs of goods and services. These goods and services have to be purchased from approved supply sources, and conform to required levels of quality and delivery schedules. *Supply* manages resources that are held within the organization, and which are moved outside, and is concerned not only with the inputs but also with the transformation and management of goods and services through the organization.

New pressures on operations management

There are four new pressures on operations management:

1 *Globalization.* Organizations compete in international markets, and face competition from international competitors in their own home markets.
2 *Employees.* Operations managers are increasingly responsible for motivating and empowering employees. One reason is that organizations depend increasingly on the flow of ideas for improvement from staff.
3 *Ethics.* Many of the ethical dilemmas facing organizations are directly related to operations, and this will be discussed further in Chapter 11. For example, Shell's decision in 1996 to dump the Brent Spar oil platform at sea once it had no further use for it sparked Europe-wide boycotts of Shell products. Other organizations have been 'named and shamed' because they or their subcontractors have employed under-age ('child') labourers. Operations may also be directly or indirectly involved with other ethical issues such as animal testing of products, or supply chain issues.

4 *Environment.* Operations directly or indirectly account for the majority of the environmental impacts of organizations. The processes by which products are created result in waste products and emissions. Goods and services also affect the environment – for example, McDonald's has switched from styrofoam packaging for its fast-food sandwiches to paper containers, substantially reducing the amount of non-recyclable waste generated by its stores.

New imperatives

There are major imperatives for operations managers, including:

- *Performance objectives*: as you will see throughout this book, the performance challenges for operations have changed over time. During the 1950s, operations performance was primarily judged by cost. During the 1980s, quality was added to cost, particularly in manufactured products where markets were under increasing pressure from Japanese products. Expectations of continuous improvements to product and service quality increased dramatically. Today, many industries have added the need to innovate new products and services as well as to deliver products and services faster, more reliably and to individual customer requirements.
- *Utilizing communications and computers*: the use of computers and communications technologies has affected operations on a par with (if not more than) other areas of the organization. Organizations use personal computers, servers and networks to link different activities internally, allowing work to be performed wherever it makes sense, and making it possible to bring operations closer to customers.

Challenges for service operations management

Like manufacturing, the service sector is undergoing rapid change. First, as in most management activities, global competition and technological change are creating pressures that affect industries, firms and individuals. Many previously unpaid activities – for example, personal services such as housecleaning or childcare – are now being performed outside the household for pay, and are formally measured as economic activities. Along with this growth in the service sector, techniques learned from manufacturing are being applied to new and existing services to increase productivity.

Along with changes in service businesses, there have been many changes to not-for-profit services, including the government and voluntary sectors. In most countries the not-for-profit sector provides a variety of services to individuals, businesses and other parts of the public sector. This provision is shifting to the private sector or being eliminated in many countries, which has a major effect on budgets and taxes.

Organizations themselves are using services as a source of competitive advantage, to differentiate their products or to increase revenues. When physical goods are identical or offer similar benefits, they can then be differentiated through the type or quality of services associated with them. For example, there may be little difference between personal computers offered by different vendors, but after-sales support services such as customer support hotlines can create differences in customer experiences. Another example is Dell Computer's Internet marketing site: customers or potential customers can configure their own personal computer to their exact specification, and be given prices and delivery dates, all based on sophisticated information technology. Why bother going to a store or dealing with sales personnel if you know what you want?

The service content of products is also increasing. For example, purchasers of the Ford Model T were expected to perform maintenance and repair activities themselves; purchasers of the Toyota Lexus have their automobile picked up from their homes, not only maintained and repaired but also valeted, and then returned to their homes. They also automatically become members of the Lexus Club, which includes many benefits not directly associated with car ownership, such as discounts on travel, gifts, wine and theatre tickets. Along with this, many customers now expect complete service solutions from providers. Package holiday providers arrange not only transportation, but also lodging, entertainment, food and excursions for their clients. As well as selling ingredients and packaged dishes, supermarkets such as Waitrose and Sainsbury are now providing gourmet meals created (if not prepared) by celebrity chefs, so that customers can vicariously dine in top restaurants in their own dining rooms.

Challenges for manufacturing operations

A major development since the 1970s has been the increase in growth within the service sector, often at the expense of the manufacturing base in many Western countries. Not surprisingly, the number of manufacturing jobs has declined in many countries in the West. For example, in the USA manufacturing jobs accounted for 33 per cent of all workers in the 1950s; this fell to 30 per cent in the 1960s, 20 per cent in the 1980s, and by 1995 the figure was lower than 17 per cent. The implications of this decline are explored by a number of writers. One of the most powerful discussions is in the book *America: What Went Wrong?* (Bartlett and Steele, 1992).

The problem is that the manufacturing element has often been ignored or downplayed in the total provision of goods and services. Indeed, there has often been a view of the manufacturing element as a secondary consideration within the total provision of goods and services, as Garvin (1992, p. xiv) describes:

> All too often, top managers regard manufacturing as a necessary evil. In their eyes, it adds little to a company's competitive advantage. Manufacturing, after all, merely 'makes stuff'; its primary role is the transformation of parts and materials into finished products. To do so it follows the dictates of other departments.

Brown (1996) suggests that the key reasons behind the relegation of manufacturing include:

- Downgrading the importance of manufacturing at societal/government levels
- Failing to educate school students sufficiently in technical/commercial areas
- Business schools teaching 'quick-fix' management tools, rather than providing a strategic framework
- Failing, both at national and company level, to invest in appropriate management development and training
- Failing at company level to view manufacturing in terms of strategic importance
- Having a view of the business which is governed essentially by short-term financial criteria.

Garvin (1992, p. xiv) argues that the definition of manufacturing operations has to be seen in a wider context than might often have been assumed in the past, and he quotes the Manufacturing Studies Board publication *Toward a New Era in US Manufacturing*, in which it is stated:

> Part of the problem of US manufacturing is that a common definition of it has been too narrow. Manufacturing is not limited to the material

transformation performed in the factory. It is a system encompassing design, engineering, purchasing, quality control, marketing, and customer service as well.

We need only to look at the contribution of manufacturing to both the Fortune 500 (firms in the USA) and the Fortune Global 500 in order to confirm how vital manufacturing can be. We should bear in mind that it is not only those firms that we might automatically associate with being a 'manufacturing company' which are important. The giant retail outlets within the Fortune 500 are also very dependent upon manufactured goods – this may seem obvious, but often people will classify retail as a service industry, as if, somehow, it is a sector that is entirely independent from manufacturing. The fact is, retail is very dependent upon the manufacturing base.

There are two important issues here. The first is that manufacturing and service firms often link together and are dependent upon each other in order to complete the transfer from inputs to outputs of goods and services to customers. The second issue is that services firms have not replaced manufacturing organizations when it comes to balance of payments and exports. Service exports have not managed to plug the gap between manufactured imports and exports in many countries. Operations management practices therefore also impact not only on corporate success, but also on the economic success of nations.

 # THE PLAN OF THIS BOOK

The topics within operations management are inter-related. The design of this book presents the chapters so that the major ideas are unfolded in a logical sequence, around the policies, practices, and performance objectives of the organization. Figure 1.10 shows this sequence.

Following the overview, the first part introduces the basic elements of operations policies.

This discussion provides the groundwork for the second part, which is about the practices that organizations put into place to realize these policies.

The third part looks at the performance side of operations. It concludes with some ideas about managing operations for sustainable competitive advantage, and future directions that operations is taking.

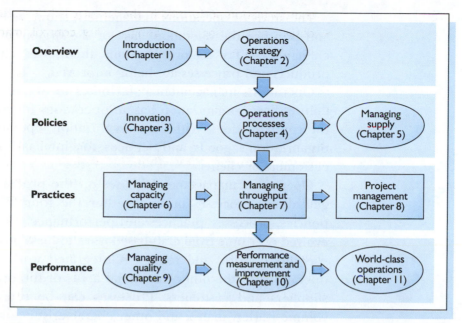

Figure 1.10 Plan of the book.

Finally, the supplementary chapters give an insight into some basic numerical techniques that can be used to help solve simple problems that we often encounter within firms.

Plan of each chapter

Each chapter begins with a short case or vignette taken from real-life operations. The theory and models that are relevant to the chapter topic are introduced next. Each chapter ends with a summary of key points, a case study, key questions and a list of key terms and concepts.

SUMMARY

Operations management is important because when an operation works well, goods and services are delivered to customers when they want them, with something extra that delights the customer and creates customer loyalty. The challenge for operations managers is to make this happen. If an organization has outstanding financials, human resources and market plans, and utilizes the very latest IT system but can't deliver products and services, then it will not succeed. Operations management makes this happen.

The study of operations management shows us how to accomplish and improve the operations task of the organization. Operations is changing as fast as organizations themselves change – everyday, products and processes are being improved.

Operations management contributes to organizational success or failure. Every organization has an operations function, which is what the company does. Within an organization, operations produces the organization's goods and services for internal and organizational customers or clients.

Operations management focuses on the processes by which work gets done. Processes bring together the four 'P's of operations – policies, processes, practices and performance. These processes have evolved over time from craft-based work to mass production and other specialized work, and today's reintegrated work. Processes also tie operations to the other functional areas of the organization, and to suppliers and customers. Processes can be categorized using the volume–variety matrix and other characteristics.

Operations managers are responsible for managing human resources, assets and costs. Operations managers must also consider a range of imperatives, including ethical and environmental considerations, and new technologies such as the Internet.

The operations process itself can be described using the transformation model, which applies to both services and manufacturing. In the wider perspective, operations managers bring together resources, knowledge and market opportunities, as shown in the dynamic convergence model.

Case study

Toyota: archetypal operational excellence

At the beginning of this chapter we asked the question, 'Who comes to mind when you think of successful organizations?' There's no doubt that when we speak about excellence in operations within the motor industry, Toyota comes to mind. This is because Toyota has constantly aimed to improve all areas of operations. For example, in the 1970s people were attracted to Toyota cars for many reasons, but the main one was usually that they were excellent value for money. During the 1980s, Toyota acquired a reputation for building cars that were very reliable, as well as providing many of the features that other manufacturers would include as optional extras as standard. During the 1990s, they were seen in the car market to have retained their value and quality (never outside the top 10 in the JD Power survey of reliability in the UK). However, they had also become highly innovative, developing new models in around half the time of their competitors in the western automotive sector. Their marketing slogan in the UK and elsewhere: '*The car in front is a Toyota*'.

It is not through clever marketing that Toyota's success (consistent growth and profitability) has been achieved; rather, outstanding operational capability has been at the root of their success, through the application of the principles of the *Toyota Production System (TPS)*. These were set out by Eiji Toyoda and Taiichi Ohno after World War II and were fully operational by the 1960s. Many of the principles, such as the elimination of waste, were a matter of expediency rather than any great invention at the time. Japan had very few natural resources, limited space and, at the time, little foreign currency to buy machinery. Other principles are the use of the innovation potential of every one of their employees and the close relationships (often involving cross-holdings of shares) with suppliers.

By the early 1990s, the name 'Toyota' had become synonymous with excellence in operations management. Studies have repeatedly used Toyota as the benchmark against which performance is judged, consistently showing quality performance significantly better (less than one-hundredth of the defects of other car producers in one study) and productivity higher than competitors (2 : 1 differences are not unusual). The importance of the TPS is highlighted by its imitators, not just in corporate Japan but around the world. No self-respecting automotive company or supplier today is without its version of the TPS. Yet none have been truly able to imitate the system, because while these competitors are imitating one version, continuous improvement means that Toyota are on to the next.

In 2000, Toyota announced plans to expand their capacity by 2 million vehicles a year, in an already saturated global market. This will put significant cost pressure on their competitors, and the consolidation evident in the rest of the automotive industry is likely to continue. It also highlights the firm's grip on the competitive characteristics of the market in which they operate.

Key questions

1 Describe how the input/output/feedback model can be used in each of the following:
   a. A university
   b. A hospital
   c. A car plant.
2 List five firms, and then examine how they line up within Chase's manufacturing/service continuum.
3 List three household products and describe how elements of both manufacturing and service have played a part in the purchase of these items.
4 List six examples of both *craft* and *mass* production.

Key terms

Craft production
Closed system
Mass production
Open system
Operations
Operations management
Operations managers
Scientific management

References

Bartlett, D. and Steele, J. (1992). *America: What Went Wrong?* Andrews and McMeel.

Brown, S. (1996). *Strategic Manufacturing for Competitive Advantage.* Prentice Hall.

Chase, R.B. and Tansik, D. A. (1983). The customer contact model for organisation design. *Man. Sci.,* **29(9)**, 1037–50.

Galloway, L. (1998). *Principles of Operations Management,* 2nd edn. Thompson.

Garvin, D. (1992). *Operations Strategy, Text and Cases.* Prentice Hall.

Hamel, G. and Prahalad, C. (1994). *Competing For The Future.* Harvard Business School Press.

Hounshell, D. (1984). *From the American System to Mass Production, 1800–1932*. Johns Hopkins University Press.

Normann, R. (1991). *Service Management*. John Wiley.

Pfeffer, J. (1998). *The Human Equation: Building Profits by Putting People First*. Harvard Business School Press.

Porter, M. (1980). *Competitive Strategy*. Free Press.

Ridderstrale, J. and Nordstrom, K. (2000) *Funky Business: Talent Makes Capital Dance*. FT Books.

Russell, R. S. and Taylor, C. W. (2000). *Operations Management*. Allyn and Bacon.

Schroeder, R. (1999). *Operations Management*, 6th edn. McGraw-Hill.

Smith, A. (1986). *The Wealth of Nations*. Penguin Books (first published 1776).

Voss, C. A., Ahlstrom, P. and Blackman, K. (1997). Benchmarking and operational performance: some empirical results. *Int. J. Operations Man.*, **17(9/10)**, 1046–58.

Whitston, K. (1997). The reception of scientific management by British engineers, 1890–1914. *Business History Rev.*, **71**, 207–29.

Wilson, J. M. (1995). An historical perspective on operations management. *Production Inventory Man. J.*, 61–6.

Wilson, J. M. (1996). Henry Ford: a just-in-time pioneer. *Production Inventory Man. J.*, 26–31.

Wilson, J. M. (1998). A comparison of the 'American system of manufactures' circa 1850 with just-in-time methods. *J. Operations Man.*, **16**, 77–90.

Womack, J., Jones, D. and Roos, D. (1990). *The Machine That Changed the World*. Rawson Associates.

Zeithaml, V. and Bitner, M. J. (2000). *Services Marketing*, 2nd edn. McGraw-Hill.

CHAPTER 2

Operations strategy: the strategic role of operations

INTRODUCTION

Case study

Peters and Waterman's popular management book *In Search of Excellence* (1982) portrayed IBM as not only meeting but also surpassing all eight of their attributes of excellent companies. As Peters admitted in 1990, 'We seemed to suggest that all 400 000 IBM-ers could be seen walking on water!' In retrospect, the IBM that lost one-third of its PC market share to Apple Computers and the Compaq Corporation (neither of which had featured in the book) seemed not to be quite so excellent.

What happened to IBM between 1982 and 1990? Like many other firms, it lost ground to more aggressive competitors. IBM's traditional market segment was large corporations: Apple and Compaq outperformed IBM in home computing, small business computing and education.

Similarly, in the UK motorcycle industry, Honda and other Japanese manufacturers first attacked Triumph Motorcycles, the traditional market leader, in the low-end 50 cc and 125 cc model ranges. Over time they gradually introduced more powerful models, gradually eroding Triumph's market share where it was strongest.

In the USA General Motors' domestic market share declined from 60 per cent in 1979 to 30 per cent in 2000, when other firms more aggressively developed market segments such as minivans, sports-utility vehicles, four-wheel drives and turbos.

A common theme of these examples is that market leaders are vulnerable to attack in non-core segments, where they are often not paying attention. Once new entrants have established a peripheral market position, they can attack the leader in its core businesses. This relies on using operations as a strategic weapon, because capabilities have to be put in place. However, once particular capabilities are in place – for example, fast innovation, quality, and low cost production – they can then be utilized to gain a powerful advantage for an organization.

Aims and objectives

This chapter explores strategy, and in particular its relevance to operations and operations management. Strategy and operations strategy are first defined, and then the developments of operations strategy are explored.

After reading this chapter, you will be able to:

- Define the strategic role of operations and operations managers
- Appreciate the importance of strategy to operations and operations management
- Describe the major types of strategies and strategy processes
- Explain the key developments in operations strategy in both service and manufacturing contexts.

WHAT IS STRATEGY?

Operations capabilities are at the heart of the success of companies such as Dell, Nokia and Sony, mentioned in Chapter 1. Although other areas such as marketing and human resource (HR) management are also important, even with the best marketing or HR plans in the world, without operations capabilities an organization will flounder because it cannot deliver on its promises to customers.

Organizations can no longer compete on a single dimension such as low cost, high quality, or delivery, but must provide all of these (and

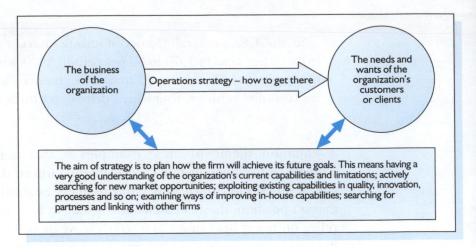

Figure 2.1 The basic aim of strategy.

more!) simultaneously. Operations managers must put in place a strategy to develop and maintain the operations capabilities to support these competitive objectives, which traditional approaches to strategy do not do. In essence, strategy is about the 'how' of an organization's aims – how it will go from its current state to its intended future position, as illustrated in Figure 2.1.

The origins of strategy

The concept of strategy originated in military terminology, where strategy refers to plans devised to outmanoeuvre the opposition. In business, firms attack where and when other firms are vulnerable.

In the earth-moving industry, Komatsu attacked Caterpillar initially in market segments that Caterpillar considered unimportant. Komatsu used a typical Japanese tactic, miniaturization (much used by Sony). Komatsu's smaller earth-moving machines were more nimble on site than Caterpillar's larger, more cumbersome ones. Komatsu also introduced models that could go underwater, another of Caterpillar's weak areas. Komatsu's stated intent was to 'Surround and then kill the cat!'

Caterpillar, however, was motivated by Komatsu's attack to defend itself. The company developed and implemented a strategy that allowed its plants to compete on a range of strategic operations capabilities simultaneously. By 2000, Caterpillar's market share in Japan was higher than Komatsu's share in the USA.

New strategies often result from competitive threats. The new strategy must be made clear and be understood by employees, and must be supported by operations capabilities in order to work. At Honda, for example (Whittington, 1993, pp. 69–70):

> [When] Honda was overtaken by Yamaha as Japan's number one motorbike manufacturer, the company responded by declaring 'Yamaha so tsubu su!' (We will crush, squash and slaughter Yamaha!). There followed a stream of no less than eighty-one new products in eighteen months. The massive effort nearly bankrupted the company, but in the end left Honda as top dog once more.

Honda's strategic operations capabilities allowed it to launch a range and volume of new products within a short time. Otherwise, it would have been arrogant and pointless to think that the company would overtake Yamaha.

When Steve Jobs returned to Apple Computers, he also used strategy as an offensive weapon (*Financial Times*, 12 November 1997):

> Mr Jobs ... declared 'war' on Dell Computers, one of Apple's most successful competitors. 'We are coming after you, buddy', Mr Jobs declared as he displayed a huge image of Michael Dell, Dell founder and chief executive, with a target superimposed on his face. Mr Dell became the target of Apple's ire, Mr Jobs said, because he had refused to retract a statement that Apple should be dissolved. 'I'd shut it down and give the money back to the shareholders', Mr Dell said.

Again, Apple had to put in place a clear operations strategy to go after Dell, and by 1999 Apple had vastly improved its operations capabilities.

Strategy formulation

There is, not surprisingly, no single best way of developing a strategy. The major elements of the strategic planning process are indicated in Table 2.1.

Every organization must plan and implement strategy to fit with its vision and mission. Important elements that need to be in place, both internal and external, are illustrated in Figure 2.2.

The traditional approach to formulating strategy simply seeks to match the firm's existing capabilities with a particular market segment that best exploits this capability. This focuses on the 'strategic fit' between resources (particular operations capability) and attractive markets.

Table 2.1   Factors in strategic decision-making (adapted from Johnson and Scholes, 1999)

- The scope of an organization's activities
- Matching those activities with the organization's environment
- Matching activities with the resource capabilities
- Allocation of resources
- Values, expectations and goals of those influencing strategy
- The direction that the organization will move in the long term
- Implications for change *throughout* the organization

Another approach is to be more 'visionary' in formulating strategy, perhaps through devising future scenarios that go beyond matching resources to 'strategic stretch'. For example, alliances can be formed with other firms.

Although strategy is complex, it is essentially about three goals. First, strategy is about satisfying (and, in some cases, delighting) customers. Here, the strategist searches for market requirements. Second, strategy is about making the best use of resources, either alone or with

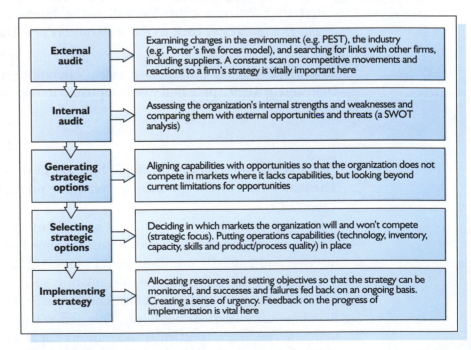

Figure 2.2 An example of the strategy planning process.

partners. Partners may initially be seen as competitors, but alliances help diminish threats from other competitors. Third, strategy is about developing superior capabilities, which competitors either cannot (or find it extremely difficult to) copy. For a firm to thrive, it must be able to manage these three strategic dimensions simultaneously.

The best firms learn, adopt and utilize world-class operations capabilities through seeking out and accumulating capabilities. Otherwise, there is a gap between strategic intent and strategic capability.

The strategy planning process answers the following key questions:

- What business is the firm really in?
- What does it do best?
- Should it outsource any current activities, and if so why, where and how?
- How can opportunities be exploited quickly and how can threats be warded off?

Strategy therefore relies on continuously gathering information to support analysis, choice and implementation. Feedback helps position the firm where it is most competitive. Strategy also creates an appreciation of the capabilities and limitations of the firm's resources, together with its responsibility to stakeholders.

Who is involved?

Everyone in the organization is ultimately affected by strategy. Who should be involved in forming strategy in the first place? Both the top-down approach to strategic planning and the bottom-up approach have been advocated, and many organizations combine the two. It is easier to suggest a particular strategy, however, then actually to realize it. To achieve a particular business goal, strategies have to be in place throughout the entire organization.

One of the writers of this book (Brown, 2000) is highly critical of top-down approaches:

> Strategy is seen by some as something which is devised at the highest levels of the firm – where ... in some firms there may not be *any* senior-level manufacturing, or operations management presence – and then simply 'passed down' through levels of hierarchy – with all the filters and blockages to accomplishing the strategy that this may bring. Pick up any textbook of strategy and the same old models seem to appear time after time. The model goes like this. Strategy starts at the

top (the corporate level); it then passes DOWN to business levels (where business strategy is devised) and then passes DOWN again to functional levels, including operations. Some publications say that there should, ideally, be dialogue in the process – particularly where a resource-driven (not necessarily including operations capabilities, by the way) strategy is being pursued. However, in the main, the top-down model of strategy remains the dominant model – you will see it articulated, especially, when a new CEO is put in place. All eyes will be on how the person at the top of the hierarchy will create a strategy. But the model is fatally flawed. It is flawed because of a number of reasons including:

- It enforces the idea of different realms of strategy – each with its own agenda – within the three levels of the firm.
- It assumes that corporate decisions will, somehow, line up with business and functional strategies to make some sort of perfect fit between them.
- It also assumes that corporate managers actually know something about operations capabilities and are able to leverage these capabilities as part of the strategic plan. However ... such an assumption is, often, totally without any foundation whatsoever.
- It encourages a hierarchical, top-down approach where, as a result, there may be little or no ownership of the planning process and the subsequent strategic plan.

In top-down strategic planning, a very few people make decisions that affect many people. If the top-down approach is used, excellent communication processes also need to be in place so that all employees 'own' the change. Strategic management writers often endorse the top-down view, resulting in a false division between 'corporate' and 'operations strategies. The outcome is described by Brown (1996):

1 Corporate strategy books tend to ignore the *strategic* importance and contribution of operations in corporate decisions.
2 Operations books – with rare exceptions – also ignore the strategic importance of operations in corporate decisions, and concentrate on tools and techniques of day-to-day operations management.

As you can see, business and operations strategies need to be closely aligned for organizations to thrive in the modern competitive era.

Market-led versus resource-based strategies

Strategy is sometimes seen as an either/or scenario. The firm can *either* compete on its capabilities – a resource-based strategy – *or* pursue a market-driven strategy. There has been considerable debate on the conflict between the two strategies. The latter can be seen as an 'outside-in' approach (market-driven); the former can be viewed as an 'inside-out' approach (resource-driven). Each approach has distinct advantages and disadvantages.

The 'outside-in', market-based strategies were popularized by Michael Porter in *Competitive Strategy* (1980) and *Competitive Advantage* (1985). Perhaps not surprisingly, its main advocates today are those who concentrate on marketing strategy.

The market-based view of strategy proposes that the firm should seek external opportunities in new and existing markets, or market niches, and then aligns the firm with these opportunities. This requires evaluating which markets are attractive and which markets the firm should exit.

A market-led strategy does not ignore a firm's capabilities. Indeed, a market-led strategy demands that a coherent, unifying and integrative framework needs to be in place if the transition from market requirements to in-house capabilities is to be realized. However, this is done only when particular market opportunities have been deemed to be 'attractive' for the firm. The danger with market-led strategies is that the firm may end up competing in markets in which it may not have sufficient capabilities to do so effectively. Thus there will be a strategic gap between what the firm would like to do (and may have chosen to do) and what it can actually do!

In contrast to the market-led approach to strategy are the resource-based strategies. The strategic importance of resources, both tangible and intangible, is not a new idea. For example, Penrose (1959) argued that firms were collections of productive resources that provide firms with their uniqueness and, by implication, their means of competitive advantage. The role of internal resource-based strategies gained prominence again in the early 1990s with the emphasis on 'core competencies', which argued that *the* chief means of sustaining competitive advantage for a firm comes from developing and guarding core capabilities and competencies.

A successful resource-based strategy process requires that strategists need to be fully aware of, and make the best possible use of, the firm's capabilities. This may seem obvious but, as we shall see in the next section, those who make strategic decisions may not understand the capabilities that reside within their plants' operations. In essence, these capabilities can provide strategic advantage only if the firm succeed in both outperforming competitors and satisfying customers. The dangers of adopting a resource-based strategy are summarized by Verdin and Williamson (1994, p.10):

> Basing strategy on existing resources, looking inwards, risks building a company that achieves excellence in providing products and services that nobody wants ... market-based strategy, with stretching visions and missions, can reinforce and complement competence or capability-based competition. And that successful strategy comes from matching competences to the market.

THE STRATEGIC ROLE OF OPERATIONS AND OPERATIONS MANAGERS

Operations managers are responsible for managing human resources, assets and costs, as shown in Chapter 1. Operations managers also ensure that the organization can compete effectively. Strategy is important because it maps how the organization will compete. For example, in 1991 Hewlett Packard announced that it would compete in the PC market as well as producing printers. To do so it would concentrate on assembly, not manufacture. This required Hewlett Packard to form, develop and nurture strategic relationships with suppliers, rather than manufacturing everything in-house. Hewlett Packard's business was focused as a result.

The elements of strategy

The day-to-day tasks that operations managers are responsible for (described in Chapter 1) have strategic consequences, because they are necessary to how operations supports the firm in its chosen markets. Brown *et al.* (2000, p. 57) identified a list of strategic imperatives:

- *Process choice* – selecting the right approach to producing goods or delivering services
- *Innovation* – adapting or renewing the organization's processes or outputs to adapt to changes in the external environment
- *Supply chain management* – managing external relationships with suppliers so that inputs are supplied effectively and efficiently
- *Resource control* – managing inventories

- *Production control* – managing processes effectively and efficiently
- *Work organization* – managing and organizing the operations workforce
- *Customer satisfaction* – managing quality.

Mismanaging any of these strategic imperatives will jeopardize the organization's future.

An operations strategy must include at least the following:

- The *capacity* required by the organization
- The range and location of *facilities*
- The investment in product and process *technology*
- The formation of strategic buyer–supplier *relationships*
- The introduction of *new* products or services
- The organizational *structure* of operations.

STRATEGY IN CONTEXT: MANUFACTURING AND SERVICE STRATEGIES

Manufacturing strategy

In Chapter 1 we described the change in manufacturing from craft to mass production. This transition also deeply affected how organizations developed strategies. Four strategic factors emerged.

First, in craft production manufacturing processes and the *business* of the firm were inextricably linked, but under mass production operations became a functional area. As enterprises grew in size and became functionally organized, operations managers lost their presence in the most senior levels of the firm despite the contribution of operations to the firm's capabilities (highlighted in the resource-based approach).

Second, the role of operations managers often became that of technical specialist, as opposed to an involvement in the strategic business of the firm. Thus operations' contribution was often ignored until *strategic plans had already been formulated* by an elite planning group whose understanding of the specifics of manufacturing or assembly was very limited.

Third, strategy formulation and planning became the prerogative of senior managers and, as we have noted, operations personnel were, typically, excluded from the process. Thus, operations strategies – if they existed at all! – were merely the means by which an already existing business strategy became translated into plant operations. As we shall see later in the chapter, this may have been appropriate for the relatively 'static' market conditions in mass production, but market requirements are now entirely different.

Fourth, there was a mismatch in the synchronization of timing between business strategy and – where it existed at all – operations strategy within firms. Timing remains a key ingredient in strategic planning, particularly in creating a sense of urgency for strategic implementation.

These four changes were, perhaps, inevitable due to the growth of large, multi-divisional enterprises within the USA. Increased size led to increased levels of hierarchy within the firm. Excluding operations personnel from the strategic direction of the firm thus created tensions between conflicting goals within the firm.

As a result, strategy and operations criteria began to diverge. Senior level strategists were now often driven by short-term financial criteria. Consequently, a trend developed of measuring the wrong things in operations. For example, a common measure is productivity, which is outputs divided by inputs. This can be an important measurement, but it is very easy to distort this. How? Simply by not investing.

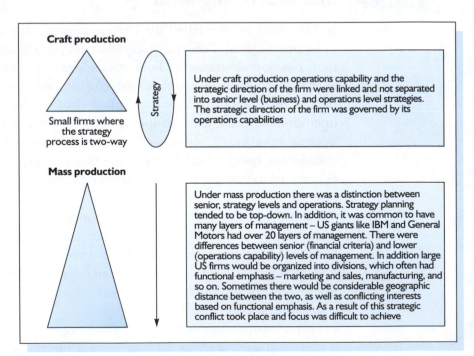

Craft production

Small firms where the strategy process is two-way

Strategy

Under craft production operations capability and the strategic direction of the firm were linked and not separated into senior level (business) and operations level strategies. The strategic direction of the firm was governed by its operations capabilities

Mass production

Under mass production there was a distinction between senior, strategy levels and operations. Strategy planning tended to be top-down. In addition, it was common to have many layers of management – US giants like IBM and General Motors had over 20 layers of management. There were differences between senior (financial criteria) and lower (operations capability) levels of management. In addition large US firms would be organized into divisions, which often had functional emphasis – marketing and sales, manufacturing, and so on. Sometimes there would be considerable geographic distance between the two, as well as conflicting interests based on functional emphasis. As a result of this strategic conflict took place and focus was difficult to achieve

Figure 2.3 Changes in strategy from craft to mass production.

The same is true of the accounting ratio – return on net assets. For sure, it makes good sense to map and compare with other competitors how money is being utilized. However, like the productivity ratio, this can be made to look artificially good simply by *not* investing. Investment in technology cannot be justified by a series of accounting ratios. Such ratios do not account for the cost of *not* investing.

The biggest problem with such accounting ratios is in rewarding manufacturing management purely on the basis of efficiency and cost minimization, which in turn, encourages high levels of utilization, economies of scale and specialized equipment. These are exactly the *wrong* parameters of measurement in an era that, as we shall see, includes mass customization and agility. The changes between craft and mass production in relation to strategy is shown in Figure 2.3.

The emergence of the strategic importance of operations

Major changes since the 1970s have undermined mass production, mainly due to increased levels of competition, which have resulted in greater choice for customers. Henry Ford's often-quoted opinion that Ford's customers 'can have any color of car provided it's black' is now long gone. Now the customer can have any colour, can have additional customer-specific requirements, and can have it delivered more speedily than ever before.

This shift places greater emphasis on operations capabilities than ever before. However, in some firms manufacturing/operations is still seen as a function and is separate from the business and corporate strategy process. This was common under mass production. The heightened levels of competition in many industries demand flexibility, delivery speed and innovation. D'Aveni (1994) used 'hypercompetition' to describe the rapidly escalating competition characterizing many industries. Strategic operations need to be in place in order to deal with such dramatic change.

A number of writers have provided important insight into the changes that need to be made. Skinner (1969, 1974) linked manufacturing operations with strategic decisions made at corporate level. The volume of literature on manufacturing/operations strategy has increased since the mid 1980s, but it is not always clear as to where and when manufacturing strategy might appear in the overall strategic planning process of the firm. Mills *et al.* (1995, p. 17) summarize the confusion concerning operations strategy manufacturing when they ask:

What is a manufacturing strategy nowadays – is it world-class, lean production, JIT, cells or TQM? Is it none of them, some of them or all of them?'

This perceived confusion with manufacturing strategy is discussed by Kim and Arnold (1996), who likewise conclude that managers often find it hard to distinguish between approaches such as JIT and other issues that might be included in manufacturing strategy. However, important insights have been made by a number of writers. For example, Hayes and Wheelwright (1984) speak of four stages where manufacturing strategy can appear in, and contribute to, the firm's planning process:

- Stage 1, which they call *internally neutral* – the role here is to ensure that manufacturing will not disrupt the intention of the firm and manufacturing's role is purely reactive to an already devised strategy.
- Stage 2, *externally neutral* – the role here is for manufacturing to look externally and to ensure that it is able to achieve parity with competitors.
- Stage 3, *internally supportive* – here manufacturing exists to support business strategy. Manufacturing capabilities are audited and the impact of a proposed business strategy upon manufacturing is considered.
- Stage 4, *externally supportive* – here manufacturing is central in determining the nature of business strategy and its involvement is much more proactive.

Hayes and Wheelwright mapped how manufacturing's role linked with business strategy, from being passive and reactive (stage 1) to a full, pivotal, involvement in the planning stages of business strategy (stage 4). The model is important as a mapping exercise so that firms can realize where manufacturing/operations lines up within the business strategy process.

Hayes and Wheelwright's (1984, p. 32) contribution is also important because it helps to explain what a manufacturing strategy should *contain*:

> . . . manufacturing strategy consists of a sequence of decisions that, over time, enables a business unit to achieve a desired manufacturing structure, infrastructure and set of specific capabilities.

The scope of structural/infrastructure areas that can form part of manufacturing strategy is wide-ranging and can include quality capabilities (including quality requirements that a plant might demand from its supplier base), manufacturing processes, investment requirements, skills audits, capacity requirements, inventory management throughout the supply chain, and new product innovation. Manufacturing strategy is concerned with combining responsibility for resource management (internal factors) as well as achieving business (external) requirements.

Skinner (1985) linked the role of manufacturing capability to the firm's strategic planning, describing manufacturing capabilities – if properly utilized – as a 'competitive weapon'.

Manufacturing's strategic role in satisfying market requirements has been developed over time. Skinner (1978) introduced the idea of the 'focused factory', and he spoke of the need to have a trade-off between cost, quality, delivery and flexibility. The idea of manufacturing strategy as a choice between trade-offs may have been appropriate in the context of 1970s, and was certainly a means of dealing with the perceived confusion in running a plant. As Schonberger stated in 1990, though, as time moved on and competition increased from firms able to satisfy a wide range of customer requirements, the trade-off solution was not a solution after all (Schonberger, 1990, p. 21):

> World class strategies require chucking the [trade-off] notion. The right strategy has no optimum, only continual improvement in all things.

Hill (1995) created specific links between corporate, marketing and manufacturing strategies. He stated that firms needed to understand market requirements by differentiating between *order-qualifying* and *order-winning* criteria. The former merely allows the firm to compete at all in the market place, since without these the firm would lose orders. However, order-winning criteria are factors that enable the firm to win in the marketplace.

Although Hill's distinction became adopted in manufacturing strategy literature, Spring and Boaden (1997), for example, question the premise 'how do *products* win orders in the market?' – suggesting, as did Brown *et al.* (2000), that it is the firm (with all of its attendant reputation, experience and architecture) and not just products themselves that wins business. In other words, firms must go beyond the idea of competing purely on products and provide a range of outstanding capabilities including low cost, high process and product quality, speed of delivery, and excellence in service.

The modern era

Today highly capable competitors from all over the globe provide more choice to customers than ever before. Various terms used to describe the current era include:

- *Mass customization*, which states the need for volume, combined with recognition of customers' (or 'consumers') wishes.
- *Flexible specialization*, which relates to the manufacturing strategy of firms (especially small firms) to focus on parts of the value-adding process and collaborate within networks to produce whole products.
- *Lean production*, which came to light in the book *The Machine That Changed the World* (Womack *et al.*, 1990) (which described the massively successful Toyota Production System) and focuses on the removal of all forms of waste from a system (some of them difficult to see).
- *Agility*, which is an approach that emphasizes the need for an organization to be able to switch frequently from one market-driven objective to another.
- *Strategic operations*, in which the need for the operations to be framed in a strategy is seen as a critical issue in order for firms to compete in the volatile era.

Regardless of its name, the current competitive era demands high volume and variety together with high levels of quality as the norm, and rapid, ongoing innovation in many markets. It is, as mass production was a hundred years ago, an innovation that makes the system it replaces largely redundant.

Intense competition requires that competencies and capabilities must include flexibility and 'organizational agility', whereby a range of dynamic capabilities can be utilized to face future competition. The ability to achieve the wide-ranging requirements of the current era does not come about by luck or chance; it is derived from accumulated learning and know-how gained by the firm over time, and at the core of the current era is a view of operations as *strategic*. While having a strategic view of operations may not guarantee that firms succeed, treating operations capabilities as a side issue to strategic areas is likely to mean that the firm will suffer in the current era of rapid change and volatility.

The current era has placed ever greater responsibilities on operations managers, and *The Economist* summarized the position very well (20 June 1998, p. 58):

Manufacturing used to be pretty simple. The factory manager or the production director rarely had to think about suppliers or customers. All he did was to make sure that his machinery was producing widgets at the maximum hourly rate. Once he had worked out how to stick to that 'standard rate' of production, he could sit back and relax. Customer needs? Delivery times? Efficient purchasing? That was what the purchasing department and the sales department were there for. Piles of inventory lying around, both raw materials and finished goods? Not his problem. Now it is. The 1980s was the decade of lean production and right-first-time quality management. In the 1990s the game has grown even tougher. Customers are more and more demanding. They increasingly want the basic product to be enhanced by some individual variation, or some special service. Companies sweat to keep up with their demands, in terms both of the actual products and of the way they are delivered.

The role of the operations manager is now more strategic than before, particularly under mass production. For example, Samson and Sohal (1993) argue that:

... manufacturing managers must become more than just implementers of engineering and marketing instructions on the shop floor. Raising the status of the manufacturing function involves getting the manufacturing manager involved in the business development/market competitiveness debate. Manufacturing managers need to be interfaced with and have an understanding of the firm's customers

and:

In the world's leading manufacturers, the production management function has become a high-status activity and is the powerhouse that energizes the competitive advantage that the marketing function can achieve in the marketplace.

Agility can be a powerful competitive weapon for the firm. As Roth (1996) states:

The ability to rapidly alter the production of diverse products can provide manufacturers with a distinct competitive advantage. Companies adopting flexible manufacturing technology rather than conventional manufacturing technology can react more quickly to market changes, provide certain economies, enhance customer satisfaction and increase profitability. Research shows the adoption and use of technological bases determines an organization's future level of competitiveness. Corporate strategy based on flexible manufacturing technology enables firms to be better positioned in the battles that lie ahead in the global arena.

However, agility is not just concerned with manufacturing. In services, technology (especially computer technology) has radically altered many of the transformation processes associated with service provision. This applies especially to back-of-house activities – for example, cheque processing in banks, reservations in hotels, and inventory management in retail stores.

The other 'revolution' in services might be seen as the opposite of a 'high technology'– the significant growth of self-service. Many people have seen and continue to see this as a lowering of quality standards as a means of reducing costs. Significant savings in labour cost may be achieved if the customer does things previously done by a service worker. In effect, this is perceived as a trade-off, similar to that described by Skinner. However, increasingly it is being understood that quality is enhanced if customers participate in their own service. For instance, diners who serves themselves from a restaurant salad bar enjoy a product individually customized to their personal tastes, appetite and value perception.

Many firms struggle with equipping operations in a way that will enable the firm to compete successfully against other firms. The result has been that industries are littered with firms who have had to exit because of their incapability within operations.

How do firms make changes to ensure that their operations are strategic? The role of the Chief Executive Officer is crucial here. What has become clear is that, in recent times, world-class firms have Chief Executive Officers (CEOs) who are, at the same time, also Chief Operating Officers (COOs) – as *Fortune* indicated (21 June 1999, p. 68):

Note how many of today's best CEOs, the master executors, don't even have a COO: Craig Barrett of Intel ... Michael Dell of Dell, Gerstner of IBM, Nasser of Ford ... That's a multi-industry all-star team of CEOs who've put themselves squarely in charge of meeting their commitments and getting things done ... The problem is that our age's fascination with strategy and vision feeds the mistaken belief that developing exactly the right strategy will enable a company to rocket past competitors. In reality that's less than half the battle.

The real battle is in constantly ensuring that *strategic resonance* takes place between those decisions made at senior levels of the firm and the firm's capabilities; and also between the firm's capabilities and customer requirements. Having *strategic operations in* place is the means by which strategy becomes operationalized.

Strategic resonance: the key to successful strategy

Brown (2000) has coined the term *strategic resonance* to describe how world-class firms devise and implement strategies. World-class firms do not see strategy as either a market-driven or a resource-based process, but create resonance between the two. World-class firms both seek new market opportunities and have in place capabilities poised to be used. Dell Computers is a perfect example. In Dell and Friedmans' book *Direct from Dell: Strategies that Revolutionized an Industry* (1999, p. 25), Michael Dell describes how he reacted to taunts from the revitalized Apple Computer Company:

> We reacted by continuing to do what we always have: focusing on the customer, not the competition.

This is more than a bland dismissal of Apple by Dell. Dell knows that his strategy works because market opportunities are met by powerful, strategic operations capabilities (*Business Week*, 8 March 1999, p. 20):

> 'By spending time with your customer where they do business, you can learn more than by bringing them to where you do business', he [Dell] writes. Visiting British Petroleum Co. in London, for example, Dell watched workers configure their machines with new software and networking capabilities – at considerable cost. BP asked Dell if he could do the work for them. The result was a new multimillion dollar business involving many such customers.

Was this a market-led strategy, or was it resource-based? The answer, of course, is that it is both simultaneously. In other words, *strategic resonance* had occurred..

World-class firms are those that cause *strategic resonance* to occur. Strategic resonance is an ongoing, dynamic, strategic process whereby customer requirements and organizational capabilities are in harmony and resonate. Strategic resonance is more than *strategic fit* – a term that we mentioned earlier to describe the 'fit' between the firms' capabilities and the market that it serves. Strategic resonance goes beyond that. Strategic fit may be likened to a jigsaw where all parts fit together; this is a useful view, but it can have – and this was noted in interviews with key staff in this research – a very static feel to it. In strategic fit it is as if, once the 'bits' are in place, the strategic planning is done. By contrast, strategic resonance is a dynamic, organic process, which is about ensuring continuous linkages and harmonization between:

- The market and the firm's operations capabilities
- The firm's strategy and its operations capabilities
- All functions and all levels within the firm.

Firms need to find and exploit their strategic resonance – between markets and the firm; within the firm itself; and between senior level strategists and plant-level, operations capabilities. Therein lies the problem – sometimes those who are in the position to make strategic decisions know little or nothing about the strategic opportunities and strategic power that lie within its operations' resources and capabilities. As a result there is no strategic resonance between strategy and operations, and consequently senior level strategists articulate a

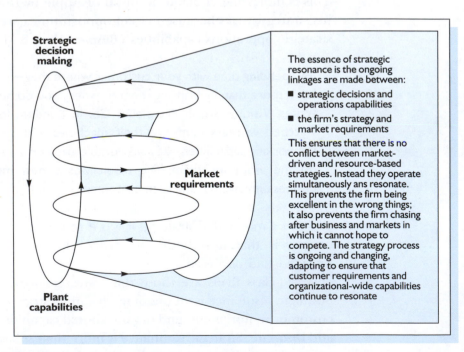

Figure 2.4 Planning strategic resonance between market requirements and operations capabilities (from Brown, 2000).

mission and a strategy that has no chance of being realized. It will not be realized because the firm does not *know* what the capabilities are in the first place, or the firm simply does not *possess* the necessary operations know-how and capability, or the firm seems incapable of seeking partnerships with other firms that do.

Strategic Resonance is illustrated in Figure 2.4.

Service operations strategies

Service sector firms face some of the same challenges as manufacturing firms, and some unique challenges of their own.

First, services are increasingly either managed or traded internationally, and so service firms need to devise plans for how this will be accomplished. Where services and manufacturing are closely linked in the overall provision to customers, the role of services can be vital. In the past, companies often located manufacturing facilities in different countries to take advantage of local resources and wage rates and the emphasis was on the manufacturing element. However, today multinational corporations are locating *services* where they can access highly-trained workers at reasonable costs – for example in India and in Eire.

Such effects can also be observed at the regional level within countries. For example, in the UK many call centres have located in Yorkshire, where local accents have been judged to be the 'most friendly' and to come across well over the telephone; others have located in isolated rural areas of Scotland, where there are large untapped resources of an educated workforce without much competing local employment.

Service organizations may choose one of three generic strategies:

1 *Customer-oriented focus* – providing a wide range of services to a limited range of customers, using a customer-centred database and developing new offerings to existing customers (e.g. Rentokil)
2 *Service-oriented focus* – providing a focused, 'limited menu' of services to a wide range of customers, usually through specialization in a narrow range of services (e.g. Midas Mufflers)
3 *Customer- and service-oriented focus* – providing a limited range of services to a highly targeted set of customers (e.g. McDonald's).

Ensuring service quality is a key competitive objective for most service organizations. Unlike manufacturing, customer contact in services means that both front-line employees and customers influence the quality and perception of the service. Service failures occur when the service is unavailable, too slow, or does not meet organizational or customer standards. Two ways that companies can mitigate service failures are service guarantees and service recovery.

Many companies now offer service guarantees as a way of ensuring customer satisfaction. For example, overnight document delivery service Federal Express guarantees delivery of packages by 10.30 am the morning after the package was mailed, otherwise the entire cost will be refunded.

Although most organizations strive for 100 per cent 'right-first-time' performance, occasionally something goes wrong. Service recovery describes how the company makes up for problems with the service. Research suggests that effective service recovery can in fact lead to more loyal customers (quoted in Zeithaml and Bitner, 2000).

One trend in service is to have customers become partners in the service delivery system by transferring at least part of production to them, variously known as co-production or consumerization of production. For example, in France's TGV high-speed passenger train services, customers check themselves in and validate their tickets using ticket machines located on the concourse between the main train station and the platform. Other familiar examples include:

- Fast-food restaurants – customers collect their food from the counter, transport it to where they will eat it, and clear away afterwards
- Petrol stations – customers pump their own petrol and may pay for it at the pump, eliminating all contact with employees
- Banks – customers use automated teller machines (ATMs) to perform many activities formerly requiring tellers, including cash deposits and withdrawals and account status queries
- Airlines – customers can order tickets on-line.

In becoming part of the production process, making the client productive can take place in four ways. The first way to make clients productive is to involve them in the *specification* of custom-tailored services. There are many familiar services that rely on customer specification, such as kitchen design.

A second way is to include customers in the production of the service, thus turning them into 'involuntary unpaid labour'. Most of us have become accustomed to eating at least occasionally in fast-food restaurants, where we (instead of employees) are responsible for clearing tables, etc. In return, these offer (at least in theory) faster service and lower costs, since employees have less work to perform.

A third way is to make the customer responsible for *quality control*. A popular restaurant trend has been restaurants such as the 'Mongolian Wok' chain, where customers select their own ingredients from a buffet, and then hand them over to a chef for stir-frying – they can include their favourite ingredients and exclude those they dislike, rather than accepting a standard range.

SUMMARY

Strategy matters, because without it a firm does not have direction. Consequently, any successes that it may gain will be by fluke. For sure, there are success stories that appear to have been achieved by pure chance – or so the stories would have us believe. However, if you get to the core of the success you will nearly always find that a firm was poised and ready with its capabilities and then met a market opportunity. It was able to respond more quickly, or with better quality or with a greater range of offerings, than its competitors. All of these capabilities are what the firm *does*, and does via its company-wide operations. This ability to learn, adopt and utilize world-class operations capabilities does not come about by chance; instead it comes about by seeking out and accumulating capabilities. If a firm does not do this, there will be a gap between strategic intent and strategic capability. It is this gap between intent and capability that remains a massive hurdle for firms, and it has cost many CEOs their jobs. CEOs in the modern era will be judged on their ability to understand, develop and utilize world-class operations in a manner that creates advantage – in other words, to use strategic operations. As we shall see in the following cases, some CEOs can do so while others cannot.

Case study

The role of the CEO in managing operations

The following is adapted from *Fortune* magazine, 21 June 1999:

What got Eckhard Pfeiffer fired? What fault did in Bob Allen? Or Gil Amelio, Bob Stempel, John Akers, or any of the dozens of other chief executives who took public pratfalls in this unforgiving decade? Suppose what brought down all these powerful and undeniably talented executives was just one common failing? It's an intriguing question and one of deep importance not just to CEOs and their boards, but also to investors, customers, suppliers, alliance partners, employees, and the many others who suffer when the top man stumbles . . . Consider the Pfeiffer episode. The pundits opined, as they usually do in these cases, that his problem was with grand-scale vision and strategy. Compaq's board removed the CEO for lack of 'an Internet vision', said *USA Today*. Yep, agreed the *New York Times*, Pfeiffer had to go because of 'a strategy that appeared to pull the company in opposite directions'.

But was flawed strategy really Pfeiffer's sin? Not according to the man who led the coup, Compaq Chairman Benjamin Rosen. 'The change [will not be in] our fundamental strategy – we think that strategy is sound – but in execution', Rosen said. 'Our plans are to speed up decision-making and make the company more efficient.'

You'd never guess it from reading the papers or talking to your broker or studying most business books, but what's true at Compaq is true at most companies where the CEO fails. In the majority of cases – we estimate 70 per cent – the real problem isn't the high-concept boners the boffins love to talk about.

It's bad execution. As simple as that: not getting things done, being indecisive, not delivering on commitments . . . It's clear, as well, that getting execution right will only become more crucial. The worldwide revolution of free markets, open economies, and lowered trade barriers and the advent of e-commerce has made virtually every business far more brutally competitive . . . Yet you needn't be ruthless to get things done. Ron Allen's willingness to swing the ax so antagonized Delta's work force that the board asked him to leave. When Lou Gerstner parachuted in to fix the shambles John Akers had left of IBM, famously declaring that 'the last thing IBM needs right now is a vision', he focused on execution, decisiveness, simplifying the organization for speed, and breaking the gridlock. Many expected heads to roll, yet initially Gerstner changed only the CFO, the HR chief, and three key line executives – and he has multiplied the stock's value tenfold . . . GE's Jack Welch loves to spot people early, follow them, grow them, and stretch them in jobs of increasing complexity. 'We spend all our time on people', he says. 'The day we screw up the people thing, this company is over.' He receives volumes of information – good and bad, from multiple sources – and he and his senior team track executives' progress in detail through a system of regular reviews. His written feedback to subordinates is legendary: specific, constructive, to the point. Of course some come up short. When Welch committed the company to achieving six-sigma quality a few years ago, he evaluated how the beliefs of high-level executives aligned with six-sigma values. He confronted those who weren't on board and told them GE was not the place for them.

This continual pruning and nurturing gives GE a powerful competitive advantage few companies understand and even fewer achieve ... Decision gridlock can happen to anyone, but it happens most often to CEOs who've spent a career with one company, especially a successful one. The processes have worked, they're part of the company's day-to-day life – so it takes real courage to blow them up. Listen to Elmer Johnson, a top GM executive, describe this problem to the executive committee: 'The meetings of our many committees and policy groups have become little more than time-consuming formalities. The outcomes are almost never in doubt ... There is a dearth of discussion, and almost never anything amounting to lively consideration ... It is a system that results in lengthy delays and faulty decisions by paralyzing the operating people ...'. That was in 1988, during Roger Smith's troubled tenure, and the problem persisted through Stempel's brief reign. Neither man could break the process machine, and both must be considered failed CEOs ... Keeping track of all critical assignments, following up on them, evaluating them – isn't that kind of ... boring? We may as well say it: Yes. It's boring. It's a grind. At least, plenty of really intelligent, accomplished, failed CEOs have found it so, and you can't blame them. They just shouldn't have been CEOs.

The big problem for them is not brains or even ability to identify the key problems or objectives of the company. When Kodak ousted Kay Whitmore, conventional wisdom said it was because he hadn't answered the big strategic questions about Kodak's role in a digital world. In fact, Kodak had created, though not publicized, a remarkably aggressive plan to remake itself as a digital imaging company. Whitmore reportedly embraced it. But he couldn't even begin to make it happen. Same story with William Agee at Morrison Knudsen – plausible strategy, no execution.

The problem for these CEOs is in the psyche. They find no reward in continually improving operations ... Any way you look at it, mastering execution turns out to be the odds-on best way for a CEO to keep his job. So what's the right way to think about that sexier obsession, strategy? It's vitally important – obviously. The problem is that our age's fascination with strategy and vision feeds the mistaken belief that developing exactly the right strategy will enable a company to rocket past competitors. In reality, that's less than half the battle.

This shouldn't be surprising. Strategies quickly become public property. Ask Michael Dell the source of his competitive advantage, and he replies, 'Our direct business model'. Okay, Michael, but that's not exactly a secret. Everyone has known about it for years. How can it be a competitive advantage? His answer: 'We execute it. It's all about knowledge and execution'. Toyota offers anyone, including competitors, free, in-depth tours of its main US operations – including product development and distributor relations. Why? The company knows visitors will never figure out its real advantage, the way it executes. Southwest Airlines is the only airline that has made money every year for the past 27 years. Everyone knows its strategy, yet no company has successfully copied its execution.

Key questions

1 From the above case, why is it so important that the Chief Executive Officer really understands operations management?
2 Why is it vital for operations and marketing to understand each other's roles within the firm?
3 Why is there still conflict between business and operations strategies?

Key terms

Agile production
Manufacturing Strategy
Mass customization
Service operations strategies
Strategy
Strategic operations

References

Brown, S. (1996). *Strategic Manufacturing for Competitive Advantage.* Prentice Hall.
Brown, S. (2000). *Manufacturing the Future – Strategic Resonance for Enlightened Manufacturing.* Financial Times Books.

Brown, S., Lamming, R., Bessant, J. and Jones, P. (2000). *Strategic Operations Management.* Butterworth-Heinemann.

Business Week (1999). 8 March.

D'Aveni, R. (1994). *Hypercompetition: Managing the Dynamics of Strategic Maneuvering.* Free Press.

Dell, M. and Friedman, C. (1999). *Direct From Dell: Strategies That Revolutionized an Industry.* Harper Business.

The Economist (1998). June 20.

Financial Times (1997). November 12.

Fortune (1999). Why CEOs fail: It's rarely for lack of smarts or vision. Most unsuccessful CEOs stumble because of one simple, fatal shortcoming. *Fortune*, 21 June, **139(12)**, 68.

Hayes, R. and Wheelwright, S. (1984). *Restoring Our Competitive Edge.* Wiley & Sons.

Hill, T. (1995). *Manufacturing Strategy.* Macmillan.

Johnson, G. and Scholes, K. (1999). *Exploring Corporate Strategy*, 5th edn. Prentice Hall.

Kim, J. S. and Arnold, P. (1996). Operationalizing manufacturing strategy: An exploratory study of constructs and linkage. *Int. J. Operations Product. Man.*, **16(12)**, 45–65.

Mills, J. F., Neely, A., Platts, K. and Gregory, M. (1995). A framework for the design of manufacturing strategy processes: toward a contingency approach. *Int. J. Operations Product. Man.*, **15(4)**, 17–49.

Penrose, E. T. (1959). *The Theory of the Growth of the Firm*, 1996 reprint. Oxford University Press.

Peters, T. and Waterman, R. H. (1982). *In Search of Excellence: Lessons from America's Best Run Companies.* Harper & Row.

Porter, M. (1980). *Competitive Strategy.* Free Press.

Porter, M. (1985). *Competitive Advantage.* Free Press.

Roth, A. V. (1996). Achieving strategic agility through economics of knowledge. *Strategy Leadership*, **24(2)**, 21–32.

Samson, D. and Sohal, A. (1993). Manufacturing myopia and strategy in the manufacturing function: a problem driven agenda. Special issue on 'Manufacturing technology: diffusion, implementation and management'. *Int. J. Technol. Man.*, **8(3/4/5)**, 216–29.

Schonberger, R. (1990). *Building a Chain of Customers.* Hutchinson Business Books.

Skinner, W. (1969). Manufacturing – the missing link in corporate strategy. *Harvard Bus. Rev.*, **May–June,** 136–45.

Skinner, W. (1974). The focused factory. *Harvard Bus. Rev.*, **May–June,** 113–21.

Skinner, W. (1978). *Manufacturing in the Corporate Strategy.* John Wiley & Sons.

Skinner, W. (1985). *Manufacturing, The Formidable Competitive Weapon.* John Wiley & Sons.

Spring, M. and Boaden, R. (1997). One more time: how do you win orders?: a critical reappraisal of the Hill manufacturing strategy framework. *Int. J. Operations Prod. Man.,* **17(8)**

Spring, M. and Dalrymple, J. F. (2000). Product customisation and manufacturing strategy. *Int. J. Operations Product. Man.,* **20(4),** 451–70.

Verdin, P. and Williamson, P. (1994). Successful strategy: stargazing or self-examination? *Eur. Man. J.,* **12(1),** 10–19.

Whittington, R. (1993). *What is Strategy – and Does it Matter?* Routledge.

Womack, J., Jones, D. and Roos, D. (1990). *The Machine That Changed the World.* Rawson Associates. Womack, J., Jones, D. and Roos, D. (1990). *The Machine That Changed the World.* Rawson Associates.

Zeithaml, V. and Bitner, M. J. (2000). *Services Marketing,* 2nd edn. McGraw-Hill.

Further reading

Anderson, J., Schroeder, R. and Cleveland, G. (1991). The process of manufacturing strategy. *Int. J. Product. Operations Man.,* **11(3)**.

Clark, K. (1996). Competing through manufacturing and the new manufacturing paradigm: is manufacturing strategy passé? *Product. Operations Man.,* **5(1)**.

Collis, D. and Montgomery, C. (1995). Competing on resources: strategy in the 1990s. *Harvard Bus. Rev.,* **73(4),** 118–28..

Corsten, H. and Will, T. (1994). Simultaneously supporting generic competitive strategies by production management. *Technovation,* **14(2),** 111–20.

Hayes, R. (1985). Strategic planning: forward in reverse? *Harvard Bus. Rev.,* **Nov–Dec**, 111–19.

Hayes, R. and Pisano, G. (1994). Beyond world-class: the new manufacturing strategy. *Harvard Bus. Rev.,* **Jan–Feb,** 77–86.

Hayes, R. and Pisano, G. (1996). Manufacturing strategy: at the intersection of two paradigm shifts. *Product. Operations Man.,* **5(1)**.

Mills, J., Platts, K. and Gregory, M. (1995). A framework for the design of manufacturing strategy process. *Int. J. Operations Product. Man.,* **15(4),** 17–49.

Voss, C. (1992). *Manufacturing Strategy.* Chapman and Hall.

PART TWO

POLICY

CHAPTER 3

Innovation: developing new products and services

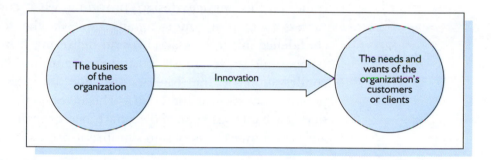

▶ INTRODUCTION

Case study

First Direct Bank, HSBC's UK call centre based banking arm, has been phenomenally successful in attracting customers away from high street banks to telephone banking. It provides customers with 24 hours a day, 365 days a year access to their accounts from wherever they may be. When a customer telephones, the operator asks a series of questions to verify customer identity. The first question – postcode – narrows down the customer's location. The operator only has to key the six or seven characters of the postcode into the computer to reduce the location to one of three houses in the UK. The postcode generates a menu of names, from which the operator selects the correct name. A final check is made by taking letters from a password. All this takes only a few seconds, and then the customer can transact his or her business. At the end of the call, the operator reads back a summary of the transactions so that the customer can check that every thing has been done correctly.

Although the First Direct system takes more customer contact time than automated systems, which rely either on voice recognition or data entered by customers using the telephone key-pad, this customer contact time is valuable to the company; the opportunity can be taken to explore other product needs that customers may have. First Direct customers are regularly asked about their needs for other financial products that the firm offers (credit cards, loans, mortgages etc.), and the ratings for customer satisfaction are rarely beaten (Consumers Association, 2000). As a result of this service design providing what customers want (access to their accounts at any time via the telephone and confidence in the transaction) and delivering it in the best way (short time to establish customer identification and giving confirmation of the transaction), the business has been a phenomenal success for HSBC. The investment in establishing this new bank was reported to have been repaid in 18 months, and it continues to generate significant profits for its owners.

Compared with other operations activities, innovation can often involve more interactions with other parties – as identified in the convergent model of operations in Chapter 1. These include working with customers, suppliers and other functions within the organization in the process of developing 'good ideas' into marketable products and services. Whilst innovation applies to process and products, the focus of this chapter is on the development of products. Innovation in processes will be discussed in Chapter 4 and throughout the rest of this book.

Aims and objectives of this chapter

This chapter will introduce the activities associated with new product development (NPD), including NPD practices that have been associated with competitive advantage, and their implications for all types of organizations (including those without direct competitors).

After reading this chapter you will be able to:

- Define NPD
- Explain how NPD contributes to organizational competitiveness
- Describe the activities associated with NPD
- Identify what constitutes good design
- Describe current best practice in NPD
- Identify the role of intellectual property as a source of ideas and a means of protection.

WHAT IS NPD?

All the goods that are around you, including the clothes you wear and this book, are the results of a development process. The services that we use are likewise the result of a development process. The process took a 'good idea' and converted it into the reality that we experience. It is a conversion process, like many others in operations, but the difference here is that there is a degree of novelty to the outcome of the process – hence the term 'innovation'. To describe this further, we can classify the nature of this process as resulting in:

1 Products or services that are new to the world – i.e. they have never been offered previously by anyone
2 Products or services that are new to the firm – they are currently offered by others in the market
3 Revisions of existing products or services.

The first of these is termed *invention,* and occurs less frequently than the other two. Because of the high degree of novelty, the costs of development can be significant – in the pharmaceutical industry, for instance, developing new drugs costs hundreds of millions of £/Euros. The last of these, revisions of existing products or services, occurs regularly as firms attempt to extend the time within the life of the product during which it is generating considerable profit for the firm. This is usually during the *maturity* phase of the life cycle, as shown in Figure 3.1. All products have a life cycle, although the length of the phases differs widely. The shortest life cycle products are either fashionable or related to very fast-moving industries. For example, in the computer printer market it is not unusual for products to be on the market for less than a year. In the music business, when a new single or CD is launched its life in the charts may be very short. In other

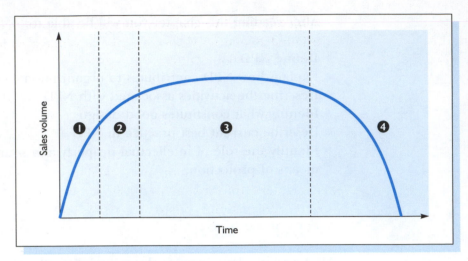

Figure 3.1 The product life cycle.

markets, life cycles may be very long. Consider the bank manager who, when discussing current accounts, stated that: 'The life cycle of these products is many hundreds of years. They do what we have always done – help people by offering savings and borrowing facilities'. Whilst this is certainly true for the underlying products, the method of delivery is changing significantly – as shown by the emergence and popularity of Internet-based accounts.

Figure 3.1 shows four parts to the life-cycle:

1 *Introduction* – the product is introduced to a new market. The customers are those who want to be the first to try the new innovation, and so require that the product meets their needs very closely. They are also likely to be enthusiasts and to want rapid introduction of further new products.
2 *Growth* – the volume of sales increases as more customers are attracted to the product. Whilst sales volume increases, the nature of the customer changes as the novelty is no longer sufficient to sell the product. Other attributes, including quality and price, become more important.
3 *Maturity* – the product reaches a level of stability in terms of volumes. This is often where products must really 'earn their keep', to repay the significant investment in their development and to fund the next generation of product development.
4 *Decline* – the product is coming towards the end of its life, and this process needs to be managed. There is significant potential for the extraction of further profit from the product, and many have

achieved this. Volkswagen shipped the production line for the original Beetle to Mexico to take advantage of local markets and favourable labour rates.

Innovation of the product therefore takes place throughout its life cycle – prior to introduction, in the introduction phase (changes to find the major markets) and during maturity (to arrest the onset of the decline phase).

NPD is a transformation process, like many others in operations management. Information is transformed by the process, and the basic flow of information is as shown in Figure 3.2.

Figure 3.2 shows a market-led approach to product design (see later discussion for other variants on this process) and the challenges that this poses, particularly with all the 'interpreting' that is present in the process. Customers are asked about their needs/wants through, for example, focus groups. These are traditionally run by the marketing function, who present the results in the form of an outline specification for the new product. Designers are then required to start to put some form to this and produce a detailed operational specification. This is then interpreted into the delivered product or service. Given all these stages of interpretation, it is possibly surprising

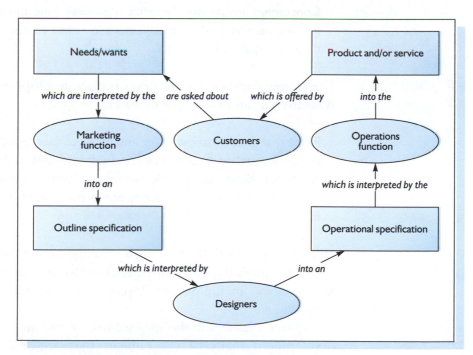

Figure 3.2 The flow of information in NPD.

that firms produce anything even vaguely resembling the products that the customers originally wanted. A key challenge for NPD managers is therefore to ensure that the 'voice of the customer' is kept consistent throughout the process. The task is to integrate the different steps and, by doing so, enhance the speed of innovation of the new product or service.

 ## WHY NPD IS IMPORTANT

NPD is critically important for an organization. The urgency for ongoing innovation is discussed by Lancaster and Massingham (1993, p. 128):

> Today, most organizations must either innovate or go out of business. Clearly, then, innovation and the new product development which such innovation gives rise to is not just desirable but is essential to long-term market and competitive success.

Davidson (1987, p. 185) puts this more bluntly:

> The most important principle of product development, beside which all others pale, is that no other corporate activity matters more. Consumers buy product benefits, not advertising and promotions, and the surest, and sometimes the easiest, route to corporate growth is through product superiority.

The strategic importance of new product development is described by Wheelwright and Clark (1992, p. 1):

> Firms that get to market faster and more efficiently with products that are well matched to the needs and expectations of target customers create significant competitive leverage. Firms [that do not] ... are destined to see their market position erode and financial performance falter.

NPD provides one of operations management's most vital contributions to organizational competitiveness. Reinventing what the organization does, including developing new products, contributes to flexibility.

Another reason for the importance of the process is that during development many of the choices that are made determine the eventual competitiveness of a product. Eighty per cent or more of a product's costs, for example, are set at the design stage, and once designs are accepted it can be difficult to reduce product costs without major redesign.

Furthermore, the new product must meet the standard that customers expect, yet provide an improvement over both previous versions and competitors' products. Operations and operations managers have a crucial role to play in determining whether the products provide a competitive advantage, or whether investment in NPD is repaid slowly or wasted altogether. However, financial performance is only one of the categories of key measures for NPD success (see Table 3.1), along with customer acceptance, product-level, and firm-level measures. Whilst these measures are highly interdependent (e.g. launching on time will certainly affect the ability of the organization to meet revenue goals), these categories illustrate the range of issues associated with NPD.

The measures in Table 3.1 provide long-term *metrics* for the process and its outcomes. In the past, operations managers were mainly concerned with product-level measures – the only ones that they could directly control. As their roles have changed, their influence in the other categories has increased and managing NPD has become more complex. Operations managers must still ensure that key product measures are achieved, but also contribute to performance in each of the other categories. It requires considerable skill and ability to bring the right parties together and to make this process happen.

Table 3.1   Success measures for NPD (Griffin and Page, 1993)

Customer acceptance measures	*Product-level measures*
Customer acceptance	Development cost
Customer satisfaction	Launched on time
Met revenue goals	Product performance level
Revenue growth	Met quality guidelines
Met market share goals	Speed to market

Financial performance	*Firm-level measures*
Break-even time	Percentage of sales by new products
Attain margin goals	
Attain profitability goals	
Internal Rate of Return (IRR)/Return on Investment (ROI)	

The metrics that are important to organizations are highly dependent on their environment. One that has attracted much attention from many parts of management and is crucial to many organizations is that of time-to-market.

Time-to-market

Time-to-market is the length of time between when an organization first decides to develop a new product and when the product becomes commercially available. It is a key objective in many markets, but particularly in those that are hypercompetitive. There are three aspects of this – speed, the dependability/timeliness of the introduction, and the need for not just one but a stream of new products to be available.

The first of these is the advantage that can be gained from fast development. For example, the emergence of a new technology may require a firm to respond rapidly, such as when Intel releases a new computer chip. Computer manufacturers must incorporate the new chip into their products as quickly as possible. In such cases time to market is critical, as it will yield *first-mover advantage*. In the UK, Direct Line launched their telephone insurance brokerage first and secured significant market share before the existing brokers (mainly high street-based) could respond. Similarly, Amazon.com have gained a customer base in the UK ten times that of their closest competitor (2 million customers versus 200 000) through early entry into online bookselling. Time-to-market is especially critical in delivering services online. Motorola clearly demonstrated the importance of speed as a competitive advantage when it produced its pocket-sized cellular phone in 1989. By the time other competitors had entered, in 1991, Motorola had sold over $1 billion worth of phones. As Clive Mather, chief executive of Shell Services International (the energy group's information technology business) puts it, 'Put simply, speed wins'.

The second is the ability of a firm to deliver a new product on time. Products are usually 'sold-in' to a market in advance of their actual release, which creates an expectation amongst potential customers. It also causes the demand for existing products that will be made obsolete by the new one to fall considerably. The financial consequences of such timeliness are serious. In the computer printer market, McKinsey and Company (1989) calculated that a printer brought to market 6 months late but within the targeted development costs will lose the organization 33 per cent of the potential profit for that product; bringing the product to market on time but 30 per cent over budget will cut profits by only 2.3 per cent.

The last of these aspects is that a firm is unlikely to be able to survive on one product, but instead requires a stream of new products. Reducing the time between new product introductions, as well as the time to develop each new product, is another important competitive objective. Research in the automotive sector shows that Japanese automotive producers have been replacing models every 4 years, whilst their Western rivals were only attaining 5–8-year cycles. Andersen Consulting (1992) showed that the best firms in the automotive industry had launched 44 per cent of their products within the past year, whilst American and European producers achieved only 17 per cent. A surge in demand for Japanese cars was associated with the availability of these new models, as well as a corresponding reduction in the demand for American and European vehicles.

Reducing the time to develop new products, bringing them to market in-line with expectations and reducing the time between new products are important competitive objectives. Later in this chapter we will discuss some practices that organizations use to speed up their NPD processes.

The failure factor in new product innovation

There are many reasons why new product innovations fail. Kay (1993) suggests that there are three main problems in innovation:

1 The process itself is costly and uncertain – a technically successful innovation might not be profitable
2 The process is hard to manage – innovating firms require special skills
3 Rewards of success are hard to appropriate – innovations can be copied and bettered by competitors.

Failure sometimes occurs because there has been a gap between design and operations when a new product is launched. We will look at how these problems can be avoided later in the chapter. Failing with innovations can have dire consequences. For example, Kay (1993, p. 101) mentions how EMI declined in televisions, computers and radiology scanner technology. This was in spite of the fact that:

> EMI was one of the most effectively innovative companies there has ever been. It was a pioneer in television, a leader in computers, its music business was at the centre of a revolution in popular culture, and its scanner technology transformed radiology. Today only its music business survives.

The failure rate of new products is enormous. Reasons for failure include:

- Launching a new product which, although innovative, is replaced by another entrant's product that then becomes the 'standard'. The VHS became the standard over RCA's play-only videodisc and the Beta format in video. Once the standard had been established, this then allowed Matsushita (responsible for establishing the VHS standard) to fend off the threat of another type of video format, the 8-mm alternative.

- Failure to develop from the 'laboratory' to manufacture. Ampex's attempts at the video recorder, where the manufacture of the tape-head made product quality difficult to control, is such a case. The transfer from 'one-off' laboratory conditions to volume manufacture is a massive challenge, and without it successful innovation will not take place. Failing to make this transfer from prototype to volume manufacture has cost some companies dearly (Derouzos *et al.*, 1989, p. 73):

The expensive and complex recording machinery developed by Ampex and other American manufacturers had to be converted into a practical consumer product. The Japanese efforts were characterized by close coordination of design and manufacturing and an intense and sustained effort to develop simplified designs for both the product and the process. In contrast, the three U.S. efforts to develop a consumer VCR ran into serious manufacturing problems, which were never overcome.

THE NPD PROCESS

There are many ways of describing the NPD process, in terms of where it starts, the drivers for the process and the nature of the outcome. Table 3.2 shows the basis of the major variants of the development process.

Market pull is the traditional view of how organizations serve their markets, and was shown in Figure 3.2. In this approach the organization searches for ways to provide customer or potential customer needs. This is the basis of what is termed the *generic* process of NPD. As we saw in Chapter 1, this was the basis that Henry Ford initially worked from when he identified the market opportunity for a cheap automobile. He then provided the technology in terms of product and process to meet this need.

Table 3.2   Variants of generic development processes (source: Ulrich and Eppinger, 1999)

	Generic (market pull)	Technology push	Platform products	Process intensive	Customization
Description	The firm begins with a market opportunity, then finds an appropriate technology to meet customer needs	The firm begins with a new technology, then finds an appropriate market	The firm assumes that the new product will be built around the same technological subsystem as an existing product	Characteristics of the product are highly constrained by the production process	New products are slight variations of existing configurations
Distinctions with respect to generic process	Additional initial activity of marching technology and market. Concept development assumes a given technology	Concept development assumes a technology platform	Both processes and products must be developed together from the very beginning, or an existing production process must be specified from the beginning	Similarity of projects allows for a highly structured development process. Development process is almost like a production process.	
Examples	Sporting goods, furniture, tools	Gore-Tex rainwear, Dyson vacuum cleaner	Consumer electronics, computers, printers, automotive industry	Snack foods, chemicals, semiconductors, razors	Motors, containers

Technology push differs from the market-led approach. Technology push is where the firm has a technology that it is trying to place into an appropriate market. The technology may have emerged from internal R&D as a new idea, or may have existed for some time. Technology push and market pull both play a key role and the success of each is dependent upon an integrated approach, as Twiss (1990, p. 9) suggests:

> ... both technology push and market pull have an important part to play in successful innovation ... this can only be achieved by a close relationship between the technologist and the marketer.

Platform products are based around a central product technology. In the case of Swatch watches, the central product technology is the movement. Swatch invested heavily in setting up the process to make these. The extensive variety of products for which Swatch became famous was added through the lower cost and lower complexity parts of the product – the case, face and hands. Most of the global automotive players use platforms for their vehicles – VAG use the same platform for the Audi A4, VW Passat and Skoda Octavia. This allowed the significant investment necessary to generate such a platform to be spread across three ranges of vehicles.

Process intensive developments occur where there is significant investment in process technology required. Gillette invested $1 billion in the production system for their Mach 3 product. It requires the delivery process to be designed at the same time as the product, as occurs in service delivery systems. Other process-based industries, such as chemicals (see Chapter 4), have similar constraints to their developments.

Customization is where an existing product can be modified and tailored to particular applications. Land Rover has the capability to customize a vehicle, through a special developments unit, to your exact specification. Many other firms leave this work to third-party specialists.

Regardless of the type of the process, the basic model is the same in most cases although the emphasis on different parts of the process will be different. Figure 3.3 shows how products move from concept through to delivery. At each stage of the process there is a filter to remove ideas that do not satisfy one or more criteria. These criteria may be *financial* (the product may not result in a positive cash flow), *strategic* (the product may not fit with current strategy), or *operational* (the product cannot be made or delivered). Most models of the NPD process use the 'boxes and arrows' approach to show the stages of the NPD process, which suggests that one stage logically succeeds another and that the information flow is one-way. Such diagrams rarely represent the complexity of NPD, which is better represented by a series of loops around which developers must go. These are caused by inevitable problems along the way, which mean that work has to be referred back to a previous stage. For instance, parts of a design may be too complex to be delivered, and this may not be discovered until the organization starts training people to deliver it. This will require a review of the design. Hence the curved arrows indicate that there are likely to be reviews, and indeed several attempts at each stage, before the process can continue. In the rest of this section, we will look at each of these stages in more detail.

Operations managers often find that managing NPD creates considerable conflict between the need to control the NPD process and

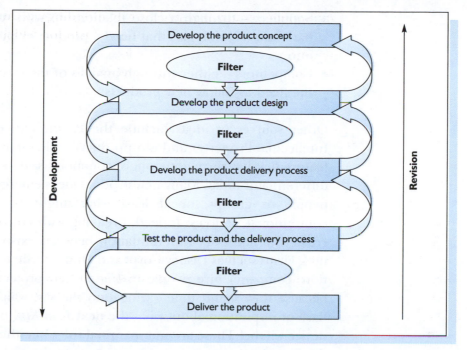

Figure 3.3 A generic model of the NPD process.

allowing those creating to have the necessary 'space' for them to be creative. How this is 'managed' in practice will be discussed below.

Developing the product concept

Developing the *product concept* is the first stage in the process. The product concept contains the basic outline of what the product or service is going to be and how it is going to be delivered.

New products and services concepts arise in many different ways and from a number of sources, including:

- Customers – many organizations have found it invaluable to harness the power of customer suggestions, customers being the people who are best placed to suggest what they want from the products and services that they use. Most usually, this is through the intervention of the marketing function within an organization.
- Internal Research and Development (R&D) departments – these used to be a feature of most large firms, but increasingly this function is being outsourced to specialist development firms
- Staff – a great source for ideas from the people who often know the products and processes better than anyone

- Suppliers – through a close relationship with suppliers, who may have new technologies that need a product or product range to go into
- Competitors – either through analysis of their current offerings or the need to follow new products.

Other sources of ideas include the Patent Office (see section on Intellectual Property) and old products, which may have contained a feature that has since gone out of common usage but would provide a differentiator today. Many new product ideas emerge from off-the-wall people or groups, or at least what might be considered 'non-conventional' sources. Indeed, breaking with convention lets people create the necessary differentiation between existing and new products. Firms such as Disney Corp. and Orange (the mobile communications company) hire people to *blue-sky* new project ideas – so called because they spend time gazing into the sky, waiting for a blinding flash of inspiration about what the next *Lion King* or communications device will be! These are not marginal roles in either firm. In Orange, the blue-sky department is located next to the main board offices.

The type of process for idea creation should depend on what the organization is trying to achieve. Many firms, particularly those that operate in niche markets, are happy to evolve their products and services continuously. Indeed, many larger firms prefer this gentle evolution to a more radical approach – often referred to as *discontinuous*, because it is not based on any previous experience of the firm. However, at the outset of the process the objective is to create as many new ideas as possible, both for radical and evolutionary innovation. Traditional work environments rarely provide the degree of inspiration for such creativity. Many organizations, including Disney and Orange, have seen it necessary to create apparent chaos by stripping away many of the constraints to creative work, and have targeted the working environment as one of these constraints. Creativity has become a key attribute for many modern businesses.

In addition to the outcome of apparent chaos, new products may be developed as a result of *basic research* – fundamental research into the nature of science (such as bio-tech companies striving to provide a complete mapping of the human genome). Basic research is expensive, highly risky (there is no guarantee of a successful outcome) and pre-competitive – i.e. there will be several stages and a considerable time-lag between this work and a commercial product. Such work is often funded by governments, as it would not be immediately attractive to commercial organizations.

Many books on NPD show the process as a funnel where ideas are filtered. This is rarely a good model of the concept development stage. Far from narrowing down the possibilities, the whole objective is to create as many strong ideas as possible. The most innovative firms only filter these once serious levels of investment in time or money are required. But what happens to those ideas that are filtered out and therefore will not be developed by the firm? Some should, quite rightly, be discarded. Others may have considerable potential, but just not at this time or by this firm. The sale of such ideas for others to develop is a major source of revenue for companies such as 3M Corporation. Other ideas may be recycled for further development or combination with other new ideas. If the idea looks promising, some firms will now provide the start-up capital for the employees responsible for the idea to go and start a business with that idea. In this way, the impact of the idea on the existing business is limited, but it might just result in a great new business that the organization can benefit from. This new model of the process is shown in Figure 3.4.

This process often appears very mechanistic, as though the creativity will just happen within organizations. More often that not, this creativity is the result of an individual and the product of what is often termed *creative frustration*. In the UK, James Dyson created an innovation in vacuum cleaners applying *dual-cyclone* technology to the vacuum cleaners. This technology eliminates the need for the more traditional bag, which rapidly becomes clogged and loses efficiency.

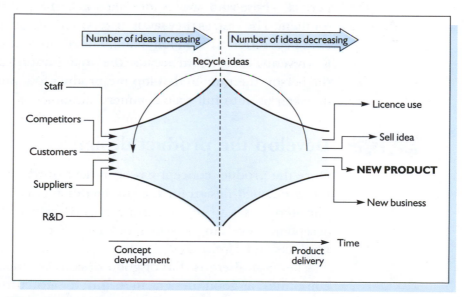

Figure 3.4 Concept input and output.

Dyson's insights were based on the systems being used in paint spray booths to remove any solid particles of paint before the air was vented to the environment. Spinning air containing particles in a container at high speed causes the particles to get thrown to the outside of the container, where they fall out of the air stream and into a collection vessel. Dyson's frustration with the inefficiencies of his normal vacuum cleaner led him to apply the technique to removing dust particles. In trying to perfect the method for domestic use, he constructed and tested over 600 prototypes before he launched his DC01 in 1992. (The story of this innovation and others with which he had been involved is told in his autobiography, *Against the Odds.*) This illustrates very clearly the role of such frustrations in starting the process.

However, the process of generating new ideas is futile if the people who generate them have no stake in the outcome, or if they are not supported in developing their ideas. 3M's original product range involved applying thin films of adhesive to paper to make products such as abrasive papers and adhesive tapes. You probably know 3M better through their most famous development in recent times, the Post-It note – a small piece of paper with a thin film of adhesive at one edge, which will attach to most surfaces and can be easily removed afterwards. Corporate folklore has it that the adhesive had been developed for another purpose and rejected for its lack of permanent adhesion. An employee who sang in a church choir used the glue to attach a piece of paper to mark the pages in his hymnbook. Since these pages were thin and easily damaged, a non-permanent glue was perfect. Those who saw his idea liked it, and asked him to make some for them. The rest, as they say, is history. The glue that failed generated 3M Corporation $1.2 billion in annual revenues in the late 1990s, and this revenue came about because the organization was prepared to give the person the time to develop the product to a point where it could be taken on into full-scale commercialization.

Develop the product design

Once the product concept has been developed it needs to be turned into a detailed design for the product or service so that it can move one step closer to becoming a reality. Design determines customer acceptance levels in particular, but also affects overall deliverability of products and services.

A key issue here is that of good design. We need to identify what constitutes a good design to begin to structure the operational requirements for NPD.

For operations managers, designing the service product with the customer in mind is of fundamental importance. In service design, well-designed products meet two often conflicting needs; the first is customer needs, the second is the need practically (and economically) to be able to deliver the service. The First Direct system would not work unless operators could quickly identify and verify customers using computer and communications technology, otherwise the costs would be prohibitive.

Designers face a similar challenge in designing tangible products. The Sydney Opera House, one of the most recognizable buildings in the world, was designed by Jørn Utzon. Utzon's design for the exterior was based on two overturned boat hulls – his father was a yacht designer – and required innovative engineering solutions. Amongst other problems, his design suffered from escalating costs as it was being built, and in order to trim the costs Utzon's design for the interior of the opera house was discarded in favour of a less expensive design, which has been compared with a 1960s bingo hall.

Product design therefore has an additional element: the elegance of the design solution. For some customers such elegance forms part of their perception of quality. Elegance may influence the decision to purchase. For example, the elegance of Apple Computer's PCs, with innovative, exciting colours, helped to transform the company at the end of the 1990s. This element adds the human or creative element to the design process, but it also creates a further set of potential conflicts to be resolved. Caroll (1993, p. 147) describes what happened at Compaq:

> [Compaq] turned everybody loose on the problem at once. The process was as messy as a dog fight, but it cut months out of the time it took to get a product on the market.

Clearly the interpretation of the end result for a customer is a highly personal issue and one that, like quality, it is challenging to analyse. Figure 3.5 summarizes the discussion.

The first element to be incorporated into the design is that of *customer needs and preferences*. This should consider how products perform in use, and the different ways that people can use them. For Quicken, writers of the leading personal financial management software, a key element in the popularity of the software is its robustness. Customers do not always read the instructions before using the product, and yet the product must still work or face incurring dissatisfaction. Many people feel that designers do not pay sufficient

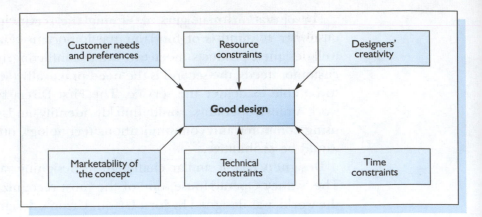

Figure 3.5 How design relates to customers.

attention to their needs – for example, who in the world designed television remote controls with so many buttons?

Resource constraints require that a design is deliverable, often with only minor changes to the existing operational resources of the organization. For example, whilst basic banking services have not changed much over time, the technologies available to deliver these services have changed significantly. NPD involves matching the needs of the product to the capabilities of the technology. Banks are totally reliant on their IT systems for their service provision, and so will be constrained by what can be delivered by the IT providers. In addition, there will only be limited resources available to the firm.

The need for creative design to maximize the differentiation of the product or service offering is a consideration in the *marketability of the concept*. Marketers have learned to promote elements that go beyond the mere functionality of products. An old marketing adage is 'Sell the sizzle, not the steak'. Cars, for example, have associated images that confer on their owners safety, sportiness, sophistication, individuality or fun. This will need to be developed alongside the product, and will be a major determinant of the success or otherwise of the product.

Technical constraints refer to a specific set of issues concerning tangible products in particular. Product designers are prone to over-promising the possibilities of their technology, and then can't deliver the promises within the required timescales. The designer therefore needs to incorporate technology that is sufficiently *leading edge* to provide a credible competitive advantage, yet which contains sufficiently well-proven technology to make the development achievable within the time constraints.

This leads to the last element – *time*. If more development time were available, many more innovations would be possible. Since firms need to earn profits, developers have to provide the best possible solution within a limited amount of time. This is particularly challenging where several technologies must be integrated for the product to function. For instance, a washing machine has mechanical components (e.g. the drum assembly), electrical components (e.g. the motor that spins the drum) and electronic components (e.g. the control circuitry that runs the machine). All of these must work together for the product to operate successfully.

Testing and delivery

Once the design has been developed, the next stage is testing, followed by developing the product delivery process (which will be discussed in Chapter 4). Testing takes a number of forms. At this stage, if not earlier, it is normal for a model of the proposed product or service encounter to be produced. This may be a physical model or *prototype*, or one based on a computer simulation. Further discussion of the technology of *rapid prototyping* is included later in this chapter.

BEST-PRACTICE IN NPD

The nature of best practice in NPD processes has changed. Current best practice requires individual contributors to the process to work together in a far more integrated manner than they have in the past. The most advanced processes today have a number of characteristics. Karlsson and Åhlström (1996) consider a package of measures which they label as '*Lean NPD*'. These include:

- Supplier involvement
- Heavyweight cross-functional teams
- Concurrent engineering
- Process integration
- Strategic management of development projects.

The firms that initially developed and implemented these measures had taken many years to do so, and firms imitating their practices were trying to achieve parity in a much shorter space of time. Omitted from this list is the role that technology can play in the development process. Operationally, this has had enormous implications for operations managers concerning the way in which processes are organized and resourced.

Supplier involvement

Supplier involvement in NPD has gradually increased in many industries in recent times. Previously, suppliers were kept at arm's length. Integration of suppliers in NPD has been through customer organizations knowing better the capabilities of their suppliers so that they can more readily use these capabilities. This has often been extended to suppliers providing *solutions* (greater parts of the finished product) rather than simply components. For VW's bus production in Brazil, this has resulted in suppliers being responsible for designing and installing systems (engines, drive-trains, braking), whereas previously this would have been done by VW engineers. Such supplier involvement has been rewarded in many cases by guaranteed purchase contracts, though with full access granted to the customer to see the accounts (through open-book arrangements) to ensure that only agreed levels of profits are being made.

Heavyweight cross-functional teams

A major operational issue concerns the structure of the organization that is created for NPD. Whilst many operations activities are functional (under the direct control of the operations manager), NPD involves many other parts of the organization (particularly marketing, R&D and finance), and often people and resources outside the organization (particularly suppliers and customers). A success story using this approach was in the development of the Ford Taurus, which replaced the Honda Accord as the biggest selling car in the USA in 1992. Ford used Team Taurus to bring together representatives from design, engineering, manufacturing, sales, marketing and service and suppliers in the earliest stages of the car's design to bring about this success.

Heavyweight cross-functional teams are drawn from many functions within the organization, but arranged so that the NPD manager has direct authority over them, over and above that of their own functional managers. In effect, for the duration of that NPD project, those people are transferred to the NPD team full-time. The role of the NPD manager can change in this instance from one of coordination to one of having full control over the team. Sobek *et al.* (1998) present a different view of how innovative firms (in this case Toyota) structure their NPD teams. The main power rests with functional areas – in Toyota's case, this is broken down by systems for a vehicle – electrical, braking, styling, drive-trains etc. Each NPD project has a product champion, usually someone who has many years service with the firm, who is made responsible for integrating the technologies necessary to produce the vehicle. This allows each of the functions to retain their specialization and apply knowledge across projects. Staff are also regularly rotated between functions to increase their networks of contacts as well as areas of interest.

Concurrent engineering

The role of operations in functions was discussed in Chapter 1, and the point made that customers buy the output of processes, not of functions. Consistent with this process-based view is the move from scheduling activities sequentially in the process to run in parallel wherever possible. This not only saves time over the traditional sequential approach, but also reduces the number of iterations that designs have to go through. It is more aptly termed *concurrent new product development* (CNPD), as it involves far more of the development stream than simply the engineering of the product. Concurrency involves the issues both of scheduling (process organization) and information transfer. The information transfer involves a forcing of early communications between the different parties in the NPD 'value-stream', as shown in Figure 3.6.

What does concurrent engineering imply for operations?

First, concurrent innovation processes require people from different functions to communicate – previously they could concentrate on their part of the process in isolation from the rest of the process – as demonstrated by Figure 3.2. Second, the overlapping reduces the size of the cycles of iteration – issues can be discussed and downstream

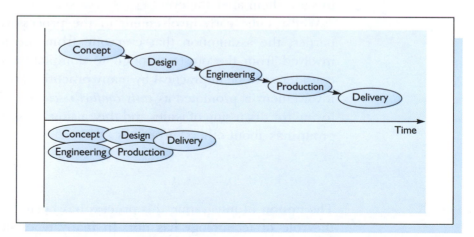

Figure 3.6 A comparison of traditional and concurrent engineering.

problems prevented. Finally, the timescale of the project is shortened, reducing time-to-market, which is a key objective for many firms.

The direct benefits of concurrent methods of working have included (in ranked order) improved matching of product with customer needs, reductions in time-to-market, improvements in product quality and lower product costs. The improvements in product cost and quality come through the greater involvement of manufacturing personnel earlier in the design cycle, to provide their input before designs become completely committed. Sobek *et al.* (1998, p. 38) describe how this can work:

> In designing a new model of the Celica sports car several years ago, the styling department suggested a longer front quarter panel. The change would have increased the panel's extension into the top of the front door, allowing the door to curve back at the top, creating an angular and more exciting look. The manufacturing engineer assigned to door panels opposed the change because the altered panel would be difficult to produce. After substantial argument, the two sides reached an innovative compromise that achieved the cutaway look that styling wanted with an acceptable level of manufacturability.

In the past, manufacturing operations personnel rarely became involved in the design process. The result was that they would have been required to make designs that had low levels of manufacturability – the ability to make products in volume. However, as a result of activities in the process running concurrently, manufacturing and other downstream staff (including people involved in product servicing in many cases) are able to prevent problems rather than try to solve them after the event.

Whilst some early involvement in the process is beneficial to all parties, the assumption that everyone from the team needs to be involved from the outset through to completion is dubious and is considered to be impractical by many practitioners. Instead, the early involvement is promoted as *early conflict resolution* (ECR), providing a forum for discussion of issues and the raising of assumptions that each group has about others' processes.

Process integration

The notion of integrating this process has been discussed above, but the role of technology has not. In many types of operation, from construction to sheet-metal fabrication and from packaging design to *haute couture*, the use of technology has revolutionized NPD, especially where engineering drawings are used in the NPD process to transfer information from one stage of design to another. These drawings precisely detail the product, including the dimensions, materials, etc. The detailed design is then passed to the manufacturing engineers, who devise a process or routing through an existing process to make the product. Their work is then passed to those who would make it.

Some examples of how technology can be used for integration illustrate the point. In construction, rather than producing drawings by hand, computer-aided design (CAD) allows the designer to work on-screen with the details stored in an electronic database. This not only speeds the production of initial drawings but also greatly facilitates changes to the drawings, which can be a very lengthy process (which deters changes) when done manually. Once the basic geometric information has been stored, it is possible for the designer to construct views of what the final building will look like and even to allow a virtual walk-through. This helps customers to envision the final product, reducing the changes during construction, since altering a computer model is far easier and cheaper. Such CAD systems can also improve subcomponent design, since interfaces can be designed and problems resolved before construction starts. Ensuring that services such as electricity and heating can be installed without major alteration to structural elements is a benefit.

Clothing design was once a very lengthy process, because once a design was produced, cloth would have to be sourced and printed, the garment made and then shown to the prospective buyer. Even minor changes would require repeating the whole process, leading to significant expense and time delay. However, being able to show a design on a virtual model on screen allows changes to be made without any garments being made. Only the final design will be fabricated.

However, possibly the most integrated processes are those in metal parts manufacturing. Having drawn the components on a CAD system and checked their fit with other parts, the geometric data can be processed through a computer aided manufacturing (CAM) system to generate machine instructions to make the part. Alternatively, CAD data can be used to produce *rapid prototypes*, where the part is made in a resin material. CAD enables a number of tests to take place, including simulations of loads and stress details on products.

In service design, such modelling systems are used by supermarkets to ensure that the necessary zones are developed within the stores, and to perform walk-throughs to test different layouts and displays. For example, the area just inside the door of a supermarket is often left as a relatively open space. This is to let customers slow down and make the transition from crossing the car park to browsing the aisles. Systems can model the flow-rates of people with trolleys through aisles, and optimize the dimensions and positioning of displays accordingly.

As you have seen, CAD technology supports process integration by enabling modelling of finished products, making it possible to agree product details at a much earlier stage. This enables downstream activities (particularly those in the delivery process) to consider the implications of these decisions earlier and make their contribution to the process. Furthermore, in many cases all parties to the process can work from the same design database, rather than having to transfer the data between one form and another.

Strategic management of development projects

Development projects are key in terms of a firm developing competitive advantage through its operations. Moving development projects from an isolated area of the firm into a mainstream process requires a different approach to their management. As Cooper (1988) commented:

> The new product strategy is the master plan that guides the firm's product innovation efforts and links NPD to the corporate plan.

It is this integration with the corporate plan that is a common theme throughout the discussion of modern operations management. NPD is no exception to this.

In taking this strategy and operationalizing it, there are a large number of considerations for the NPD manager. These include the number and type of tools and techniques that the NPD team will use to assist in the process. CAD/CAM has already been discussed, and the role of project management will be considered in Chapter 8. The following section considers some tools and techniques that have proved popular recently.

Modern tools and techniques

Table 3.3 briefly summarizes some of the tools and techniques that firms use in the NPD process.

Table 3.3   Modern tools and techniques of NPD

Tool	Description	Claimed benefits
Quality function deployment (QFD)	A matrix method (see below) for relating prioritized customer attributes to engineering characteristics	Facilitates trade-off decision-making in product design
Zenbara	The dismantling of old products to obtain ideas for new ones	It can save significant investment in overly-complex technology that may not provide competitive advantage, in addition to reducing development time
Guest engineers	The temporary allocation of staff either from a supplier to a customer or *vice versa* for the purpose of encouraging information transfer between the parties. An increasing feature of arrangements where suppliers are more heavily involved in their customers' processes	By increasing the possibilities for information transfer, the chance of a design being 'right first time' is increased
Design for manufacture	In principle, this is the purposeful consideration of manufacturing constraints early and throughout the design process	Improves manufacturability and so reduce product costs
Design for assembly	As for DFM, but where the process is predominantly assembly, there are a large number of features of designs that can greatly aid their efficient assembly.	This can lead to reduced product costs, and improved product quality
Taguchi methods	The application of the principles of experimental design to determine the effect of a set of interacting variables on an outcome of interest	Claimed to save much unnecessary experimentation during development, and make products more robust (less susceptible to process variation)
Failure mode effect analysis (FMEA)	This involves the rating of three factors associated with a product or a process – namely the risk of a failure occurring, its visibility and its consequences. Rating each of these out of ten and multiplying the three factors together provides a Risk Priority Number	Ranking the Risk Priority Numbers provides a prioritized list for remedial action or control, resulting in improved product quality or more reliable processes
Value analysis	The identification of features of products and their costs against customer benefit	Reduces product costs whilst retaining its utility to the customer

Quality function deployment

Quality function deployment (QFD) is a matrix method for helping NPD managers and designers to make decisions, typically based on the trade-off between cost and performance, or other design parameters. QFD provides a graphical means for relating customer requirements to attributes that the product/service provider understands. Conveying this information is a vital part of the strategy process; without it there are too many assumptions made by project staff in relation to the needs of the customer.

An example of a basic QFD grid, which was used in a project to develop a new international MBA programme, is shown in Figure 3.7. It was vital that the faculty understood the needs of the market (the *customer attributes*), the characteristics of the course that they could control (number of staff, etc.) and the relationship between these. They would then be in a position to make design decisions regarding the degree. Before they did this however, they needed three more pieces of information. The first was the relationships between the different course characteristics. These are shown at the very top of the grid. The second concerns customer perceptions of the current programme offered by the faculty (marked by a *B* on the right hand side of the figure) relative to their major competitor (marked *A*). These are given on a 1–5 scale in the box on the right. The third piece of information concerns the measures that are included at the bottom of the figure. These are measures of actual characteristics of the courses from the existing programme and their competitor.

The customer attributes were derived through a two-stage process. The first determined the main features that were pertinent to prospective customers of the programme. The second phase required them to rank them in order of importance on a 0–10 scale. These results were then used to show the average relative importance of the attributes. As shown in the figure, the reputation of the school was the most important, achieving a relative importance of 10. 'Location' was the next highest factor, with 'cost of the course' way down in seventh place.

Considering the relationship between the course characteristics and the customer attributes, the grid shows that the higher the percentage of visiting faculty, the better the reputation of the school. However, it was not clear what the relationship between the 'number of students in the group' and 'reputation' would be. One view was that the more students in the group, the more successful the course appeared. Another view stated that small groups improved the quality of the contact between the students and the staff, and that this would improve the reputation. The relationship is therefore marked as 'requiring further investigation'.

Considering the relationships between course characteristics, there is a negative relationship between 'student qualifications' and 'number of students in the group.' Put simply, the higher you set the entry requirement for the course, the fewer students you have to choose from, hence the smaller group.

From this exercise, the course designers had a much better picture of what would make their course successful. They now had some priorities to work from and could see the impact of different factors under their control.

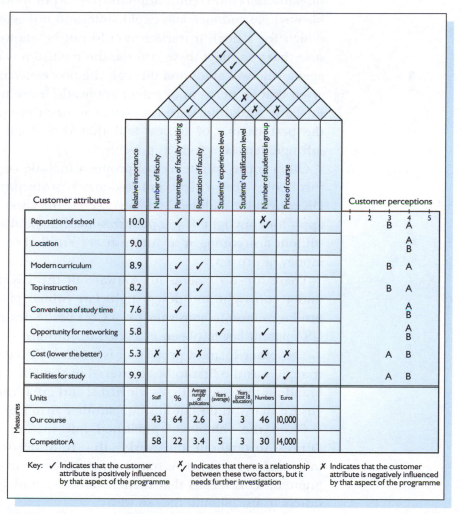

Customer attributes	Relative importance	Number of faculty	Percentage of faculty visiting	Reputation of faculty	Students' experience level	Students' qualification level	Number of students in group	Price of course			Customer perceptions
Reputation of school	10.0	✓	✓				✗✓				3 B / 4 A
Location	9.0										A / B
Modern curriculum	8.9	✓	✓								B A
Top instruction	8.2	✓	✓								B A
Convenience of study time	7.6	✓									A / B
Opportunity for networking	5.8				✓		✓				A / B
Cost (lower the better)	5.3	✗	✗	✗			✗	✗			A B
Facilities for study	9.9						✓	✓			A B

Units		Staff	%	Average number of publications	Years (average)	Years (post 18 education)	Numbers	Euros			
Our course		43	64	2.6	3	3	46	10,000			
Competitor A		58	22	3.4	5	3	30	14,000			

Measures

Key: ✓ Indicates that the customer attribute is positively influenced by that aspect of the programme ✗✓ Indicates that there is a relationship between these two factors, but it needs further investigation ✗ Indicates that the customer attribute is negatively influenced by that aspect of the programme

Figure 3.7 The QFD matrix.

Suppose you have just come up with a brilliant idea for the latest must-have gadget, which will improve the life of everyone who buys it (the bath plug that changes colour with the temperature of the bath water has already been done!). The only way to ensure that you get any financial benefit from your idea is to patent it. A patent is the sole right to exploit your idea, granted by a National Patent Office, which gives you legal redress should someone infringe your idea. You have 20 years to exploit the idea, which may involve granting a firm the right to make your product. The person who invented the original ring-pull for the drinks earned 0.01 p every time someone somewhere in the world made a can using his design. This may not seem like a lot of money, until you consider the hundreds of millions of cans that are made every year!

The requirements of a patent are that the idea must have an *inventive step* (sufficiently different from previous ideas in a demonstrable way), be commercially exploitable, and not be excluded (your new design for a nuclear warhead would not be allowed!). Once you are sure that you meet these criteria, the next step is to contact a patent agent, who will guide you through the process. This can be costly but, given that 95 per cent of patent applications are not granted (usually for fairly straightforward reasons), you need to ensure that you have the best chance of success and that your legal protection against infringement is as wide as possible.

Other forms of intellectual property include copyright (as protects this book), design right and trademark protection. Currently, in the UK copyright (and the © symbol) are *natural* laws – you do not have to apply for copyright. If you publish something and someone else uses it without accrediting it to you, you are entitled to legal redress (read money, if proven).

There are no patents for software in the UK as yet; it is covered under copyright and design right law (which protects the look of a product – most famously the Coca Cola bottle design). However, in the USA patent law has been extended to software.

The other form of protection is trademark registration (Bass's red triangle was the first to be registered in the UK). Due to the value of branding this is a vital area for firms, and great care must be taken to ensure that you do not infringe another firm's brand.

Given the volume of published information available at Patent Offices throughout the world, this is a major source of design information for firms. As stated above, 95 per cent of patents are never granted. This means that their details are available on the shelf for others to use, should they so wish.

For further information, see http://www.patent-office.gov.uk/

SUMMARY

NPD is an economically important value-stream to most organizations, and the way that it is managed can have significant consequences on the ability of the organization to compete. It covers the invention of new products, which occurs relatively rarely compared to the introduction of products new to an organization and the improvement of existing ones. The process involves the transformation of information from a concept to a completed product, and involves much cross-functional and cross-organizational activity. Customers are at the heart of the process, and suppliers have a vital role to play from the early stages of NPD onwards. At the outset of the process, the NPD manager needs to create a degree of chaos to encourage the development of a large number of new ideas. In the latter stages, the rapid filtering and development of the remaining ideas is vital. Ideas that do not contribute immediately to new products may provide an important source of revenue for the firm by being exploited in other ways. Good design is vital to customers and the organization alike, and modern best practices to assist in providing good design include concurrent engineering. Like other process in operations management, NPD has a significant strategic element. The outcome of the information transformation process is termed *intellectual property*, and this can be legally protected through patents, registered designs, copyright and trademarks in many countries.

Case study

Triumph Motorcycles

Triumph Motorcyles was a great name in bikes until the mid 1980s, when the firm finally went out of business. The reason was an inability to compete with predominantly Japanese bikes that were more sophisticated and generally better made. This was somewhat ironic, as the bikes that the Japanese firms (Honda, Yamaha, Kawasaki and Suzuki) had originally made were virtual carbon copies of the British bikes of the time. They had used the process of *reverse engineering* – or dismantling products to see how they worked – to minimize their own development time, and had made gradual improvements to the products over time. In 1985, the Triumph name was bought out and a team of developers started work on developing a range of bikes that would compete with the best Japanese and European products. The budget was miniscule by global automotive standards – £50 million to develop three bikes (Ford at the same time spent £500 million developing one engine). The bikes (the *Trophy*, a sports-touring bike; *Daytona*, the sports machine; and the *Trident*, a retro-styled street-bike) were launched to some acclaim in 1991, and the firm has gone from strength to strength since. How did they manage to develop three different machines on such a relatively small budget? They used a number of techniques, including *reverse engineering* (which ironically had been used on the original Triumph so effectively 20 years previously) and *modular design*.

Modular design in this case meant that instead of designing every part for every bike specifically, a high degree of commonality existed between the parts (86 per cent of the parts were common across all three bikes). In doing this, the firm saved significantly on manufacturing set-up costs and minimized the inventory required of each. Whilst this standardization of parts can lead to some design compromises, in this case the designers appeared to have been able to accommodate these and still produce products that performed well.

Key questions

1 Why is NPD considered to be 'an economically important activity'?
2 What are the limitations of box and arrow models of the NPD process?
3 What can the NPD manager do to ensure the best chances of success of a new product, and how would you determine success?
4 What are the limitations of using reverse engineering?
5 Why might modular design and the use of standardized components compromise the performance of the end product?
6 How would using modular design be applied to other industries? For example, would it be appropriate for other vehicle design, construction, aerospace, services and computer software design?

Key terms

Concurrent engineering
Cross-functional teams
Filters
Intellectual property
Process integration
Product life cycle
Product platforms
Quality function deployment
Time-to-market

References

Andersen Consulting (1992). *The Lean Enterprise Benchmarking Report*. Andersen Consulting.

Carroll, P. (1993). *Big Blues: The Unmaking of IBM*. Crown.

Consumers Association (2000). How does your bank rate? *Which?*, **Oct,** 35–7.

Cooper, R. G. (1988). The new product process: a decision guide for management. *J. Marketing Man.*, **3(3),** 238–55.

Davidson, H. (1987). *Offensive Marketing*. Penguin.

Dertouzos, M., Lester, R. and Solow, R. (1989). *Made In America*. MIT Press.

Dyson, J. (1997). *Against the Odds: An Autobiography*. Orion Press.

Financial Times (2000).

Griffin, A. and Page, A. L. (1993). An interim report on measuring product development success and failure. *J. Product Innov. Man.*, **10,** 291–308.

Karlsson, C. and Åhlström, P. (1996). The difficult path to lean product development. *J. Product Innov. Man.*, **13,** 283–95.

Kay, J. (1993). *Foundations of Corporate Success*. Oxford University Press.

Lancaster, G. and Massingham, L. (1993). *Marketing Management*. McGraw Hill.

McKinsey & Company (1989). Reported in: Dunaine, B.: How managers can succeed through speed. *Fortune Magazine*, **13 Feb,** 54–9.

Sobek, D. K. II, Liker, J. K. and Ward, A. C. (1998). Another look at how Toyota integrates product development. *Harvard Bus. Rev.*, **Jul–Aug,** 36–49.

Twiss, B. (1990). *Managing Technological Innovation.* Pitman Publishing.

Ulrich, K. T. and Eppinger, S. D. (1999). *Product Design and Development,* 2nd edn. McGraw-Hill.

Wheelwright, S. and Clark, K. (1992). *Revolutionizing Product Development.* Free Press.

Further reading

Booz, Allen and Hamilton Consultants (1982). *New Product Management for the 1980s.* Booz, Allen and Hamilton Consultants.

Clark, K. B. and Fujimoto, T. (1991). *Product Development Performance: Strategy, Organization and Management in the World Automotive Industry.* HBS Press.

Tidd, J., Bessant, J. and Pavitt, K. (1997). *Managing Innovation: Integrating Technological, Organizational and Market Change.* John Wiley.

Ulrich, K. T. and Eppinger, S. D. (1999). *Product Design and Development,* 2nd edn. McGraw Hill.

Von Hippel, E., Thomke, S. and Sonnack, M. (1999). Creating breakthroughs at 3M. *Harvard Bus. Rev.*, **Sep–Oct,** 47–57.

CHAPTER 4

Operations processes: process choice and layout; developing new products and services

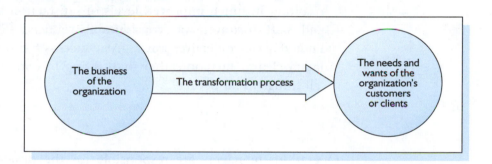

The business of the organization → The transformation process → The needs and wants of the organization's customers or clients

INTRODUCTION

Botchit and Leggit is a large law firm. Ten years ago, they had only a few solicitors and partners. Today, they employ over 400 people. Their markets for both commercial and domestic legal work have become highly competitive, with large international law firms competing for a wider range of work than they would previously have been interested in, and many small specialist firms taking on much of the low complexity work such as the domestic conveyancing for buying and selling houses. This twin-pronged attack on their markets meant that they needed to fundamentally review how they delivered services to their clients.

Botchit and Leggit was organized in the same way as many other specialist professional service organizations – with lawyers and other support staff grouped into functions. Work coming in would be passed through each of the functions in turn, depending on the specialism that was required at that time. This was fine when the objective was to have a specialist on the case at all times. The downside was that the process was very slow and expensive, and as a result customers were deserting the firm. A basic marketing analysis identified three major market groups. When these were investigated, three different types of work and sets of competitive objectives were defined. The firm reorganized by splitting the main operations into three areas, allowing each to focus on their main tasks and customer group. The results were startling – customers had their needs met far more closely, resulting in much improved levels of satisfaction and retention, and staff turnover was considerably reduced. Focusing on a limited set of objectives was a great success for staff, who had a much clearer mission rather than trying to compromise and be 'all things to all people'.

Operations managers are responsible for the design, and as in the above case, redesign of processes. Through processes, we *operationalize* strategies (turn them into reality) and create and deliver the product/service offerings required. The operations manager's role is vitally important in integrating all the contributors into the design/redesign process. As seen in Chapter 1, the nature of the transformation process in terms of volume and variety configurations is an important part of operations.

Aims and objectives

This chapter will introduce how new processes are designed, and how existing processes are redesigned in response to changing market needs and/or changing operational capabilities.

After reading this chapter you will be able to:

- Identify the role of process design/redesign in operations management and discuss the factors affecting the process design decision
- Describe the different process types for manufacturing and service operations
- Describe the different layouts that organizations can use and the benefits and limitations of each
- Explain the implications of high technology, and agile, lean and mass-customization approaches to process design
- Apply appropriate tools and techniques for process analysis.

THE FACTORS AFFECTING PROCESS DESIGN

The operations manager has a key decision to make regarding process design that will determine the future success or failure of the operation. Specific decisions are made concerning the *capacities* and *capabilities* that the operation should have. The inputs to this process are shown in Figure 4.1.

One input is *operations strategy*, the combination of the organization's and the customer's requirements. Operations strategy is expressed in terms of:

- *Scope of operations* – how much of the task will be done by the firm, in-house, and how much by suppliers and customers

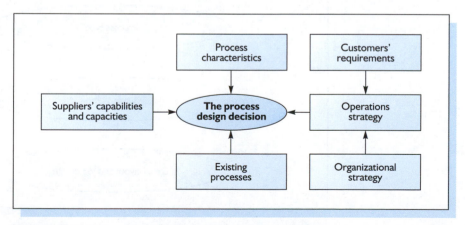

Figure 4.1 The inputs to the process design decision.

- *Scale of operations* – the required capacity of the operation (e.g. how many products per hour or customers per day the system is required to handle)
- The *cost* of the products and services
- The time allowable for *delivery* of products and services to customers.

Each of these will in turn be influenced by the organizational strategy – including the level of investment that the organization is prepared to make in these processes.

Process characteristics include the nature of what is to be transformed. The production of large-scale engineering products is clearly a quite different matter from the delivery of Internet-based services. However, these characteristics will change with time, particularly with advances in new technology – for example, the way that metal products are made today in highly automated processes is very different from the processes that existed even 30 years ago.

Existing processes provide a major input to the design decision. The level of investment that many firms have made in processes can and does provide a level of *inertia*, which can work against change or improvement. A production line or any piece of technology may take many years to repay the investment made in it. Furthermore, a process may have been in existence for some time and the firm has gained considerable knowledge about how it works. Thus there can sometimes be a dangerous mentality of 'if it ain't broke, don't fix it', and this is totally alien to practices of continuous improvement, which will be discussed in Chapter 8.

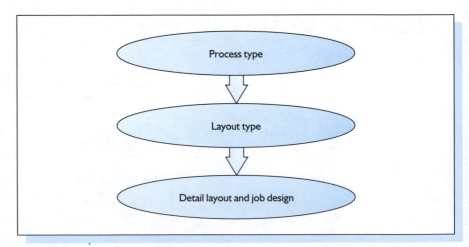

Figure 4.2 The process choice hierarchy.

Supplier capacity and capabilities is the last major input to this decision. As well as considering the operation itself, process decisions should include a consideration of the entire supply network of which the operation is a part. Greater levels of integration with suppliers and their inclusion as part of the process design are powerful and important inputs to process design.

Once we know what the requirements are, we can select the best process type for those requirements. As with product design the decision will rarely be clear-cut, and we will have to make trade-off decisions, such as between unit cost and flexibility. Once the best process type has been decided, the best layout type can be matched to the process type. The final step is detailed process layout design, where individual operations are allocated to particular operators. How integrated tasks should be – whether people do a small part of an operation or a larger element – is also determined at this stage. This process is shown in Figure 4.2.

Process type and physical layout

Process type refers to broad categories of operations configurations, which are available for the operations manager to select from. *Physical layout* describes the actual placement of people or machines that take part in the transformation process.

In the first part of this section we will consider the five process types; in the second part we will look at physical layout. Process choice and physical layout are closely linked; process choice will to a large extent dictate the physical layout of the transformation process.

THE FIVE GENERIC PROCESS TYPES

The five generic process types are project, job, batch, line and continuous. Figure 4.3 shows how each of these relates to the volume and variety of the transformation process. Each process type is associated with a particular combination of volume and variety. You saw in Chapter 1 how the volume/variety configuration provides clues to the nature of the firm's core operations. Organizations who compete on cost usually rely on high volumes to achieve the low unit costs through *economies of scale*, which will be examined in more detail in Chapter 6. These result from the operation being able to use larger machines or more specialized workers. Economies also arise from the ability to purchase in bulk and have more control over the supply chain.

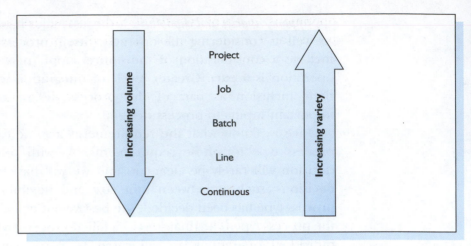

Figure 4.3 The five generic process choices.

The choice of process type is strategically important, because firms are limited in what they can and cannot do once this has been decided. To a large extent the process determines what the organization's capabilities are, and how it delivers products and services to customers or clients.

Within an organization, different stages of production or different service activities may use different process types. For example, Carrefour, the French hypermarket chain, will predominantly sell goods in very high volumes, but within Carrefour's stores some variety is available in the delicatessen areas within the shop, where each customer can select the quantity required of a particular item. Other supermarkets have begun to adopt this approach. Typically, though, a dominant process choice will be associated with the core process – in Carrefour's case, high volume, low variety processes.

We will now consider each of the process types in turn, starting with the lowest volume processes, projects, and moving to the line and continuous flow processes.

Project

You are probably familiar with some high-profile activities, such as the construction of the London Eye, or the Sydney Olympics. The best process type for large-scale, complex products, or services that are low-volume or unique, is nearly always *project*. In manufacturing, aerospace and other high-tech products such as flight simulators, as well as most civil engineering and construction (e.g. bridges and tunnels), organize operations as projects. In services, most consulting and other professional services can be classified as project work, because the relationship with each client is unique.

Whilst there is a degree of uniqueness associated with projects that does not exist for other process types, we still refer to it as a *process*. That is, some common elements will be used from one project to the next. These common elements include the techniques used for project planning and scheduling. Easy-to-use tools such as Gantt charts are often employed for simple projects, whilst more sophisticated tools such as project network planning may be used for complex projects (this is discussed in more detail in Chapter 9). These are used to ensure that the individual nature of the customer requirements can be delivered.

In project environments, highly flexible and mobile staff are required. Consultants are often required to go where the work is – that is, they work around the client. Similarly, people working on major construction projects, such as dams, may travel all over the world.

Job

Many products are manufactured and services provided in very small quantities, sometimes as 'one-offs'. The process choice associated with this is *jobbing*. Whilst projects are also associated with low-volume high-variety outputs, the variety of work is generally more limited than the complete individuality of projects, and there would at least be a largely common process between jobs. This is illustrated by the following examples.

A freelance graphic designer or book editor will provide jobbing services to advertising agencies and publishers respectively. In manufacturing, jobbing is the closest process choice to traditional craft manufacturing. You would be likely to find jobbing used in making prototypes of new products and in making unique products, such as machines, tools and fixtures to make other products. Another example would be making clothing in the *haute-couture* industry.

As for projects, workers in jobbing work will need to be highly flexible. In manufacturing, because only small quantities of a single product are being processed at a time – and sometimes even 'one-offs' – the organization will generally invest in general-purpose machines rather than ones designed for a narrow range of products.

To support jobbing, detailed planning is required to decide what sequence each product will follow through the operation.

Batch

Batch production describes a process where products or services are produced in groups of similar (or mostly similar) outputs at higher volume and lower variety than in jobbing. The following example illustrates the difference between jobbing and batch processes. A jobbing printer would be able to copy a small quantity of notes for a lecture programme, with no expectation that the work would be repeated. Set-up costs would be low, but the unit cost would be high. Batch printing would become appropriate where the same lecture programme was being run many times. There would be some set-up costs (e.g. for typesetting), and for each course a number could be produced but at a much lower unit cost.

Some businesses have no choice but to run batch processes. These are particularly evident where the product is in seasonal markets. Wine producers have to harvest their grapes, usually during just a few days each year, and get the product into production as quickly as possible. They run an 'annual batch', or vintage.

Other examples of batch operations include a local bakery and all types of moulding, where a 'master mould' is created and products are pulled from the mould. A surgeon in a hospital will routinely batch together certain complementary surgical procedures to allow other specialists all to be present at the same time.

In batch production, particularly at the low-volume end (such as hand-laminating glass-reinforced plastics), we again find general-purpose machines. Operators may need to be able to perform multiple functions, as in jobbing, and especially be able to move to different workstations as and when required. Scheduling can be complicated, especially when new products and one-offs also have to be scheduled. At higher volumes more automation may be appropriate, and special purpose machines may be used instead of general purpose. Batch is quite complicated to manage. One of the ways to help manage a range of products is to divide them into relatively high and low volumes. Low-volume batch production will resemble job processes; high-volume batch production will resemble a line process.

Line

At greater volumes than batch operations, products and services are usually highly standardized, with little variation between one unit of output and the next. *Line* operations are usually found when the process can focus on a conversion activity that results in a single type of output, but where each stage of the process between input and output is distinct from the other stages.

High-volume, standardized products such as particular car models, televisions, stereos, DVDs and computers are particularly suited to line production. In services, line processes are used in the preparation of fast food or in handling standard financial paperwork such as mortgage applications. In either case, there is a set sequence of events in the conversion process.

The highly standardized products found in line processes are also associated with higher investments in technology, which may be unique to a firm or even a specific product line. Gillette's $1 billion spend on developing the Mach 3 razor was predominantly taken up by development of the production process to make this product. This process is the subject of great secrecy and provides something their competitors have so far been unable to copy – three blades on a razor.

There are several disadvantages to using line production for any but the most standard products. The first is that line production is dedicated to a single product; the introduction of new products using the existing line is difficult. As discussed later in this chapter, operations managers now have a number of possibilities open to them should they need to increase the variety of products whilst still maintaining the advantages of a high-volume line process – in particular, low unit cost.

Continuous

Unlike the other four process types, *continuous* production does not result in discrete outputs (we cannot count or separate units of output within the production process). It is typically found where a process can be set up to run without stopping – some continuous processes run all day, every day, for a year or longer. Continuous production is applicable where products are totally standardized, such as in power generation, chemical refining, steel production and some food processing, but there are few service operations that are located in this high-volume, low-variety area. It is associated with very high investment in dedicated facilities and equipment, with work mainly automated and low levels of labour input beyond control and monitoring.

Continuous production differs from line production because the latter can be stopped at a particular stage of production and the production process can be restarted again without affecting the product, whilst stopping a continuous process is generally avoided because production cannot easily be restarted without having to discard all of the materials being processed. In addition, there may be significant costs associated with the stoppage – shutting down blast-furnaces used in steel production generally requires that the furnace be re-lined, at a cost of many tens of thousands of pounds.

The process types given above are summarized in Table 4.1.

Whilst we can differentiate services according to the same process types as manufacturing organizations, other classifications shed more light on the nature of the processes we are describing.

The choice of process and layout has clear links with the product life cycle. The life-cycle diagram serves to show where a particular product is in its life cycle and where, consequently, it should be placed in terms of process choice. In the early stages of the product's life the 'focused'

Table 4.1   Summary of process types

Process type	Process characteristics
Project	Highly flexible. Individualized output results in high unit costs. Mobile and flexible staff required. Quality determined by individual customer requirements
Jobbing	Significant flexibility required, though the volume is generally higher than when compared to projects. Some repetition in the system, and many more common elements to the process than occur with projects. High unit costs relative to higher volume processes, but low set-up costs
Batch	Some flexibility to handle differences between batches still necessary, requiring some investment in set-up for each batch. Higher levels of specialization required in both people and machines
Line	Highly specialized people and machines allow high rates of throughput and low unit costs. Limited flexibility usually associated with this process. Quality levels consistent.
Continuous	Usually non-discrete products produced over a significant period of time. Very high levels of investment required and limited possibility for flexibility due to highly dedicated processes. Commonly highly automated

area of manufacture will be in a low-volume batch group; it may return to another low-volume focused area at the decline stage of its 'life'. In the growth, maturity and saturation stages the product is best manufactured in a group of high-volume batch, and as volume increases single line processes are most appropriate, generally in 'U'-shaped lines. The product life cycle and the link to process choice is shown in Figure 4.4:

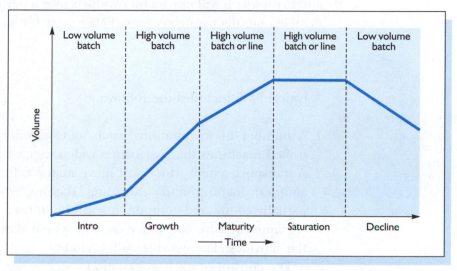

Figure 4.4 The change of process choice in a product life cycle.

There are two things to bear in mind with the product life cycle:

1 Not all products will go through each stage of the life cycle – in the UK the Sinclair C5 died very early in its product 'life'
2 The length of time that a product may remain in a particular stage of the cycle will vary – the stages are not the same lengths of time for every product.

A firm must link manufacturing processes with product requirements and so movement from one process choice to another might take place when any of the following factors are present:

● A new or substantially modified product is being introduced
● Competitive factors and priorities have changed
● Volume changes occur
● The current performance of a product is inadequate
● Competitors are gaining advantage by a better process approach or new technology.

The point of the product life cycle in relation to manufacturing is that it reveals that, due to the changes in volume in a product's life cycle, one fixed process is not necessarily sufficient or indeed applicable for a product for the duration of its life. As a result, flexible systems have to be in place to facilitate this change over a period of time. Investment in these processes, although expensive, is increasingly viewed as a competitive requirement. It is clear, therefore, that a standard line cannot hope to satisfy the market requirements of variety, flexibility and so on which will impact on products over a period of time. Instead, flexible manufacturing systems (FMS) cater for such variety.

 ## Flexible manufacturing systems

A typical FMS includes the following:

1 A number of workstations, such as Computer Numerically Controlled machines that perform a wide range of operations
2 A transport system which will move material from one machine to another; loading and unloading stations where completed or partially completed components will be housed and worked upon
3 A comprehensive computer control system that will coordinate all the activities. The activities will include:
   - The control of each workstation
   - Distribution of control instructions to workstations
   - Production control
   - Traffic control
   - Tool control
   - System performance monitoring.

FMS enables speed and flexibility – in terms of rapid changes to products – to be made with precision and consistency of reliability. FMS cells are arranged around a group of products where some variety of the product is required even though volume is high. If the volume was very high and the product variability was minimal, then a line process would be most applicable. FMS allows a product to be made in a number of variations and in different volumes over a period of time. This has clear benefits for both manufacturer and customer (Bateman and Zeithaml, 1993, p. 680):

Mazda's production plans for a Monday are final on Friday afternoon, compared to the three weeks' lag time at General Motors ... Dies can be changed in minutes, whereas in US plants changing dies took hours or even a full workday . . . Mazda can deliver a tailor-made car in one week, compared to three weeks for US manufacturers. With the advantages of speed, quality and customized products, flexible manufacturing appears to be a mode of operations that auto makers must adopt for long-term survival.

However, success with FMS is not just about investment in technology. Any organization has to invest in human resources to gain benefits from FMS, as Bessant (1991, p. 121) indicates:

> . . . a point which emerges from a number of studies is that the benefits of FMS investment often come more from the organizational changes which it catalyses than from a narrow set of physical equipment which is installed. It forces a 'new way of thinking' on the firm and it is this change in approach which is critical in obtaining the full benefits.

Thus far we have discussed manufacturing processes. Clearly service processes are core to many types of organizations, and so we need to understand the different types of processes within service environments.

Service processes

Four process choices have been identified by Schmenner (1986) that are useful for classifying service process choices. These are the service shop, service factory, mass service and professional service, as shown in Figure 4.5.

It is possible to match these service process types with the generic process types discussed above. *Professional services* are often organized as projects, with the consultants (or whoever is involved in the service delivery process) working around the customer. There is a high level of labour intensity, as there is little scope for automation of the service, and high levels of customer interaction (to obtain and deliver the required information).

Service shops are often associated with jobbing operations, including car repairs and hospital activities. Here, there is a similar degree of individuality in the way that the service is delivered – every person or job is different, but the labour intensity is markedly lower.

Both service shops and mass services may use batch processes, depending on the level of customization of outputs for individual customers.

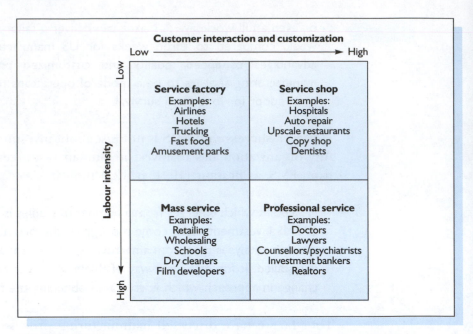

Figure 4.5 Schmenner's service matrix (based on Schmenner, 1986).

Mass services provide a highly standardized service to their customers, though this still requires some labour input to each customer.

Service factories are often set up around line production, and require minimal input to individuals. Theme parks may put on characters who will give a 'veneer of individuality', but in reality this is only a very small part of the overall service that they are providing.

One type of process that has not been included in this analysis is that most basic unit of activity, the craft process. Here, one person performs the vast majority of the task, relying on his or her skills and knowledge of the area to do so. Examples of this type of work include independent financial advisors, blacksmiths and other very small businesses – usually based around one individual. The process choice in such cases is limited to the scale and scope that the individual can provide, although some of the detail layout issues will be pertinent. For the operations manager selecting a craft process may be an option when considering how work is to be performed, though in larger organizations, this will be used as part of one of the core process types.

Having determined the process type that we need to have, as described above, the next decision for the operations manager is the layout that needs to be in place, and this is discussed in the following section.

Connecting process choice and layout

Process choice and layout are closely linked. Table 4.2 summarizes the predominant linkages.

Table 4.2 shows that the predominant relationship between process and layout choices is clustered around the diagonal. This is not necessarily the only case, indicating that in many cases there are a number of options available to the operations manager. The other factors of operations strategy, process characteristics, existing processes and suppliers will all guide the choice. Of these, the role of the competitive objectives that the organization is striving to achieve will be a key concern.

As noted earlier, process choice largely determines how the firm competes in the marketplace. Project and jobbing processes are associated with a wide variety of products or designs, which can be customized for individual customers or clients. Volumes are small or products may even be 'one-offs'. New products or product improvements may be required on an ongoing basis. The firm competes based on flexibility, including design and innovation.

Line and continuous processes, on the other hand, are associated with the delivery of a narrow range of standard outputs in high volume. Introducing new products or services takes longer than in project and job production, because the process is dedicated to specific products.

Although the project–fixed layout, jobbing–process layout, and line or continuous–product layout connections are straightforward, batch production is linked to different physical layouts depending on factors besides volume and variety (scope and scale).

Table 4.2 The link between process choice and layout.

LAYOUT TYPE	PROCESS TYPE				
	Project	Jobbing	Batch	Line	Continuous
Fixed-position	•••	••	•		
Process	•	•••	•••		
Cell	•	•••	•••	•	
Product			•	•••	•••

•, a possible link; ••, a likely link; •••, the most likely linkage between the layout and the process type.

The most common process choice is batch, but it is difficult to build strategic competitive advantage around batch processes – it is often 'stuck in the middle'. Managers often focus their attention on finding the optimum batch size, rather than on customer service. New techniques such as *mass customization* and *agile* manufacturing offer a way of copying the characteristics of either jobbing or high-volume process choices to batch production. These techniques will be discussed later in this chapter.

A danger for both manufacturing and service organizations is that redesign of processes can cause a mismatch between the process choice and customer expectations. In a professional services setting (or in job production) customers expect high customization as well as high labour inputs. However, if the service provider (e.g. legal or medical services) begins to use batch production to reduce costs, customization may become compromised. In the example given at the start of this chapter, the focusing of the business into several smaller operations that handled the needs of that particular customer group better than the original 'one-size-fits-all' approach, the redesign enabled the operation to deliver its competitive objectives.

The following considers the overall layouts that can be used. As will be seen, the choice has considerable influence on the nature of the work done in each case, the type of equipment that will be required and the nature of the flow of work through the operation.

PHYSICAL LAYOUT

The process type is reflected in how the operation arranges its activities, or its layout. Specifically, we now have to decide how the tasks that make up the operation are to be delivered. The process type determines the nature of the tasks that will be performed – for example, will these be project activities or will they be part of the work in a line process? The layout determines where and in what sequence activities that make up a process are located. The four basic layout types – fixed, process, product and hybrid or cell layouts – were identified in Table 4.2. The following describes each in more detail.

Fixed-position layout

In a *fixed-position layout* the product or person being acted on remains in one place whilst operations take place around it. Workers come to the product (or to the production location) instead of the product moving between workers and/or work centres, and workers carry out single or multiple activities to modify a product or provide a service until completion.

Fixed-position layouts are used in services, e.g. in dental or surgical treatments where the patient remains in a single location whilst being treated. In manufacturing, the production of heavy, bulky or fragile products, such as ships and aeroplanes, and most construction projects take place with the people and machines moving around the 'product'.

Fixed-position layouts are associated generally with lower volume process types – most usually projects (as in construction), but sometimes with jobbing processes (specialized contractors in construction) and batch processes (as with the production of aeroplanes or construction of many types of the same house on a housing development).

Process layout

In a *process layout*, specific types of operations are grouped together within the manufacturing or service facility. There is no pre-specified 'standard' flow. Products move around according to processing requirements, as shown in Figure 4.6. This layout type is commonly used in hospitals, where specialisms are grouped together – e.g. accident and emergency, X-ray facilities, paediatrics etc. Since few patients will have identical problems and so will not receive identical treatment, wards and departments are laid out to accommodate a wide range of potential patient requirements. Many retail operations, especially department stores, use a process layout, where the customers move between areas dedicated to different goods, such as kitchenware, furniture and clothing.

The same occurs in manufacturing operations such as precision engineering, where the product does not move in a specified sequence but is moved to particular areas as and when required, allowing a variety of products to be made. In manufacturing, a process layout is commonly associated with jobbing production, where low volumes of products such as furniture, high-fashion clothing and jewellery are produced to individual requirements. In general, low-volume batch production will also be associated with process layout, although high-volume batch production may follow the product layout that is described next.

This layout is ideal for handling small batches of 'products' or a wide variety of tasks, each of which require specialist people or machines.

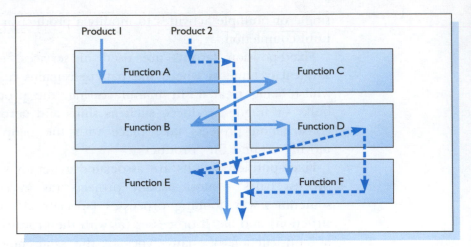

Figure 4.6 Process layout in a *functional* approach.

Process layouts are associated with flexible equipment and workers, so that even if a single operation breaks down the whole process does not have to stop. The problem, as Figure 4.6 demonstrates, is that even with only two products running through this system the *flow* becomes complex and difficult to manage. If you move between the different functions, such as in a hospital, you may have to queue before being 'processed' by each of the specialist functions. This functional approach therefore is usually not the fastest at handling throughput, and often requires people to 'progress chase' items through the system, or develop complex IT systems to keep track of the location of particular items.

The law firm in the example described at the start of this chapter originally used a process layout. The redesign involved splitting the process to meet the needs of different client groups, and the following two designs were used to provide the necessary focus for each micro-operation (or *operation within an operation*).

Product layout

The product layout was developed during mass production, as an extension of the principles of scientific management in the context of assembly-line production. In a product layout, people and machines are dedicated to a single product or small range of similar products. Each workstation is laid out in a sequence that matches the requirements of the product exactly, and each stage is separate from the next stage, as shown in Figure 4.7.

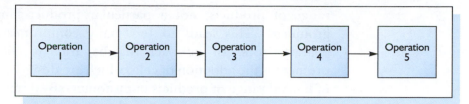

Figure 4.7 Product layout.

The sequence of operations in a product layout follows a straightforward sequence, where one activity in the line cannot be started unless the previous activity has already been completed. In manufacturing, the product layout is common in automobile assembly and other high-volume applications. In services, this layout can be found in high-volume, standard services, especially where there is a tangible element, such as fast-food preparation. IKEA, the furniture retailer, has a product layout for its stores. People have to follow a pre-defined route through the store, from one area to another. In this way IKEA achieve rates of customer throughput (see Chapter 7) that few other retailers can match.

The operation does not need to be laid out in this manner – indeed, space restrictions often dictate that a straight line cannot be used. Keeping the divisions between the operations remains, but the overall layout can take a 'U' or an 'S' shape.

In line operations, workstations should be located close together to minimize materials movement. Materials flow and control is critical, especially in ensuring that there is a steady flow of work to do and that both stock-outs (where materials run out) and large piles of work-in-process (WIP) are minimized. Because each workstation is dependent on the next, the speed of the entire line is determined by the workstation with the lowest capacity. Furthermore, if a single work centre is not operating the entire line comes to a halt very rapidly. Japanese automotive manufacturers have made a feature of this for some time – if there is a problem with any part of the operation, any worker can stop the line. This focuses attention on removing and preventing recurrence of the problem, which would be hidden if the line were allowed to continue working.

The hybrid process/product cell

In large or complex operations, neither the process nor product layout may be entirely satisfactory. The machines or work centres (operating theatres, departments in a store) are designed to accommodate a range of products, not a particular product family (or customer grouping). This leads to too many compromises in the process characteristics. An approach that has tried to eliminate these compromises is the adoption of cells, which are designed to meet the needs of limited range of products or customers. By doing so they can be far more focused on those needs, rather than trying to meet a much wider range.

As shown in Figure 4.8, the cell layout has a number of features. These include the layout in a U-shape, which allows one operator to carry out more than one function and to maintain all operations within sight of each other (facilitates communication and control). The facilities are more flexible than would be found in a product layout and the operators are multi-skilled (they can carry out more than one task).

There are other aspects of cell working that firms have found beneficial. These include the team-working benefits that go with having a small group of people working together, and the increased autonomy that such cells permit. They can, for example, considerably simplify the scheduling process, allowing managers to schedule by cell rather than by scheduling each machine. In addition, it is often found that the work moves faster through cells than is the case in more traditional line processes, thus achieving short lead-times for customers.

In manufacturing, machines are grouped together in a cell to support the production of a single product family. This approach is

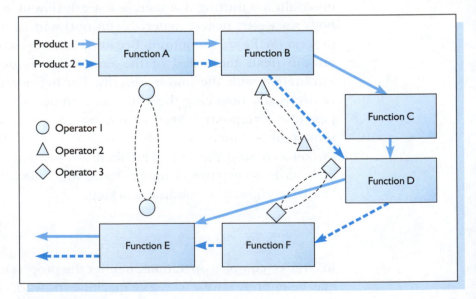

Figure 4.8 Cell layout.

common in high-tech manufacturing environments, where high volume and moderate variety can be achieved simultaneously. In services, activities are grouped together to produce similar services or handle the requirements of a particular customer group. Some high-volume, batch-type services such as call centres use a cell layout, where calls are routed through to specific areas. Department stores are clusters of cells, where each holds the goods needed by a particular customer group. They also have the capability to deal with the entire customer transaction, including taking payment and dealing with any after-sales issues.

Process choice and competitive objectives

As discussed in Chapter 2, Hill (1995) distinguished between 'order-qualifying' and 'order-winning' criteria. Order-qualifying criteria are those factors that an organization needs in order to be considered at all by customers, and order-winning criteria are those factors that a company needs to win customer orders. Hill suggested that order-qualifying and order-winning criteria can be mapped on to process choice, as shown in Figure 4.9.

Organizations can use this framework to analyse how process choice limits their ability to compete on certain competitive objectives. Process choice, however, is a broad decision, and only by going for a layout type that is different from that of competitors can firms achieve advantage through it. For instance, the predominant layout in car production is the product layout. Volvo Cars decided to break with this and create advantage by using a cell layout at their Udvalla plant. The benefits of fast throughput and team working would, they argued, outweigh the disadvantages of lack of specialization amongst their

	Project	Job	Batch	Line	Continuous
Order-winning criteria	Delivery Quality Design capability	Delivery Quality Design capability	⟷	Price	Price
Qualifying criteria	Price	Price	⟷	Delivery Quality Design capability	Delivery Quality Design capability

Figure 4.9 Linking process choice and order-qualifying/order-winning criteria.

assembly workers. The outcome was not positive for the company, but this was a bold move in an attempt to create advantage through layout.

Choosing the layout for a process is a basic operational decision that needs to be made and revisited regularly to check whether a change to layout would indeed yield advantage. Alternatively, competitive advantage can be pursued through other means, including through the detailed layout decisions discussed below. The choice is never totally straightforward, however. A firm may produce the same type of product for two markets under one process choice. The particular needs of each market may differ, even though the process choice is the same. For example, a firm producing flight simulator units supplies two markets, commercial and military. The requirements for the two are entirely different in terms of cost, delivery reliability and features, even though each simulator product is made under a project process choice. Under the process choice mapping model we would expect the competitive requirements to be the same because they share the same process choice, but this is not the case.

The layout decision is rarely a simple one, as the above has demonstrated. The information that operations managers have to work with will also be imprecise, particularly when it comes to working with forecasts for demand. This changes the nature of the very task that operations managers have to perform from the highly scientific approaches that were advocated by the management scientists (often called *operations researchers*, when related to this field) of the past to one that is highly creative. This is most obvious when they have to deal with the many apparent conflicts in the process – e.g. the choice between a layout that would deliver a service cheaply and one that would provide the necessary levels of customer interaction.

TRENDS IN PROCESS DESIGN

Manufacturing

In many industries, mass production (and the inherent product layouts) is still the dominant way of organizing the production of high volumes of standardized products. A major change is that recently in many markets customers or competitors have forced mass producers to change their approach to process design, to allow them to compete in new ways. These new approaches have been made possible through the application of computer and communications technology, coupled with new ways of thinking about operations. Two new approaches to designing process have created new options. Many operations are actively pursuing one or both of the following alternatives to traditional mass production:

- Mass customization
- Agile manufacturing.

Mass customization

Mass customization describes the provision of what customers perceive as customized goods and services in high volume, but the operation can create and deliver without incurring additional costs to change the output's design or appearance. The idea is simple; make exactly what the customer wants in the quantity that he or she desires. This can be created through limited design variety based around a single product platform or related variants of that platform (see Chapter 3). Cellular phone and pager manufacturers are taking advantage of mass customization when they offer customers the ability to select an 'individual' (out of a finite range) faceplate. Similarly, web sites can use 'cookies' to customize web sites for return visitors, a technique used to great advantage by Internet book and gift retailer Amazon.com, who provide customers with recommendations based on the their past purchases.

Mass customization attempts to combine the benefits to customers of higher variety whilst retaining the benefits, in terms of costs in particular, of high volumes.

Hewlett-Packard is one firm that has experimented with using *mass customization* to deliver products to customers in a cost-efficient and timely manner. Products such as Hewlett-Packard's computers are designed around independent modules that can be assembled into different products easily and inexpensively. Since final assembly of these modules can be postponed until the very last stages of the process, customization can be undertaken in close proximity to their dealers, who can request a specific model. This has achieved savings on transport and logistics costs. In 1999, in order to attempt to emulate the success of Dell Computer's direct sales strategy, Hewlett-Packard moved to providing the same service to end customers rather than just to dealers, extending their need and capability for mass customization.

Mass customization requires more than rethinking product design and assembly. However a firm pursues *mass customization*, a strategic plan needs to be in place simply because capabilities will not be developed by mere chance. Mass customization requires marketing and operations cooperation, as well as a comprehensive operations strategy being in place, before mass customization is attempted. Many firms have attempted mass customization and failed, because it requires a strategic leap from mass production rather than tinkering with the final stages of an operation. Clearly *mass customization* is based on operations capabilities, but it is more than simply enhancing the existing technologies and competencies that a particular firm may possess. Instead, whole supply chains may need to be reconfigured and, in doing so, greater responsibility might be placed on firms within the supply chain or supply network.

A key issue here is the ability to respond to customer requirements and to do so quickly. Many in the car industry believe that it is only a matter of time before you will be able to order a car to your specification one day, and have the exact car delivered, made to order (as opposed to delivered from stock) within 48 hours.

Agile manufacturing

Agile manufacturing has been proposed as an alternative approach to mass production or mass customization (Kidd, 1994). Bessant *et al.* (2001, p. 24) offer a useful definition of *agility*:

> Agility in manufacturing involves being able to respond quickly and effectively to the current configuration of market demand, and also to be proactive in developing and retaining markets in the face of extensive competitive forces.

They further argue that agility can be defined by what it is *not*. Agility is *not*:

- just about adoption of specific technology
- available in a single panacea
- simply following fashion
- just adoption *per se* – implementation has profound importance
- merely equipment-based
- always about radical change
- the province of specialists.

To achieve agility, the operation must deploy agile strategy, processes, linkages and people. *Agile strategy* describes the processes for understanding the firm's situation within its sector, committing to agile strategy, aligning it to a fast moving market, and communicating and deploying it effectively. *Agile processes* refer to the provision of the actual facilities and processes to allow agile functioning of the organization. *Agile linkages* include intensively working with and learning from others outside the company, especially customers and suppliers. *Agile people* consist of a flexible and multi-skilled workforce, working with a culture that allows initiative, creativity and supportiveness to thrive throughout the organization.

Mass customization and agility compared

Whilst customization within mass markets is nothing new, the degree to which customization is demanded in industrial markets is now greater than before, and similar requirements are now evident within consumer markets. Both *mass customization* and *agility* require more than fine-tuning existing operations capabilities; they are instead major changes, which may demand radical configurations and redesign of operations within the firm's plants. The impact of rapid change and increased competition providing greater choice for customers has now placed enormous responsibilities on operations managers.

The role of technology in process design

Some firms have tried to satisfy simultaneous demands for low cost, flexibility, speed and variety simply by investing in process technology. In many businesses the use of *Enterprise Resource Planning* (ERP) systems provides the information infrastructure to meet the needs of fast response to customer requirements. In manufacturing, many firms have made substantial investments in technology, including:

- *Flexible Manufacturing Systems (FMS)* – small groups of machine tools linked together by robotized loading and transportation facilities
- *Computer-aided Design and Manufacturing (CAD/CAM)* – see Chapter 3
- *Computer-integrated Manufacturing (CIM)* – where entire processes are linked through a single controlling computer.

These have often accompanied the modification of existing processes though cell layouts. However, such approaches, although possibly providing opportunities for the firm to develop competencies, are not sufficient in themselves. General Motors spent $80 billion on technology during the 1980s, only to see their domestic market share shrink from around 56 per cent in 1979 to around 30 per cent by 1999.

Turning technology into competitive advantage is a major challenge for firms. Operations must manage the capabilities of both staff and systems (including suppliers) prior to investment in technology in order to prepare for the new capabilities and limitations of these systems. Failure to do so will often result in wasted investment. Indeed, there is a need for a comprehensive, coherent strategic framework to be in place within firms if investment in process technology is to contribute to competitive advantage. During the 1980s, firms investing in flexible manufacturing systems found that the processes were often not fulfilling their potential for improving productivity and reducing costs, due to:

- Operator error – the controlling computers were usually complex to operate and required considerably more operator training than firms were prepared to pay for
- Poor materials – the requirements for consistency of materials was far greater; a robotized handling systems at that time was markedly less able to handle any variety (such as small dimensional changes) in the materials than a human-operated system
- Maintenance problems – when you have a highly complex machine that employs computer controls, electronics systems, electrical systems and usually some hydraulics that all come from different manufacturers, and something goes wrong, who do you call to come and fix it?

The problem is often that firms do not take the time to learn; they expect and budget for instant results. There are many cases of firms that spent sufficient sums but failed to take the time to learn from successes and failures in using technology. As a result, investments became financial millstones. For others, such investment created leverage, brought about by advanced technology allied to enhanced skills, know-how and learning.

Clearly, managing the process transformation is an enormously important challenge for operations managers in both service and manufacturing settings. Success does not come about purely by having the right technology. Other factors, including the way that it is used and integrated into the layouts and overall processes, may be more important.

SUMMARY

The five basic types of process choice are: project, job, batch, line and continuous. The basic types of layout are: fixed, process, hybrid (cell) and product, and there are links between the layout (the physicality of operations) and process choice (the transformation). A process choice will indicate what a firm *can and cannot* do. Process choice may significantly influence what the company sells and what it is able to offer.

Process technology is not a quick-fix solution, and investment must be made alongside skills and capabilities. Any investment has to be made to support the company in its chosen market, and should not be at the whim of a particular technical specialist but a holistic decision for the company.

Understanding processes is as important to services as it is to manufacturing. The five types of processes can be mapped on to services, but the Schmenner matrix model also helps to aid understanding into the nature of service processes.

Case study

Service processes at Social Services

Oakmead is the area head office of a Social Services department in the South of England. Its catchment area deals with around 100 000 people. The range of services includes an 'intake' unit, devoted to initial assessments, care for the elderly, child care, help for the disabled and support for mental health clients. The demands placed upon Social Services can be enormous, and social workers are often in no-win situations in a range of critical areas. For example, if a child is brought into care then Social Services may be accused of breaking up the family unit; if on the other hand a tragic event happens within a family during the time when Social Services were beginning to be involved, the consequences can be devastating for all concerned. Moreover, both the local and national press seem keen to highlight instances when things go wrong. Perhaps the most well known of these came in 1988 in the North of England, where there was a series of reports of what were perceived as 'bad practice' relating to detecting child abuse.

Like all Social Services Oakmead is subject to a shortage of funds, and this calls for the very best of operations management to make the greatest use of limited resources, in particular with regard to how to manage a range of different operations processes. Back in 1995 the Oakmead office had been arranged by four geographic areas – North, South, East and West – in order to cover the geographic region. Each area had its own specialist teams, but the arrangement placed emphasis on area rather than on process. By 1997 the Oakmead office was struggling to meet clients' needs, and in 1998 the County Council Head Office hired management consultants to assess the current position in order to make suggestions for improvements throughout the region. When the management teams in Oakmead were asked to work with consultants, a number of key problems came to light. The first was a layout problem. Consultants had been surprised, when reading the breakdown of figures for types of clients, to see that there was a low referral rate for both elderly and disabled clients. However, when they came to the Oakmead office the reason for this became clear; the reception area was on the third floor in a building that had no lift! The other problem was that there was confusion with process flows, resulting in duplication of process tasks throughout the office. For example, when a potential client telephoned the office the approach was very resource-driven rather than client-led. Great emphasis was placed upon *where* the person lived rather than what the needs of the client were. Once the need had been determined the client would be forwarded to a particular geographic grouping, and would then need to provide the same details that had been given in the initial telephone conversation.

After agreeing with senior-level managers that there were problems with how processes were managed, the following changes took place. First, the physical aspects needed to be changed, and so the reception area was moved to the ground floor. Not surprisingly it was then found that the number of elderly and disabled clients increased dramatically in the following 12 months – by 32 per cent for elderly and 56 per cent for disabled clients, who had formerly been put off by having to climb stairs. Second, walls that had created barriers between geographic teams were demolished. Three months after the changes were made, the area manager commented: 'immediately, the atmosphere changed – we got things done by talking with each other rather than being huddled in our separate offices'.

In addition to changing the physical aspects of the layout, Social Services were fundamentally reorganized around focused process groupings rather than by the former geographic layout. For example, when examining the flow of operations it became clear that the intake process was the high-volume centre of the system. As a result of this assessment, additional staff were recruited to deal with the high number of intake calls. The process was rearranged so that the intake team (a high-volume, service factory process) would now quickly forward the clients' details to a specialist group. Once the call was put through, the process then became that of a professional service – a unique encounter between the client and the service provider. The specialist process groups – care for the elderly, childcare, help for the disabled and support for mental health clients – would deal with needs across the region rather than within specific geographic boundaries.

The improvements were dramatic, including response times to child-at-risk situations cut by a half; and the number of disabled people seen over a year period increased by 36 per cent.

Clearly, understanding the nature of the service delivery and then managing processes by grouping around focused areas has enormous benefits for service and manufacturing environments.

Key questions

1 Describe the process choice and layout that you would expect to find in the following:
   a. A fast food restaurant
   b. A general hospital
   c. A car repair workshop.
2 Explain why flexible manufacturing systems are now in place in many high volume industries.
3 Provide three examples of each of the following:
   a. A professional service
   b. A mass service
   c. A service factory.

Key terms

Cellular layouts
Continuous process
Job
Line
Mass Service
Process choice
Process technology
Professional services
Project
Service factory

References

Bateman, T. and Zeithaml, C. (1993). *Management: Function and Strategy*. Irwin.

Bessant, J. (1991). *Managing Advanced Manufacturing Technology*. Blackwell.

Bessant, J., Brown, S., Francis, D. and Meredith, S. (2001). Developing manufacturing agility in SMEs. *Int. J. Technol. Man.*, **1–3,** 12–33.

Hill, T. (1995). *Manufacturing Strategy*. Macmillan.

Kidd, P. (1994). *Agile Manufacturing – Forging New Frontiers*. Addison Wesley.

Schmenner, R.W. (1986). How can services business survive and prosper? *Sloan Man. Rev.*, **27(3),** 21–32.

Further reading

Åhlström, P. and Westbrook, R. (1999). Implications of mass customization for operations management. An exploratory survey. *Int. J. Operations Product. Man.*, **19(2)**.

Bessant, J. (1993). The lessons of failure: learning to manage new manufacturing technology. Special issue on Manufacturing Technology. *Int. J. Technol. Man.*, **8(2/3/4),** 197–215.

Buchanan, D. A. and Boddy, D. (1983). *Organizations in the Computer Age: Technological Imperatives and Strategic Choice*. Gower.

Burgess, T. (1994). Making the leap to agility. *Int. J. Operations Product. Man.*, **14(11),** 23–34.

Duguay, C., Landry, S. and Pasin, F. (1997). From mass production to flexible/agile production. *Int. J. Operations Product. Man.*, **17(12)**, 1183–95.

Feitzinger, E. and Lee, H. (1997). Mass customization at Hewlett-Packard: the power of postponement. *Harvard Bus. Rev.*, **75(1)**, 116–22.

Lau, R. (1999) Critical factors for achieving manufacturing flexibility. *Int. J. Operations Product. Man.*, **19(3)**.

Lei, D., Hitt, M. and Goldhar, J. D. (1996). Advanced manufacturing technology: organizational design and strategic flexibility. *Org. Stud.*, **17(3)**, 501(23).

Leonard-Barton, D. (1993). Core capabilities and core rigidities: a paradox in managing new product development. *Strategic Man. J.*, **13**, 111–25.

Pine, B. J. (1993). *Mass Customization: The New Frontier in Business Competition.* Harvard Business School

Pine, B. J., Victor, B. and Boynton, A. C. (1993). Making mass customization work. *Harvard Bus. Rev.*, **Sep-Oct**.

Piore, M. J. and Sabel, C. F. (1984). *The Second Industrial Divide: Possibilities for Prosperity.* Basic Books.

Upton, D. (1994). The management of manufacturing flexibility. *California Man. Rev.*, **36(2)**, 72–89.

Victor, B. and Boynton, A. C. (1998). *Invented Here: Maximizing Your Organization's Internal Growth and Profitability, A Practical Guide to Transforming Work.* Harvard Business School Press.

CHAPTER 5

Managing supply

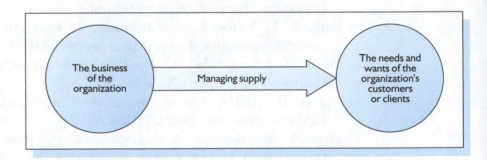

The business of the organization → Managing supply → The needs and wants of the organization's customers or clients

INTRODUCTION

Case study

RS Components (Radio Spares) is a good example of an organization integrating its entire supply chain activities. RS provides a catalogue service to industrial and service firms. The catalogue covers all manner of items, ranging from transistors and resistors through to large-scale transformers and other heavy-duty equipment. This firm viewed itself as primarily a logistics and marketing operation, with purchasing performing the service role of providing the goods at the right time, right price and right quality. RS competes in a market with two other major firms, all using the same type of marketing channel (catalogue), and found that their sales were declining, and they were unable to differentiate themselves within the market place. They could not see how to overcome this problem, and could not understand how the purchasing function could possibly add any further value, other than logistical and inventory management. The key to their problem was that of strategic focus – i.e., where was value being added in the business? The company decided to form a 'supply chain management' team consisting of purchasing, marketing and logistics. After close analysis of their business they discovered that, whilst they could not offer suppliers joint risk sharing and value engineering work, they could offer market intelligence.

Essentially, RS were the link between the customers' future requirements and their suppliers (manufacturers). If this communication flow could be optimized by clear and efficient communication, RS would be able to place new items in its catalogue almost 6 months before its competitors. This new approach had the effect of increasing customer loyalty and differentiating RS as a responsive supplier to market demands.

Why is purchasing and supply management such an important topic area? There are several reasons. First, the purchasing function has the responsibility for managing the timely delivery, quality and prices of the firm's inputs, including raw materials, services and sub-assemblies, into the organization. When we consider that many firms purchase around 80 per cent of their products and services, this is no small task. Secondly, any savings achieved by purchasing are reflected directly in the company's bottom line. In other words, as soon as a price saving is made this will have a direct impact on the firm's cost structure. In fact, it is often said that a 1 per cent saving in purchasing is equivalent to a 10 per cent increase in sales. Thirdly, purchasing and supply have links with all aspects of operations management, and so we need to understand their importance. Finally, the way a company controls its sourcing strategy will have a direct impact on how the firm does business. For example, the firm will sometimes 'outsource' elements of its business – including catering, travel, and aspects of information technology. The implementation and development of these approaches relies heavily on purchasing's expertise. It is important to understand how purchasing and supply are linked with operations management in the provision of goods and services to the end customer.

Aims and objectives

This chapter will discuss supply management and how it affects business.

After reading this chapter you will be able to:

- Explain the development of purchasing into strategic supply
- Outline the various sourcing strategies available to the firm
- Explain when, why and where each strategy should be used.

UNDERSTANDING SUPPLY

The easiest way to think about how purchasing affects the firm is by using a simple input–transformation–output model or systems model such as that we first saw in Figure 1.3. We have modified this in Figure 5.1.

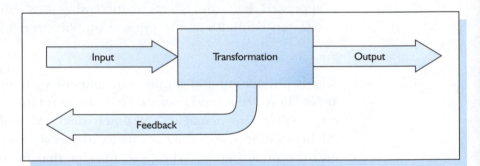

Figure 5.1 Input–transformation–output model.

The first key point is to understand the distinction between purchasing and supply. Purchasing is defined as managing the inputs into the organization's transformation (production) process. Supply, on the other hand, is the process of planning the most efficient and effective ways of structuring the supply process itself. This not only includes inputs but also, to a large extent, the transformation process itself.

Purchasing's role has traditionally been seen as a service provider to the other functions within the business. The primary task of purchasing was to buy the goods and services from approved sources of supply, making sure that they conformed to the required levels of quality and performance, delivery schedules and the most competitive price.

This view of purchasing as a service department, performing predominantly a clerical role, is changing rapidly. Purchasing (or supply as it is now more commonly known) is viewed as an important and strategic process. In order to reflect this important role, many large organizations have divided the purchasing and supply elements of the business into two distinct parts:

1 Purchasing, which deals with the day-to-day buying activities of the firm; and
2 Supply, which is concerned with the strategic planning, goal setting and strategy development in optimizing how the firm better manages its supply process.

The role of strategic supply is to assess the options for outsourcing elements of the business. It examines how the supply structure should be organized and deals with strategic questions, including whether the business should buy from many suppliers, or have fewer suppliers who make up larger elements of the business. Once these questions have been answered, specific strategies then need to be put in place. One such strategy is known as supply tiers, and the trend for 'mega' or 'first-tier suppliers' is currently being pursued by a number of firms. For example, in both aerospace and automotive manufacturing there are now many 'first-tier' suppliers. 'Mega' suppliers are responsible for providing an entire subsystem (for example the entire wing or gearbox), as opposed to the traditional method, where many suppliers would provide their individual element and the manufacturer would assemble the parts. The idea is that a first-tier supplier will now do the majority of the coordination and assembly work for the customer, and the prime manufacturer then simply slots the elements together to form the finished product. In doing so they have re-evaluated what is core to their business and then used the supply strategy to allow them to focus upon this. This change in the focus of a company's business allows it to become more flexible and to concentrate on what it does best. It is through taking a strategic supply focus that these changes are achieved.

Motivations for the development of purchasing towards supply management.

There are many reasons for the transition of purchasing form a clerical to a more strategic focus. Purchasing has had a range of pressures upon it that have forced it to change. A simple PEST (political,

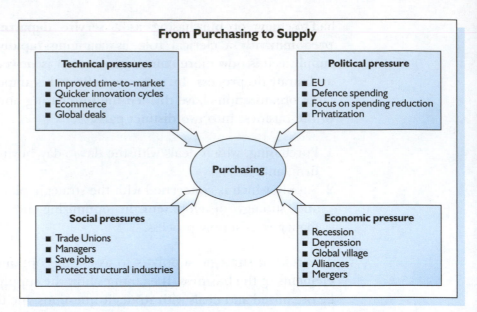

Figure 5.2 Pressures on purchasing to change.

economic, social and technological) model can be used to illustrate this point. Figure 5.2 illustrates the PEST analysis, showing the forces of change on purchasing that have acted as a catalyst to move it from a clerical function to a strategic process.

Political factors

Political pressures have caused changes in both the *focus of supply* – for example, the change of emphasis from price to cost focus – and the *change in the structure of industries*. This has become evident in government policy on privatization in many public services. The introduction of the Public Private Finance (PPF) initiative has had a major impact on how public sector firms now fund major projects. Instead of the government being the sole source of funds, public bodies now form relationships with the private sector to fund the projects jointly (with government guarantees). These major policy changes have meant that within certain industrial economic sectors the focus of the organization as a whole has had to change. This has developed from defining the 'best' specification possible towards finding the lowest cost solution. For example, defence spending reductions, combined with a policy change allowing sourcing of components to come from non-domestic manufacturers, caused a massive shockwave throughout that industry. The aerospace industry had to change from its traditional 'cost plus' focus and concentrate on 'value-for-money', thus moving towards a cost-focused approach. Cost and price are not used interchangeably here. Price refers to the process of driving down the quoted price of the goods, and this will often have the net effect of reducing the supplier's margin. Cost is a more sophisticated approach, which focuses on understanding the entire cost of the product (including process) and then jointly finding ways to reduce this.

Further policy changes (such as privatization) moved public sector services into the private sector, where the pressures of competition and cost competitiveness are much higher.

Economic factors

Economic pressures also forced organizations to examine the way that they managed supply. Recessions and depressions, together with competition on a global as opposed to a domestic level, meant that increased costs could not be passed onto the final consumer. Instead they had to be either absorbed, resulting in lower profits, or passed back, which often meant that suppliers would go out of business; alternatively, these costs had to be eliminated. This era of the late 1980s and early 1990s saw the development of concepts such as lean manufacturing and lean supply management. The focus with all of these approaches was primarily on improving efficiency and reducing waste both within the organization and within the firm's supply chain, thus resulting in overall cost reductions to the firm.

Social/image changes

Social pressures have also forced purchasing to change. If purchasing wanted to enhance its image, it would need to utilize professional and well-qualified personnel. In order to attract these types of people into the area it would need to present a professional profile similar to that of finance or marketing. Purchasing's main problem was that it was not seen as 'sexy'.

Wickens (1987, p. 162) commented how image was a problem in the 1980s for production and supply:

> The best graduates want to go into merchant banking, the professions, the Civil Service, the finance sector. If they think of industry or commerce it is in the areas of marketing, sales, finance or personnel that attract.

This view is now beginning to change as purchasing achieves higher strategic status within the organization. In addition, purchasing now has a professionally chartered institute, along with other major functions such as marketing, production and finance. All of these elements help in raising the profile of purchasing. Further social pressure on the firm by other stakeholders to save money, and therefore jobs, was exerted by trade union groups and various pressure groups both within and external to the firms.

Technology factors

The development of new and innovative technologies has meant that purchasing can communicate and involve a much wider range of the organization in the supply process. For example, it is now possible, via the Internet, to allow anyone (subject to their being authorized budget holders) to purchase against an E-catalogue. Purchase cards (credit cards for managers) are also revolutionizing the way that we do business. In addition to technologies that facilitate the purchasing process, firms are also requiring improved times-to-market of their own products. This can only be achieved if the supply structure is able to deliver quality suppliers that can work with the buyer.

The need to be increasingly competitive, flexible and efficient has been exacerbated by the global village phenomenon, with domestic firms having to benchmark with the best in the world.

Throughout the 1980s and 1990s, many firms adopted in-vogue production techniques and concepts such as just-in-time (JIT) and total quality management (TQM), which will be discussed in later chapters. During the early to mid-1980s the concept of the value chain was first proposed, which, being a systems model, involved the purchasing (input) function. Firms began to realize that the concepts of JIT, TQM and world class manufacturing (WCM) would only work if the supply process were also closely managed. This led to the development of a new buzzword, 'partnership sourcing'. The CBI and DTI created an entire organization to promote partnership sourcing throughout UK industry.

THE EVOLUTION FROM PURCHASING TO SUPPLY MANAGEMENT

How we think about supply management has changed, and this is illustrated in Figure 5.3. Initially, purchasing focused on the dyadic linkage between a buyer and supplier. In the late 1980s, supply chain

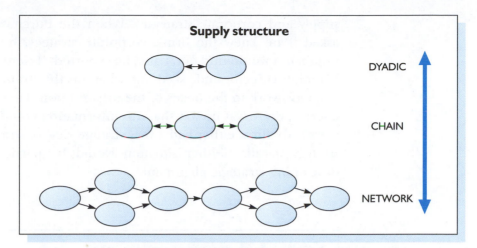

Figure 5.3 The supply structure (source: Harland *et al.*, 1999).

management focused on supply as a *chain* or *pipeline*, taking account of the buyer, supplier and final customer relationships. Finally, strategic supply views supply as a network of relationships across an entire industry sector, where buyer and supplier roles can be interchanged several times during the network.

Managing supply is difficult, because it relies heavily on cross-functional cooperation. Often buyers do not consider the entire supply chain and its interfaces – supplier/buyer, buyer/customer, and internal buyer/buyer. Organizations need to form linkages throughout the entire supply network, as shown in the following example of an integrated supply network.

Supply: a strategic process?

The creation of strategic purchasing departments has transformed purchasing from a clerical function to a strategic business process. However, there is a difference between implementing strategies and being strategic. As Ellram and Carr (1994) point out:

> It is critical to understand that there is a difference between purchasing strategy and purchasing performing as a strategic function. When purchasing is viewed as a strategic function, it is included as a key decision maker and participant in the firm's strategic planning process.

For example, a major aerospace company was developing a procurement strategy, and needed to confirm that it was aligned with the supply and corporate strategies. When the Purchasing Director was asked if he knew the firm's corporate strategy, he replied that he didn't, but would find out. Later, he reported: 'I went to the Corporate Planning Director and asked him what was the strategy so that I could align my work to the needs of the organization. He replied that it was a secret, there was no way that this information could be given to me!' Clearly the firm either had a very strange view of strategy, or it had no strategy at all. Neither situation would be particularly helpful in developing strategic alignment.

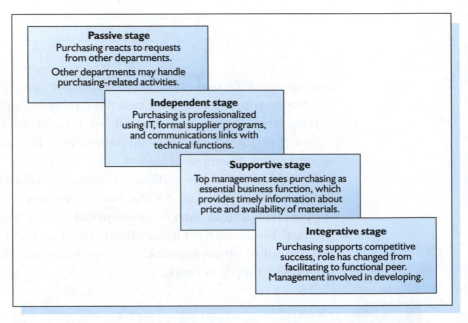

Figure 5.4 Strategic positioning tool (adapted from Reck and Long, 1988).

What, then, is the difference between implementing a strategy and acting strategically? Several tools and frameworks measure how strategic a purchasing department is. One is Reck and Long's (1988) four-phase positioning tool, shown in Figure 5.4. This positions purchasing capability from 'passive' through to 'integrative' within the overall business. This tool can be used as a detailed benchmarking mechanism for firms to position themselves in order to make changes.

Another way to examine the strategic contribution of supply is in the strategic alignment model in Figure 5.5, which shows how supply strategy should be aligned with corporate strategy. It also shows that both of these must be supported (and aligned with) performance

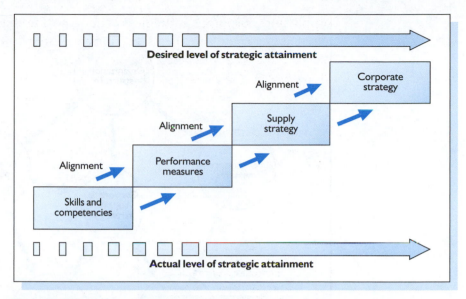

Figure 5.5 The strategic alignment model.

measurement systems and the skills and competencies of the people in purchasing.

Many companies focus on aligning supply and corporate strategy, and ignore performance measures and skills and competencies. In most 'strategic' purchasing departments performance is still measured by 'lead time, quality and rejects', which are tactical measures. Tactical measures encourage tactical behaviour. Strategic purchasing relies on strategic measurements. For example, cross-functional teams should be measured on team output, not on individual performance.

The strategic supply wheel in Figure 5.6 illustrates an integrated approach to supply strategy. Strategic supply must balance all of the elements in the wheel, rather than concentrating on a single element. A firm cannot focus only on relationship management without also considering skills and competencies, performance measures, costs and benefits and so on. The supply wheel and strategic sourcing strategies will be explained in detail later in this book.

The strategic supply wheel is used to show that in order for supply to be viewed as strategic, it must balance out all of the elements of the model. It is insufficient to concentrate on just one element within the model; in addition it is about finding appropriate strategies within the model. It is not sufficient for a firm to focus its efforts on relationship management without also considering all of the other key factors now discussed.

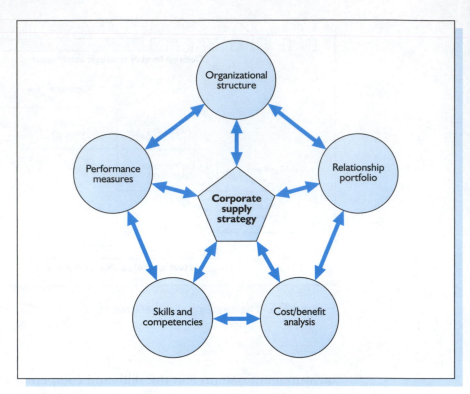

Figure 5.6 The strategic supply wheel (from Cousins, 2000).

Key issues in the supply wheel

Performance measures: One of the central issues within any firm is the concept of performance measures. These can be thought of as both internal and external measures. Within supply, external measures are often referred to as 'vendor assessment' schemes. These are mechanisms that firms use to assess the performance of their suppliers. For example, they are likely to measure a range of capabilities, including delivery performance, price competitiveness, and quality and defect rates. There will also be internal measures focused on the buyers; these will generally focus on price, delivery and quality. The key here is to make sure that the internal and external measures align. In addition, measures should be appropriate, so if we are buying nuts, bolts and rivets (low value, high volume items) it is likely that we are going to measure how quickly these things are being bought; these are known as efficiency measures. On the other hand, if we are buying more complex and expensive items – for example, a computer system (low volume, high value) – it is less likely that we are interested in how quickly the item is bought; rather, we shall measure in terms of how the product has met our design specifications. These types of measures are known as effectiveness measures, which focus on how well we are achieving against our strategy as opposed to how quickly are we doing things.

It is vitally important that these measures are aligned with the strategy that the firm wants to pursue. If the firm is looking to build long-term relationships, then it will need to develop more effectiveness-focused relationships. If it is into short-term cost savings, then it will need to focus more on efficiency measures. It is, however, likely that the firm will be need to pursue both strategies, depending on what it is buying. We will see later on in this chapter how this can be achieved through using a product position matrix.

Relationship portfolio. This refers to the range of relationships that a firm can have with its suppliers. These can be very adversarial and traditional in nature. In this scenario, the relationship is focused on driving hard deals based (usually) around price. Alternatively, at the other end of the spectrum, the relationships can be much more collaboratively focused. This is where the firms will work with each other to try and find ways of reducing costs (the use of *cost transparency*, i.e. sharing joint cost of information). They may also share technologies and innovation ideas, jointly developing products between them. The process is sometimes referred to as 'partnership sourcing'. Again it is vital that these strategies match with what the firm wants to achieve and that the measures, which motivate people, are focused on delivering the correct relationship strategy. Traditional relationships will generally focus on efficiency-based measures, whereas the more complex collaborative relationships will require much more effectiveness-based measures.

Cost/benefit. This refers to the amount of money that will be saved by pursuing a given strategy, and the cost to the firm of following that route. If the cost is more than the given benefit, then it is unlikely that the firm will follow the strategy. If the reverse is true, it seems like a good strategy to follow. Therefore, whatever strategy is considered the firm should be clear about possible outcomes. For example, if a firm wishes to pursue the collaborative relationship strategy, then questions must be asked about the costs involved in setting up the teams, the risk of focusing on only one supplier, exposing cost information, and so on. We must then evaluate the potential benefits of pursuing such a strategy. This may include reduced overall costs for both firms, improving time-to-market, developing new technologies and so on.

Organizational structure. This refers to the type of control mechanism the firm is using. Whilst there is a range of different structures that could be discussed, they can basically be classed into three distinct groups; centralized, decentralized and hybrid. Table 5.1 summarizes the main characteristics of each.

The way a function is structured will affect the way it interacts with other functions within the firm (dynamics). There has been a trend for firms to centralize purchasing, thereby realizing economies of scale from bulk purchasing. This has the disadvantage of potentially not satisfying local customer needs and wants. The reverse trend then followed, which was to decentralize, thus securing customer satisfaction. This in turn lost some of the economies of scale and management.

Table 5.1   Characteristics of organization structure

Organization structure	Characteristics	Advantages	Disadvantages
Centralized	This is where purchasing activity is centralized in one major location. Head office is responsible for all of the purchasing for the firm	The main advantages are: economies of scale, centralized expertise, easier management of the process, experts are easy to find. Global sourcing as opposed to local sourcing. Therefore, find the best deal	The main disadvantages are: does not tend to be customer focused, can become bureaucratic, buyers have to constantly travel to meet supplier, customers etc.
Decentralized	Purchasing is conducted at a divisional level. Each division will have a budget and will focus on its own individual requirements	Tends to be very customer-focused. Very responsive to customer needs. Source locally and manage quality levels locally	Tends to be more expensive, miss out on global deals. Less strategic and more transaction focused. Lacks economies of scale
Hybrid	The hybrid is a middle ground model, which is both centralized and decentralized. This will consist of a centralized purchasing area that focuses on supply chain effectiveness. They will negotiate corporate deals and examine ways of optimizing supply chain efficiency. Day-to-day procurement is handled by the divisions	This model allows for the advantages of both the centralized and decentralized model to be realized	The main disadvantage of this model is that it is very difficult to control. When it works well the returns are very high, if it works badly the reverse is true!

The current trend would appear to be a hybrid structure. This structure is both centralized and decentralized at the same time. Whilst this is naturally more complex to manage, if operated properly the benefits of both structures can be realized.

Skills and competencies. To pursue any of the chosen strategies at the centre of the strategic supply wheel model, the firm will need to have the appropriate skills and competencies within its employees. If the firm decides that it wants to develop long-term relationships with its suppliers, then it will need to make sure that the various supply personnel are trained in the correct manner. In essence, they will need to think strategically.

As with all of the previous circles in the strategic supply wheel, the appropriate skills and competencies must match the strategic direction, be supported by appropriate measures, operate within an appropriate organizational structure and aim to achieve a range of benefits at minimal cost. The strategic wheel is a useful diagnostic tool for considering the strategic nature and intent of the firm.

Another model that provides insight is the Strategic Transition model. This model (Figure 5.7) shows the various supply strategies available to a firm, which are are summarized in five main forms: flat pricing, total cost focus, supply-side management, strategic sourcing, and network and relationship management.

The model shows the movement from a purchasing focus on 'flat pricing' at one extreme towards 'network and relationship management' at the other end of the spectrum. Each of these five phases has a given output, and a set of characteristics that defines it. This model identifies nine key elements involved in purchasing

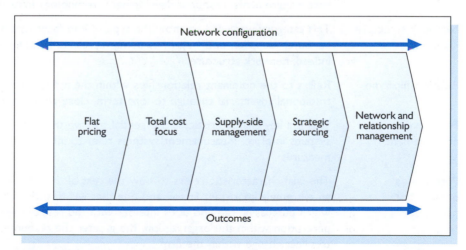

Figure 5.7 The transition model.

strategy: key objectives, supply mechanism, supply structure, strategic approach, why fails, key issues, network structure, performance measurement and purchasing's perception within the organization (see Table 5.2).

The factors are then mapped against the overall 'Transition model', which enables a matrix to be produced that allows firms to see their relative positioning. The matrix is shown in Table 5.3.

Table 5.2 Purchasing assessment factors

Factor	Definition
Key objectives	Refers to the main goal of the purchasing functions i.e. price reduction, cost improvement, relationship development etc.
Supply mechanism	Shows how the purchasing function uses its position within the supply chain to achieve the key objectives, such as price leverage, cost transparency, benchmarking etc.
Supply structure	Refers to the structure of the supply market – for example, is it multi-sourced, single sourced, dominant supplier, buyers' market etc.
Strategic approach	This is the focus of the purchasing organization; is it predominantly short term, fire-fighting and tactical, or longer term, proactive and strategic?
Why fails	This category was placed in the model as respondents felt that in order to move on to the next phase they needed to understand why their current approach was not sustainable. Reasons for failure could be the focus of the approach was more on price than on cost, less on quality than on service and so on
Key issues	Refers to common problem areas realized with these strategies, such as skill base requirements, resource development, technology infrastructure etc.
Network structure	This category was used to show the type of interfaces that are most prevalent, i.e. buyer–supplier, one-way, or two-way, customer–supplier–customer, or indeed, network structure
Relationship type	Refers to the dominant relationships within the model, such as traditional/adversarial through to long term, close collaborative
Performance measurement	This is a key characteristic; it is essential to have the correct measurement systems in place. Measurement systems refer to internal as well as external measures
Purchasing's organization perception	The final characteristic refers to how the rest of the firm sees purchasing. This is an extremely important factor, and one that will directly influence the way in which purchasing can and does interact with the rest of the firm. The higher the perception within the organization, the greater the resource allocation and ability to effect change within the firm

Table 5.3   Transition positioning matrix

Stages of excellence	Stage 1	Stage 2	Stage 3	Stage 4	Stage 5
Approach	Flat pricing	Total cost focus	Supply-side management	Strategic sourcing	Network and relationship management
Description	Adversarial, tactical, focus on price, transactional	Focus on total cost, distant relationship with suppliers	Focus on supply service package, develop closer relationships with suppliers	Cooperative strategic focus on supply, commitment to single/few suppliers	Focus on supply, demand and mutual development, total commitment
Key objectives	To contain price	To contain cost over total product life	To gain from suppliers their specialist expertise and skills	To work jointly with suppliers to increase value in supply chain	To improve total understanding, mutual network development
Supply mechanism	Volume leverage	Cost leverage	Total service leverage, benchmarking supplier development	Leverage through cooperation	Network leverage
Supply structure	Multi-supply, multi-relationship	Multi-supply, multi-relationship	Fewer suppliers	Single/few key suppliers	Network of key single suppliers
Strategic approach	Tactical	Tactical	Moving from tactical to strategic	Strategic	Strategic
Why fails	Focus on price not cost	Focus on cost not on quality and service	Resistance or failure to share relevant information with suppliers, focus on competition not cooperation	Focus on cooperation not involvement	Too expensive, needs high level of trust/dependency
Key issues	Low skills, low information, low-level decision-making	Relatively low skilled, information-based	Less purchasing but greater 'management' skills required, greater information flow between firms	High level of information flow between firms, high level of commitment	Highly skilled, complete information openness, high-level/complex decision-making
Network structure	Buyer-competitive suppliers	Buyer-selected suppliers	Buyer and first- and second-tier suppliers	Supply chain	Network of relationships
Relationship type	Adversarial	Distant	Involved	Committed	Trust
Performance measures	Basic measurements based on price differences from year before	1. Process activity mapping; 2. Production variety matrix; 3. Decision point analysis; 4. Cost Transparency	1. Communications analysis; 2. Supplier development matrix; 3. Quality function deployment	1. Supply chain response matrix; 2. Quality filter mapping; 3. Performance measurement of purchasing	1. Value stream mapping; 2. Advanced communications analysis
Purchasing's organization perception:	Passive	Supportive	Independent	Integrative	Differentiator

Application of the Transition model

This model has three clear implementation stages: assessment, strategy development and benchmarking. These are summarized in Table 5.4.

This model allows for a more comprehensive assessment of purchasing's strategic ability. This type of benchmarking creates a tool for managers to improve the effectiveness of purchasing activities. These types of approaches lead to the improvement of the overall focus of the purchasing department, and also can improve the organization's perception of the function. Once activities have been positioned and assessed against the 'Transition model', managers are then able to allocate time and resources most effectively to the activities under their control.

Table 5.4   Stages of implementation of the Transition model

Stage	Purpose	Description
1	Assessment	The purchasing organization should benchmark where it currently sees itself against the characteristics and criteria listed within the model
2	Strategy development	Purchasing should consider where it wants to be and examine the gaps in its approach vis-à-vis what the model is telling it, and should then develop a strategy to take the function forward
3	Benchmarking	The final stage is to use the model to review current progress and see how the function is developing

The use of the 'Transition model' allows purchasing managers to understand clearly how the management of the purchasing activities needs to be changed, how resources can be distributed most effectively and can adjust the profile of the department within the organization.

SOURCING STRATEGIES

There are a variety of ways that a firm can organize the supply process into the organization, and these are known as sourcing strategies. The rationale for these different approaches will come from a variety of factors, including the evaluation of how important the goods or services of strategic supply are to the firm and determining the competitive nature of the market place. In addition, the firm must also consider the level of technical complexity within the product.

Kraljic (1983) developed a positioning matrix to help consider these and other factors to help buyers and suppliers in their sourcing and competitive positioning strategies. He identified four key purchasing approaches or strategies: routine, bottlenecks, leverage and critical. These are represented on the following matrix. These strategies are positioned against the level of supply exposure and/or technical risk compared with the strategic nature of the product or service – i.e. the level of value or cost exposure to the buying firm. Figure 5.8 illustrates the basic positioning matrix in which buyers can position the types of products and services that they purchase. These groups are termed 'sourcing groups, which refers to a range of products or services that might be purchased. For example, nuts, bolts and rivets are often referred to as a Maxmin sourcing group. This is because the buyer will order to maximum and minimum stock levels.

This matrix is very simple but also very powerful, and has proved to be invaluable to firms in enabling them to focus on their procurement approaches.

The technical or supply risk can be derived from a few key factors. First, if there are only a few suppliers in the market place then the

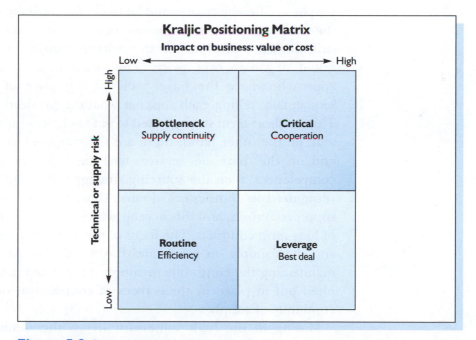

Figure 5.8 Strategic positioning matrix.

supply exposure is likely to be very high (the supplier will have all of the power in the market place). Alternatively, the supplier may possess superior technological skills, competencies and/or capabilities. This will give them a competitive advantage in the market place and therefore create higher degrees of dependency. With respect to the matrix, the buyer must weigh up the relative scale of high versus low (which is always an inherent weakness of this sort of model) and establish where the supplier best fits. The horizontal axis refers to the level of impact that the supplier's product or service has upon the customer's (buyer's) ability to deliver the final product. Value or cost is used because the item could be of relatively low cost, but of high 'strategic' value to the buyer's product. For example, in the aerospace industry a helicopter's gearbox is held in place primarily by several large bolts. Whilst these bolts are relatively inexpensive compared to other elements of the aircraft, i.e. avionic systems, they are of high strategic importance and value, because without them the gearbox would fall out!

The strategic positioning matrix suggests several strategies that the buyer might choose to follow. If the product/service is of low value/cost and low technical/supply risk, it is seen as a low level part or commodity type product. Examples include nuts, bolts and rivets in manufacturing. Types of stationary or low level temporary labour hire would also fall into this category, and should be sourced from the most efficient suppliers. The objective would be to get the most competitive price for the product, whilst maintaining delivery and quality standards. As switching costs are low and the market is highly competitive, buyers would negotiate over price. This often involves a Dutch auction approach, where the buyer will bid the price of the parts down sequentially, telling each supplier what the previous supplier has bid. This is a short-term strategy used to get low prices for the product.

If, on the other hand, there are few suppliers in the market place and/or the part or service has high degree of technological competences, then the sourcing strategy will be different. These are recognized as 'bottleneck' items. Here the strategy is to maintain supply continuity, and this may be achieved through the establishment of long-term contracts. The focus of the buyer will tend to be more on cost than simply on price, and the buyer will also be interested in maintaining the continuity of supply. Liquidated damages clauses are often put in place in these types of contracts in order to maintain continuity of supply.

Moving to the high value/cost items, the model suggests using different strategies depending on technical and/or supply exposure to the market place. For example, where the buyer perceives the exposure to the market place to be low yet the cost or value of the item is high – in automotive, for example, this may be a product such as car seats – the strategy would be to negotiate the 'best' deal. This can be obtained through the use of 'leverage' strategies (Porter, 1980).

Leveraging involves pulling together a range of similar products (or sometimes the same product bought at different locations throughout the firm) and making a larger contract as a result. The aim of this approach is to increase bargaining power, thus establishing a much stronger negotiating position. For example, the buyer of seats, instead of sourcing Model A with Supplier 1, Model B with Supplier 2 and so on, would source both models from the same supplier. This will give the buyer the advantage of economies of scale, thus allowing a stronger negotiation position from which to leverage. Firms who are pursuing a strategy of cost reduction consistently follow this strategy. This approach to purchasing can and often does change the nature of the supply market exposure.

The supply market exposure will tend to increase as the buyer moves from several suppliers to one major source, and this will increase the dependency relationship and tend to move the supplier into the top right-hand box of Figure 5.8. This process often occurs without the buying company realizing the effect of the strategy, and there are many examples of this in recent years, with companies pursuing cost minimization programmes leading to large-scale supply base

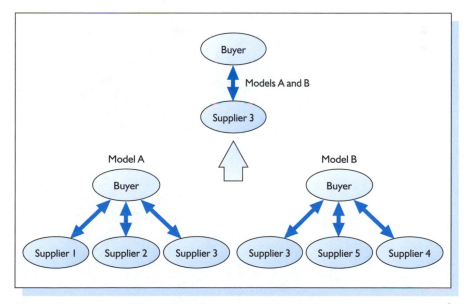

Figure 5.9 Leveraging strategies.

consolidation (Cousins, 1999). This leads to the final quadrant, where there is high exposure to the supplier and high impact upon the business (value and/or cost). These products or services are often seen as critical or strategic to the business. These would tend to be high value items, often with mega suppliers created through leveraging strategies. Examples of these types of products would be modular assembly supplies (from first-tier suppliers and key technology suppliers). In services there are many examples of major outsource providers, such as key suppliers of information technology – companies such as EDS and CSC Index take over the operations of the firm's entire IT network. These relationships tend to be single or sole sourced. This is mainly due to the large amount of investment required; switching costs are generally prohibitively high, with mutual dependencies. These relationships need to be managed very carefully, and they are seen as very long-term with the focus on partnership as opposed to buyer/supplier.

Supply structure and design

For each of the quadrants on the model, the sourcing strategy will need a requisite sourcing or supply structure. It is important to choose the correct design of structure to suit the strategy and type of

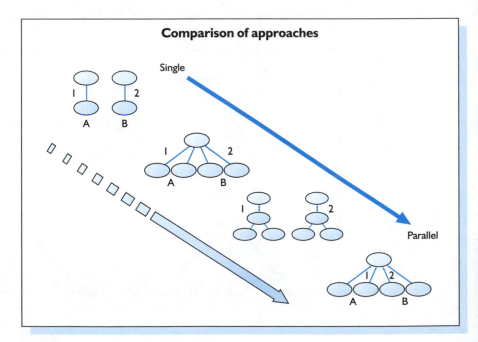

Figure 5.10 The four main sourcing structures

procurement. There are four primary sourcing structures that can be used (plus some amount of variation on these): single, multiple, delegated and parallel (see Figure 5.10).

The above figure illustrates the complexity of the various sourcing approaches, ranging from the simplest structure, single or sole sourced, to the more complex structures of delegated and parallel sourced. It is the role of the buyer to decide when and where to apply each of these structures, and this will be dependent upon the needs and wants of the firm, the types of relationship desired and the levels of dependency that both buyer and supplier are prepared to take. It is interesting to note that the most dependent relationship is found in the simplest structure – i.e. the sole or single sourced arrangement.

Single sourcing

This structure is where the buyer has only one source of supply (Figure 5.11). This could come from a decision to use one source because of the high cost of the item or because of the strategic importance to the end product.

The most common reason for sole sourcing is that there is only one source of supply. Using the strategic positioning matrix (Figure 5.8), this type of approach would put the supplier in either the top right (critical) or top left (bottleneck) box. The advantages of managing this type of relationship are that there is only one supplier; it is therefore easier to exchange ideas and cost structures and to look for ways of mutual improvement of the product and processes. It is also easier to instigate a long-term arrangement. The disadvantage is that there is only one source of supply, and this could put the buyer in a

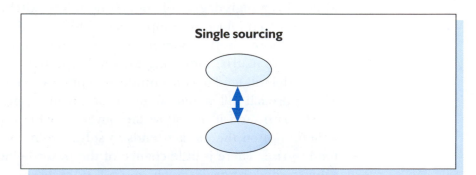

Figure 5.11 Single sourcing strategy.

position of weakness or over-reliance if not managed properly. In addition, if the supply source were to cease business for whatever reason, the customer would be highly exposed in the market place.

 ## Multiple sourcing.

Multiple sourcing is defined as having several supply sources to supply the product, and is illustrated in Figure 5.12. The structure is often used to maintain competition in a given market place.

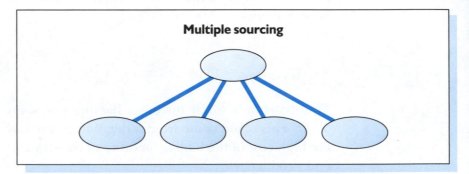

Figure 5.12 Multiple sourcing strategy.

The buyer will have a range of suppliers to choose from, and will carefully balance capacity constraints with individual supplier performance when placing orders. The old adage, 'don't put all your eggs in one basket', is often used to describe this supply structure. Buyers will also frequently enter into the 'Dutch auction' mentality and bid suppliers off against each other to achieve the best price. This is often seen as an adversarial approach and is most common in market places where this a high degree of competition, low switching costs and low levels of technological competence. This structure would tend to appear more in the bottom left (routine) box of the strategic positioning matrix, indicating low-level type purchases. Buyers using this model will tend to concentrate on a price as opposed to cost focus. This approach will enable some continuity of supply (certainly in the short term), and it will allow the buyer to achieve price reductions, although often the market tends to suffer from collusion and prices tend to rise. There is little chance of the buyer being able to operate sophisticated strategies such as cost transparency and partnership sourcing approaches. This model has traditionally been the mainstay of procurement strategy, but it is currently being replaced by more sophisticated and value adding approaches such as delegated and parallel sourcing.

Delegated sourcing strategy

This approach became very popular in the mid 1990s across a wide range of industries, and is illustrated in Figure 5.13. It was first pioneered in the aerospace and automotive industries, as a more efficient way of managing supply (Cousins, 1999).

This structure involves making one supplier responsible for the delivery of an entire sub-assembly as opposed to an individual part, and the customer delegates authority to a key supplier. This supplier is known as a *first-tier* supplier. The principle is that the customer only manages one supplier, and that the supplier manages the other suppliers that provide parts to complete the product – as is shown in the following example.

A major car manufacturer was investigating how it could reduce the amount of suppliers to its business, but still maintain quality, cost and delivery requirements. They decided to implement a tiered structure approach to supply management. This would mean that they would be able to work closely with one key or first-tier supplier, and could exchange learning and also develop a clear integrated cost structure. The buyer firm would also not have to assemble the part themselves, because it would arrive complete and thus be inserted directly onto the vehicle.

The buyer decided to choose a major product area, which was the wheel assembly. After looking closely at the suppliers it was decided that the bearing manufacturer should be the prime or first-tier

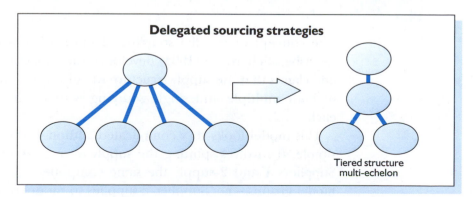

Figure 5.13 Delegated sourcing.

supplier. It was this manufacturer's responsibility to provide the buyer with a completed wheel assembly. This resulted in moving from a multiple sourced to a delegated sourcing strategy.

The move significantly reduced the amount of suppliers to the customer (95 per cent reduction). It also enabled the manufacturer to focus its resources on the first-tier supplier.

Delegated sourcing has a number of advantages for both the customer and the supplier. Focusing on one supplier gives the buyer the opportunity to work closely with this supply source instead of many, thus reducing day-to-day transaction costs. The increased dependency on one supplier results in the buyer and supplier exchanging more detailed information, particularly around cost issues (implementing cost transparency techniques is commonplace, otherwise known as 'open book'). The buyer will pass on capabilities and technologies to the supplier to enable production the required sub-assembly. The supplier in turn becomes a major player for the buyer. This also increases the dependency from the supplier's perspective, giving the supplier more authority and control over the delivery and production of the sub-assembly. The process of delegated sourcing tends to create 'mega' suppliers. These suppliers, if not managed properly, can became very powerful and then exert their power over the buyer, usually in the form of price increases. It is vitally important for the buyer to make sure that when these arrangements are put in place, the dependencies are well understood and managed. This strategy would often be found initially in the 'leverage' section of the matrix, and in the medium term, due to the high dependency and high switching costs, it would move into the 'critical' area (top right).

Parallel sourcing

The concept of parallel sourcing (Figure 5.14) is quite difficult to describe. Richardson (1994) developed the concept in the early 1990s, and claims that the supply structure will give the buyer the advantages of both multiple and single sourcing without the disadvantages of each.

This model looks very complicated, although the principle is quite simple. It involves splitting the supply over a variety of models; thus Suppliers 1 and 2 supply the same component, but across different model groups – i.e. Supplier 2 supplies to model one, and Supplier 1 to model two. This allows the buyer to maintain competition

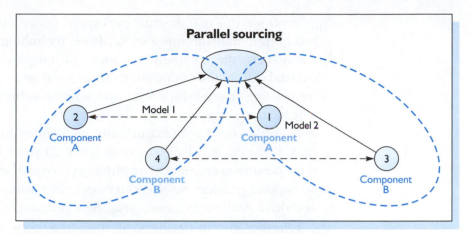

Figure 5.14 Parallel sourcing.

across model groups; it also facilitates benchmarking of price and performance. This is a complex structure to manage, but does have the advantage of maintaining competition. This structure would generally be found in the 'leverage' box of the strategic positioning matrix.

SUMMARY

The area of purchasing and supply management is of growing importance to organizations. With the pressures of increased competition, improved time-to-market and cost reduction, organizations have to respond by re-engineering their supply structures to match the strategic pressures and priorities that are being placed on the firm. Firms can do this in a variety of ways, but they must consider the appropriateness of each of these approaches and in turn balance them with the other enabling elements with the strategic process.

Case study

'No business as usual'

In British Petroleum's principal area of upstream activity in the North Sea, drastic reductions in development costs had become imperative if the region was to continue to attract oil company investment in an increasingly competitive global market. BP recognized that advances in offshore technology alone would not achieve the company's commercial targets; a fundamental cultural shift in the oil industry's traditional and often adversarial contracting relationships was also essential to break through the cost barrier.

To serve as the breakthrough challenge, BP selected the Andrew field, an oil discovery that for 20 years had refused to show positive economics. The question now was, would a new way of working provide the necessary boost in business performance and drive Andrew to commercial development?

Together with its partners, BP formed a pioneering alliance in 1993 with seven contracting companies to develop Andrew's offshore production facilities. Focused on a common business goal, the alliance resolved to step away from the constraints of 'business as usual' in its quest to transform Andrew into a valued producing asset. Corporate alignment to the challenge came through the sharing of risks and rewards, where company profits were firmly tied to the project's financial outcomes. For individuals, the opportunity to work in a unified team with the freedom to question conventional solutions unlocked previously untapped potential for innovation and cooperation.

The power of the alliance was to surprise even its most ardent supporters by the unexpected magnitude of commercial success that it came to deliver, surpassing all anticipated levels of performance to set new benchmarks for the industry!

Key questions

1 What is the difference between purchasing as a tactical function, and supply as a strategic process?

2 Assume you are a consultant and have been asked to help in the development of a tactically focused purchasing organization to a strategically focused supply process. How might you approach this task? What do you see as the key problem areas?

3 Explain the different sourcing structures that can be used. Which structures should be used in which situations?

4 Discuss the concept of appropriateness within the supply wheel. What is meant by strategic alignment?

Key terms

Lean supply management
'Mega' suppliers
Single, multiple, delegated and parallel strategies
Strategic supply wheel
Strategic Transition model
Supply structure and design
Transition position matrix

References

Cousins, P. D. (1999). An investigation into supply base restructuring. *Eur. J. Purchasing Supply Man.*, **5(2)**, 143–55.

Cousins, P. D. (2000). Supply base rationalisation: myth or reality?' *Eur. J. Purchasing Supply Man.*, **3(4)**, 199–207.

Ellram, L. and Carr, A. (1994). Strategic purchasing: a history and review of the literature. *Int. J. Purchasing Materials Man.*, Spring, 23–35.

Harland, C., Lamming, R. and Cousins, P. (1999). Developing the concept of supply strategy. *Int. J. Production Operations Man.*, **19(7)**, 650–73.

Kraljic, P. (1983). Purchasing must become supply management. *Harvard Bus. Rev.*, **5**, 109–17.

Porter, M. (1980). *Competitive Strategy.* Free Press.

Reck, R. F. and Long, B. G. (1988). Purchasing: a competitive weapon. *Int. J. Purchasing Materials Man.*, **Fall,** 2–8.

Richardson, J. (1994). Parallel sourcing and supplier performance in the Japanese automobile industry. *Strategic Man. J.*, **14**, 339–50.

Wickens, P. (1987). *The Road to Nissan.* Macmillan.

Further reading

Browning, J. M., Zabriskie, N. B. and Heullmantel, A. B. (1983). Strategic purchasing planning. *J. Purchasing Materials Man.*, **Spring,** 19–24.

Burt, D. and Doyle, M. (1994). *The American Keiretsu: A Strategic Weapon for Global Competitiveness.* Irwin.

Burt, D. and Soukup, W. R. (1985). Purchasing's role in new product development. *Harvard Bus. Rev.*, **Sep–Oct,** 90–96.

Caddick, J. R. and Dale, B. G. (1987). The determination of purchasing objectives and strategies: some key influences. *Int. J. Physical Dist. Materials Man.*, **17(3),** 5–16.

Cousins, P. D. (1997). Partnership sourcing: a misused concept. In: *Strategic Procurement Management in the 1990s: Concepts and Cases,* (R. Lamming and A. Cox, eds), p.35–43.

Cox, A. (1996). Relational competence and strategic procurement management. *Eur. J. Purchasing Supply Man,* **2(1),** 57–70.

Farmer, D. and Van Ploos, A. (1993). *Effective Pipeline Management.* Gower Publications.

Hines, P. (1994). *Creating World Class Suppliers: Unlocking Mutual Competitive Advantage.* Pitman Publishing.

Hines, P., Cousins, P., Lamming, R. *et al.* (2000). *Value Stream Management.* Financial Times Publications.

Lamming, R. (1993). *Beyond Partnerships: Strategies for Innovation and Lean Supply.* Prentice-Hall.

Lamming, R. and Cox, A. (1997). Managing supply in the firm of the future. *Eur. J. Purchasing Supply Man.*, **1,** 53–62.

Laneros, R. and Monckza, R. M. (1989). Co-operative buyer–supplier relationships and a firm's competitive strategy. *J. Purchasing Materials Man.*, **25(3),** 9–18.

MacBeth, D. and Ferguson, N. (1994). *Partnership Sourcing: An Integrated Supply Chain Approach.* Pitman Publishing.

Nishiguchi, T. (1994). *Strategic Industrial Sourcing: The Japanese Advantage.* Oxford University Press.

Saunders, M. (1994). *Strategic Purchasing and Supply Chain Management.* Pitman Publishing.

Speckman, R. (1989). A strategic approach to procurement planning. *J. Purchasing Materials Man.*, **Winter,** 3–9.

St. John, C. and Young, S. (1991). The strategic consistency between purchasing and production. *Int. J. Purchasing Materials Man.*, **Spring,** 15–20.

PART THREE
PRACTICE

CHAPTER 6

Managing capacity: managing transforming resources

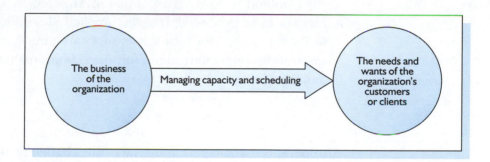

INTRODUCTION

Case study

The automobile industry is the world's largest manufacturing business. However, there are a number of major concerns for auto firms and there are vast differences between competitors in terms of their size, capabilities and financial performance. A small number have large cash reserves, but the weaker members are saddled with huge amounts of debt, and at the beginning of the new millennium only a quarter of the world's 40 car-makers were profitable. Competition has become far more intense due to increased globalization efforts coupled with saturated capacity in several major geographic areas. Perhaps *the* key issue for the industry is over-capacity; in total, the car producers can produce 20 million more cars and trucks a year than it sells. Put bluntly, every car plant in North America could close, and the world would still have too many cars. The capacity problem is made even more acute because the Asia-Pacific region will add capacity to make an additional 6 million cars by 2005. Different firms will deal with the problem of over-capacity in various ways, but an important development has been in the surge of mergers and acquisitions. For example, the merger between Daimler and Chrysler in 1999 created the world's fifth largest car company by volume, with combined annual revenues of around $130 billion. As well as mergers and acquisitions, various alliances took place that allowed major car firms to create a stronger presence than before in previously undeveloped territories. Renault invested $350 million in OAO Avtoframos in Moscow, by which 120 000 cars would be produced. Daewoo invested $1.3 billion in AvtoZAZ in the Ukraine. All of these measures are aimed at dealing with profoundly important areas for operations managers: capacity and scheduling.

All operations managers must face the challenge of managing the organization's resources so that outputs are delivered to customers and clients in the right amount, at the right time. In particular, operations managers are responsible for managing the resources used in the transformation process so that the supply of the operation's outputs is aligned with customer or client demand for goods and services. When this not performed well, outputs are produced for which there is no immediate demand, or not enough outputs are produced to meet demand. Sometimes this can be a deliberate strategy – there is always one toy at Christmas whose desirability is enhanced by its short supply – but a mismatch either way often means lost revenues or increased costs for the organization.

We saw at the beginning of this chapter how the automobile industry suffers from over-capacity. However, interestingly, on one occasion DaimlerChrysler had the opposite problem; customer demand for Chrysler's PT Cruisers was much higher than the company's production capacity. The popularity of the retro-styled automobile caught everyone by surprise – some dealers were even charging double or triple the manufacturer's recommended price for the few ones they could get. The company's factory in Toluca, Mexico, could produce around 120 000 model year 2001 PT Cruisers, but many customers who had placed orders with dealers had been waiting for months without even knowing whether they would receive their car.

Aims and objectives

In this chapter, we will consider how operations managers measure and manage transforming resources in operations environments. Managing these resources is important because once decisions have been made about the outputs that will be produced and the processes used to produce them, the next constraint that determines the level of work that the organization can perform is the availability of these transforming resources, which provide the organization's capacity. Good capacity management ensures that the organization doesn't make promises to customers or clients that it can't deliver.

After reading this chapter you will be able to:

- Explain how the operation's transforming resources determine what level of output the organization can sustain
- Explain the relationship between demand and supply, including how and why demand varies
- Compare different strategies for dealing with variations in demand, over different time frames and in different operations environments
- Understand, and be able to apply, some of the good rules of scheduling.

UNDERSTANDING CAPACITY

Capacity decisions are one of the key policy decision areas for operations. Like other policy decisions, this involves making trade-offs between investing in productive resources and making the best use of them. On the one hand, transforming resources such as facilities, technology, and people are generally expensive and take time to acquire or create, so the organization wants to use them wisely. On the other, materials, information and effort may be wasted if they are acquired or transformed when there is no demand for them, while sales may be lost if outputs are not available when needed by consumers.

Defining capacity

In operations management, the term *capacity* describes the level of output that the organization can achieve over a specified period of time. Capacity can be defined in several different ways, and some of these are described below.

Theoretical capacity

One definition of capacity is the maximum level of output that can be attained by the organization, *theoretical capacity*, which is the level of output that can be achieved if the organization's resources are used fully. This would mean operating 24 hours per day, 7 days per week, 365 days per year, and for all but continuous production this is clearly unrealistic.

Many manufacturing operations and most service operations operate either during fixed hours, such as 9 am to 5 pm, Monday to Friday, or have some periods where operations are minimal. A university might be able to double or triple the level of students through scheduling lectures around the clock, including weekends and holidays, which would make very efficient use of its lecture theatres; however, it wouldn't be very popular with students or faculty!

Design capacity

Even facilities running continuously find it difficult to achieve 100 per cent productive time; they must generally shut down at least periodically for maintenance and cleaning. A second definition of capacity is *design capacity*. This is the level of output that the operation was designed to have, which includes allowances for planned non-productive time. For example, a cinema might calculate its capacity based not only on the length of the average film, but also including the time for the audience to leave at the end of the film, the room to be cleaned and the audience for the next film to be seated. This level of capacity is usually the one selected for planning purposes. However, a drawback of design capacity is that that it does not include unplanned productive time, such as unscheduled outages. These can result from internal factors, such as unplanned staff shortages, or external factors, such as extreme weather or transportation disruptions.

Given these considerations, a practical definition of capacity might be *the amount of resource inputs relative to output requirements at a particular time* (Chase and Aquilano, 1995, p. 319).

Actual capacity

Operations managers and other decision-makers often need to know what level of outputs an operation has produced or will produce over a certain period – its actual capacity – as well as what it can produce theoretically or by design. This shown in Figure 6.1.

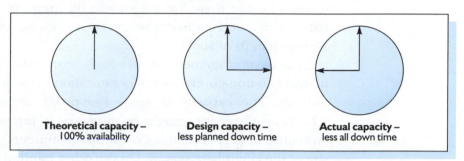

| Theoretical capacity – 100% availability | Design capacity – less planned down time | Actual capacity – less all down time |

Figure 6.1 Theoretical, design and actual capacity.

Measuring capacity

How do operations managers measure capacity? Since operations draw on a variety of different resources, each of which might be capable of producing a different amount of outputs, the answer is not usually very simple.

Capacity is generally measured using a combination of measures, including time and money. Money relates to common business measures such as sales revenues and profits, whilst time relates to measures of how much time is taken to complete products or services. (In operations management, time is often the most important measure for outputs, and money for inputs.)

Capacity measurement is usually most straightforward in *manufacturing operations*, where capacity is generally measured in terms of the maximum number of physical units of goods that the operation can produce during a given period of time. Thus, an automobile assembler will measure its capacity as the number of cars produced during a day (or month or year), a mobile phone manufacturer as the number of phones produced, and so on.

Many activities in *service operations* cannot be initiated except by customers. Here, either the operations must wait for customers (idle time) or customers must wait for the operation (queuing). Although appointment or reservation systems can help, the demand is often erratic. Therefore service operations generally measure their capacity in terms of the potential to provide services rather than actually processing capacity, since they often operate below capacity.

Hotels, for example, might measure their capacity in terms of the number of rooms and/or beds, since they cannot be certain that customers will always turn up to fill them. Similarly, capacity comparisons for hospitals are generally presented as number of beds, whether or not there are patients to fill them, or as the number of patients on average who can be seen in a given period of time, or as the average length of stay.

Capacity management in *non-profit organizations*, such as governmental and non-governmental organizations, is sometimes particularly difficult. The capacity of some non-profit organizations, such as schools or universities, might be measured in terms of the number of customers or clients (in this case pupils or students), or in terms of the size of the client base served. On the other hand, it often makes sense for these operations to report capacity in terms of the level of outputs relative to the level of inputs, since the demand for outputs is often unlimited and the level of resources available to support the operation is often limited and/or fixed. A library, for example, might state its capacity as the number of books that it holds, rather than the number of readers it can serve. Equally, their opening hours indicate the timing capacity that is available for its customers.

Like service and non-profit operations, *supply operations* are also dependent on arrivals – in this case customer orders – rather than being able to measure capacity precisely.

Inputs to capacity

An organization's ability to transform inputs into outputs is determined by the level of its transforming resources (Figure 6.2), which include its:

- Facilities
- Technology
- Workforce
- Ability to acquire inputs, including financial resources.

When capacity management decisions are being made, the effects of each type of input on the operation's ability to perform work must be considered. For example, the number of patients that can be seen in a hospital department depends on the number of staff employed, the

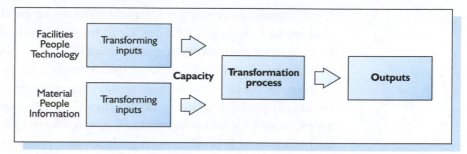

Figure 6.2 The effect of capacity in the transformation model.

number of beds available, and the availability of operating theatres and other specialized technologies. The number of automobiles that an assembly plant can produce will be limited by the number of workers, the process technology, and the availability of inventory.

Facilities

At the level of a manufacturing plant or service facility, operations management is concerned with determining the level of resources necessary to support strategy or alternately maximizing the level of outputs at a given level of resources. Capacity management here will be concerned with both the absolute level at which the operation can produce outputs and the range and/or mix of outputs that can be produced. This is important because one of the ultimate goals of a business organization is to generate profits, not to maximize investment in assets.

In the long term, organizations match capacity with demand through changing the number, location and processing capacity of facilities. At the organizational level, the number and location of facilities is a strategically important decision that will affect the total output of the organization. At the operational level, a major influence on the capacity of an individual manufacturing or service facility is the physical space available.

Facility location is important for operations that involve either production facilities manufacturing physical goods or service facilities that need to serve customers through direct customer contact. Facility location decisions are influenced by various factors, including the locations of customers, suppliers and workers, how local conditions affect business operations, and costs of doing business (including infrastructure). A good review of these factors can be found in Michael Porter's book *The Competitive Advantage of Nations* (Porter, 1990).

An organization may decide to centralize the production of all of its outputs in a single large facility, or to invest in multiple facilities, either located close to markets or specializing in a particular output or range of outputs. Organizations may use a 'hub and spoke' network for linking facilities; this is a popular arrangement for airlines and overnight package delivery companies. The London Underground is an example of a highly centralized system; nearly all the tube lines are laid out so that it is difficult to go from one point on the periphery to another without passing through the centre of London (with the exception of stations on the Circle line).

Physical location is no longer central for some types of operations. The rise of virtual organizations and the increasing amount of transactions conducted over the telephone, dedicated communications systems and the Internet means that availability to customers through electronically-mediated means, rather than physical location, is becoming increasingly important to customer choice. We have already discussed the ability of banks to deliver financial services through multiple channels, including face-to-face transactions, ATMs, telephone banking, dial-up services, and over the Internet. Support services such as call centres and data processing can be located anywhere – some remote fishing villages in Scotland have become major players in call processing, and data processing for major organizations can be done in India overnight for records updating. Work is also being done within organizations on a remote basis; teleworking and telecommuting are becoming popular alternatives to commuting to the office via crowded roads or railways.

Economies of scale

In deciding the best size for a manufacturing or service facility, managers generally try to select a size that minimizes the average cost per unit of output over the life of the facility. You should already be familiar with the concept of fixed and variable costs (Figure 6.3). Fixed costs remain constant over a range of volume of outputs, whilst variable costs are proportional to the volume of outputs.

The concept of economies of scale suggests that costs decrease as the volume of outputs increase, because fixed costs can be spread over a greater number of units of output whilst variable costs remain the same. Organizations often use the concept of economies of scale to find an optimum size of facilities based on the decrease in average cost per unit of output as the volume increases. However, average cost per unit doesn't decrease forever, because the price of many inputs will increase in a 'lumpy' way with increasing volume, especially when

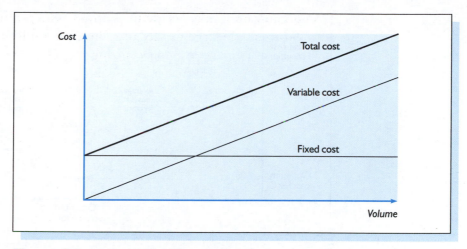

Figure 6.3 Fixed and variable contributions to total cost.

resources must be acquired externally. For example, heating and air conditioning equipment comes in standard sizes rather than being customized.

The optimum family size, according to food manufacturers, is four or six, as we can see from the fact that food products are generally packed in lots of four or six, but never five! Similarly, transportation vehicles such as coaches come in fairly standard passenger ranges (although the passenger capacity of an aeroplane can be varied by allocating more or less space to economy, business and first-class compartments, and by varying the space between seats and the width of the seats).

Figure 6.4 shows how economies of scale influence facility size. The average cost per unit of output has been plotted across a range of capacities for facilities A, B, C and D of increasing size. Within each plant, there is an optimum level of capacity that minimizes the average per unit cost for that plant. Across all the plants there may be an operating level that offers a lower average per unit cost than the other plants; however, this plant and operating level will be selected only if it is also the best match for the level of market demand.

The power of economies of scale is illustrated by the rise of superstores and hypermarkets in retailing. The retail organization can spread overhead costs across a much larger range of products and wider customer base, so that the cost per item sold is much lower than in conventionally-sized retail stores. They are also generally built outside town centres, not only because more space is available there, but also because land and building costs are cheaper. With a much

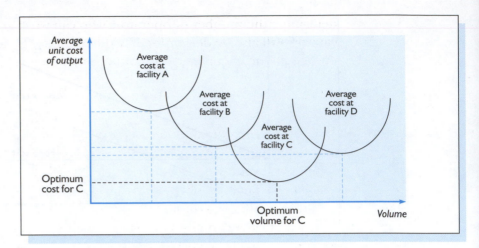

Figure 6.4 Economies of scale for different-sized facilities.

lower cost structure, these stores can undercut town-centre shops; this has led to the 'hollowing' of many high streets in the UK. (You might also know that recently there has been a move by the same companies whose superstores caused a migration of stores and shoppers from town centres back into town centres, with much smaller outlets such as Tesco Metro.)

In general, the concept of economies of scale suggests that there is an optimum level of capacity that minimizes the average per unit cost for all types of organizations. However, manufacturing facilities tend to be large in scale and centralized, whilst customer-processing facilities tend to be smaller in scale and close to their customers. That said, service operations that support customer processing (such as call centres, data-processing or other facilities) are more like manufacturing operations, and may be large, central sites supporting many other local sites.

Layout

In many services, customers are involved in some aspects of the transformation process. In a retail bank, counter personnel deal directly with customers to handle transactions and customer inquiries, whilst other staff deal with processing cheques, etc., and are rarely in contact with customers. Many operations separate high-contact and low-contact operations in time and/or in space. When separated, high-contact operations are described as *front-room* operations, whilst low-contact operations are called *back-room* operations.

Obviously, physical space alone will not completely determine capacity. For example, the physical space available at a call centre will determine the number of operators who can work at a given time, but capacity will also be determined by the number of telephone lines that the telephone exchange can handle simultaneously.

Technology

As Chapter 4 highlighted, process choice, including process type and layout, is highly related to where the operation is positioned on volume and variety.

After the facility's physical size, a second influence on capacity is technology, which was discussed in Chapter 4. Technology includes the investments in machines, equipment, computer and communications systems, and technological know-how.

Technology costs can add significantly to the investment required in productive resources. These costs include not only that of purchasing the technology, but also the associated operating costs, including staff training. In addition, obsolete or worn-out equipment must be upgraded or replaced. This can be as often as every 1–2 years for computer and communications equipment.

Workforce

The third major determinant of an operation's capacity is the size and capabilities of its workforce. Organizations consist of both direct and indirect workers. *Direct workers* participate directly in the productive process. In manufacturing, these include people who operate machines, assemble components or transport materials. In services, this usually describes the front-line employees who are in direct contact with customers or clients, and the back-room employees who support their work. *Indirect workers* include everyone else, and are there to support the direct workers.

The organization's workforce includes permanent, part-time workers and temporary workers. In many countries, changes to the permanent workforce are restricted by law. The workforce may work overtime (or extra shifts) to increase capacity. The organization may also use subcontracting to extend its capabilities. Many organizations have begun to distinguish between core and peripheral workers, who cannot necessarily be distinguished by the length of their association with the organization. Microsoft, the computer software company, has traditionally employed a high proportion of its workers on a temporary contract basis, both for flexibility and to avoid paying high levels of benefits.

In some organizations, multi-skilling – training workers in more than one job so that if someone is absent or otherwise occupied another worker can step in to perform that task – can be used to maintain capacity.

In manufacturing, the use of highly integrated equipment and information technology means that fewer and fewer workers are needed to produce a given level of output. In the 1970s the trend toward increasing automation was argued to be leading inevitably towards 'lightless factories' – production facilities with no employees that could be started up and run unattended.

Service organizations generally (but not always) rely more on employees than on capital equipment. Normann (2000) describes services by whether they are personality-intensive or not. Services rely on employees who are skilled with information technology.

Measuring workforce capacity

Unlike machines and other automated equipment, workers tend not to work at a programmed, uniform pace. First, the actions and activities performed by humans are rarely as repeatable or repetitive as those performed by machines. Furthermore, one machine is usually very much the same as other machines of the same type, but people often vary considerably in the level of work that they can achieve. Finally, people usually need time off, whereas machines and systems can often be run continuously over a long period.

People are also more flexible than automated systems in responding to changing needs and variations in the environment. In a famous study, Sutton and Rafaeli (1988) found that when stores are busy and there are many people queuing, convenience store clerks tend to spend less time serving customers and engage less in friendly behaviours such as smiling or thanking customers. On the other hand, when times were slow, the clerks and/or customers initiated small talk and engaged in more friendly behaviours in order to make work more interesting. In other words, the clerks focused on efficiency when there were a lot of customers queuing, but on social interaction when things were less pressured.

Because of this inherent variability in people's work pace, special sets of tools and techniques have been developed to measure what work levels people can achieve under normal circumstances. *Time and work measurement* describes a set of tools used by operations managers to estimate the time taken to perform a task. The two goals of time and work measurement are to identify and eliminate wasted time, and to set time standards for tasks. *Method study* aims to eliminate unnecessary operations and waste.

Work measurement techniques include time study and pre-determined motion time studies (PMTS). The data for such studies can come from records of past output, observations of work being done, or recordings of work being done. *Standard time* can be defined as the total time in which a job should be performed, including rest time.

Work study is often linked to the principles of *scientific management*, which was developed by F. W. Taylor during the 1880s and 1890s. Taylor started out by studying ways to improve production in machine shops, where skilled machinists acted as subcontracts rather than workers as we understand today.

Based on his beliefs about how to organize machining operations efficiently, Taylor developed an approach to the organization of work that treated workers as another element in the machine that was the organization. A *job* comprised all the tasks performed by a worker. Taylor broke jobs down into their simplest activities and simplified job designs so that each worker would only execute a limited range of skills in a particular job. *Tasks* could be broken down into individual activities called *elements*, and elements were made up of *job motions*, or basic physical movements.

The idea of *specialization of labour* was nothing new, as discussed in Chapter 1, but it was extended into a new context. The main idea underlying scientific management was that once jobs had been analysed and reorganized, precise time standards and production targets could be set up. Since workers were generally paid on a piece-rate system, where extra money could be earned by exceeding the standard target, setting piece-rate standards and pay was important to company profits. Taylor was probably more naïve than malevolent in devising his system of scientific management, but in practice scientific management systems were often implemented as a means of reducing the amount paid to workers, and by 1920 labour resistance to Taylor's methods in the USA was significant; European countries had not widely adopted Taylorism anyway.

Work study can help modern operations in many ways. For example, Brown (1994) observed how Work study methods were being used in quality initiatives in a number of plants in the USA and UK, and Adler (1993) reported how the General Motors/Toyota plant (NUMMI) used Work study as a central feature to manufacturing performance.

The 'image' problem with work study

If you have seen the film *Schindler's List*, you will have seen the dark side of work study techniques. There is a scene where a Nazi officer records the time of a worker. The worker makes a hinge and the stopwatch accurately tracks the time to make the product. The worker is then dragged outside to be shot (thankfully the gun doesn't work!) because he is non-productive. Although this is a horrific extreme, we should point out that there's no doubt work study was used as a technique in the 'bad old days' of the worker/manager divide, when industrial relationships in many companies were poor. Clearly, the worker/manager divide – the 'them' and 'us' syndrome – is alien and destructive to modern operations management. However, work study in itself is not responsible for creating the atmosphere in which this is likely to occur. Schonberger and Knod (1991, p. 701) state how important work study is to modern operations:

> Some writers have said that the rejection of Taylorism is one reason for Japan's industrial success. That is nonsense . . . The Japanese are the most fervent believers in industrial engineering in the world . . . In the just-in-time approach problems surface and then people apply methods study (and quality improvement) concepts to solve the problems. Time standards are widely used in Japanese industry . . . to plan how long to expect a job to take, assign the right amount of labor, and compare methods.

In Adler's (1993) observation on the NUMMI project, he states that (p. 101):

> NUMMI's intensely Taylorist procedures appear to encourage rather than discourage organizational learning and, therefore, continuous improvement.

and concludes that:

> time-and-motion discipline . . . need not lead to rigidity and alienation. NUMMI points the way beyond Taylor-as-villain to the design of a truly learning-orientated bureaucracy.'

Work study divides into two complementary areas: method study and work measurement.

Method study

Method study, in essence, is looking critically at processes in order to improve performance. The method study approach of 'SREDIM' can be a very practical help in modern operations management. The acronym SREDIM stands for:

- *Select* a specific area of work or process in order to improve it
- *Record* all relevant facts of the particular area or process
- *Examine* all factors in the present process
- *Develop* a better approach or process
- *Install* the new method as a standard of excellence
- *Maintain* this new standard as the minimum whilst actively seeking for further improvements on a continuous basis.

The five symbols used in method study can serve as a simple yet powerful approach to measuring current processes, in terms of time and other factors, in order to make improvements: The five symbols are:

O	Operation	∇	Controlled storage
D	Delay	$\rightarrow$	Transport
□	Inspection		

The aim is to have as much pure 'operation' activity as possible as this is the *only* activity that adds value; the others are, essentially, non-productive 'cost' factors and will prevent utilization of capacity. Method study can be a powerful approach to continuous improvement, and can benefit key areas such as:

- Department layout
- Workplace layout
- Materials handling
- Tools design
- Product design
- Quality standards
- Process design.

Work measurement

In addition to method study, the other ingredient in work study is work measurement. Work measurement can have direct impact on the following areas:

- Costing systems
- Incentive schemes
- Manpower planning
- Machine utilization
- Production scheduling
- Capacity planning.

For example, Lincoln Electric, a leading maker of arc-welding equipment, uses work study methods as a means of determining compensation: workers are responsible for their own quality, and this approach has caused the exit of several major companies from the industry.

Ford used its own 'Modular Arrangement of Predetermined Time Standards' (MODAPTS) as part of their commitment to improved productivity. The success at the Norfolk, Virginia, plant resulted in similar techniques being utilized and adapted to many of its other North American plants.

Henry Ford was the first industrialist to exploit the full power of Taylor's ideas, in assembling the Model T Ford. In conjunction with the use of the moving assembly line to pace work, Ford divided tasks between workers and set up the system so that each worker repeated a very simple task on a very frequent basis over and over again. This allowed him to employ workers with very low levels of mechanical skills, many of whom were either fresh off the farm or new immigrants to the USA, achieving unheard-of levels of productivity whilst paying workers much higher daily rates than other firms or other industries. Today we recognize that this repetitiveness has profound physical and psychological effects on workers, including repetitive strain injuries (RSI) and problems with motivation.

Today, operations managers are responsible for managing the workforce, taking advantage of what we've learnt since Taylor's and Ford's day.

Learning curves A final aspect of the workforce that can affect capacity is the idea that workers get better at particular tasks with experience. The mathematical representation of this is the *learning curve*. The learning curve was first identified in the manufacture of aeroplanes during World War II, where production engineers noticed that every time cumulative output doubled, the time to produce the nth aeroplane was reduced by 20 per cent. Figure 6.5 shows a theoretical example of a learning curve, where the first unit took 100 hours to complete and there is an 80 per cent learning curve. Note that because of the doubling effect the average time decrease per consecutive unit starts out as very large and then decreases very slowly. A handy technique for analysing real data is to plot observed times and cumulative numbers of units on logarithmic scales (powers of ten), where the distribution of times will approach a straight line. (If you're not handy with logarithms, then you might want to use a learning curve table where the values have already been calculated for you.)

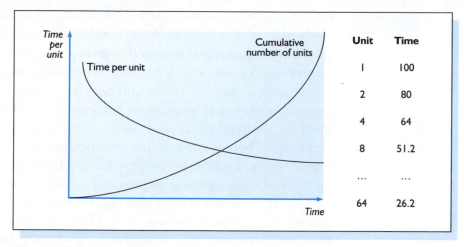

Figure 6.5 The learning curve.

The concept of learning curves is thus important to capacity, because organizations can expect to achieve higher levels of output with the same amount of resources as the cumulative number of units increases.

Acquiring inputs and distributing outputs

The final determinant of the organization's capacity is its ability to acquire inputs and distribute outputs. As mentioned above, public sector organizations such as governmental and other-not-for-profit agencies may be operating with fixed levels of financial and/or human resources, and their goal is to serve as many clients as possible, making the best use of those resources. For businesses, the availability of financial resources for purchasing inputs, equipment and facilities, and for hiring workforce, may limit capacity. Other inputs themselves may be limited.

The alcoholic beverage tequila (used by students in celebrating birthdays and other momentous occasions!) is currently in short supply because of a scarcity of its main ingredient, the agave cactus. The growing demand for tequila wasn't recognized far enough in advance, and the agave cactus, which only grows in a limited area of Mexico and needs to be planted and cultivated decades in advance of its harvest, is in short supply – thus tequila prices are rising as stocks fall.

Summary

It is clear from this first section that an organization's capacity depends on the level of resources – facilities, technology, workforce and inputs – that it has in place to create and deliver outputs. Capacity constrains the options open to operations because it is difficult to increase or decrease the level of transforming resources (especially facilities and equipment, but in many situations workforce) on a short-term basis. Furthermore, capacity measurement may be related to either staff or facilities and equipment, depending on the relative importance of each in the transformation process. In many operations skilled staff provide the product or service, with plant or equipment being used to facilitate their work. This is notable in operations that provide one-off or very small quantities of unique outputs, such as project or jobbing manufacturing operations or service shops. In such operations, staff hours are the most common measurement of capacity used.

In many other operations, plant and equipment make the product and people support their task. These operations typically produce large quantities of standardized products, using line or continuous processes for manufacturing, or mass services for services. Here, the quantity the process itself is able to produce will be the most common measurement of capacity. For example, in tyre manufacturing a typical capacity measurement will be the number of tyres a factory is able to produce over a particular period. In services, similarly, airline capacity is often measured in terms of seats, and restaurant capacity is measured in terms of customers that can be served.

In intermediate operations, such as batch operations in manufacturing, either people or plant and equipment will be the most important determinant of output, so either type of capacity measure will be used.

As seen in previous chapters, the guiding principle of mass production was to put high levels of standardized resources in place to produce high volumes of standardized output at the lowest long-run average cost. On the other hand, craft production operated with a minimum level of resources in order to create low volumes of customized outputs to meet customer demand exactly, although at a much higher per-unit cost. In between these two extremes, operations managers are responsible for managing capacity planning.

In order for strategic capacity planning to take place, organizations and managers must understand, as far as possible, what levels of outputs are currently required by customers and clients, and what their requirement will be in the future. A review of the determinants of demand follows.

THE DETERMINANTS OF DEMAND

The main driver of strategic capacity planning is the demand for the organization's outputs. Demand is usually forecast by sales or marketing, based on historical data and predictions about the future.

To manage demand, an organization must consider all potential and actual sources of demand for its goods and services. *Demand management* requires managing both internal and external demand for the organization's outputs. *External demand* comes from customers; *internal demand* comes from elsewhere in the organization.

In general, demand for goods and services follows a predictable pattern that can be described by the product life cycle, which was introduced in Chapter 3. This describes a general pattern of demand that is true for most products directed towards end consumers: demand increases during the introductory and growth phases, levels off during maturity, and decreases during the decline phase.

However, knowing where the organization's output is in the product life cycle alone is not usually enough to predict demand. First, most facilities are not dedicated to a single product in a specific phase of the product life cycle, but produce a range of outputs specifically to avoid dependence on a single product.

Furthermore, for most organizations demand is not the same from time period to time period, but is affected by long-term and short-term fluctuations. Long-term changes in demand result from changes in the basic factors that determine demand, such as political, social, economic and technological changes, which change the *baseline* of demand. The PEST framework for analysing an organization's environment is a useful way of monitoring these long-term changes.

Short-term changes in demand result from changes around this baseline. For services, variations in demand often occur over very short periods – for example, early morning and late afternoon rush hours over the course of a day, and weekend versus weekday variations.

Forecasting

There is usually uncertainty in predicting demand due to random fluctuations and other factors. Forecasting experts usually describe demand as being able to be 'decomposed' into a number of components:

- *Trend* is a gradual change in demand over time, whether an increase or decrease

- A *cycle* is a change in demand that repeats itself over time, and can be long term or short term
- Short-term cycles include *seasonal* variations in demand
- *Random variations* are 'noise' that 'get in the way' of predicting.

Demand forecasting uses information about past demand levels and possible changes in demand to make predictions about future demand levels. Forecasting provides the basis for predicting resource requirements, preparing production plans and co-ordinating supply and delivery. Organizations use forecasting in order to identify future demand for outputs, and such techniques will be discussed in the latter part of the book.

Techniques for forecasting

Operations managers draw on a variety of techniques for forecasting demand. The three basic types of forecasting methods are time series, causal, and qualitative methods. If the operation has collected enough data about past levels of demand or outputs, then mathematical techniques such as simple averages, moving averages or exponential smoothing can be applied. Figure 6.6 presents a typical process for forecasting.

Time series methods are methods based on how demand varies over time, whilst *causal methods* are based on how demand varies based on some other factor. *Qualitative methods* use judgement and expert opinion (called the Delphi technique) as the basis for forecasting.

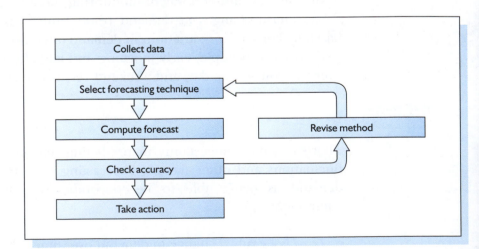

Figure 6.6 A process for forecasting.

Although a complete discussion of forecasting is beyond the scope of this chapter, some commonly encountered forecasting methods are described briefly below.

Time series methods

Time series methods use historical data, assuming that the causes of demand variation for the future will be the same as for the past.

The simplest technique for forecasting demand is by *averages* – predicting the next period's demand based on this period's demand. For example, if this semester's enrolment in a management class is 60 students, the forecast for next semester's enrolment is set at 60 students. This technique is useful when demand tends not to change much from period to period, or if all fluctuations are random.

Forecasting using the *simple average* technique is nearly as straightforward: the next period's demand is calculated as the average of the demand for previous periods. So if demand for the past three weeks was 4, 5 and 3, then the predicted level of demand in week 4 is $(4+5+3)/3 = 12/3 = 4$. If demand is relatively constant the simple average is useful, but if demand has been changing or if some periods are unrepresentative of current demand, then more sophisticated forecasting techniques are appropriate. The *moving average* technique computes the average based only on a certain number of the most recent demand periods, discarding older data. Note that the moving average that considers only one period's demand is the first technique that we started with.

Moving averages can weight each past period equally (simple moving average) or unequally (weighted moving average); a more sophisticated version of this is exponential smoothing.

In Table 6.1 you can see that these techniques vary in their accuracy. The simple average technique is better than the past period technique,

Table 6.1   Forecasting using averaging

Period	Actual demand	Past period	Simple average	Moving average
0	100			
1	110	100 (−10)	100 (−10)	
2	100	110 (+10)	105 (+5)	
3	120	100 (−20)	103 (−17)	
4	110	120 (+10)	107.5 (−2.5)	107.5 (−2.5)
5	110	110 (0)	108 (−2)	110 (0)

because it uses more of the information provided, and the moving average technique outperforms the simple average technique when the early period data is less relevant than data from more recent periods.

Causal methods

Causal methods are used to forecast demand when demand or outputs can be associated with factors besides time and outside the organization's control, such as economic indicators. These usually rely on statistical techniques such as *linear regression*. Linear regression calculates demand based on the relationship between demand and one (simple linear regression) or more (multiple linear regression) variables.

Qualitative techniques

Consumer/market research are often used to estimate demand for completely new products or services, where no data are available or close enough for quantitative forecasting methods to be applied. In the case of technology-push products or services (discussed in Chapter 3), these can be highly inaccurate; it is often said that market research for the original Sony Walkman suggested that nobody could see the point of such a personal stereo and it was concluded that the market would be too small to be profitable!

The *Delphi technique* is an established technique for tapping expert opinions about events or trends that are far into the future or highly speculative.

Many organizations employ *futurists*, people whose job is to think widely into the future. Often these predictions are wrong. For example, when the Supersonic Transport project that resulted in the Concorde was in full swing, the widespread use of supersonic transport for passenger transport was predicted by the year 2000 (Veiga, 2000). Another well-known erroneous prediction was that nuclear power would be such a low-cost source of electricity that it would be too cheap to meter.

STRATEGIES FOR MATCHING SUPPLY AND DEMAND

As well as managing the static level of resources for creating and delivering outputs, operations managers are also responsible for managing the availability of these resources in time (and in space). In part these concerns will be covered in Chapter 7, but here we will examine those aspects that are tightly linked to the availability of the organization's fixed resources of facilities, technology and workforce.

The objective of *strategic capacity planning* is to (Chase and Aquilano, 1995):

> Specify the overall capacity level of resources – facilities, equipment and labour force size – that best supports the company's long-range competitive strategy for production.

Given the constraints that are discussed above, the total output of an operation will be determined by higher-level organizational decisions, including the location and layout of individual facilities. That given, how do organizations decide what capacity level is best? This is where planning and control is important.

Planning and control

The importance of matching the output of the organization's outputs and the resources for producing those outputs is one of the key drivers of any organization's planning and control activities.

In this chapter, planning and control will be treated as two separate activities. *Planning* describes the activities that take place in order for the transformation process to occur (Figure 6.7), whilst *control* describes those activities that take place during the conversion of inputs into outputs. However, you should be aware that in practice it is not always possible to separate planning activities and control activities.

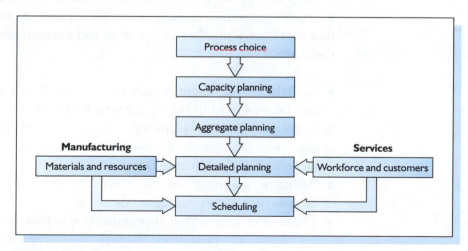

Figure 6.7 An overview of the planning cycle.

Long-range plans are usually reviewed on an annual basis. In the *medium term,* organizations match capacity with demand by acquiring flexible resources or varying their use, such as hiring or firing workers, buying additional equipment or subcontracting. These plans are usually reviewed every quarter, or sometimes every month. In the *short term,* organizations can adjust capacity by extending the utilization of existing resources, for example through the use of overtime. However, this is expensive and limited. These plans are usually reviewed weekly (Figure 6.8).

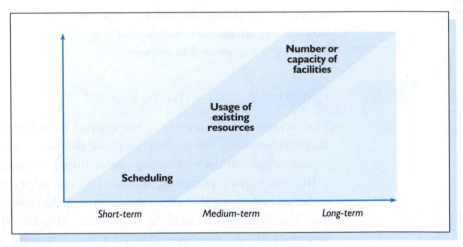

Figure 6.8 Time horizons for strategic capacity planning.

Chapter 7 presents a typical framework for planning and control in a large organization making a complex product, and it can be seen that there are a number of key tasks in planning and control. Briefly, these are:

- Capacity management, which is concerned with matching capacity and demand within the operations function
- Aggregate capacity planning, which is a medium- to long-term statement of capacity requirements to satisfy total demand, period by period, for product groups
- Resource planning, which considers the amount of resources necessary to satisfy aggregate demand
- The master production (operations) schedule, which breaks down the aggregate plan into time periods, resource categories and individual orders

- Rough-cut capacity planning, which is a detailed schedule for all jobs or orders to be completed in the planning period
- Detailed operations schedule breakdown, which is concerned with the loading, sequencing and scheduling tasks for all jobs during the period
- Shop floor control, which is short-term rescheduling and prioritizing to deal with unexpected variation from plans.

Whilst in very small operations all of this may be done informally, in medium- to large-sized organizations computer systems are generally used to tie planning and control together.

In total, planning and control cover an extensive set of activities that allow an organization to match its capabilities with the market demands. The design of the planning and control system will depend on:

- The complexity of the product or service
- The extent to which products or services are standardized or customized
- The choice of the process for producing goods or services
- The extent to which the company makes or buys different elements of the products or services
- The strategy that the company uses for matching demand for the product or service and the amount that it supplies.

Long-range capacity planning

Operations managers are responsible for developing long-range capacity plans that address the capacity strategy of the organization over the long term – for the next 1–5 years. The issue that drives long-range capacity planning is, 'What will happen to demand over this period?'

Long-term capacity planning helps organizations to make decisions about resources that take a long time to build or acquire.

Long-range capacity plans are generally based on forecast demand, rather than known demand. These forecasts are usually made at the level of *aggregate demand*, which is the demand for product groups rather than individual products. Product groups include products with similar materials inputs and processing needs.

Medium-range capacity planning

Medium-range capacity planning covers the time frame 6–18 months in the future. In this time period facilities, products and processes cannot usually be changed, so they are assumed to be fixed.

185

Medium-range capacity planning thus concerns short-term measures such as overtime, contracting, and other ways to use existing facilities. Plans focus on individual products, and on monthly or even weekly requirements.

 ## Three capacity management strategies

As seen above, a critical task for operations managers is to match demand and supply. Three strategies that are used across organizations to manage fluctuations in demand and supply are:

1 Providing the same level of supply, no matter what the demand level. This strategy may be called *demand smoothing* in service operations, or *level production* in manufacturing operations.
2 Exactly matching the level of supply to the level of demand. This strategy is usually called *chase demand*.
3 Adjusting demand to better match supply. This strategy is called *demand management*.

Level capacity strategies

One strategy that organizations use to match demand and supply is to produce and store outputs in advance of demand (Figure 6.9). These strategies rely on building inventory. Other types of operations, such as service operations, have only limited recourse to inventory-building strategies. In many service organizations, mismatches between supply and demand will result in *queues*.

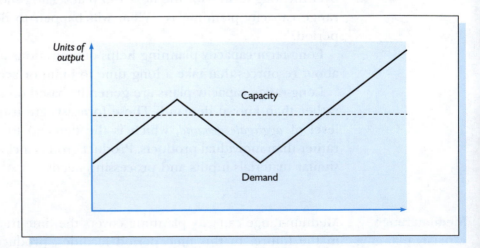

Figure 6.9 A level capacity strategy.

Chase strategies   Organizations that use chase strategies adjust their activity levels to reflect the fluctuations in demand (Figure 6.10).

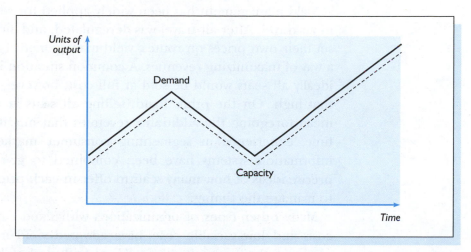

Figure 6.10 A chase capacity strategy.

Demand management strategies   Organizations that use demand management try to change demand to smooth high and low periods (Figure 6.11).

   Yield management is a particular type of demand management that attempts to maximize revenues by using different techniques to change demand, especially by varying prices. In Oakland, California, the Parkway Theatre decided to increase its business on Monday nights, traditionally a slow night, by making it a weekly 'Baby Brigade' night. Babies under the age of 1 year get in free, although their parents have to

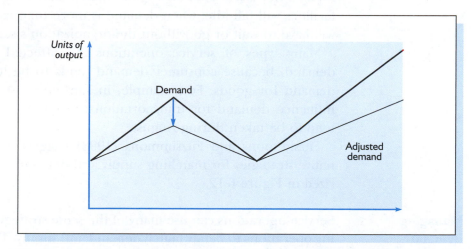

Figure 6.11 A comparison of the three types of capacity management policies.

pay $5 each. Although some other cinemas allow babies, parents usually have to leave if someone complains about the noise; others force parents to buy a full-price ticket for the baby (Locke, 2000).

Yield management has been widely applied for setting ticket prices in air travel. After air travel was deregulated, and airlines were able to set their own prices on routes, yield management became popular as a way of maximizing revenues. A common situation in air travel is that ideally all seats would be sold at full cost; however, demand is rarely that high. On the other hand, selling all seats at a discount would mean foregoing the additional revenues that might be gained. Over time, experience in segmenting consumer markets and powerful information systems have been combined to give companies very precise ideas of how many seats to offer in each price range, and how to manage the timing.

Many other types of organizations with fixed capacity, high fixed costs and low variable costs have adopted yield management techniques in their own situations. These include hotels, car-rental firms and so on. During the past few years new intermediary companies, such as Internet-based companies like lastminute.com and travel consolidators, have sprung up to take advantage of information economies in yield management.

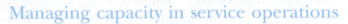

Managing capacity in service operations

Unlike manufacturing operations, where goods can be produced in advance and stored in warehouses awaiting future consumption, services are consumed simultaneously with production. When demand for a service is less than the organization's service capacity, servers and facilities will fall idle; when demand is more than capacity, customers will have to wait or go without the organization's services.

Many types of service operations are affected by variations in demand, because consumer demand tends to be less uniform than demand for goods. For example, in Europe most vacations (which influence demand for transportation as well as hospitality services) tend to be taken during August.

Fitzsimmons and Fitzsimmons (1998) suggest a number of alternative strategies for matching supply and demand, which are summarized in Figure 6.12.

Managing demand

Service operations can use many of the same strategies as manufacturing operations to better match demand and supply. They can apply the level production strategy by smoothing demand – reducing the

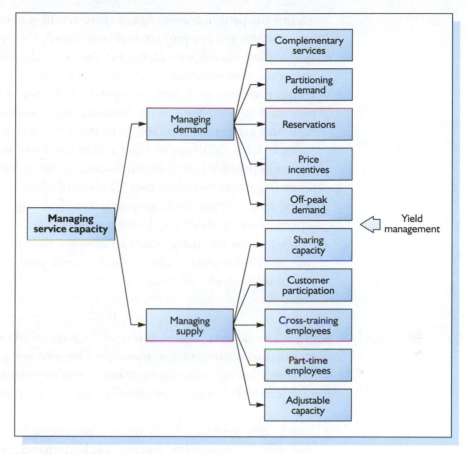

Figure 6.12 Strategies for matching demand and capacity in service operations (based on Fitzsimmons and Fitzsimmons, 1998).

variation in customer arrivals – rather than by producing to stock at the same level of production over time. Methods include:

- Partitioning demand – analysing the patterns of demand from planned arrivals and random arrivals and scheduling both groups to smooth total demand, e.g. through appointments or office hours.
- Offering price incentives – using higher and lower prices for the same service at different times, to give an incentive for using non-peak services. Transportation services commonly use price incentives. For example, rail companies offer Saver and Supersaver rates to passengers who can travel outside the peak morning and afternoon rush hours, or on the weekends. Hotels offer special price deals to fill rooms in low seasons.
- Promoting off-peak demand – as well as shifting demand away from peak periods, organizations often try to increase demand

during off-peak periods. Again, hotels will use this approach by a 'stay for three days, pay for two' package.

● Developing complementary services – restaurants often use bars to hold customers in advance of seating them.
● Using reservation systems – reservations are a way to pre-sell a potential service and limit demand. Reservations reduce waiting time and guarantee availability to their holders, although no-shows (people who don't show up to honour their reservations) are a common problem for entertainment and transportation. As a result, many organizations keep careful track of when and where no-shows occur, and may use strategies such as penalizing no-shows (discount airlines such as Go! and Easyjet mainly issue only non-refundable tickets) or overbooking (most airlines sell tickets to more passengers than they have seats available during peak periods, and hotels often overbook rooms).

Managing supply   Service operations often use the strategies above for managing demand, but strategies for managing supply are equally important, since many service operations cannot smooth demand (or only to a limited extent). Some strategies that are often employed include:

● Using daily workshift scheduling – providing higher levels of server and facility availability during high demand periods, and lower during off-peak periods. Part-time employees may also be used to cover demand during peak periods during the day, or on peak days during the week.
● Increasing customer participation – encouraging customers to perform part of the service provision themselves, such as serving themselves from self-service salad bars in restaurants, pumping their own petrol, or clearing their own tables in fast-food restaurants (co-production). Customers expect benefits in return, such as less expensive meals or faster service.
● Creating adjustable capacity – varying capacity for different services or different customers segments, such as changing the allocation of tables between bar service only and meals in a pub, or changing the number of first-class and economy class seats on an aeroplane.
● Sharing capacity – sharing scarce resources between different operations, such as shared seating areas in a food court.
● Cross-training employees – training employees in several different operations, so that they can be shifted between them as demand varies. In supermarkets, employees often restock shelves during low

demand periods, but take over tills when customer queues start to build up. (This sometimes has the side benefit of making employees' work more interesting.)

Service organizations may use more than one technique for matching demand and supply simultaneously. For example, road tax discs in Great Britain must be renewed by the first of the month, in order for drivers to remain legally on the road. Since an average of one-twelfth of road tax discs must be renewed during an average month (in actuality, the current system encourages a single major peak in the autumn), various strategies have been devised to prevent all renewals being made on a single day. Some people may choose to renew through the post. Discs can be renewed up to 14 days in advance, so some people may choose to go early and avoid the rush. Finally, some post offices open additional windows, and pre-process aspects of the renewal process whilst people wait in line, to make peak day processing as efficient as possible.

Managing capacity in supply operations

When we consider capacity strategies in the context of the supply network, compared with managing a single manufacturing facility or single service facility, the operations manager's job becomes much more complex. For supply operations managers, matching demand and capacity determines the difference between success and failure, since downstream operations are very heavily dependent on their fulfilling promised deliveries and service levels. Because suppliers and customers in a supply network are dynamically linked (Figure 6.13), the effects of mismatches in supply and capacity are even more pronounced than within a manufacturing or service operation.

Major industrial and consumer products suppliers have found striking levels of variability in their supply chains. The MIT professor Jay Forrester graphically illustrates the effects of a sudden increase in demand by retail customers of 10 per cent in his book, *Industrial*

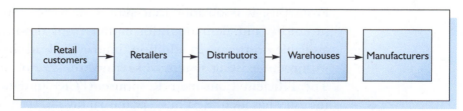

Figure 6.13 A simplified supply network.

Dynamics. As retailers react to the increase in orders and pass the information upstream (in Forrester's systems dynamics model) each level experiences an even greater increase in orders: retailers order 16 per cent more from distributors, distributors order 28 per cent more from the factory warehouse, and the factory production output increases by 40 per cent (Forrester, 1961). Consequently, if demand has increased by only 10 per cent, the factory will be left with a large number of unfilled orders. These boom and bust cycles in multistage supply networks are experienced by customers as alternative periods of product shortages and oversupply, both of which are costly to the company. This becomes especially bad when organizations can only pass information to and receive it from their immediate customers and suppliers; communication over greater distances in the supply network helps reduce these extremes.

You might already have seen this *bullwhip* effect in supply chains demonstrated through playing the 'Beer Game', or reading about it in Peter Senge's popular management book *The Fifth Discipline* (Senge, 1990). In the Beer Game, students play the roles of consumers, retailers, wholesalers and manufacturers of a brand of beer. Because they can't communicate with each other directly, they must rely on orders from the next downstream player as inputs for making decisions.

Lee *et al.* (1997) have identified four causes of the bullwhip effect:

1 Demand forecast updating – increasing fluctuations are created by forecasting methods, safety stock and lead-times along the supply chain
2 Order batching – increasing fluctuations are created by order cycles based on periodic ordering (e.g. MRP monthly cycles) and push ordering (sales quotas) by customers
3 Price fluctuations – downstream customers engage in forward buying to take advantage of price discounts and other promotions
4 Rationing and shortage gaming – if products are in short supply, customers with larger orders will receive more product if they are allocated proportional to orders.

From this, it is obvious that supply networks will operate better if inventory and demand information from downstream echelons is available upstream. In addition, improving lead times and batch sizes within the existing system will reduce the size of the bullwhip effect. The Efficient Consumer Response (ECR) initiative in the grocery industry has identified huge potential savings from reducing information distortions.

While changing existing systems will help reduce the size of the bullwhip effect, really getting to the root of the problem means educating everyone in the supply network about its causes and effects. Eliminating the bullwhip effect will require changing buyer behaviour through education, not only in purchasing and supply, but also in those responsible for managing marketing practices that create some of the bullwhip effects.

Scheduling

Operations *scheduling* is concerned with the short-term control of activities concerned with the provision of goods and services. The link between capacity management and scheduling in relation to time is shown in Figure 6.14.

The output of scheduling is a timetable for performing work. In materials processing, scheduling can be used to avoid bottlenecks and to use equipment, labour and machines to ensure the smooth flow of outputs to customers. In customer processing, scheduling can be used to:

- Schedule the timing and sequencing of activities
- Establish which workers perform these activities, and when
- Arrange deliveries of raw materials
- Arrange deliveries of finished goods.

Special techniques have been developed for project scheduling, which deals with both short-term and long-term activities, and these will be discussed in Chapter 9.

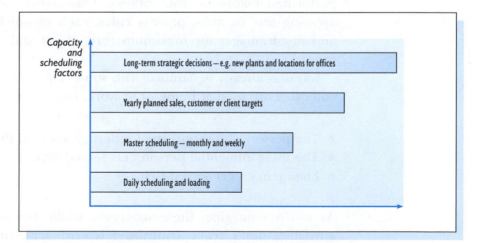

Figure 6.14 The time factor – linking capacity and scheduling management.

As mentioned above, in many types of operations, processing is either completely or partly performed to specific customer orders – make-to-order is a typical example. In such operations, a major task for operations management is to determine when and in what order to perform customer jobs, which falls into the area of operations scheduling and control. An operations scheduling and control system generally involves three types of activities:

1 Loading – determining the amount of work to be assigned in each stage of the process, whether to work centres or staff groups
2 Sequencing – deciding on the order in which jobs will be initiated and processed at each stage
3 Scheduling – allocating start and finishing times to each job.

Loading assigns jobs to work centres, within the limits of the maximum amount of work that the work centre can perform. There are two types of loading. *Finite loading* refers to assigning work to a work centre with a fixed capacity limit, such as a machine with a maximum processing rate. *Infinite loading* applies where there is no maximum capacity limit at a particular work centre or activity, such as a queue at a cash machine (ATM) that is allowed to grow longer and longer. Loading must take account of time not worked, set-ups and changeovers, and machine down time, which can limit both the planned time available and the actual time available.

A common situation in operations occurs when more than one job or customer can be processed at a given time. *Sequencing* determines in what order to process jobs or customers, i.e. which task should be performed before or after others. This usually takes the form of applying one or more priority rules, each of which has advantages and disadvantages for maximum throughput and customer waiting time.

You may already be familiar with some 'rule of thumb' sequencing rules that are used at home or at work, including:

● The person who shouts the loudest gets served first
● The most influential person gets served first
● Emergencies get served first.

As you can imagine, these strategies, while they may be politically advisable, don't really contribute toward achieving organizational objectives or efficient performance. As a result, more rational ways of organizing work are usually desirable. When scheduling is important, typical measures that are used to determine how well the organization's policies are working include:

- Meeting due dates – getting jobs done in time to meet promises made to internal or external customers and minimizing lateness
- Using resources efficiently – time as well as physical resources
- Fairness – treating all jobs or customers equally.

Instead of these rules, operations scheduling attempts to find rules that balance the efficient use of resources to process jobs or serve customers with customer satisfaction. Rules that are commonly used for sequencing jobs or customer processing include:

1 First come, first served (FCFS). The first job or customer to arrive at a workstation will be the next one processed. This is a fair rule when people or jobs arrive randomly and have similar requirements. All customers are treated equally in the sense that priorities are assigned in order of arrival, but no allowance is made for the fact that some jobs or customers are more important or need to be finished sooner than others.

2 Earliest due date (EDD). The job or customer with the earliest due date will be processed next. This minimizes the total lateness of all jobs or customers being processed. This rule highlights the importance of due dates, and therefore may be more in line with customer needs. On the other hand, where service is unreliable or consistently late customers often learn to 'play the system' and submit jobs with artificially early due dates.

3 Shortest processing time (SPT). The job or customer that will take the least time to process is the next processed. This minimizes the total waiting time, but long jobs or more urgent jobs may not be processed quickly. This rule maximizes the throughput measured as number of jobs processed, and is therefore commonly used by operations whose goal is to maximize cash flow, since these flows come earlier in the process and therefore are discounted less.

4 Longest processing time (LPT). This is the opposite of shortest processing time. This rule may be applied when the operation is not concerned with early cash flows, but can be associated with interim (stage) payments for partly completed work.

5 Last arrived, first processed (LAFP). The opposite of first come, first served. This is seldom an efficient rule, because it means that jobs

currently in the system will have to wait even longer to be processed. However, overworked administrators often apply this rule because the job that has arrived latest is usually associated with a living, breathing customer!

6 Least slack time. The job with the least time between the time it will take to process the job and the due date (slack or float time) will be processed next.

7 Critical ratio (CR). A more sophisticated version of least slack time, since it computes the ratio of time remaining to the work remaining, so that jobs or customers with varying processing times can be compared more easily.

8 Start the job with the shortest first processing time. This is managed by breaking up the total work content into the operations that are required, and the operations manager then chooses the job with the shortest first operation. The rationale for this is to 'get up and running' with jobs, and this ploy may be used where firms have invested recently in new technology. The problem with this approach is that, like others we have discussed, this rule pays no attention to customer requirements. The other problem is that although firms may wish to be 'busy' and to utilize technology, this may simply encourage work in process and not result in finished goods. This in turn may mean that the firm cannot invoice, and so cash may be drained.

9 Start the job with the longest last operation. This is quite difficult to execute, but some companies do it. The reason for this is that the last thing that a firm wants is to progress jobs and then have them held up at the last process. What this rule tries to do is to avoid bottlenecks occurring at the last stage (which is the most expensive stage of the overall job, because all other costs have been accrued by this stage).

The Gantt chart

The Gantt chart is a simple and common tool for scheduling activities. We will discuss its application to projects in more depth in Chapter 9, but a note is relevant here. The Gantt chart is a bar chart that shows what work is scheduled for a given time period, with the activities shown on the vertical axis and the time frame shown on the horizontal axis (Figure 6.15). To prepare a Gantt chart, you will need to know what jobs need to be done, when each job can be started and how long it takes.

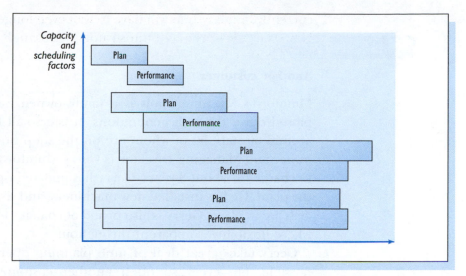

Figure 6.15 A basic Gantt chart.

Gantt charts are useful because they are simple to use and easily understood by managers and workers, who can quickly see whether jobs are on schedule and where resources need to be reallocated to keep jobs on time.

SUMMARY

Capacity management is vital for the entire organization because it will determine, to a large extent, what it can do as well as what it *cannot* do. Successful capacity management will prevent an organization from making promises to customers (in terms of quantities and delivery times) that it cannot accomplish. In that sense, therefore, capacity management is fundamentally important, because it can enhance the firm's reputation for on-time delivery to customers.

Matching demand and supply is an ongoing challenge for operations managers, especially in service, non-profit and supply operations, where building inventory in advance of demand may not be feasible. Three strategies for matching demand and supply in manufacturing operations are level production (which may be known as demand smoothing in other operations), chase production and yield management.

Operations managers are responsible not only for high-level planning, but also for managing ongoing operations, including shop-floor scheduling.

Case study

Another customer

Mumford's Machine Tools is a family-owned business that has passed down through generations. It is a small firm employing around 60 staff, 50 of whom are on the shop floor. The current owner and Managing Director is Gerry Mumford, who has been in charge for about 3 years. Gerry has updated operations within the plant. He has installed new machinery, and six manufacturing cells are in place. Gerry is also proud of changes to the workforce, where flexibility is apparent throughout.

Gerry takes great deal of time planning operations as far as possible, but every so often another customer calls entirely unexpectedly, and this is one of those days. A fax has just come through with the following message:

> Hi Gerry, I hope you're well. I haven't been in touch for a while but I need a favour. As you know we've increased our business in aerospace and we need to have some flanges made by you so that we can use them in a new product here. The specification is the same as before but we need 10 more. Please let us know if the price for this is the same as before. Also please let us know when we can have these. You can fax me or email me on the email address below – I wasn't sure if you had email yet. Thanks Steve Goodwin.

Gerry looked at the previous schedule and remembered that the sequence needed to go through particular cells: cell 2, followed by cell 4 and then cell 3. Each of the 10 units would need three hours on cell 2, followed by five hours on cell 4 and finally four hours on cell 3.

The problem for Gerry was, when should he schedule the new order for Steve Goodwin? His plant has six cells, but there are other customers whose jobs have not begun.

The customers details are as follows:

Customer	Quantity required	Cell sequence for each job (Each component in the quantity column must go through the particular cell sequence; the hours for each component are in brackets)
McKinsey Enginerring	5	Cell 2 (5) Cell 4 (4) Cell 3 (5) Cell 2 (3)
Simpsons	10	Cell 3 (2) Cell 4 (10) Cell 6 (3)
Kelly's Automation	6	Cell 4 (3) Cell 1 (2) Cell 2 (5) Cell 6 (1)
Elliot's Tools	8	Cell 1 (3) Cell 2 (4) Cell 1 (2) Cell 3 (4)
Griffith's Precision	5	Cell 2 (2) Cell 6 (4) Cell 3 (1)

Using the scheduling techniques you have seen in this chapter, when would you schedule Steve Goodwin's work, and why?

Key questions

1 Describe the difference between theoretical and design capacity.
2 Why is capacity sometimes more difficult to plan in a service environment than it is in manufacturing?
3 What is meant by chase demand? Describe how this may be applied in three different settings.

Key terms

Capacity
Causal methods
Chase demand
Demand

Demand forecasting
Demand management
Economies of scale
Facilities
Forecasting
Gantt chart
Learning curves
Level demand
Method study
Random variations
Scheduling
Technology
Time series
Workforce
Work measurement
Work study
Yield management

References

Adler, P: (1993). Time and motion regained. *Harvard Bus. Rev.*, **Jan–Feb,** 95–110.

Brown, S. (1994). TQM and work study: partners in excellence. *Product. Inventory Man. J.*, **35(3),** 34–49.

Chase, R. B. and Aquilano, N. J. (1995). *Production and Operations Management: Manufacturing and Services.* Irwin.

Fitzsimmons, J. A. and Fitzsimmons, M. J. (1998). *Service Management: Operations, Strategy, and Information Technology,* 2nd edn. Irwin McGraw-Hill.

Forrester, J. W. (1961). *Industrial Dynamics.* The MIT Press.

Lee, H. L., Padmanabhan, V. and Whang, S. (1997). The bullwhip effect in supply chains. *Sloan Man. Rev.*, **Spring,** 93–102.

Locke, M. (2000). Oakland movie theatre cries: Get that crying kid in here! *Associated Press,* 4 October.

Normann, R. (2000) *Service Management,* 3rd edn. John Wiley & Sons.

Porter, M. E. (1990). *The Competitive Advantage of Nations.* The Free Press. (Summarized in Porter, M. E. (1990). The competitive advantage of nations. *Harvard Bus. Rev.*, **Mar–Apr,** 73–93.

Schonberger, R. and Knod, E: (1991). *Operations Management: Improving Customer Service.* Irwin.

Senge, P. (1990). *The Fifth Discipline.* Doubleday.

Sutton, R. I. and Rafaeli, A. (1988). Untangling the relationship between displayed emotions and organizational sales: the case of convenience stores. *Academy Man. J.,* **31(3),** 461–87.

Veiga, A. (2000). Some predictions don't stand the test of time. *AP Online,* 26 October. (http://www.nandotimes.com/technology/0,1634,500272458–500425058–502656882–0.00/htm)

Further reading

Bennett, D. J. (1981). Operations planning and control. In: *Operations Management in Practice* (C. D. Lewis, ed.), p. 205. Philip Allan.

Betts, A., Meadows, M. and Walley, P. (2000). Call centre capacity management. *Int. J. Service Industry Man.;* **11(2),** pp. 185–96.

Goldratt, E. M. and Cox, J. (1986). *The Goal.* North River Press.

Schmenner, R. W. and Swink, M. (1998). On theory in operations management. *J. Operations Man.,* **17,** 97–113.

Suzaki, K. (1987). *The New Manufacturing Challenge: Techniques for Continuous Improvement.* Free Press.

Westbrook, R. (1994). Priority management: new theory for operations management. *Int. J. Operations Product Man.,* **14(6),** 4–24.

CHAPTER 7

Managing throughput: improving material, customer and information flows

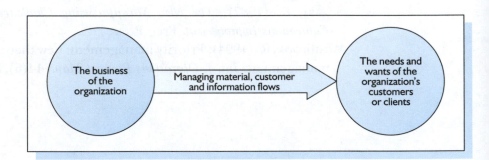

 INTRODUCTION

Case study

The money spent on health care represents a significant proportion of the total spending (Gross National Product) of most Western nations. This is driven at least in part by aging populations, increased expectations for health provision, and the development of new and costly procedures for increasing life span and the quality of life.

Hospitals form an important element of Britain's National Health Service, and represent a significant investment in facilities, technology and workforce. Despite this investment, patients' waiting time for operations and other treatments is a persistent political hot potato. One of the main constraints on treating non-emergency patients is the availability of hospital beds, rather than surgeons or operating theatres (although these are also in limited supply). A considerable amount of research by hospitals therefore goes into ways of getting patients into and out of hospital more quickly.

Hospital managers in the USA, driven by pressures from Health Maintenance Organizations (HMOs), who arrange payment for the bulk of health care in the USA, have come up with many innovative ideas for reducing the time that hospital patients spend not being actively treated. Outpatient surgery means that patients can be operated on for many routine ailments and recover at home, rather than in a hospital bed, freeing up that bed for a more seriously ill patient. Less invasive surgical procedures, such as 'bellybutton' or 'keyhole' surgery, mean that patients recover more quickly and can be released sooner. Where patients can be treated as outpatients but need to be observed in a clinical setting, after-case specialists (who combine aspects of hotels and trained nursing) have become a popular option for cosmetic surgery, etc. 'Just-in-case' precautions, such as the length of time that new mothers spend in the maternity ward, have been drastically reduced over the past few years.

What happens in the USA inevitably arrives in the UK after a short time lag. NHS drop-in clinics can treat minor injuries and illnesses, freeing up hospital A&E departments to treat more serious cases.

Operations managers are responsible for making the best use of resources under their control in support of the corporate strategy. Chapters 3–6 described the sequence of decisions made by operations managers in designing the manufacturing or service system, including the choice of goods and services to be provided by the operation, the processes through which those goods and services are created and delivered, and the resources that are put in place to deliver them. Chapter 6 described the operations decisions involved in acquiring or building the resources that the organization invests in to create and deliver goods and services to customers and clients. These resources include the facilities, technology, workforce, and systems for acquiring inputs and distributing outputs. Operations managers must balance the demand for the operation's outputs and the operation's ability to provide those outputs.

Once these decisions have been made and the resources have been put into place for producing goods and services, the operations manager is responsible for managing and improving ongoing operations. As Chapter 1 noted, the three main types of inputs to operations are materials, information and customers. Operations managers manage the flow of these resources through the system so that the desired level of output (to meet customer demand) is achieved in the most efficient way.

This chapter looks at how products and services are created and delivered – the ongoing processes through which inputs are acquired, transformed into outputs, and distributed to customers and clients. This is the core of operations management, and the bulk of managerial attention is devoted to managing within ongoing operations.

Building on this chapter, Chapter 8 will focus on a particular issue in managing throughput: how to manage the creation and delivery of goods and services so that the operations objective of 'right first time' is achieved. This objective in turn supports the other performance objectives.

 ## Aims and objectives

This chapter has two objectives. The first is to introduce you to the management of the flow of transformed resources through the productive system as products and services are created and delivered. We will consider flows of customers, materials and information in turn. The second objective is to provide an overview of approaches that are used in operations to improve the productive system.

After reading this chapter you will be able to:

- Identify the key issues in managing the processing of customers, materials and information
- Describe the purpose and management of inventory
- Compare the three major approaches to improving throughput – MRP, JIT and TOC.

MANAGING OPERATIONS FLOWS

A key performance objective for most operations is to reduce throughput time, which is the total time required to order, manufacture and distribute goods, or to provide services to customers. Most goods actually spend more time waiting to be transformed, being moved or being stored than they do actually being transformed – which is where the real value is added. Within service operations, customers often spend more time waiting to be served than they do being served, and sometimes even in consuming the service itself!

If we think of a transformation process as being a 'pipeline' through which goods and services are delivered to customers and clients, then the challenge to operations managers becomes clear: to shorten the pipeline and increase the velocity through it.

We will look at issues associated with customer flows, material flows and information flows in turn. We start by looking at the flow of customers in the high-customer contact parts of service operations – the front room. We then consider materials flows, which are common to both back-room service operations and manufacturing. We conclude this section by briefly looking at information flows associated with ongoing operations.

Customer flows

As you have seen, key differences between manufacturing and service operations arise from the intangibility of services and the need for customer contact during all or part of the transformation process. Customer contact usually takes place in the front room of the service operations, whilst activities that can be performed without the customer being present go on in the service back room. Figure 7.1 shows the flows that might take place in a fast-food restaurant such as a fish and chip shop.

Both customers and service operations managers have a similar goal: for customers to spend the maximum time possible during the transformation process in value-added activity, and to be processed with as little waste as possible, including time and other non-recoverable wastes. The design of amusement parks shows the trade-off between value-added and non-value-added time; visitors may wait as long as 30 minutes to board the 4-minute Oblivion Ride at Alton Towers.

Of course, if the primary purpose of the operation is storage (for example warehouses store materials, databases store information and hotels 'store' clients for a specified period of time), then customers

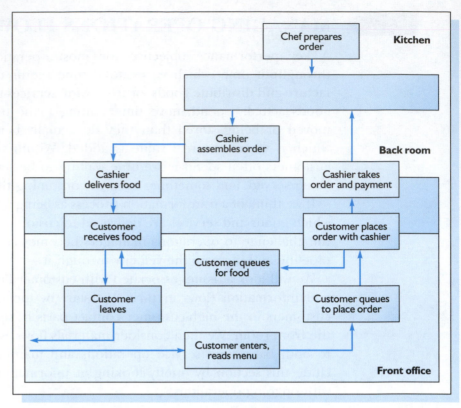

Figure 7.1 A map of the flows in a fast-food restaurant.

will still want to spend as little time as possible in non-value-added processes, such as checking in and out of the hotel. This is why hotels now offer many ways to speed up both processes, such as a video checkout.

Queuing

We shall deal in more depth with queuing techniques in the latter part of the book, but a few words are relevant here. Customers and clients tend to arrive at many service operations in an unpredictable fashion, so capacity and demand are often unbalanced. When the demand for customer processing exceeds the capacity of the service operation to process them, queues result. These queues can be physical – customers queuing at a till to place orders or pay for purchases – or virtual – customers in telephone queues waiting to speak with a call centre operator.

Some of the queues that we wait in take other forms. The ticketing system in use at some supermarket counters is another type of queuing system, where customers take a number instead of standing in line. Customers may also go for a drink in the bar whilst they are waiting for a table in a restaurant rather than standing in a waiting line.

The design and layout of service operations must be done with the processing needs and flows of customers in mind. Chapter 4 described the generic types of processes (project, jobbing, batch, line and continuous) and operations layouts (fixed, process, cell and product).

Number of queues versus number of servers

If there is more than one customer-processing operation, each can be provided with its own queue, or a single queue can serve multiple processing operations (Figure 7.2). This is useful when the time taken for an individual customer transaction varies rather than being roughly uniform. Bank queues, for example, often use a single-queue, multiple-server system, since customer transactions may last only a few seconds or several minutes. Fast-food restaurants, on the other hand, often use a multiple-queue, multiple-server system, since most transactions take about the same amount of time. McDonalds are committed to serving you as quickly as possible, and the multiple-queue, multiple-server approach is used for that purpose.

Another advantage of single-queue, multiple-server systems is that customers appear to move more quickly (although the customer processing time should be the same in either system), since the chances of being stuck in the queue behind the person counting out pennies or carrying out a complicated transaction are reduced. On the other hand, the single queue looks longer than multiple queues, so customers may be reluctant to join it.

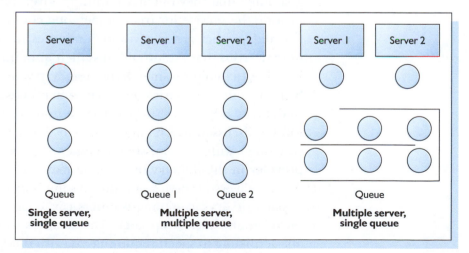

Figure 7.2 Single and multiple queue systems

Single-stage versus multiple-stage queues

Simple service operations consist of a single queue serving a single customer-processing unit, but many service operations are designed around multiple processing units linked by queues. In a self-service petrol station, customers may queue for petrol and then again to pay for their purchases.

Three strategies involving customer waiting time (besides queuing) that service operations can use are:

1 Operating according to a fixed timetable. Many mass services operate to a fixed timetable rather than responding to specific customer demand. Many mass services operate this way – buses and trains are scheduled, whilst taxis respond to specific customer demand.

2 Using an appointment system. Most professional services operate using an appointments system. Customers thus provide a ready-to-use pool of 'raw materials', so that the doctor, lawyer, accountant or other professional experiences the minimum amount of time *not* processing clients.

- The NHS Drop-in Centres, as well as the NHSDirect Internet and call centre-based health resources, provide a means for patients to be treated without going through the appointment system.

- An example of an unreliable appointment system is the wait for the arrival of someone to repair a home appliance or deliver a package. This often means a long wait and/or a wasted day, as the service provider rarely narrows down the delivery window to less than mornings or evenings, and often the person fails to show up when promised – or even at all. In the USA, with the use of hand-held computers and cellphones, some service companies can guarantee that they will arrive within a given half-hour period, or provide the service for free. In fact, one company suggested that it could predict arrivals within 5 minutes or so, but customers were nervous that they would miss their appointments. In the UK, KeyLine, a builders' merchant, totally transformed itself from being resource-driven to being customer-focused in its approach to delivery reliability. KeyLine used a number of techniques that will be discussed in Chapter 9, and in doing so achieved its aim contained within its mission statement: to be the most reliable provider in the delivery of building materials in the UK.

3 Delayed delivery of service outputs. In some service operations, such as repairs or dry-cleaning, customers can drop off the item to be worked on and pick it up later. The cleaners will charge different tariffs according to speed requirements, with the 1-hour turnaround typically being premium priced.

Services as customer processing

Many service operations take a processing-oriented view towards customers. Harvard professor Theodore Levitt first identified the 'production-line approach' as a new approach to service operations in 1972. More recently, the sociologist George Ritzer (2000) has identified four ways that service operations maximize customer processing in search of profit maximization: efficiency, calculability, predictability, and control through non-human technology.

Efficiency, in this context, means providing the optimum method for satisfying a customer need or want. Domino's pizza used to promise delivery within half-an-hour or a refund/discount (however, this was discontinued because too many teenage delivery drivers were involved in automobile accidents).

Calculability describes a quantitative approach to both the tangible aspects of the service offering and the intangible aspects of the service itself. Theme parks such as EuroDisney provide a predesigned 'experience' for visitors, where every aspect of the visit, from parking to hotels, catering and rides, is controlled down to minute details.

Predictability means the assurance that products and services are the same over time and in all related service outlets. Both outputs and the workforce itself must be standardized in order to minimize variation – the routinization of services, for example through scripts. Call centres and other voice-to-voice interactions use computer-prompted scripts to ensure that customers are processed thoroughly and quickly, and that there is little variance between operators. This consistency is a major selling point of franchise restaurants and global products (e.g. Starbuck's): they are the same *anywhere* in the world.

Control through non-human technology is exerted on both the customers and the workforce within the service system. This control can be subtle (creating layouts that channel customers into the correct location and prepare them to interact efficiently with the service) or extremely obvious (the mechanized systems in fast-food restaurants for controlling drink portions, cooking and serving french fries, etc.).

Materials flows in manufacturing and service operations

Thinking about operations as a system of inputs, transformations and outputs can be applied to any operation that produces tangible outputs. For manufacturing operations, tangible outputs are the main output of the operation; for service operations, tangible outputs can be either core or peripheral to the service being provided.

Managing materials flows

The choices made about the operation's dominant process type (see Chapter 4 for details) will limit the flows of materials, information and customers through the operation.

In *line* and *continuous flow*, the product moves sequentially from inputs to finished products. Goods made using continuous-flow processes are often produced in bulk, and are only packaged into discrete items in the final stage of production. Once production has been started up, it is difficult to make any changes to the product or processes without shutting down production for an extended time. This limits the flexibility of the production system, especially for making changes to products. The two main challenges in line and continuous flow are first to design the system to achieve optimum flow, and secondly to balance the flow at every workstation and between workstations to achieve the optimum pace of output.

In *batch flow*, each batch of the product flows from one work centre to the next. Each batch can take a different route through the system, so specialized computer systems or departments are required for routing jobs.

In *project flow*, both the resources used to do work and the resources on which work is done are brought together specifically for the project.

Materials flows are typically analysed using assembly drawings, assembly charts, routing sheets and flow-process charts, which together specify how a product is to be manufactured.

Information flows

Operations managers are also concerned with information flows, often in the form of feedback about the transformation process.

Planning and control systems are used by organizations to coordinate the convergence of transformed and transforming resources to meet customer demands.

In *aggregate planning*, organizations match the time frame of plans to the level of product analysis. Longer timeframes usually involve very general groupings of the operation's outputs, which are the subject of aggregate planning. Long-term plans are usually made for all of the operation's outputs, or for general product or service groupings. Medium-term plans are more detailed, and usually concern product families or service offerings. Short-term plans for manufacturing usually involve individual products, components or customer orders, whilst short-term plans for services are usually made for individual workforce and customers.

The complexity of products, processes and operations makes it necessary for many organizations to use computer-based systems for managing information. Information technology describes the computer-based information systems used to collect and distribute information to support decision-making. Generic types of information systems found in operations management include:

- Management information systems – systems for collecting and processing data
- Decision support systems – information systems designed to support managerial decision-making
- Expert systems – systems for making decisions based on expert knowledge
- Artificial intelligence – systems for diagnosing and solving problems using neural networks, genetic algorithms and fuzzy logic
- Enterprise software – systems for managing a wide range of business processes, often based on client/server architecture
- Advanced communications, e.g. EDI, electronic funds transfer, the Internet, intranets and extranets, teleconferencing and telecommuting, virtual reality.

The acquisition of inputs and distribution of outputs

Chapter 6 described the importance of having systems in place for acquiring inputs and distributing outputs, as well as the financial resources for acquiring the transforming and transformed resources. Both capacity (transforming resources) and inputs to be transformed (transformed resources) must be in place before goods and services can be created.

INVENTORY

Analysing materials flow using the pipeline perspective also involves analysing the time that materials are not flowing through the production system. When the inputs and outputs of an operation are held for future consumption by customers and clients, they are classed as *inventory*, which describes any resource held by the organization that is intended for future use.

In manufacturing operations, inventory is usually classified for accounting purposes into raw materials, supplies, work-in-process, or finished-goods inventory.

Raw materials inventories are the inputs to operations that have been acquired for conversion into goods or tangible outputs of a service operation. Raw materials are sometimes divided into component parts, items which have been partly processed outside the operation, and raw materials, which have not yet been processed, such as crude oil for cracking into petrol and other petroleum products, or potatoes for processing into crisps.

Supplies are inventory items that are not directly used in the production process, but are necessary to production. Supplies include cleaning materials, maintenance equipment and other items, including disposables, that do not become part of the finished product or tangible output of a service operation.

Work-in-process inventories are goods at an intermediate stage between raw materials inputs to the process and finished goods. The design of the production process will greatly influence the level of work-in-process inventory, as will be seen later in this chapter.

Finished-goods inventories are outputs whose transformation has been completed and which are ready to be delivered to or acquired by customers or clients.

Whilst organizations can reduce the level of raw materials and components being held to supply the productive process, and the level of finished goods, some level of work-in-process (WIP) inventory is nearly inevitable. Some WIP inventory is held because it is being moved between production stages. *Buffer inventory* is a stock of partially completed items kept between stages of a production process that is held so that any interruption to the process can be minimized through feeding already completed work into the process.

Where inventory is held

An operation may choose to hold inventory in raw materials, work-in-process or finished-goods inventories in order to satisfy customers with different needs for customization and different delivery requirements.

Even a simple service operation such as a sandwich shop can choose different ways of holding sandwiches. Prêt a Manger, a London-based chain of sandwich shops, only offers its customers pre-packaged sandwiches, which gives customers speedy service – they need only select and pay for the sandwiches – but they can only choose from what is on offer. Café Aroma, a competitor, also holds the sandwiches as finished-goods inventory at store level, but instead of making the sandwiches in the store they assemble them at a central facility, keeping costs low and minimizing the complexity of the distribution network. In contrast, the Subway sandwich shop lets customers select sandwiches from a standard range and customize them with ingredients such as lettuce, pickles, onions, oil and vinegar, and so on. At the shop level, ingredients are held as a combination of raw materials and work-in-process, as combinations of ingredients for popular sandwiches are packaged together (Upbin, 1999).

Some inventories may be held deliberately as part of adding value to products – neither Cheddar cheese nor Parma ham would be as delicious in their un-aged state – but most work-in-process inventory is the result of unbalanced flows rather than deliberate strategy.

The decision regarding where best to acquire resources, hold inventory, and produce to customer orders is common to manufacturing and service operations. In *make-to-order*, resources are acquired but no work is done until receipt of a customer order. For example, a shop that custom assembles bicycles might keep a stock of frames, wheels, seats and so on, but not assemble them into a finished bicycle until a customer orders a specific assemblage of parts. This strategy requires less elapsed time to meet customer delivery requirements, but trades off some ability to customize outputs to customer wants.

In *make-to-stock,* resources are acquired and all work necessary to complete a product is performed prior to the customer order. For example, most stereo equipment is manufactured independently of any customer order and held in stock, so that customers are served from existing inventory. Compared with the other strategy, this system minimizes delivery times and often costs (except for inventory, which must be closely managed), but has the least flexibility to meet customer wants.

Whether an operations chooses resource-to-order, make-to-order or make-to-stock as the way in which it provides its products or services to the customer will have important implications, especially for its planning and control system (Figure 7.3).

For resource-to-order firms every job is different, and therefore project control will be most important. For make-to-stock firms, maintaining a smooth operations flow will be critical, so production control will be most important. For make-to-order firms, handling individual customer orders will be vital, so operations scheduling and control will be most important.

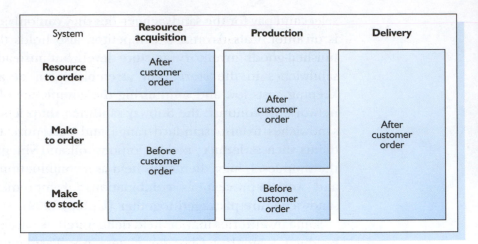

System	Resource acquisition	Production	Delivery
Resource to order	After customer order		
Make to order	Before customer order	After customer order	After customer order
Make to stock		Before customer order	

Figure 7.3 Differences between resource-to-order, make-to-order and make-to-stock

Reasons for holding inventory

Holding inventory can support the performance objectives of quality, reliability, speed, flexibility and cost in the following ways.

- *Protecting against quality problems.* Holding inventory can compensate for problems with quality in inputs to the production process, production or finished products.
- *Reliability.* Holding inventory can help an operation ensure reliable delivery to customers, no matter what happens.
- *Protecting against interruption in supply.* One of the main reasons for holding inventory is to decouple the operation from changes in the environment. This can be due to physical causes, such as earthquakes, fires or floods. It can also be due to man-made causes, such as postal strikes, underproduction by suppliers, or suppliers going out of business.
- *Smoothing production flows.* When demand varies, putting finished goods into inventory allows the organization to maintain a more constant level of input resources, especially the utilization of technology and workforce (as seen in Chapter 6).
- *Meeting higher than expected demand.* Chapter 6 described some of the problems with accurately forecasting demand. *Safety stock* is inventory that is held in excess of the expected level of demand to protect against running out of inventory, a condition known as stockout.
- *Improving delivery speed.* Organizations hold inventory so that they can immediately provide goods to customers. Retail operations try

to anticipate levels of customer demand and keep enough units in inventory to satisfy that need.

- *Flexibility.* There are three major planning and control strategies for dealing with fluctuations in demand: resource-to-order, make-to-order and make-to-stock. These differ according to the amount of work that is done prior to receipt of a customer order. In resource-to-order, the operation waits on the receipt of a customer order before acquiring resources or beginning work. An example of a resource-to-order operation is catering, where the organization will wait for the receipt of a customer order before ordering stocks of food; another is large-scale engineering and construction projects. This strategy minimizes the need to hold resources that might not be consumed, but maximizes the elapsed time between receipt of a customer order and delivery of the product or service.

- *Reducing input costs.* The cost of acquiring inputs is often reduced by purchasing larger amounts. First, the organization can spread the costs of acquiring the goods over a larger number of input units. Second, the organization may be able to take advantage of any quantity discounts that suppliers may offer. Third, the organization may need to purchase inputs in advance of price increases.

Inventory management

The purpose of *inventory management* is to provide a way to decide when and how much inventory to purchase from suppliers or to build, in-house. Holding inventory often carries significant costs. It has been suggested that the costs of purchasing and holding inventory can account for as much as 60–80 per cent of the total cost of a product or service. As you will see later in this chapter, the levels of inventories held by most companies have declined dramatically since the 1970s. This has partly been driven by the increasing costs of holding inventory, and partly by the decreased flexibility associated with holding inventory.

The costs of inventory include:

- Holding costs – the costs of having inventory, including the cost of storage facilities, the funds, and decreases in the value of items held in inventory through obsolescence, pilferage, etc.

- Ordering costs – the costs of replenishing inventory, such as the cost of preparing a purchase order, the costs of transportation and shipping, receiving, inspection, handling and storage. When the part or component is being made in-house these may be called set-up costs, which refer to the cost of preparing the production order, and any other costs associated with obtaining the materials, changing the production process or setting up equipment.

● Shortage costs – the cost of not having enough inventory on hand to meet customer demand, including lost sales, production stoppages, etc.

Organizations use various inventory management systems, including:

● Continuous inventory systems
● Periodic inventory systems
● The ABC system.

Many different types of inventory systems have been developed, and a particular organization might use different systems to manage its different types of inventory. Some of the most common types are briefly described below.

 ## Continuous inventory systems

A continuous inventory system is one where inventory levels are continually monitored, and when inventory levels drop below a predetermined level a fixed amount is ordered to replace it.

Household items are often monitored using informal continuous inventory systems. Likewise, an automobile retailer might place an order for a specific car model as a replacement each time one is sold to a customer.

Fixed-order quantity systems

A fixed-order quantity inventory system is a continuous inventory system in which a predetermined amount is ordered whenever on-hand inventory drops below the reorder point, which is the level of inventory in stock that triggers a new order. In fixed-order quantity systems every change in inventory must be recorded, so it is generally used for expensive or critical items.

Economic order quantity systems

The economic order quantity (EOQ) is a fixed order quantity that is used to minimize total inventory costs. The basic EOQ formula is given as:

$$EOQ = \sqrt{\frac{2AB}{C}}$$

where A = annual demand, B = variable ordering cost and C = variable holding cost.

For example, if A = 12 000 units; B = $20 per order; C = $10 per unit per year,

$$\text{EOQ} = \sqrt{\frac{2 \times 12\,000 \times 20}{10}}$$

$$= \sqrt{48\,000} = 219.$$

Therefore, 219 would be the number to order under the EOQ approach.

Although still used in firms, the case against the EOQ formula has been well stated over a number of years (see, for example, Burbridge, 1964) because the formula is based on the following assumptions (Brown, 1996):

1 All costs are known and do not vary, and demand for an item is also similarly known and will not vary
2 As a result of point 1, both the unit cost of an item and the reorder costs are fixed and do not change according to quantity
3 There is only one delivery for each order, which is fine on an as-required basis for just-in-time (JIT), under the EOQ approach this 'one delivery' means that the buyer will incur stock-holding costs until the materials are actually required.

The EOQ approach is alien to just-in-time management, which, as we shall see, seeks to 'pull' the exact number of materials or components to a particular workstation only when required and not before. The EOQ formula encourages buffer stock and endorses a 'just-in-case' mentality rather than a just-in-time approach.

Periodic inventory systems

A periodic inventory system is an inventory system in which the inventory level is checked after a specific time period, and a variable amount is ordered depending on the level of inventory in stock. A *fixed time period* system is a periodic inventory system in which a variable amount is ordered after a predetermined, constant amount of time has passed.

Retail operations such as supermarkets and convenience stores often use a simple inventory system where the level of stock available to customers on store shelves is monitored and replenished as necessary. For example, if there are normally 20 pepperoni pizzas in the chill cabinet and the shelf-stocker counts only 16, then four pizzas will be fetched from the store's warehouse to make up the difference.

This sort of inventory system is generally known as a *bin system*. The system described above is a one-bin system, where inventory is periodically replenished no matter how few items have been used. A slightly more sophisticated version is the two-bin system, where once the first bin has been completely used up and a replenishment order triggered, material from the second bin is used. The two bins are sized so that the second bin should just be used up when the next order arrives.

ABC classification

The ABC system is a method for classifying inventory items according to their total annual amount. ABC is based on the Pareto principle (80/20 rule), which suggests that only a few items account for most of the value of inventory.

A simple technique for managing inventory is ABC classification. ABC classification can be used to examine the distribution of inventory by value, which is useful when a large number of inventory items are in use in an organization. The goal of ABC classification is to decide which items are important and need to be tightly monitored, and which are not.

The first step in ABC classification is to develop a list of all inventory items, the cost of a single item, and the number of units of each item used in a year. The cost of each item is multiplied by its annual usage to get the annual expenditure on that item. Once the annual expenditure on all items has been calculated, the second step is to sort the list from top to bottom in descending order of annual usage. The third step is to determine the cumulative percentage of the total annual cost contributed by each inventory item (the expenditure of an item added together with all of the costs of the items above it, divided by the total expenditure on all items).

After all items have been classified, the list is divided into A, B and C items. The items with the highest annual expenditures are called A items. In general, everything to do with these items will be managed very carefully because they represent a very high investment. These items need to be managed within the close buyer–supplier relation-ships that form part of strategic supply and were discussed in Chapter 5. The items with moderate annual expenditures are called B items, and will be managed less tightly than A items. The items with the lowest annual expenditures are called C items, and very simple inventory methods may be used to control their usage. These items, such as screws and fasteners, are often purchased on a bulk basis and drawn down as needed, because it is more expensive to acquire them than to keep track of them.

A typical distribution of cumulative expenditure with items is shown in Figure 7.4. A commonly used rule of thumb is that 80 per cent of expenditure will be accounted for by 20 per cent of items (the A items), whilst the other 80 per cent of items account for the remaining 20 per cent (the B and C items).

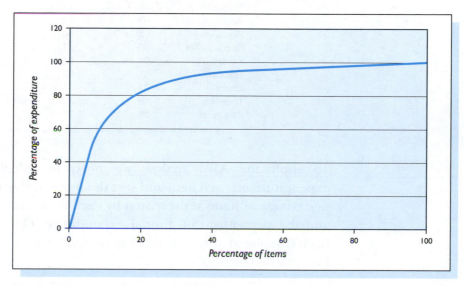

Figure 7.4 The basis for ABC classification.

If ABC classification is used, it is important to remember that this system only looks at annual expenditures and ignores all other aspects regarding how important an inventory item might be. An item that is classified as B or C might still be critical to the production or functioning of a product –– consider the importance of a fan belt to the operation of an automobile! However, when considering the complexity of managing even simple operations, such as a bookstore, ABC classification makes sense as a way of deciding where to focus attention.

Example of ABC classification

The Claverton University student store carries a range of souvenir items with the Claverton logo. Although there is a steady level of demand from students, faculty members and visitors, the store manager has noticed that some items seem to run out of stock frequently and some items are gathering dust in the backroom. Since the store's profits are used to fund scholarships, the Student Union has asked the store manager to look for a better way of managing the souvenir line. The manager has looked up the following data from sales records:

Item name	Cost per unit (£)	Monthly sales (units)
Pen	1	60
Baseball cap	16	16
Mug	65	19
Mouse pad	2	90
Fleece jacket	99	57
Sweatshirt	24	33
Tracksuit	41	97
Blazer	84	1
Trainers	69	32
Polo shirt	23	76

To apply the ABC analysis we need to calculate the monthly expenditure on each item and sort the items in descending order. The percentage of items represented by each item can then be calculated, and the percentage of annual expenditure. Once these steps have been completed, the souvenirs can be divided into A, B and C category items as follows.

	Item name	Cost per unit (£)	Monthly sales	Percentage of items	Monthly expenditure (£)	Percentage of expenditure
1	Fleece jacket	99	57	0.10	5643	0.349
2	Tracksuit	41	97	0.20	3977	0.594
3	Trainers	69	32	0.30	2208	0.731
4	Polo shirt	23	76	0.40	1748	0.839
5	Mug	65	19	0.50	1235	0.915
6	Sweatshirt	24	33	0.60	792	0.964
7	Baseball cap	16	16	0.70	256	0.980
8	Mouse pad	2	90	0.80	180	0.991
9	Blazer	84	1	0.90	84	0.996
10	Pen	1	60	1.00	60	1.000
					£16 183	

The contribution of the items to monthly sales is shown in Figure 7.5. From the analysis above, the store manager might be advised to

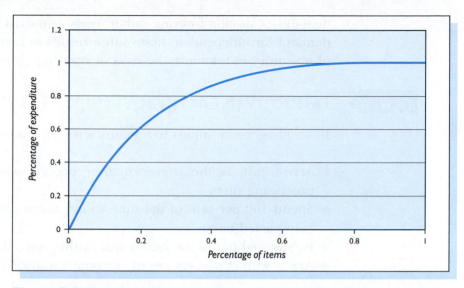

Figure 7.5 The ABC classification at the University of Claverton student store.

manage the sales of fleece jackets very carefully, whilst mugs, sweatshirts, baseball caps, mousepads, blazers and pens might need less attention.

Independent- and dependent-demand inventory

The appropriate system for managing inventory often depends on whether demand comes from external or internal customers or clients. *Independent-demand* inventory refers to items for which demand is unrelated, or independent. A personal computer assembler such as Dell Computers must respond to independent demand from customers for assembled computer systems.

By contrast, the demand for *dependent-demand inventory* is related to (and depends upon) the demand for another item. Dependent demand is characteristic of components or subsystems. For example, dependent demand would describe the demand for microprocessors, printed-circuit boards and disk drives for the computers assembled by Dell to customer order. The demand for these items by Dell would have been in turn experienced as independent demand by the microprocessor, PCB and disk-drive manufacturers.

Understanding the difference between independent and dependent demand is important, because dependent demand can be calculated from the demand for independent-demand items but independent

221

demand is usually forecast rather than known. Uncertainty in the demand for independent items often results in carrying higher levels of inventory to minimize the risks of running out.

IMPROVING OPERATIONS FLOWS

In an ideal world, inputs to a manufacturing operation would:

- Arrive just as the transformation process was ready to begin processing them
- Spend 100 per cent of the time within the transformation process being acted upon
- Be shipped out of the facility just as they were finished
- Arrive with customers just as customers wanted them.

Similarly, customers would arrive at a service operation just as the next server became free to serve them, would be acted upon 100 per cent of their time in the service operation, and then would leave just at the end of processing.

We obviously do not live in an ideal world. How then do operations improve systems so that materials are ready when needed? Some of the concepts discussed in previous chapters, such as concurrent engineering and other ways of improving innovation (Chapter 3) and mass customization and agile manufacturing (Chapter 4), affect operations flows. Here, we will specifically look at two of the most popular techniques for improving flows – the application of sophisticated computer technology and the adoption of Japanese manufacturing approaches. We will finish with another consideration; the fundamental redesign of processes themselves.

Computerized systems

Many products, such as automobiles and electronic equipment, are made up from large numbers of different parts. Clearly, bringing all of these parts together is complex, and since the 1960s various computerized systems for managing dependent-demand inventory have been developed.

Materials requirements planning systems (MRP)

During the 1970s, computer-based inventory control systems became popular as a way of trying to match supply and demand. The earliest systems for computerized production planning and control were known as *materials requirements planning* (MPR) systems (Figure 7.6). MRP systems were devised to manage component demand inventory rather than finished goods inventories. MRP systems usually were found in batch or line/mass process types of operations, where finished products were produced from a large number of component items over several production stages. The demand for components could be calculated from the demand for finished goods; hence it is dependent-demand inventory. Finished goods requirements, because they come from external customers, are termed independent-demand inventory.

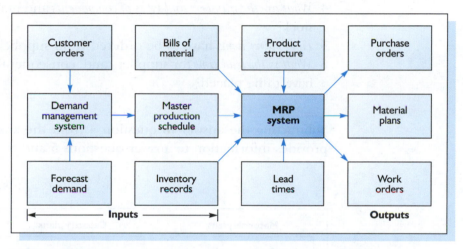

Figure 7.6 A generic MRP system (based on Slack *et al.*, 1998).

MRP is intended to have components available when they are needed, no earlier and no later. MRP treats raw materials, components and finished goods differently, so it can be used as a production scheduling and control system. In addition, it can keep track of orders so that they can be rescheduled when delays occurred.

The three important inputs to the MRP process are:

1 The master production schedule, which provides information about the quantities and scheduled outputs of end-items
2 The bill of material or the product structure file, which records parts that go into an item and the quantity required
3 The inventory master file, which describes what inventory is currently available (on hand) and on order.

An MRP system can interact with other systems to create a *capacity requirements planning* (CRP) system that identifies where there is a resource mismatch, based on when operations plans to start production of individual jobs or customer orders, the routing of these batches, and what orders or jobs yet remain to be completed (Figure 7.7). Essentially the major ingredients of MRP are quite simple, involving questions such as:

1 *How many* products are to be made?
2 *When* do these products need to be made?
3 *What is the finished product composition* in terms of materials and components?
4 *What are the numbers and types of components* and materials currently in stock?
5 *How many items* have to be ordered from suppliers?
6 *What is the lead time* for suppliers and, consequently, when do orders have to be placed?

Subtracting the answer to question 4 from the answer to question 3 provides information to answer questions 5 and 6.

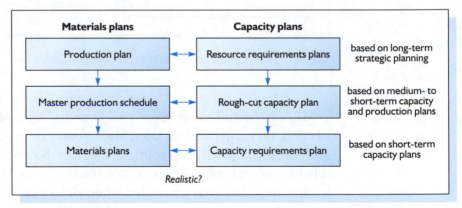

Figure 7.7 Matching capacity and production plans with MRP (based on Slack *et al.*, 1998).

If the demand for certain resources exceeds the capacity of individual work centres or the system, then the MRP plans will need to be recomputed. The CRP system provides a way of doing this by computer rather than by hand.

Manufacturing resource planning

More sophisticated versions were *manufacturing resources planning* (MRP) systems. Despite their names, these systems are used in both manufacturing *and* services. MRPII systems include additional modules (see Figure 7.8).

MRP evolved into MRPII, which in essence included MRP and added other management ingredients such as tooling, routing procedures, capacity availability and man-hour requirements.

If successfully implemented, MRP should provide the following benefits to an organization (Waters, 1992, p. 277):

- Reduced stock levels
- Higher stock turnover
- Increased customer service, with fewer delays caused by shortages of materials
- More reliable and faster quoted delivery times
- Improved utilization of facilities, as materials are always available when needed
- Less time spent on expediting and emergency orders.

If used properly, MRP should enable better relationships with suppliers to be developed over time because lead times should be

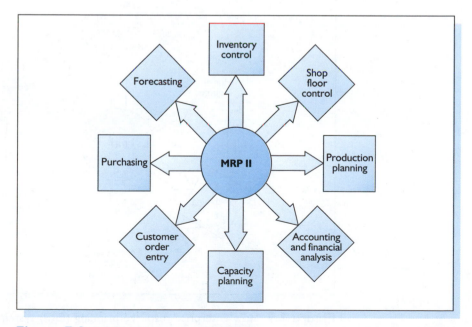

Figure 7.8 Additional elements of MRPII.

known and therefore unreasonable pressures of delivery requirements are not put on suppliers.

Enterprise resource planning

Enterprise resource planning (ERP) systems go beyond MRP and MRPII to integrate internal and external business processes. SAP AG, a German software company, sells the most popular ERP system, R/3. Although ERP systems have become popular, implementing ERP is time-consuming and costly. Like all software 'solutions', ERP has its advocates and critics alike. The basic flow of the system is shown in Figure 7.9.

The limits of MRP and allied systems

MRP is a dependent-demand system that calculates materials requirements and production plans to satisfy known and forecast sales orders. MRP helps managers to make decisions about production volumes and timings based on calculations of what will be necessary to supply demand in the future. The computer programs for MRP make a series of simple calculations about the volume and quantity of materials.

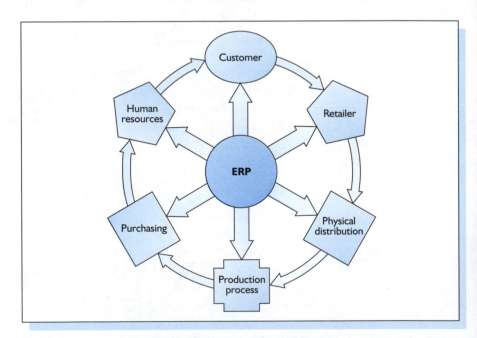

Figure 7.9 How enterprise resource planning (ERP) systems link the supply chain.

MRP has been widely taken up in industries where a large number of parts, components or subassemblies must be brought together in complicated sequences to create complex products. Managing this without computer assistance would beyond the ability of any individual or team to manage. However, a drawback to MRP in performance improvement is that the logic of MRP is based on mass production, which as we have suggested elsewhere in this book is neither universally applicable nor universally relevant in today's environment. In particular, MRP encourages a static approach to process management, batch production and holding inventory, which have been identified as leading to complacency among managers.

Just-in-time

Many Western companies have adopted the Japanese manufacturing approach known as *just-in-time* (JIT) production, whose central principle is purchasing or producing exactly the amount that is needed at the precise time it is required.

This approach is most useful in repetitive manufacturing, where there is high demand for a standard product. The goal of just-in-time is to achieve a smooth, uniform flow of small amounts of the appropriate materials through the system. Production coordination is achieved through informal local control, typically through the use of a kanban system, rather than through centralized computer control as in MRP.

This includes the flow of materials into the operation and from the operation to customers, as well as flows within the operation itself. Purchasing must work very closely with suppliers so that inputs can be delivered frequently and in small amounts, often to the production work centre itself rather than into a separate storage area.

The origins of JIT

The key ideas associated with JIT were developed at the Toyota Motor Company under the leadership of founder Eiji Toyoda, whose father had founded the successful Toyoda Spinning and Weaving Company (Toyota was selected as the company's new name to replace Toyoda, which means 'abundant rice field'). The fledgling post-war Japanese automobile manufacturing industry was then miniscule compared with the American and European automakers, and raw materials and components, as well as equipment, were scarce and expensive.

Rather than purchasing designs and know-how from foreign companies, Toyota started by taking apart imported automobiles and redesigning them to fit Japanese conditions. Similarly, Toyota observed Western production methods, but adapted them to lower production volumes and designed its own machinery, drawing on the in-house experience of designing equipment for the precision textile machinery.

The actual development of the ideas of the Toyota Production system is mainly the responsibility of Taiichi Ohno. Ohno decided that Western automobile manufacturing – especially Ford's system – had two critical flaws. First, it failed to achieve a continuous process flow, instead relying on batch manufacturing in lots of hundreds of thousands. Second, the Ford system in particular was unable to adapt to individual consumer preferences for product diversity. Ohno's solution was small-lot production, which allowed him to reduce costs through eliminating waste and idle time. Perfecting the system was not simple – he started just after World War II ended, and the elements of the entire just-in-time system took many years to perfect.

As originally conceived by Ohno, JIT is a philosophy – a way of working – as well as a set of tools and techniques. The three key elements of the JIT philosophy are:

1 Minimizing waste in all forms
2 Maintaining respect for all workers
3 Continually improving processes and systems (*kaizen*).

 The JIT production system

The main focus of the JIT production system is eliminating waste in all its forms. The major forms of waste that have been identified include:

1 Basic working processes
2 Design for manufacture
3 Simplicity, repetition and experience breed competence
4 Small, simple machines
5 Careful layout
6 Total productive maintenance
7 Set-up reduction
8 Visible management
9 Supplier involvement.

MRP and JIT systems will be compared later, but it is important to note here that one of the biggest differences between JIT and MRP or other conventional systems is that JIT is a pull production system. Push systems rely on predetermined schedules to initiate production, but pull systems rely on customer requests.

A key feature of JIT production is designing the system around flexible resources – both workers and technology. Multifunctional workers are trained to perform more than one job, so that they can replace other workers who are absent or missing, and so that they spend as little time as possible not working. Similarly, instead of special-purpose equipment, JIT production uses general-purpose machines that can perform several basic functions and thus spend as little time as possible not being used.

A second feature of JIT production is cellular layouts (see Chapter 4). Manufacturing cells bring together in a single physical location all the machines needed to manufacture a group or family of parts. The layout of the machines is often U-shaped, so that a single worker can operate several machines or processes simultaneously.

A highly visible feature of JIT is the use of kanban production control. Kanbans are the physical means of putting pull production into practice. A kanban is a 'visible signal', such as a card, that authorizes the production of a standard production quantity. Kanbans were used traditionally in Japan outside shops to signal that the shop was open for business. The idea in JIT is that the kanban indicates that an operator is 'ready for business' too, and that inventory needs to be in place so that work may begin at a particular workstation. Kanbans

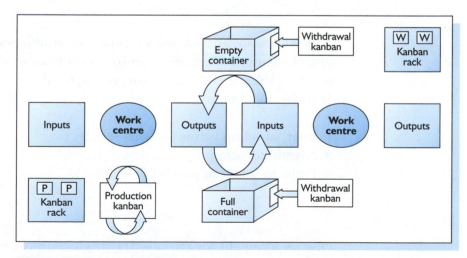

Figure 7.10 How kanban works.

are a type of two-bin inventory system, as described earlier in this chapter. Types of kanban containers include squares, racks, signals and post offices.

A kanban production system needs at least two types of kanban. A production kanban authorizes the production of goods, whilst a withdrawal kanban authorizes the movement of goods. Vendor kanbans may also be used to authorize the acquisition of inputs from suppliers. A basic diagram of the use of kanbans is shown in Figure 7.10.

Small-lot production provides a means of linking kanbans and the pull system. This reveals problems with the process or products more quickly than large lots, as illustrated in Figure 7.11.

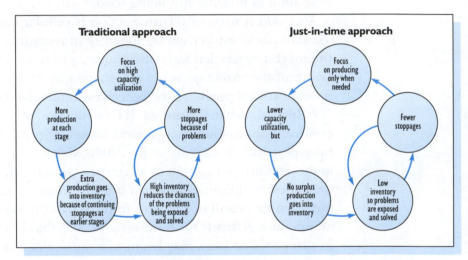

Figure 7.11 Problems are revealed by JIT (based on Slack *et al.*, 1998).

Quick set-ups are necessary to small-lot production. Shigeo Shingo, one of Ohno's colleagues at Toyota, invented specific rules for quick set-ups (Shingo, 1990), known as single-minute exchange of dies (SMED), including:

● Internal set-up versus external set-up
● Streamline set-up
● Perform set-up in parallel or eliminate.

The main requirements of JIT

One requirement for effective JIT production is uniform production levels. These result from production smoothing, which is based on reducing variability through more accurate forecasting, smoothing demand and mixed-model assembly.

The second major requirement is an organization-wide emphasis on quality. Quality at the source is supported by smaller lot sizes. The goal is zero defects.

Practices that support quality include *jikoda*, which gives workers authority to stop the production line if problems occur. *Jikoda* is often associated with *andons*, lights located above each workstation that show the station's quality status – green (normal), amber (help) and red (stop). Zero defects are supported by *pokayokes*, which are foolproof devices to prevent defects from occurring in the first place. Visual control provides direct feedback to workers.

The responsibility for quality goes beyond workers in the production process. *Kaizen* is a system for continuous improvement, which requires total employee involvement (the participation by every employee at every level).

Productive maintenance is a system of periodic maintenance and inspection designed to keep a machine in operation, rather than a machine failing and needing repairs to make it operational. Total productive maintenance is a total quality approach to maintenance.

JIT beyond the productive system

JIT relies on a small network of reliable suppliers who can deliver parts frequently without the need for inspection. Practices associated with JIT supply include:

- Locating near to the customer
- Using specially adapted vehicles
- Establishing small warehouses near the customer
- Using standardized containers
- Certification.

Other names for adaptations of JIT include stockless production (Hewlett-Packard), material as needed (Harley Davidson), and continuous-flow manufacturing (IBM). JIT forms a key part of lean production (Womack *et al.*, 1990).

JIT and MRP compared

At least superficially, MRP and JIT are not at all compatible. MRP is a push-based planning and control system designed to push work through the system. JIT is a pull-based system of planning and control, designed to pull work through the system in response to customer demand. JIT, unlike MRP, offers benefits of lower cost, increased revenues, lower investment, workforce improvements, and a structured way of uncovering problems and improving operations.

Despite these differences, MRP and JIT can work together. JIT performs best in stable conditions, including simple product structures, clearly defined material flow, and level and predictable demand. MRP, on the other hand, is good at coping with complexity and with uncertain future demand. The two systems can complement each other in two different ways. First, an operation can use JIT for managing the actual day-to-day production work and MRP for planning and control. Secondly, an operation can use JIT for managing end-products that are always (runners) or frequently (repeaters) produced, and MRP for end-products that are only infrequently produced or one-offs (strangers). In reality, MRP and JIT can, and indeed in many cases should, work well together. As Karmarker (1989, p. 125) states:

> MRPII ... initiates production of various components, releases orders, and offsets inventory reductions. MRPII grasps the final product by its parts, orders their delivery to operators, keeps track of inventory positions in all stages of production and determines what is needed to add to existing inventories. What more could JIT ask?

Theory of constraints

The *Optimized Production Technology* (OPT) system, based on Goldratt's theory of constraints, performs roughly the same functions as MRP.

To speed up flow through the pipeline, obstructions must be identified and removed. Any obstructions create bottlenecks that restrict the flow through the system, as the total output of the system can be no greater than the flow through the bottleneck(s).

Two types of bottleneck have been identified. If the bottleneck is at the final assembly (or final service) stage of the operation, then the system's capacity will be no greater than the capacity of the final assembly. On the other hand, if the bottleneck is upstream (ahead) of final assembly, then the capacity of the process (including process outputs) will be limited to the capacity of the bottleneck, but it may be difficult to identify.

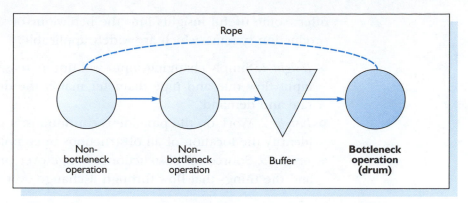

Figure 7.12 A simple drum–buffer–rope system.

Goldratt's theory of constraints has three main principles, which can be simply expressed as drum–buffer–rope (Figure 7.12):

1 The pace of the process should be set according to the capacity of the bottleneck (*drum*)
2 Since an hour lost at the bottleneck is an hour lost forever, a buffer of jobs should be maintained upstream of the bottleneck (*buffer*)
3 Jobs should be released on the receipt of order signals from the bottleneck to avoid excess jobs queuing up as WIP inventory (*rope*).

Even complex systems can be conceptualized using drum–buffer–rope, as shown in Figure 7.13.

Although fewer companies use Goldratt's OPT software for managing production than use MRP or JIT systems, the theory of constraints

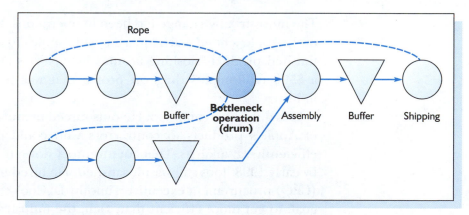

Figure 7.13 A more complex drum–buffer–rope system.

offers some useful insights into the behaviour of simple or complex production systems, which are widely applicable:

- *Insight 1.* Simply changing input will not increase output! The best input flow rate and pipe diameter match the desired output flow rate and demand
- *Insight 2.* Work on the pipeline is continuous: it is often difficult to identify the location of all obstructions in complex processes
- *Insight 3.* Sources of obstructions change over time as the pipeline and the things that flow through it change over time.

SUMMARY

Making better use of throughput – in particular with inventory – has been one of the great areas of organizational learning by many firms in the West in trying to emulate some of the Japanese practices that have underpinned Japan's success in key industries. Many Western manufacturing firms have tended to view materials management as a 'tactical' activity. Consequently, as seen in Chapter 5, purchasing and inventory management has been performed, in the main, at lower levels of the organization and has been relegated to a reactive function. In Japan, by contrast, materials management has been seen in terms of strategic importance, as part of the manufacturing arsenal, which will serve to out-compete other players in markets. However, these techniques are not wholly Japanese, and there are many cases of successful implementation of MRP and JIT in Western firms.

Case study

The changing fortunes at Apple

The most striking change has been in operations. When Jobs took over, Apple ended each quarter with some 70 days' worth of finished products sloshing around its factories and warehouses, a $500 million-plus drag on profits that was the worst in the industry.

Jobs quickly streamlined. He outsourced manufacturing of half of Apple's products to contractors who could do it far more efficiently, say analysts. That got inventory down to about a month by early 1998. Jobs still wasn't satisfied. He hired former Compaq (CPQ) procurement executive Timothy D. Cook to meet a higher goal: to get more efficient than Dell, the industry's best.

It was a daunting challenge. Cook recalls drawing a flowchart of Apple's operations, with all the linkages from suppliers to manufacturing to distributors, that 'looked like a printed circuit board' And not a very fast one. Because many of the transactions between suppliers weren't processed in real time, it could take days for a parts order to be delivered to a factory. And Cook knew he would be facing an inventory management nightmare when Jobs unveiled five different colors of iMacs.

Cook wasted no time. In his first month on the job, he outsourced production of the printed circuit cards inside Macs, easing the complexity of the manufacturing job. He closed more than 10 warehouses for finished products, making do with nine regional sites. With fewer places for stuff to sit, the less stuff there would be, he reasoned. 'If you have closets, you'll fill them up', says Cook.

Simplicity was the key. Cook trimmed Apple's list of key suppliers from more than 100 to just 24. That further eased the job of keeping track of all the parts used in Apple's products. And since it meant more business for each supplier, Apple wielded more influence with each – and better prices.

Finally, his team scrapped an off-the-shelf software program for managing manufacturing and inventories that had been limping along. Instead, Apple devised its own build-to-order system for handling online purchases.

It has worked beautifully. Pundits snickered when Jobs predicted Dell-like online efficiency at a 1997 event. 'We're coming after you, buddy', Jobs said, referring to founder Michael Dell. Today, Apple's online store is shipping 75% of orders on the day they're placed, up from 5% for the Apple of old. 'That's as good as or better than Dell or Gateway', says Salomon Smith Barney analyst Gardner.

But Cook's biggest claim to fame is getting the inventory of parts down to less than a day – obliterating the record in an industry where weeks or even months is the norm. One reason: Apple has persuaded key suppliers to set up shop close to Apple facilities, for just-in-time delivery. Another benefit of the new system: The entire production process has dropped from almost four months to just two, so Apple can more quickly move to the latest, fastest parts.

Business Week, 31 July 2000.

Key questions

1 From the above case, describe how inventory management has been used for strategic advantage.
2 What type of inventory systems might you see in the following:
   a. A hospital
   b. A fast-food restaurant
   c. A warehouse
   d. A PC manufacturer.
3 What is kanban, and why is it used in JIT?
4 What is the difference between 'push' and 'pull' systems?
5 What is the difference between MRP and MRPII?

Key terms

ABC classification
Buffer inventory
Dependent demand
Finished goods inventories
Independent-demand inventory
Just-in-time production
Kanban
Raw materials inventories
Safety stock
Stockout
Work-in-process inventories

References

Brown, S. (1996). *Strategic Manufacturing for Competitive Advantage*. Prenctice Hall.

Burbridge, J. (1964). The case against the economic batch quantity. *The Manager*, **3,** 12–20.

Karmarker, U. (1989). Getting control of just-in-time. *Harvard Bus. Rev.*, **Sep–Oct,** 122–31.

Levitt, T. (1972). A production-line approach to service. *Harvard Bus. Rev.*, **Sep–Oct,** 41–52.

Ritzer, G. (2000). *The McDonaldization of Society: New Century Edition*. Pine Forge Press.

Shingo, S. (1990). *Modern Approaches to Manufacturing Improvement.* Productivity Press.

Slack, N., Chambers, S., Harland, C., Harrison, A. and Johnston, R. (1998). *Operations Management,* 2nd edn. Pitman.

Upbin, B. (1999). Beyond burgers. *Forbes Global,* 11 January (http://www.forbes.com/global/1999/1101/0222028a.html)

Waters, C. (1992). *Inventory Control and Management.* John Wiley & Sons.

Womack, J., Jones, D. and Roos, D. (1990). *The Machine That Changed the World.* Macmillan.

Further reading

Cusumano, M. (1985). *The Japanese Automobile Industry: Technology and Management at Nissan and Toyota.* Harvard University Press.

Fitzsimmons, J. A. and Fitzsimmons, M. J. (1998). *Service Management: Operations, Strategy, and Information Technology.* Irwin McGraw-Hill.

Goldratt, E. and Cox, J. (1986) *The Goal.* Gower.

Hall, R. (1983). *Zero Inventories.* Dow Jones–Irwin.

Monden, Y. (ed.) (1986). *Applying Just-in-Time: The American/Japanese Experience.* Industrial Engineering and Management Press.

Monden, Y. (1993). *Toyota Production System,* 2nd edn. Industrial Engineering and Management Press.

Schroeder, R. G. (2000). *Operations Management: Contemporary Concepts and Cases.* Irwin McGraw-Hill.

Womack, J. and Jones, D. (1996). *Lean Thinking.* Simon & Schuster.

CHAPTER 8

Project management: content, history and current issues

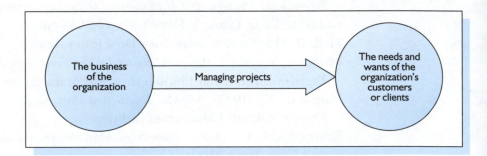

The business of the organization → Managing projects → The needs and wants of the organization's customers or clients

Introduction

Case study

The sporting excellence of over 10 000 athletes at the Sydney Olympic games was witnessed by 15 000 press representatives and countless spectators in Sydney and around the world. Less obvious were the activities and organization required for the games to take place. Organizing the games required constructing the facilities, promoting the event, managing and controlling the budget of hundreds of millions of Australian dollars, and trying to keep sponsors happy. If construction had not been completed in time, costs had gone out of control (as in Montreal in 1972) or the games had been the target of terrorist actions, the penalties for failure would have been enormous. Instead, the Sydney Olympics were heralded as a great success.

Large and high-profile events such as the Sydney Olympics represent one extreme of projects. The other extreme is projects conducted by individuals and organizations. Both types of projects can be improved using the principles that led to the success at Sydney. These principles comprise project management.

Aims and objectives

Project management is an important topic in operations management, and is a core business process in both ongoing activities and organizational change. This chapter highlights the concepts and the methods used in project management.

After reading this chapter you will be able to:

- Identify projects and their role in operations and in organizational change
- Classify project management approaches
- Break down a project into key project processes and phases
- Apply the main tools and techniques of leading-edge project management.

Projects: an introduction

Projects are low-volume, high-variety activities. Each project is at least somewhat unique in the process it uses or in the desired outcome. Because projects are finite – like the Sydney Olympics, they have a definite beginning and end – they are different from other process types (see Chapter 4), which are often repetitive processes. The importance of the project transformation processes is evident in that it is the only process type in operations management to have its own subject area.

Projects have two roles in operations; delivering what operations does, and changing the operation. Both roles within projects take place at both the individual and organizational levels.

Operational projects conducted by organizations are usually very different from individual projects. Peters (1999) estimated that about

50 per cent of all revenue-earning activities at the organizational level are conducted as projects. These include consulting contracts, advertising campaigns, new product introductions and building construction. Besides the economic contribution of projects to businesses, not-for-profits use projects to achieve their goals – for example, charity fund-raising.

Projects are also used for individual and organizational change. Individual change projects might include studying a new project, going on holiday or moving house. Organizational change projects might include redesigning key business processes, or introducing information systems or other new working systems. Table 8.1 shows some examples of both.

Organizational projects can be described using the terms that have been used to describe process design: scale, scope and competitive objectives. *Scale* describes the size of the project or the amount of resources involved. *Scope* describes the amount of work that the organization will perform directly. The *competitive objectives* for the project are provided by the operations strategy, typically as time, cost and quality objectives for the project.

Projects may also be classified by whether they are carried out:

- By one *individual*, such as a short review of a procedure or a presentation
- By one *function*, such as end-of-year reporting by Finance
- Across *functions*, such as implementing a new ERP system
- Across *organizations*, such as jointly developing e-business systems.

Many organizations are now project-based, particularly in hyper-competitive industries such as mobile communications, where in organizations such as Motorola and Vodaphone the role of project management has evolved from being peripheral to core within the business.

Table 8.1 Examples of operational and change projects

	Operational projects	Change projects
Individual	Carry out work tasks	Study a course
Organizational	Earn revenue	Introduce new methods of working

 ## Approaches to project management

Project management is critical for all functions, not just for operations. As this section shows, project management has become increasingly important, although this development has not evolved as quickly as operations management (particularly operations strategy).

Project management has developed through three stages, from no defined methods to well-defined methods to strategic project management, as shown in Table 8.2.

Table 8.2 The development of project management

Stage	Era	Characteristics
1	Pre-1950s	No generally accepted or defined methods
2	1950s	One best way approach, based on numerical methods established in the USA for managing large-scale projects
3	1990s	A contingent approach based on strategy and the convergent model of operations

Obviously, small- and large-scale projects were undertaken before the 1950s. Individuals managed events and other situations – for example, the Pyramids were constructed, wars were fought, and products were developed. However, project management as a way of integrating individuals and activities in any formalized manner did not exist until the 1950s.

During the 1950s, formal tools and techniques were developed to help manage large, complex projects that were uncertain or risky. The chemical manufacturer Du Pont developed Critical Path Analysis (CPA) for scheduling maintenance shutdowns at the company's production facilities. At the same time, the defence contractor RAND Corporation created Programme Evaluation and Review Technology (PERT) for planning missile development.

These tools focused nearly exclusively on the project planning phase, and there were no close rivals for their use. Since then other methods, such as Critical Chain Methods, have been developed that can be used for planning and controlling projects.

As well as project planning and control, the role of projects is today being reconsidered (see for example, Maylor, 1999; Gray and Larson 2000). As for other areas of operations, a strategic approach is taken to the design of the project process, rather than the highly reactive approach that has been prevalent until recently. Conventional methods developed to manage large-scale direct-value-adding projects with timescales of years, such as heavy engineering, are too cumbersome when projects require short-time scales to exploit market openings quickly, in particular in an information-based economy.

The third stage of project management emphasizes the strategic role of projects, especially the processes that the project manager must put in place to deliver the end objective of the project and satisfy the needs of all the project's customers. In this new approach project managers become project *integrators*, responsible for integrating the required resources, knowledge and processes from the project beginning to end. A key integrative skill is recognizing needs and sourcing their provision within the context of *key project processes.*

Key project processes

Projects are run through processes, as we have seen in past chapters for other aspects of operations. These processes are often common to many projects. Indeed, studies of world-class organizations show that 'the best are better at getting better', and this is achieved through continuous improvement. The 3-D model (shown in Figure 8.1) describes three phases in continuous improvement for project management:

- Phase 1: *Design it* – map out the process that will deliver the project output
- Phase 2: *Do it* – carry out the process
- Phase 3: *Develop it* – critically review all of the activities (including planning) to see what could have been done better, and capture this knowledge for future projects.

The project manager plays a different role in each project phase. In Phase 1 the project manager is concerned with the design of the project process, including project planning. The output from this phase is the plans and objectives for the project team. The project is often reviewed at the end of Phase 1 and the decision to go ahead or not is made.

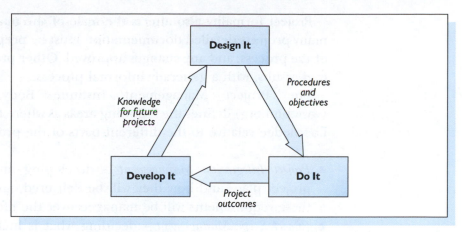

Figure 8.1 The 3-D model.

In Phase 2 (provided the project goes ahead) the project is executed.

In Phase 3 the processes and outcomes of the project are reviewed to make sure that knowledge – at least 'what worked' and 'what were the problems' – is captured and used for future projects.

Project complexity

Project complexity determines the nature of process design and the role of the operations manager. Scale and scope together describe project complexity. Project complexity can be defined as:

> Overall complexity = Organizational complexity × Resource complexity × Technological complexity

Organizational complexity results from the number of people, departments, organizations, countries, languages and time-zones that members of the project will have to deal with.

Resource complexity describes the project size or budget.

Technology complexity results from the novelty of project elements – while a technology may not be new, it may be being applied in a new way – or their interaction with other project elements.

Overall complexity is related to the scale of the project management task. A small project within a single department is generally much less complex to manage than a large, cross-organizational project such as the Channel Tunnel.

243

Project formality also affects the scale of the management task. In many projects detailed documentation must be prepared at each stage of the process, and any changes approved. Other projects focus on the end results, with a generally informal process.

The Project Management Institute Body of Knowledge (www.pmi.org) defines the following areas as where there is established knowledge relative to the different parts of the project process:

- *Project Integration Management* – developing an overview of the project plans and how they will be delivered, and how changes to these requirements will be managed over the life of the project.
- *Project Scope Management* – deciding what is included and, just as importantly, what is NOT included in the project. Scope management also leads to a process of approval or *sign-off*, where the key project customers or stakeholders agree the scope and how, if at all, it can be changed during the project.
- *Project Time Management* – taking the overview plan and breaking it into activities, which are then placed into a schedule. The time management element also includes a plan of how progress will be monitored.
- *Project Cost Management* – considering the resource requirements for the project and, by combination with the time plan, showing when they will be required. This leads to the compilation of a budget and provides a key means for cost control (such as monthly cost reporting).
- *Project Human Resource Management* – planning how the organization will be structured for the project, how to put the right team into place to work on the project, and how this team will be developed over the life of the project.
- *Project Communications Management* – planning how the objectives of the work will be communicated to the team and other parties with an interest, how information will flow (e.g. how do people know when to start doing an activity?), and how progress and team performance will be reported.
- *Project Risk Management* – identifying potential problems and their magnitude, and deciding how these can be prevented or mitigated.
- *Project Procurement Management* – considering how and when supplies are needed, the plan for their procurement, and how the process will be administered.

These provide an overview of the key processes that the project manager is concerned with. To these we would add:

- *Project Strategy* – developing the strategic role of project managers to make a positive contribution to competitive advantage through this capability (see below for further discussion of the strategy process).
- *Project Stakeholders* – managing the expectations and perceptions (as discussed in Chapter 1) of the group of stakeholders (both customers of the projects and those involved in the process).

Such aspects provide for a comprehensive consideration of the project process by the operations manager. The first task, which incorporates aspects of every one of these, is process design.

Designing the project process

A strategic approach to processes requires a direct link between the organizational strategy and operations strategy (Chapter 2), and between operations strategy and the project. The link between operations strategy and the project is expanded in Figure 8.2.

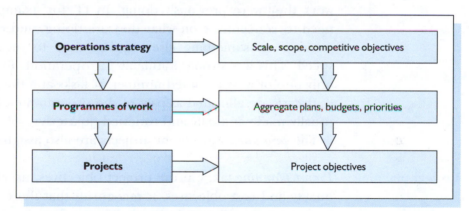

Figure 8.2 The project process.

Programme of work

A *programme of work* can be defined based on the operations strategy, which determined the scale, scope and project objectives. A programme usually includes many projects, and spells out the budgets and priorities for each one. European mobile communications providers are working to develop their third generation (3G) products. Within each 3G programme there are many individual projects being undertaken – e.g. developing the network infrastructures, the interfaces with the phone manufacturers, and the products that will be offered through this medium.

The *aggregate plan* shows the workload for people and teams for the project and other operations workload. Without an aggregate plan in place, organizations often significantly overload people and teams, causing them to become unfocused (like the operations described in Chapter 2). For example, one of the authors of this book encountered a particular organization's new product development team that had 72 projects going on at one time, with only eight people and one manager in the team. A staff member described it as chaotic, with work scheduled by 'whoever shouts loudest'. Project efficiency and staff morale were low, and stress levels were high. Aggregating the projects and matching the workloads to the available resources is capacity planning, and is used extensively in other aspects of operations (see Chapter 6).

Even if the aggregate plan is acceptable, multiple projects can reduce efficiency due to changeovers. As with operations processes, there can be significant 'set-up' costs when people switch between activities, since they often need to refamiliarize themselves with the work they were previously doing. In IT, for example, programmers need to concentrate on what they are doing, and changing them to working on something else requires time to regain their original speed. This is a strong argument for operations focus – working on only one or a very limited number of tasks at a time.

Budgets are allocated as part of the programme of work. These are usually made annually and reviewed quarterly.

The *priorities* for different projects are also assigned at this stage.

Project planning

Project planning takes in the project objectives, usually stated as time, quality and cost objectives. It recognizes that there may be trade-offs between these – for example, when you are working to tight deadlines on a personal project, you may have to compromise either on the quality of the work (not as extensive as you first wished) or on costs (hiring in outside help to complete part of the work). The most important thing at this stage is knowing whether time, cost or quality is most important, so that the process can be planned accordingly.

Once the main objective has been identified, the project manager's next responsibility is to turn these objectives into reality. This process is shown in Figure 8.3. Key questions are associated with each stage.

Once time, cost and quality objectives have been set, the project manager must show how the project will be delivered (or at least that it can be delivered). An *overview plan* states how this will be done, and

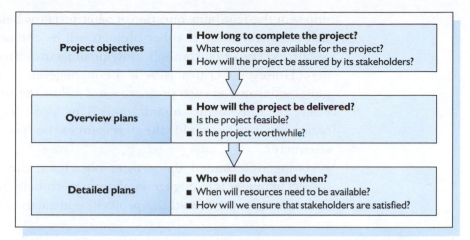

Project objectives	■ **How long to complete the project?** ■ What resources are available for the project? ■ How will the project be assured by its stakeholders?
Overview plans	■ **How will the project be delivered?** ■ Is the project feasible? ■ Is the project worthwhile?
Detailed plans	■ **Who will do what and when?** ■ When will resources need to be available? ■ How will we ensure that stakeholders are satisfied?

Figure 8.3 Turning the objectives into reality.

is required by many clients as part of awarding contracts. After the overview plan has been developed, *detailed plans* are generated by the project manager, a project planner, or other administrative support personnel in the project office.

The overview plan

The overview plan answers three questions:

1 How will the project be delivered?
2 Is the project feasible?
3 Is the project worthwhile?

If the overview plan shows that the project is possible, the project manager must also demonstrate that it is *feasible*, and that it can be carried out within the time, cost and quality constraints. Feasibility is a particular problem in project management. A goal of repetitive operations is reducing costs, but the operation has a relatively stable base since it is ongoing. No such stability exists for projects, particularly when many firms are bidding for a contract and the cost target may not be clear. Here, the project manager must balance incomplete information about the work to be done with the costs of finding out more without a definite chance of a successful contract bid.

Most organizations also require projects to be *worthwhile* – there must be some recognizable benefit relative to the resources of time, money and effort invested by the project team. Many organizations stop with the feasibility question. The criteria for being worthwhile are only partly financial, as other projects will be competing for the same resources. The organization's strategic objectives should be considered here. However, a critical issue is the managerial time and energy that must be devoted to each project – what will be the return in present or future benefits to the organization? This also raises the question of *opportunity cost* – could these resources be put to a better use elsewhere?

Having determined the project objectives, the next task for the project manager is to engage in planning – initially at an overview level and subsequently, should the project be attractive, at a detail level.

Project planning

Work breakdown structure and stage-gate planning

> How do you eat an elephant (or its vegetarian equivalent)? Just one slice at a time.

An overview plan breaks the project down into manageable units of work, known as a Work Breakdown Structure (WBS). This simple-sounding process is vital because it defines the relationship between different parts of the project. For example, a railway refurbishment project was broken down as shown in Figure 8.4.

Once the overall project has been broken down into subprojects (for example, renovate trains), each subproject can be assigned to a firm that specializes in that particular area. Each subproject may also be broken down further (level 2 and so on) until a micro-level list of tasks is identified that can be performed either by individuals over short time periods or by subcontractors, who perform them as

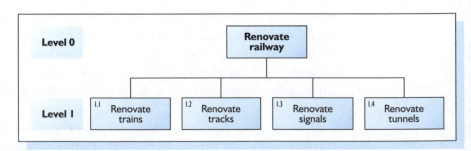

Figure 8.4 Work breakdown study of a railway refurbishment project.

projects. Tasks are numbered following the following convention, which is similar to a Bill of Materials in manufacturing planning:

1.   Renovate railway (Level 0)
1.1 Renovate trains (Level 1)
1.1.1, 1.1.2, etc. Subtasks of the above

The firm managing the railway renovation project coordinates the different subprojects and contracts. This can be challenging, as London Transport found when new trains were delivered to run in a refurbished underground line. The new trains would not fit through the refurbished tunnels, which was due to a breakdown in communication between the contractors working on the trains and those working on the tunnels. Most subprojects depend at least partly on other subprojects, and breakdowns occur when these interfaces aren't managed.

Whilst the WBS structures the *project*, there are other means for structuring the *process*. Breaking down the process for delivering the project into *phases* with gates between the phases is a way of putting checks in place to make sure the project is meeting objectives. This is known as the *stage-gate process* (Cooper, 1988), which originated in the Phased Delivery Processes (PDP) developed by the US military.

The project review at a gate will determine the answers to the following questions:

● Is the project making satisfactory progress compared with its original goals?
● Do the project objectives need changing in light of any events since the project was started (e.g.technological or market change)?
● Are there any problems that need other management attention?
● Should the project go on to the next phase (a go/no-go decision)?

Without phases and gates in place, projects can run on without meeting their objectives. In the 1970s, Sir Clive Sinclair set out to produce a family vehicle for under £1000. This would have been a real breakthrough, particularly as it was planned to be electric and therefore seen as environmentally favourable as well. The project team lost its way as the project progressed, and the C5 recumbent electrically-assisted tricycle was universally derided on its launch in 1980. Phasing the project with clear gates would have prevented the project from being completed.

249

Early gates in the project process are intended to catch 'lemons' – projects that have a low chance of success, but continue because managers become attached to them (Drucker described them in 1955 as 'investments in managerial ego'). This prevents them from consuming further resources.

Some gates are also *milestones*. These are events in the process, not only the beginning or end, but also significant intermediate events such as completion of a particular component of a new product or a particular subproject in a contract. Companies often receive interim or stage payments for the work already carried out at milestones.

Both the WBS and the stage-gate break the project into manageable units of work by the time in which the work must be completed.

The detailed plan

After the overview plan has been developed and project planning has taken place, the detailed planning stage can begin. This stage focuses on the time, cost and quality objectives.

A good saying to remember here is: 'If you fail to plan, you plan to fail'. Whilst planning alone will not guarantee project success, it can be used to model a process, which facilitates:

- Process optimization, to change the way that resources are deployed or processes arranged
- Elimination of potential problems or mitigation of their effects.

Modelling can be done away from the process (off-line) without having to create a real operational process to experiment with. This lets planners save both time and costs. Project managers can draw on a number of modelling techniques. Later in the chapter we will introduce three methods for project planning; the Gantt chart, critical path analysis, and the critical chain.

The overview plan lists activities that various contributors (individuals, functions, suppliers and contractors) to the project will carry out. This list comes from the WBS, and is phased. The next job for the project planner is to find the relationships between activities, specifically which depend on other activities to start or finish. For example, access to particular data might be required for a consultancy project. The project manager must negotiate this access so that the consultants can obtain the data in time for the investigation to proceed. These dependencies are typical of all projects, from small personal projects such as study or work assignments to very large projects. Knowing these dependencies in advance prevents unnecessary delays –

in a consulting project, consultants would not be able to do their jobs until they had access to the data.

Identifying dependencies allows the project planner to make verbal statements of these relationships – 'Complete activity A before starting activity B' or 'Complete activity C before starting activities D and E'. This is useful, but rapidly becomes unworkable with many activities and/or dependencies. Different modelling techniques can be used to describe activities and their relationships, including Gantt charts, Activity-on-Arrow diagrams and Activity-on-Node diagrams.

Gantt charts

Gantt charts were discussed briefly in Chapter 6 because they can be used in all types of operations planning. They are often used in project environments. Gantt charts were developed by Henry Gantt, a consultant who worked with F. W. Taylor, in the late 1800s. They were used for production planning as a simple way to show activities and the time they take using a horizontal bar chart. The Gantt chart proved very useful for scheduling highly routinized tasks in mass production systems, since it allowed the tasks of individual workers to be planned out in great detail (in minutes or even seconds).

The Gantt chart was first used in project management in the 1950s, and is among the most accessible of project management tools and techniques. Of course, projects aren't usually planned in minutes, but in days, months or weeks. A project to run a short course was verbally stated as:

1 We will meet on 8/01/01 to decide whether or not to go ahead with the course.
2 Following this we need to determine in detail the target market. This will take 2 days.
3 Once we have done that, we can outline the course content (3 days) and book a venue (nominally 1 day).
4 With these in place, we can develop the marketing material (5 days) and then will need a further 5 days to have it printed and sent out to our target market.
5 While we are awaiting responses and taking bookings, we can develop the actual material that will be presented on the course. The material will take 10 days to develop.
6 We need to allow 15 days for people to reply to the marketing material.
7 We will then run the course over a 2-day period.

Figure 8.5 shows a Gantt chart developed for the project. This clearly shows the benefits of using even a simple graphical technique compared with the verbal statement. Even though there are only a few activities in this example, the Gantt chart is easier to interpret because it shows both the dates and dependencies (arrows) between activities. It also shows which activities are sequential (one after the other) and which are in parallel (at the same time).

The Gantt chart, although simple and popular, does not allow much scope for optimizing the project plan or identifying potential problems. The optimum plan might be to run the course as soon as possible and to do further work to shorten the development cycle. For example, the marketing materials could be adapted from other courses, and the printing and distribution might be expedited. To prevent problems, the project manager might consider which activities are most likely to go wrong. An appropriate venue might not be ready, and the course might have to wait. If booking the venue became one of the first activities, more time would be available for this problem to be solved.

The main weakness of the Gantt chart is identifying critical activities – those activities that will hold up the process. The next two techniques are much better for this.

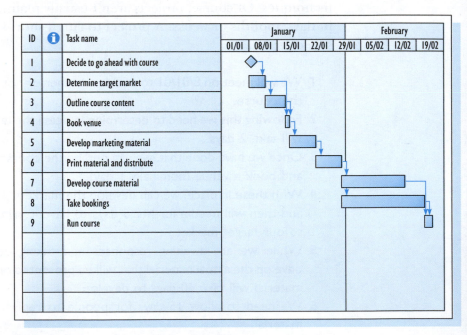

Figure 8.5 A Gantt chart for developing a short course.

Activity-on-arrow diagrams

Activity-on-arrow (AOA) diagrams are slightly more complex than Gantt charts, but are more useful for analysing projects. *Activities* are represented by arrows that run left to right between events, as shown in Figure 8.6. *Events* are points of no time duration, and are shown as circles. The completed diagram is a project network.

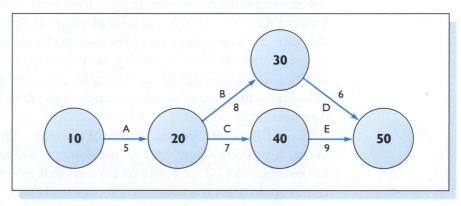

Figure 8.6 An activity-on-arrow project network.

In Figure 8.6, Activity A starts at Event 10 and lasts for 5 time units (days or weeks, as stated in the project plan). Once Activity A has been completed Event 20 occurs, which is followed by Activities B and C. Activity C must finish before Activity E begins, and Activity B must finish before Activity D starts. Event 50 marks the end of the project, once activities B and E have been completed.

Figure 8.6 also shows a useful way of numbering events – in groups of ten – which lets the project planner add an additional activity or event (for example, 15 or 35) without having to renumber the entire diagram.

The project planner will need to calculate the project duration once the AOA diagram has been drawn. Two additional pieces of information can be added to the diagram; the earliest event time (EET) and the latest event time (LET). The *earliest event time* is the earliest time that an event can occur. Conventionally, the very first event (Event 10 here) is assigned an EET of 0. The EET for the second event (Event 20) is calculated as the EET of the event where Activity A starts (Event 10) plus its duration (5 units), which makes Event 20's EET 5 units ($0+5=5$). Using the same method, the EET for Activity B is 13 ($5+8=13$) and the EET for Activity C is 12 ($5+7=12$).

What happens when an event occurs after more than one activity? There could be two possible EETs for Event 50. The EET for Event 50 following Activity D is 19 (13+6=19), and following Activity E is 21 (12+9=21). Which of these is correct? Event 50 cannot happen until Activities D and E have been completed. When Activity D stops at time 19, Activity E is still going on. Therefore, the EET for Event 50 is 21. The EET will always be the maximum of its predecessors, not the minimum.

Calculating the EETs for a project from start to finish is known as a forward pass. This tells the project manager the project duration – in this case, 21. The project manager now performs a reverse pass, from project end to project beginning, to calculate the latest event times (LETs), which are the latest time that an event can occur without delaying subsequent activities and thus affecting the project duration.

The LETs would be calculated beginning with the final project event, Event 50, whose LET is the same as its EET (21). Working backwards, the LET of Event 40 is calculated as the LET of Event 50 minus Activity E's duration, or 12 (21−9=12). Similarly, the LET of Event 30 is 15 (21−6=15).

Just as in the forward pass to calculate EETs, the LET of an event where two activities start creates a choice. The LET of Event 20 based on Activity B is 7 (15−8=7), and based on Activity C is 5 (12−7=5). Using similar reasoning to that above, the latest time that Event 20 can occur without delaying the entire project is 5, the earliest LET. If the LET were 7, then a forward pass would show that the project duration would now be 23. Finally, the LET for Event 10 must be zero (if the project planner gets any other answer, there is a mistake in the calculation).

Both the EETs and the LETs can be added to the project network diagram, as shown below in Figure 8.7. The EETs and LETs are shown in the nodes that represent events. The event label is on the left side of the circle, the top right shows the EET, and the bottom right shows the LET.

What new information does this project network give to the project planner? The path that links the events where the EET and the LET are the same (EET=LET) is known as the *critical path*. The critical path is shown in by the double arrows – the path linking Activities A, C and E. Activities on the critical path must be completed on time for the project to end on time; any delay on the critical path will delay the entire project. For the project manager, the implications of the critical path are:

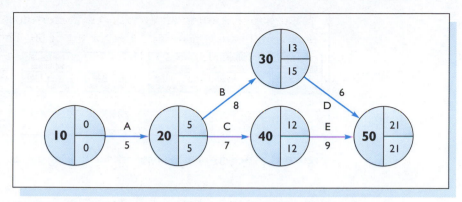

Figure 8.7 An AOA network with estimated times and critical path.

- The project planner should try to shorten activities on the critical path to make the entire project shorter
- The project manager should monitor critical path activities carefully to make sure that they are finished on time and do not delay the entire project.

The short course example described above is drawn as an AOA project network diagram in Figure 8.8.

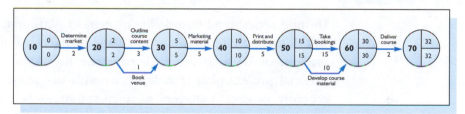

Figure 8.8 AOA project network for developing a short course.

Activity-on-node diagrams

An alternative to the AOA method is Activity-on-node (AON) diagramming. The principle is similar, but here the activities are represented by boxes and the logical links between them are shown as arrows. Again, the above example of the short course can be represented by the technique. The result is shown in Figure 8.9.

Project planning software

Professional project planners often deal with large and complicated projects that would be difficult to draw by hand, and even more

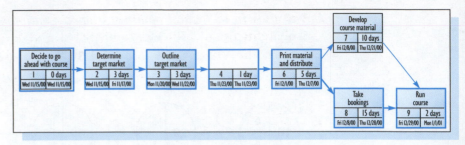

Figure 8.9 Activity-on-node network for training course.

difficult to change and update. Many software packages are available for constructing Gantt charts and network diagrams. A selection of software packages for personal computers using the Windows operating system is shown at the end of the chapter.

Although project planning software automates drawing and revising project diagrams, it cannot manage the project itself (contrary to some vendors' claims!). Many senior managers prefer instead to use whiteboards for planning. Very large-scale projects such as construction projects generally rely on software.

Critical chain project planning

Despite widespread knowledge of project planning, many projects are still delivered late or not at all. Most projects are delivered late, over budget, or both. Is the fault with the methods used to deliver the original project plan (baseline), or with the project managers? Until recently project managers were assumed to be at fault, but a new development – the critical chain method – proposes an entirely new approach to project planning.

The critical chain way of thinking is based on Eli Goldratt's Theory of Constraints, which was discussed briefly in Chapter 7. Goldratt (1997) identified four major problems with current methods of project planning:

1 *Activity durations are usually based on estimates rather than known times.* As 'best guesses' of project duration, estimates can be correct, too short or too long. When people estimate how long something will take, they may offer optimistic (too short), pessimistic (too long) or correct (just right) activity times. If these estimates apply to activities on the critical path, optimistic estimates will increase project duration and pessimistic estimates may cause waste, as the project could have been finished sooner.

2 *Any delay in the critical path will delay the entire project.* Although the probability of any individual activity being delayed depends on that activity, the effect of delay on a series of activities (even if the probability of delay of each project is low) will result in a high probability of the entire project being delayed. Therefore, calculating project duration on the critical path is not very accurate.

3 *Work is never started early.* Spare time on projects is usually dissipated because people tend to start work at the last possible minute (often later than feasible for completing the work on time) rather than at the earliest possible time. Late starts inevitably result in late finishes. This is compounded by the effects of computer failures, illness or other unforeseen events that seem to occur more frequently when time is tight – although in reality it's just that their effect is much larger.

4 *Even if some activities are finished early, the time saved is usually wasted.* Instead of the benefits of activities that complete early being passed on, methods such as the Gantt chart still lead to subsequent activities being started when originally scheduled, rather than earlier. This means that early finishes are wasted instead of being used to offset late finishes elsewhere in the project.

These four major problems affect projects even in organizations that are otherwise excellent. Lucent Technologies and various firms from the construction sector have begun to use buffered programmes, where individual activities are stripped of any safety margins created by pessimistic estimates. These safety margins are added together to create a buffer at the end of the project. Because the buffer falls at the end of the project, the problem of never starting work until the last possible time is avoided. (The further reading suggested at the end of the chapter gives more information on project control using buffered programmes.)

With this system, activities are no longer scheduled to start on particular dates but when the previous activities have finished. This creates a relay-race effect in the project, and any time saved when activities are finished early is passed on to subsequent activities.

Project managers calculate the amount of time left in the buffer to see if the project will finish on time. This is easier than calculating the start and end of all the activities left to be completed. Some firms even display the buffer time in project work areas so that people can monitor project progress themselves. This does require self-discipline. The project manager must also indicate to the team when activities must be started, and protect them from other demands so that they can complete critical path activities as soon as possible. One project team put bright orange beach balls on the desks of employees working on critical tasks to warn off anyone who might distract them! This made critical path activities visible, and was very effective.

SUMMARY

Project management has emerged as a subject vital to modern business. Within operations, projects are the means by which a significant percentage of businesses earn revenue. They are also the means by which organizations change. Project management is different from many other operations areas in a number of respects, including the level of interaction that is required with other functions and, in many cases, with parties outside the organization.

The tools for project management are now well developed to allow the delivery of projects within the key success criteria of time, cost and quality. These start with ensuring that the strategic aspects of the work are determined and that the work programme is part of an aggregate plan. The objectives are then turned into plans by identifying activities through the WBS and creating plans for time, cost and quality.

Critical path analysis is a standard tool for project managers to determine the duration of projects and which activities will delay the project if they are late. These methods are enhanced through the application of the Theory of Constraints to provide a workable buffered plan, which is readily controllable.

Case study

IT project failure at the Very Clever Software Company

The Very Clever Software Company needed to replace its best-selling product, and so started a project to design the new one. Initially a 200-page proposal was circulated, to technical staff only, in 1997. Nobody showed it to the sales or marketing people, and soon afterwards none of the technical staff were able to locate a copy of this vital document. The project faced a number of problems, including the following:

● It was being run on two sites by a project manager who was exclusively based at one of the sites, with significant antagonism between the two sites

- The project team was only part-time on the development of this new product; the rest of the time they were dealing with problems with existing products
- Right from the start work was never completed on-time, and the launch-date of the product was continually being delayed
- Nobody had a detailed plan to work from – programmers and most people 'on the ground' were making decisions about how the product would work as they went along
- Customers were promised features that could not be delivered
- Staff left due to the confusion and frustration of working on the project
- When the product was eventually released, it was defective and was so late to market that the firm was significantly behind competitors
- The process was so chaotic, it was not possible to add contract labour (additional programmers) to help speed-up the process
- The firm lost £500 000 in sales in one 3-month period alone, due to the delay with the launch.

This project became a financial disaster for the company, due to their lack of following a basic project management process. They survived due to the financial support of their parent company.

Discussion questions

1 Why should the proposal document for such a project be circulated to all relevant parties, and is it important for it to be available for the project team?
2 Why might having a dedicated project team be important to the success of such an important project?
3 How might 'process design', as discussed in this chapter, have helped this project avoid some of the problems that they faced?
4 In such a process there are trade-off decisions to be made between the objectives of time, cost and quality. In this case, suggest which of these should have been the priority.

Key questions

1 What is a project, and how does it differ from other operations activities?
2 Why is successful project management important to both organizations and individual managers?
3 How would the principles of project management be used to ensure the success of a group project that you are involved in as part of your coursework?
4 How do the methods of capacity planning in project through the aggregate project plan compare with capacity planning in other aspects of operations?
5 What are the advantages and pitfalls of using project management software in planning and controlling your projects?
6 Choose two of the packages from the list of software below. From their websites, what are the positive features of each?

Major project planning software

Supplier	Product Name	URL and comments
Microsoft Corporation	Project	http://www.microsoft.com/office/project/default.htm and see the cases of applications at http://www.microsoft.com/office/project/CaseStudies.htm
Primavera Systems Inc.	Primavera	www.primavera.com
Asta Development Corporation	PowerProject	http://www.astadev.com/content/indexm.htm
CFM Inc.	Teamflow	www.teamflow.com – a non-traditional approach to project planning, which focuses on information flow
ProChain Solutions Inc.	Prochain	www.prochain.com – lots of good information on this site and useful discussions on critical chain project management

Key terms

Activity-on-arrow diagrams
Activity-on-node diagrams
Gantt charts
Project cost management
Project risk management
Project scale
Project scope
Project time management
Stage-gate process
Work breakdown structure

References

Cooper, R. G. (1988). The new product process: a decision guide for management. *J. Marketing Man.*, **3(3),** 238–55.
Drucker, P. (1955). *Management.* Butterworth-Heinemann.
Goldratt, E. M. (1997). *The Critical Chain.* North River Press.
Gray, C. F. and Larson, E. W. (2000). *Project Management: The Managerial Process.* McGraw Hill.
Maylor, H. (1999). *Project Management,* 2nd edn. Financial Times Management.
Peters, T. (1999). *The Project 50.* Alfred A. Knopf.

Further reading

Meredith, J. R. and Mantel, S. J. (2000). *Project Management: A Managerial Approach,* 4th edn. Wiley.
Project Management Institute (1996/2000). *A Guide to the PMI Body of Knowledge.* Download from the website www.pmi.org
Project Management Journal – published quarterly by the Project Management Institute.
International Journal of Project Management – published eight times a year by Elsevier.

PART FOUR

PERFORMANCE IMPROVEMENT

CHAPTER 9

Managing quality

INTRODUCTION

The following is based on information from personal observations and from the Farmhouse Cheesemakers' Cooperative.

Today, cheeses made all over the world, from Australia to the USA, are known as Cheddar, making Cheddar the most widely purchased and eaten cheese in the world. Only West Country Farmhouse Cheddar cheese made in the west of England by the West Country Farmhouse Cheesemakers' Cooperative, however, has been awarded the Protected Designation of Origin – PDO. This accreditation has been awarded as a quality endorsement that the cheese has been made by hand, using traditional methods and local milk on the farm, and protects the name West Country Farmhouse Cheddar throughout Europe. Specific criteria are set out by the Ministry of Agriculture, Fisheries and

Foods (MAFF) for this trademark, which is intended to protect the heritage and tradition of specific foods and prevent their imitation elsewhere in the EU.

The West Country Farmhouse Cheesemakers' Cooperative of dairy farmers was formed in 1982, with the aim of making and marketing authentic, premium quality, hand-made Cheddar on their farms using inherited skills and traditional methods. Members must adhere to the basic principles of the Cooperative, which emphasize total quality and independent grading, together with hygiene and food safety.

Total quality starts at the farm, with the pastures grazed by the dairy herd producing milk for the Cheddar. The PDO acts as a quality endorsement that the cheese has been made using authenticated methods and local milk. All milk used for the production of West Country Farmhouse Cheddar must come from the four counties of southwest England – Dorset, Somerset, Devon and Cornwall. Quality continues throughout the farm operation, with Cheddar made by hand on the farm in the traditional, time-honoured way.

Besides the ingredients and the recipe, the Cheesemakers must adhere to the strict hygiene standards set out in various statutes: the Food Safety Act, Food Safety Regulations, Dairy Products Regulations and Food Labelling Regulations. All the members comply with high standards of hygiene based on the *Good Hygienic Practices for Food and Cheese Manufacture*, and observe product-testing guidelines, with all products regularly tested through independent laboratory services.

Members must submit their Cheddar for independent grading, first when the cheese has been maturing for 2 months and regularly thereafter. An experienced, independent cheese grader must carry out all grading. Total impartiality guarantees a consistency of standards for texture, colour and flavour, and ensures the customer buys only the finest quality, authentic West Country Farmhouse Cheddar. Grading will take place from around 3 months to ascertain the quality of the cheese in terms of colour, texture, smell and taste. West Country Farmhouse Cheesemakers' Cheddar is carefully matured and monitored for a further 6 months, and only then, after the final grading, does the premium cheese achieve the Farmhouse Cheesemakers' label. The cheeses will continue to mature until the cheesemaker decides that they have reached their peak, which is usually at 12 months old.

Quality is a key competitive battleground for all organizations that provide a product or service to customers or clients. Managing quality is one of operations management's most important responsibilities.

Aims and objectives

This chapter will introduce you to the basic concepts and approaches associated with the operations' perspective on quality management. This chapter begins by presenting definitions of quality, and describing the historical evolution of quality. The second section compares different applications of quality management to managing the transformation process. The last section presents a selection of tools and techniques for managing quality.

After reading this chapter you will be able to:

- Define quality from different perspectives
- Describe how quality management has evolved over time
- Identify different ways to manage quality within operations
- Apply some common techniques and tools for managing quality in manufacturing and service operations.

WHAT IS QUALITY?

In discussing the performance objectives and competitive priorities of operations (mentioned in Chapter 2), quality is often described as getting things done 'right first time, every time'. In past chapters we have discussed the physical aspects of the transformation process by which goods and services are created and delivered. In this chapter we take a closer look at why quality is important, and how 'right first time' can be achieved.

Quality has proved more difficult to define than other operations concepts. For example, Robert Pirsig spends nearly his entire book, *Zen and the Art of Motorcycle Maintenance* (Pirsig, 1974) , meditating on the nature of quality. However, a number of writers have attempted to clarify the nature of quality. Garvin (1983, p. 40) identifies five different definitions of quality:

1 *Transcendent* quality is 'innate excellence' – an absolute and universally recognizable high level of achievement. Examples of this come from various artistic achievements that have had profound emotional impact, which cannot necessarily be measured but is real

nonetheless. Transcendent quality often depends highly on intangible, subjective elements. Rolls-Royce, for example, found that replacing wood with moulded plastics in its cars subtracted a vital component from the Sedan's rich leather smell, leading customers to complain about a loss of quality. Rolls-Royce worked with a specialist supplier to develop a chemical solution to give the new Rolls-Royces the same smell as the classic 1965 Silver Cloud (Associated Press, 2000).

2 *User-based* quality 'lies in the eye of the beholder', so that each person will have a different idea of quality, based on its fitness for use by the individual. The term 'fitness for use' is associated with one of the quality gurus, Joseph Juran (1951), who stated that this was an essential requirement in delivering quality.

3 *Value-based* quality is performance or conformance at an acceptable price or cost. In a sense the distinction between 'high' and 'low' quality is largely meaningless – quality is no longer a term associated with 'high end' market tastes, but rather is measured by each particular customer segment within an overall market. Someone who owns a Lada, for example, might be equally satisfied with their car's performance as someone who owns a Mercedes, since they may be willing to put up with a lower level of finish and performance for the lower price.

4 *Product-based* quality is a precise and measurable variable, and goods can be ranked according to how they score on this measure. This allows customers and manufacturers to compare products, sometimes without even using or experiencing the product. Magazines such as *Which* are good examples of this quality focus, as they provide summary tables for different products based on measuring and comparing goods such as household appliances, automobiles and home entertainment equipment.

5 *Manufacturing-based* quality is 'conformance to requirements', adhering to a design or specification. This view of quality takes little account of customer needs or preferences. A popular example is the 'cement lifejacket': an operation could claim quality products under the manufacturing-based definition even if the products were completely useless, as long as they adhered to the standards that had been set for their manufacture.

As you can see, the latter four definitions of quality can be arranged along a continuum from the customer or client's perception of the product (or service) to the producer's perception. In reality, successful quality management is achieved by linking the needs of the customer with operations capabilities. This match was summarized by Feigenbaum (1983, p. 7), when he stated that quality is:

> ... the total composite product and service characteristics ... through which the product or service in use will meet the expectations of the customer.

and (p. 11)

> ... quality control must start with identification of customer quality requirements and end only when the product has been placed in the hands of a customer who remains satisfied.

Thus, user-based and value-based quality are defined externally to the producing organization, whilst product-based and manufacturing-based quality are defined internally. Can these two perspectives be reconciled? The bridge model in Figure 9.1 suggests a way of taking both into account.

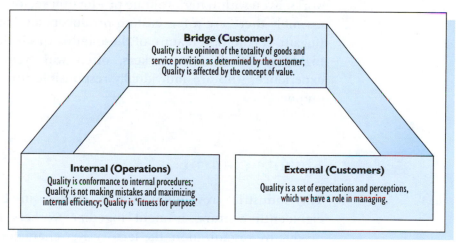

Bridge (Customer)
Quality is the opinion of the totality of goods and service provision as determined by the customer; Quality is affected by the concept of value.

Internal (Operations)
Quality is conformance to internal procedures; Quality is not making mistakes and maximizing internal efficiency; Quality is 'fitness for purpose'

External (Customers)
Quality is a set of expectations and perceptions, which we have a role in managing.

Figure 9.1 Bridge model of quality (Maylor, 2000).

This bridge model emphasizes the need for operations to manage the intangible aspects of quality as well as those definable and measurable characteristics that can be controlled or at least affected by operations, whilst marketing must have a good understanding of customer requirements. These requirements must then be fed into operations so that customer satisfaction can be achieved.

AN HISTORICAL PERSPECTIVE ON QUALITY

Chapters 1 and 2 described the historical evolution of production methods. Methods for controlling quality have also evolved over the same time, sometimes together with, and sometimes independently of, changes in production methods.

During the *craft* era, individual artisans and skilled craftsmen assured the quality of luxury goods by making them in small quantities, and inspecting them when they were finished to make sure that they met the expected standard. Craft production of valuable or skilled items was generally controlled by associations of craftsmen, called guilds, which set the standards for how work was done and by which products were judged. Thus quality was built into, and was an integral part of, the overall transformation process.

Although craft production is no longer the norm for manufactured goods, it is still found in certain sectors and in many services. High-quality glassware is still produced by hand-blowing, from the blue glass hand-blown in Bristol and Bath in the UK to Sweden's famous glass works. Even within high-volume production sectors such as automotive assembly there are a few custom producers left, such as Morgan and Bugatti. A common feature of these industries is that they still rely on highly qualified craft workers, often with years of training and experience, who are individually responsible for the quality of their outputs.

Quality control

The industrial revolution, which started in Britain during the eighteenth century, brought together workers in a new kind of productive organization, the factory. Key characteristics of the factory were the substitution of machines for human effort (powered machinery) and inanimate for animate sources of power (steam), and the use of new raw materials such as cotton and steel. The factory system changed the location of the production of many types of goods from cottages and small workshops, where work was 'put out' to individuals or families, to organized workshops and factories, where labourers were employed for wages.

In many sectors individuals were still responsible for doing their own quality inspections. At first, parts for machines or other complex items were fitted by hand, so that every machine was unique. This began to change, primarily in producing the machines for production, which led to the use of precision gauges, fixed settings and special-purpose tools. Most of these advances were based on the skills and knowledge from the clock, watch and instrument making industries, where precision was required.

By the end of the nineteenth century, industrial manufacturing had become the norm in the USA and Western Europe. Under the new 'American system of manufactures', interchangeable parts required much more precise tolerance to standards since a single part was intended to fit into any machine during assembly, without being reworked to fit. New mass-market consumer items such as sewing machines, bicycles and reapers could only be produced in high-volumes if parts could be fitted together quickly and accurately. This required the development not only of special-purpose machines, but also of precise measuring tools such as gauges.

Under this new production mode, quality became a management responsibility and the independent function of *quality control* emerged. G. S. Radford's published *The Control of Quality in Manufacturing* in 1922, which provided a guide to inspection.

Quality assurance

Quality began to move beyond inspection to *quality assurance* when Dr W. A. Shewart began applying statistical methods to quality control at the Bell Telephone Labs. The company had formed an inspection engineering department in 1924 to investigate quality problems associated with telephone network equipment. Shewart's book *Economic Control of Quality of Manufacturing*, published in 1931, was the first to present ideas about using statistics for monitoring and controlling quality during production through the control of processes, rather than outputs. Shewart and his colleagues Harold Dodge and Harry Romig developed the ideas of statistical process control (SPC) further when the Quality Assurance Department at Bell Labs was created. Quality assurance is the process of preventing, detecting and correcting quality problems.

Here, they developed important ideas about sampling and process control (discussed later in this chapter). These ideas focused mainly on manufacturing-based, product-based and user-based quality, and the detection of defects rather than their prevention.

Quality management

During the World War II, the need to improve quality in the production of armaments and other items for defence stimulated further development of sampling and process control. Two of Shewart's students, Joseph Juran and W. E. Deming, helped develop quality from quality control into *quality management*. Juran's *Quality Control Handbook*, written in 1951, provided the most comprehensive reference to quality, and is still used today. Despite this knowledge, however, few companies in the USA adopted these approaches to quality.

On the other hand, the Japanese, in the process of rebuilding their manufacturing industry following World War II, adopted many of the approaches that were initially developed in the USA and also developed new ones. In particular, in 1950 Deming was invited by the Japanese government to give a series of lectures on quality control. Deming believed that variation was the major cause of poor quality, and thus reducing variability in manufacturing would improve quality. He also thought that even though all employees should be trained to use problem-solving tools and statistical techniques for quality control, top management was responsible for improving quality. Deming had the Japanese government invite top managers from companies such as Nissan and Toyota to his lectures. Deming (1986) summarized his thinking about quality in his famous Fourteen Points for improving quality and productivity:

1 Create constancy of purpose
2 Adopt new philosophy
3 Cease dependence on inspection
4 End awarding business on price
5 Improve constantly the system of production and service
6 Institute training on the job
7 Institute leadership
8 Drive out fear
9 Break down barriers between departments
10 Eliminate slogans and exhortations
11 Eliminate quotas or work standards
12 Give people pride in their job
13 Institute education and a self-improvement programme
14 Put everyone to work to accomplish it.

He argued that improved quality leads to lower costs, because it is cheaper to get things right the first time rather than fix them later.

This idea suited Japanese production, which at the time was plagued by high costs and a reputation for poor-quality goods.

The Japanese also adopted many of Joseph Juran's ideas, particularly his ideas about quality costs. He suggested that an emphasis on preventing quality defects from occurring, for example through product design, was superior to an emphasis on detecting or remedying quality problems, since it would reduce total costs. Another American whose ideas became popular in Japan was Armand Feigenbaum, who proposed *total quality control* in 1956. This empha- sized that quality was everyone's responsibility, rather than that of a specialized department or a small group of people.

Because of their influence, especially in Japan, Deming, Juran and Feigenbaum are notable among the small number of quality advocates (sometimes known as the 'gurus' of quality) who have been influential in making quality a key concern of organizations. However, Juran has pointed out that the contribution form these gurus (including himself) may have been somewhat overstated. The common belief is that Japan was decimated after World War II, and that as a result of the intervention of a few American management gurus the economy was quickly improved. However, Juran states that the Japanese would have achieved high levels of quality in any event; the involvement from the management gurus merely resulted in speeding up this process (Juran, 1993).

Although greater advances were being made in adopting quality ideas in Japan, some advances in quality assurance continued to be made in the USA, especially in defence and aerospace, where reliability became a key concern. In the early 1960s, for example, Martin Company, an aerospace company, implemented the first 'zero defects' programme, which challenged the assumption that some level of defects was inevitable. However, zero defects focused only on quality problems at the shop-floor level, rather than addressing the larger systems or management issues. In Japan, in the meantime, many new techniques were being developed, including quality circles.

The 1980s to today

Quality has emerged as a major strategic factor due to increased competition on a global scale, which in turn has given greater amounts of choice and power to consumers. When Henry Ford declared that a customer can have a car painted any colour he likes 'as long as it is black!', he was reflecting the competitive conditions of the time; the market was immature and would do what it was told to do. However, in the new millennium many markets have numerous competitors within them.

The oil shocks of the 1970s created a crisis in mass production, which led Western firms to adopt many of the more visible elements of Japanese production (including quality) in the hopes of regaining competitive advantage. Among these were quality circles (QCs) and total quality management (TQM), along with a number of ideas developed by Japan's own quality experts, Kaoru Ishikawa and Genichi Taguchi, during the 1970s.

Both just-in-time and total quality management have been widely adopted by organizations. Today, new variants on quality, including quality awards and quality certification systems, are widely promoted as the new keys to organizational success, but their long-term worth has yet to be proved. There are as many success stories as there are stories

Table 9.1 Major events in quality evolution (based on Nicholas, 1998)

Emphasis	Major themes	Dates	Key figures
Inspection	Craft production	Prior to 1900s	
	Inspection	1900s	
	Standardized parts and gauging	1900s	
	Control charts and acceptance sampling	1920s	Walter Shewhart, Harold Dodge, Harry Romig
Statistical process control	Theory of SPC	1931	Walter Shewart
	US experts visit Japan	1940s	W. Edward Deming, Joseph Juran, Arnold Feigenbaum
Quality assurance	Cost of quality	1950s	Joseph Juran
	Total quality control		Arnold Feigenbaum
	Quality control circles in Japan	1950s	Kaoru Ishikawa, Taiichi Ohno
	Reliability engineering	1960s	
	Zero defects		
Total quality management	Robust design	1960s	Genichi Taguchi
	Quality function deployment	1970s	
	Design for manufacture/assembly	1980s	
	TQM in West	1980s–present	

of failure. Motorola, Xerox, and Ritz-Carlton Hotels are well-known examples of firms that have successfully implemented quality efforts, and where quality has become part of the organizational culture as well as a top organizational goal. A brief history of the development of quality is illustrated in Table 9.1.

APPROACHES TO QUALITY MANAGEMENT

Operations managers must ensure that the goods or services produced by the transformation process meet quality specifications. Many different techniques and tools for managing quality have emerged to support this responsibility (Figure 9.2). One way to organize the different approaches to quality management is to show where they are normally used within the transformation process.

Outputs

Quality management includes ensuring the quality of the outputs of the transformation process by sorting them into acceptable or unacceptable categories *before* they are delivered to customers or clients (Deming called them 'the final inspectors'). This is most related to Garvin's manufacturing-based definition of quality – quality as meeting specifications.

Conformity describes the degree to which the design specifications are met in the production of the product or service, and is, again, highly influenced by operations capabilities. Although specifications are initially set in the design process, operations managers are responsible for ensuring that the products and services that are delivered to customers meet those specifications.

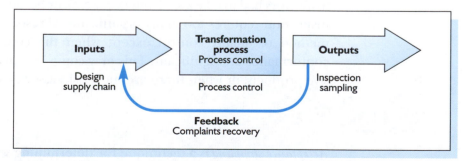

Figure 9.2 Quality management and the transformation model.

Two kinds of specifications can be identified for products or services, attributes and variables. *Attributes* are aspects of a product or service that can be checked quickly and a simple yes or no decision made as to whether the quality is acceptable. Thus, attributes are quality aspects of a product or service that are either met or not met.

Variable measures, on the other hand, are aspects of a product or service that can be measured on a continuous scale, including factors of weight, length, speed, energy consumption and so on. Variables are standards that can be met or not met as well.

The responsibility for conformity within manufacturing operations is sometimes assigned to a specific *quality control (QC) department*. The QC department may be responsible for a variety of activities, including assessing the level of quality of goods and services, and of the processes that produce those goods and services. The tools used by the QC department are described later in the chapter.

Quality control is usually associated with two types of quality management:

1 Inspection
2 Acceptance sampling.

Inspection

The most basic way of measuring quality is through inspection: measuring the level of quality of each unit of output of the operation and deciding whether it does or does not meet quality specifications. Inspection classifies each product as good or bad. Products that fail inspection may be reworked to meet quality standards, sold as seconds (at reduced prices) or scrapped altogether.

One hundred per cent inspection requires sampling of all of the unit's outputs. This is clearly impractical in many circumstances – for example, a brewery would probably go out of business quickly if inspectors had to take a sip from every cask or bottle of beer! In general, inspection requires too many organizational resources to be used as a method of quality control except when the consequences of non-conformance are significant. This may come into play with very expensive products, or when there are high risks associated with failure.

Acceptance sampling

Acceptance sampling is a technique for determining whether to accept a batch of items after inspecting a sample of the items. The level of quality of a sample taken from a batch of products or services is measured, and the decision as to whether the entire batch meets or does not meet quality specifications is based on the sample. Acceptance sampling is used instead of inspection when the cost of inspection is high relative to the consequences of accepting a defective item.

Rather than relying on guesswork, acceptance sampling is a statistical procedure based on one or more samples. Acceptance sampling begins with the development of a sampling plan, which specifies the size of the sample and the number of good items. The maximum allowable percentage of defective (non-conforming) items in a batch for it still to be considered good is called the *acceptable quality level* (AQL). This is the quality level acceptable to the consumer and the quality level the producer aims for. On the other hand, the worst level of quality that the consumer will accept is called the *lot tolerance percent defective* (LTPD) level.

Since the sample is smaller than the entire batch, then there is a risk that the sample will not correctly represent the quality of the batch. The *producer's risk* is the probability of rejecting a lot whose quality meets or exceeds the acceptable quality level (AQL). The *consumer's risk* is the probability of accepting a lot whose level of defects is at or higher than the lot tolerance per cent defective (LTPD) (Figure 9.3).

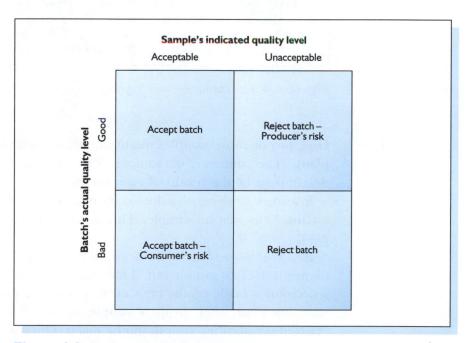

Figure 9.3 Producer's and consumer's risk.

These may sometimes be described as Type I (alpha) and Type II (beta) errors, terms that are derived from statistical theory.

In order to be useful, a sampling plan must balance the risk of mistakenly rejecting a good batch (producer's risk) and the risk of mistakenly accepting a bad batch (consumer's risk). Together, the AQL, LTPD and the two levels of risk define an *operating characteristics curve* (OC), which is a statistical representation of the probability of accepting a batch based on the actual percentage defective. Figure 9.4 presents an operating characteristics curve where the producer's risk has been set at 0.05 and the consumer's risk has been set at 0.10. The acceptable quality level is 20 per cent defectives, and the lot tolerance percentage defective is 80 per cent defective.

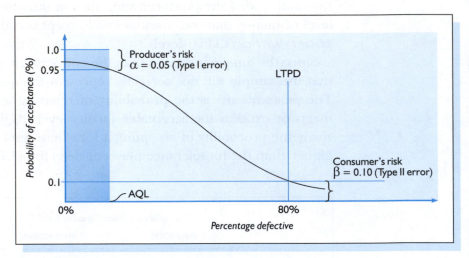

Figure 9.4 An acceptance sampling plan.

Sampling plans

One, two or more samples might be taken under different sampling plans. The number of samples can be known in advance or determined by the results of each sample.

In a *single sampling plan* the decision to accept or reject a lot is made on the basis of one sample. This is the simplest type of sampling plan.

In a *double sampling plan* a decision to accept or reject a lot can be made on the first sample but, if it is not, a second sample is taken and a decision is made on the basis of the combined samples. In a double sampling plan, after the first sample the batch will be accepted or rejected, or another sample will be taken. Once a second sample has been taken, the lot will be either accepted or rejected.

A sequential sampling plan extends the logic of the double sampling plan. Each time an item is inspected, a decision is made to accept the lot, reject the lot, or continue sampling.

Cost of quality

Inspection and conformance sampling are two quality management techniques whose main emphasis is on conformity. The level of quality aimed for in conformity-centred approaches is often determined using economic analyses of the costs of quality.

Quality creates a significant level of cost to the organization. Juran (1951) argued in his *Quality Control Handbook* that managers must know the costs of quality in order to manage quality effectively. These costs can be divided into the costs of making sure that quality mistakes do not happen, and the costs of fixing quality mistakes. The costs of making sure mistakes do not happen can be divided into the costs of appraisal and prevention.

Prevention costs are those costs of all activities needed to prevent defects, including identifying the causes of defects, corrective actions, and redesign. Managers must put in place measures to prevent defects occurring – including company-wide training, planning and implementing quality procedures. In Garvin's (1983) study of Japanese versus American manufacturing, he found that the added cost of prevention (which resulted in better quality Japanese goods) was half the cost of rectifying defective goods made by American manufacturers.

Appraisal costs are the costs of inspections and tests and any other activities needed to make sure that the product or process meets the specified level of quality. Quality laboratories may also be part of the appraisal process, whereby a product or component is analysed outside of the immediate production area. Inspection, in addition to in-built statistical processes, will often take place in the early stages of a 'quality drive' in critical areas of production, for example:

- In operations that have historically caused problems
- Before costly operations take place – reworking on a costly area is particularly expensive
- Before an assembly operation which would make 'disassembly' difficult
- With regard to finished goods – the extent of inspection of finished goods will diminish over a period of time as the disciplines of quality management become integral to the operational process.

The costs of fixing quality mistakes can be classified as the costs of internal and external failures. The costs of *internal failures* include the costs of defects that are detected before products or services reach the consumer, such as reworking or scrapping defective products. The cost of this will appear as an overhead, which will impact on pricing strategy. The costs of *external failures* are those costs of defects once they have reached the consumer, including replacements, warranty and repair costs, and the loss of customer goodwill. Hutchins (1988, p. 39) makes an important point on the real cost of external failure:

> It is most unusual to find any computations which take into account the consequential losses. For example, there is the time spent in placating an irate customer; the loss of machine time; the effect on scheduling; the costs associated with the purchase of replacement materials . . . the cost of stockholding associated products which must be held in temporary storage awaiting the arrival of satisfactory replacement parts is never included in the figures. Neither are any estimates relating to the loss of sales revenue.

Figure 9.5 suggests that the optimum level of quality will always be set so that some level of defects is acceptable, since the costs of prevention approach infinity as 100 per cent conformance is approached. However, under the quality management philosophy of zero defects the ultimate goal of operations is 100 per cent conformity. In

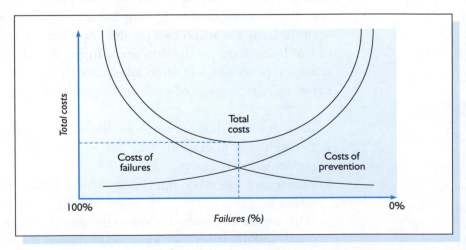

Figure 9.5 A cost of quality model of optimum level of quality.

part, this is based on Philip Crosby's idea that 'quality is free', in which he argues that the benefits from improving quality more than pay for their costs (Crosby, 1979, p. 2):

> Quality is free. It is not a gift, but it is free. What costs money are the unquality things – all the actions that involve not doing jobs right the first time.

Crosby discusses how firms can evolve into becoming enlightened. He spoke of five stages of development, and in the first stage the cost of quality was reckoned to be about 20 per cent of sales. At this first stage, Crosby argued, management has no real comprehension of quality. However, by the fifth stage, the final stage, the cost of quality should fall to about 2.5 per cent.

When an organization commits to quality, costs will come down. However, it is not just the total sum of the costs that is important; the composition of these costs also provides insight. Under traditional approaches, the largest cost will be external failure – with all of the strategic losses this may bring. As firms evolve into becoming enlightened in quality, the largest portion of cost changes from external failure to that of prevention (Figure 9.6).

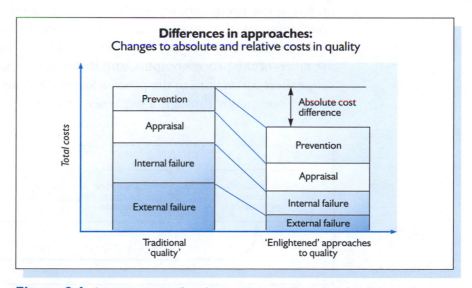

Figure 9.6 A comparison of quality costs in traditional and enlightened approaches to quality.

Process control

The conformity-based approaches to quality management described above merely sort acceptable from unacceptable outputs, but do not address the underlying causes of poor quality. Quality management can be more proactive through addressing quality defects *during* the production process, rather than *after* it.

Take a simple example; eating a meal out in a restaurant. If the server waited until the end of the meal to see if there were any complaints or problems, then he or she wouldn't have a chance to correct any problems that had occurred. However, if checks were made regularly during the meal – that the food is what has been ordered, that it has arrived without too much delay, and that it is of the right temperature and tastes good – then any problems could be dealt with immediately.

The key concepts associated with process control were developed by Walter Shewart at Bell Laboratories in the 1920s. Some important techniques associated with process control include:

- statistical process control
- quality at the sources.

Statistical process control

Statistical process control (SPC) measures the performance of a process. Statistical process control (SPC) can be used to monitor and correct quality as the product or service is being produced, rather than at the conclusion of the process. SPC uses control charts to track the performance of one or more quality variables or attributes. Samples are taken of the process outputs, and if they fall outside the acceptable range then corrections to the process are made. This allows operations to improve quality through a sequence of activities (Figure 9.7).

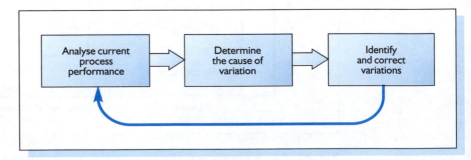

Figure 9.7 Process control activities.

Control charts

Control charts support process control through the graphical presentation of process measures over time. They show both current data and past data as a time series. Both upper and lower *process control limits* are shown for the process that is being controlled. If the data being plotted fall outside of these limits, then the process is described as being 'out of control'.

The statistical basis of control charts, and the insight that led to statistical process control rather than process control based on guesswork or rule of thumb, is that the variation in process outputs can be described statistically. Process variation results from one of two causes: common (internal) factors or random (external) causes. Although there will always be some variation in the process due to random or uncontrollable changes in factors that influence the process, such as temperature, etc., there will also be changes due to factors that can be controlled or corrected, including machine wear, adjustments and so on.

The goal of SPC is for the process to remain in control as much of the time as possible, which means reducing or eliminating those causes of variation that can be controlled. For example, wear over time can lead to a process going out of control.

Process control charts

SPC relies on a very simple graphical tool, the control chart, to track process variation. Control charts plot the result of the average of small samples from the process over time, so that trends can be easily identified. Managers are interested in the following:

- Is the mean stable over time?
- Is the standard deviation stable over time?

Two different types of control chart have been developed, for measurements of variables and measurements of attributes.

Control charts for variables

Two kinds of control chart are usually associated with variable measures of quality, which include physical measures of weight or length. Sample measurements can be described as a normal distribution with a mean (μ) and a standard (s) deviation (the mean describes the average value of the process, and the standard deviation describes the variation around the mean). The mean and standard deviation of the process can be used to determine whether a process is staying within its tolerance range, the acceptance range of performance for the operation.

Control charts are based on sampling means (X) and ranges (R) for every 'n' items and 'm' samples. Besides the norm for the process, both upper and control limits that the process should not exceed are also defined. Control limits are usually set at three standard deviations on either side of the population mean. In addition, warning lines may be in place so that operators can see a trend in the sampling process that might result in movement toward either the upper or lower control settings.

An *x-chart* plots the sample mean to determine whether it is in control, or whether the mean of the process samples is changing from the desired mean. Manufacturers often measure product weights, such as bags of flour, to make sure that the right amount (on average) is packaged. Figure 9.8 shows an x-chart for a process where the desired process is set at 10. Samples of five items were taken at regular intervals, and the average weight of the five items was calculated and plotted on the chart. The middle line plots the long-run average of the process output. The upper and lower control limits, which are set at three standard deviations from the average, are shown on either side.

From Figure 9.8 it can be seen that the sample means vary around the long-run process mean, but they stay within the upper and control

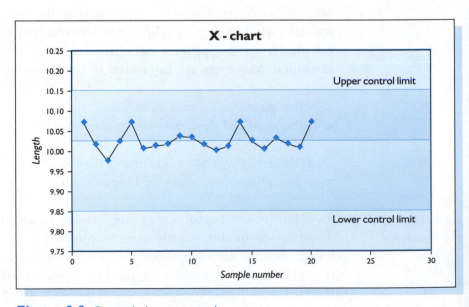

Figure 9.8 Control charts: an x-chart.

limits, so the process is said to be in control. If the means of one or more samples had been outside the control limits, then the process would have been out of control and it would have been necessary for the process operator to take some action to get it back in control.

Managers may also be interested in how much the variance of the process is changing – that is, whether the process range (highest to lowest) is stable. A *range chart* (*R-chart*, Figure 9.9) for variable measures plots the average range (the difference between the largest and smallest values in a sample) on a chart to determine whether it is in control. The purpose is to detect changes in the variation of the process.

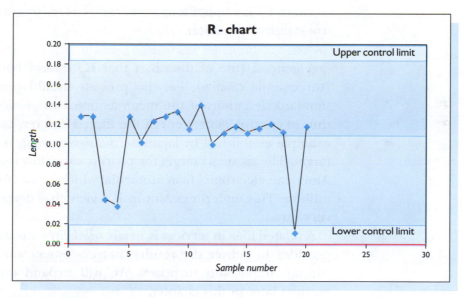

Figure 9.9 Control charts: a range chart.

As you can see in Figure 9.9, the range exceeds the lower control limit towards the end of the observation period. The process operator would need to take corrective action to bring the process back into control.

Attribute charts

Process control using control charts can be done for attributes as well as variable measures. A *p-chart* plots the sample proportion defective to determine whether the process is in control. The population mean percentage defective (p) can be calculated from the average percentage defective (p) of m samples of n items, as can the standard deviation (σs). This sort of chart is similar to the x-chart described above.

Statistical process control (SPC), a manufacturing concept, has been applied to services (especially in quasi-manufacturing or back-office environments) with mixed levels of success.

Process capability

Process capability describes the extent to which a process is capable of producing items within the specification limits, and can be represented as:

$$C_p = (UTL - LTL)/6\sigma$$

where UTL = upper tolerance level, LTL = lower tolerance level and σ = standard deviation.

A general rule of thumb is that C_p should be greater than one (three-sigma quality), i.e. the process should remain within three standard deviations of the mean as much as possible. The process is thus in control 98 per cent of the time. However, based on the quality example established by Japanese, *six-sigma quality* is a more ambitious target. The six-sigma target for process capability is associated with the American electronics firm Motorola, which sets a target of 3.4 defects/ million. This underlines Motorola's view that defects should be very, very rare.

A related idea in services is *service reliability* – the ability of the service provider to deliver the results that customers want time after time, without unpleasant surprises. We will expand on ideas related to services later in this chapter.

QUALITY STANDARDS AND CERTIFICATION

A quality management approach that is often associated with quality control and conformity is quality certification to particular quality standards. *Quality standards* are codes that specify certain organizational and operational practices, and that they are in place and being followed. *Quality certification* certifies organizational compliance with industry, national or international quality standards.

One of the best-known standards is ISO 9000, which began in the UK but has been widely adopted around the world. ISO 9000 provides generic guidelines and models for accrediting the company's quality management system. Its focus is conformity to practices specified in the company's own quality systems, setting out how the company will establish, document and maintain an effective quality system that will demonstrate to its customers that it is committed to quality and is able to supply their quality needs. The company defines the quality system and can meet the requirements of the standard's elements in various ways, but all of the appropriate elements must be documented, the documentation must cover all of the requirements, and the company must do what it has documented. ISO 9000 certification follows a satisfactory audit by registrars.

ISO 9000 originated in the quality system requirements of the UK military in the 1960s, and gradually spread to other areas of defence procurement. The British Standards Institute (BSI) drew heavily on these military standards when it began to develop British Standard (BS) 5750 for quality systems for civilian use. A UK-wide national quality campaign led to the setting up of the necessary infrastructure for organizational certification. The International Standards Organization (ISO) modelled the ISO 9000 series of standards very closely on BS 5750, and the European Union has since adopted them as its common set of quality management system standards, to facilitate free trade within the European union, as EN 9000.

Proponents of ISO 9000 certification have claimed that it leads to both internal and external benefits, and to better quality through better quality systems, and that it signals that the firm has better quality systems and thus enhances the marketing of the firm's products and services. The Department of Trade and Industry (1993) even proposed that a marketing advantage from BS 5750 could result for 18 months to 2 years, simply by being the first in an industry to be registered! Internally, the systemization of processes and procedures within the organization ensures 'the continued repeatability of a set of product and service characteristics that have been explicitly or implicitly agreed to by a customer and a supplier' (Corrigan, 1994). Externally, quality certification systems give purchasers confidence in the quality of suppliers' products, since they have been certified to meet a common set of system quality standards.

On the other hand, it has been difficult to find support for these benefits (see, for example, Voss and Blackmon, 1994). As a result, many producers who require quality certification have developed their own, more stringent, standards, such as the automotive and aerospace industries' own sets of standards.

Despite the shortcomings of ISO 9000, quality standards and certifications do at least ensure that a minimum level of practices is being followed. They can be appropriate when applied in the right circumstances. The environmental standard ISO 14000 has been developed to certify environmentally responsible practices by organizations, and has been widely adopted by companies. The importance of ISO 14000 will be discussed in Chapter 11.

Whilst acceptance sampling was developed in the context of manufactured goods, these ideas can also be applied to service operations. *Service standards* are the choices made in the service design and delivery regarding quality, and may relate to any aspect of the service that is important to the market segment that the company serves. They provide a guide to determine whether servers are providing the right level of service, and support the quick detection and correction of adverse trends.

Services, as well as goods, can be sampled to see if they come up to standard. Mystery shoppers are one way to sample services. Fast-food restaurant chains often have well-developed systems for sampling the products and services provided by their restaurants, including waiting time, food temperature, size of portions and so on.

Quality at the source

As quality management shifts from process outputs to the process itself, there is a corresponding change in the responsibility for quality. Inspection and sampling techniques supported the old quality-control view that management or specialized QC personnel should be responsible for ensuring quality. SPC highlights the idea that the people actually running the process should be responsible for managing the quality associated with that process. This idea has been formalized as *quality at the source*, the idea that each person involved in the production process is responsible for making sure that their contribution meets specifications. Quality at the source is a key element of both quality assurance and total quality management.

SERVICE QUALITY

Because of intangibility and customer contact, quality in services is often defined differently to quality in manufacturing, although similar considerations may be applied to the tangible output of a service (e.g. the pizza rather than the entire pizzeria). Zeithaml *et al.* (1990, p. 26) defined the dimensions of service quality as:

- *Tangibles* – the appearance of physical facilities, equipment, personnel and communication materials. The customer perceives that all the tangible aspects of the service are fit for the task and customer-friendly.
- *Reliability* – the ability to perform the promised service dependably and accurately.
- *Responsiveness* – the willingness to help customers and provide prompt service. The customer's perception that the service provider responds quickly and accurately to his or her specific needs and demands. Customers are often held in long queues when trying to reach call centres.
- *Assurance* – the knowledge and courtesy of employees and their ability to convey trust and confidence. The customer feels that he or she is in courteous, able and competent hands.
- *Empathy* – caring, individualized attention that the firm provides for its customers. The customer feels that he or she is receiving caring services and individualized attention.

Imagine that you have gone into a video store to rent a video. You might judge the quality of the store on what you see and physically experience. Is it neat and clean, or messy and disorganized? Does it have the videos that you want to rent? How helpful are the counter personnel? Could you trust their judgement in recommending a film? Do they treat you as an individual? All of these, and more, will go into your assessment of this service.

An important aspect to note is how these service quality aspects can also be ranged from tangibles, which are measurable and observable by the organization as well as its customers and clients, to empathy, which is difficult to perceive except by the recipients of the service.

In some respects, the perception of a service is its reality. Service providers must manage the technical aspects of the service process carefully so that all technical requirements are met – for example, delivering a package within 24 hours, or providing an edible meal. The technical quality of results is the extent to which the results produced for the customer are as good as the state-of-the-art in the field allows. This means that objective measurements of service quality and standards must be based on the customers and how they pass judgement on important process dimensions – managing the evidence (Berry and Parasuraman, 1991). For example, when the Body Shop chooses its suppliers it is well known that part of the selection criteria involves the supplier's commitment to environmental issues. Perhaps what is not quite so well known is that the Body Shop also insists upon high service quality levels. For example, the Lane Group delivers products to the Body Shop and commits to do so within a 2-hour time frame. They are expected to achieve this delivery performance at a level of 99.7 per cent, which means that 997 out of every 1000 deliveries must be within this 2-hour time period. This is an example of the 'intangible' nature of service quality being judged in a tangible, measurable way – in this case, by performance delivery.

Customer satisfaction is the extent to which results produced for customers and the process they went through to secure these results meet their expectations. The relationship between expectations and perceptions is often expressed as an equation:

Customer satisfaction = Perceptions – Expectations

As well as the actual service quality in a single service encounter, customer expectations are influenced by other factors such as past experience, word-of-mouth advertising, on-site signs, and need. The zone of tolerance between expectations and perceptions of process and results (Berry *et al.*, 1994) is very small, especially after a service failure. A 'ratchet effect' has been found to exist in services: exceed a customer's expectations slightly and he or she will be pleased or even delighted. However, the next time the same customer will be merely satisfied by the extra, or disappointed by its absence. Thus, systematically exceeding expectations is not enough to delight – especially when those expectations have been raised unrealistically by marketing and advertising.

The Servqual model

Service quality can be categorized into two broad components: those dimensions that directly affect the results that customers want, and those concerned with the process customers have to put themselves through to get those results (process quality).

Most studies of service quality have been undertaken by researchers in marketing rather than those in operations management, who have concentrated more on product quality – probably because product quality is more easily measured in objective terms and service quality in perceptual terms, which involves psychology.

One of the best tools in understanding how perceptions of quality differ between customers and producers is the 'gaps model' (Figure 9.10), which was developed by Parasuraman and his colleagues in 1985. This 'gaps' model shows different points where the service that

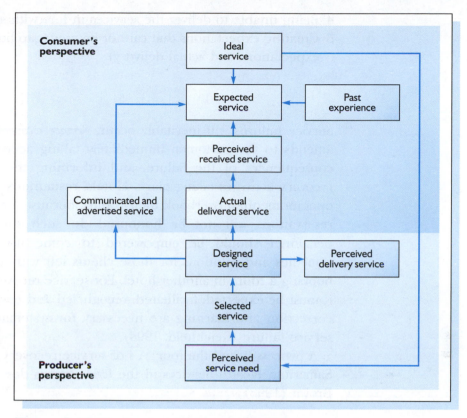

Figure 9.10 The 'gaps' model of service quality.

is designed and delivered by the producer and the service actually needed, expected and perceived by the customer differ. Some of the gaps are on the producer's side, whilst others are on the customer's side.

Servqual provides a structured approach to measuring customer satisfaction through measuring the gap between what customers expect and what they perceive of the service provided in a service encounter. Customers fill out questionnaires that ask about their perceptions and expectations, and the gap (or difference) between the two is measured.

Based on Figure 9.10, Parasuraman and his colleagues (1985) identified five gaps that can lead to service quality failures:

1 Not understanding the needs of the customers
2 Being unable to translate the needs of the customer into a service design that can address them
3 Being unable to translate the design into service expectations or standards that can be implemented

4 Being unable to deliver the services in line with specifications

5 Creating expectations that cannot be met (gap between customer's expectations and actual delivery).

Resolving problems with service quality

Service failures will inevitably occur. *Service recovery* involves making amends to the customer, immediately taking action to alleviate the consequences of the failure, and informing the customer of the recovery activities taking place. Hotels, restaurants and other service operations often overbook their rooms, because a certain number of reservations will not be honoured. In such situations, front-line personnel should be empowered to come up with on-the-spot remedies and solutions for those clients left without rooms, such as booking a room in another hotel. For service recovery to be effective, it must be expected, facilitated, recognized and rewarded. Detection, correction and learning are necessary for systematic learning from service failure (Reichheld, 1996).

A process called the four 'A's of service recovery was developed at Samaritan Health Services in the USA, and is described by Tax and Brown (1998)

1 **A**nticipate and correct problems before they occur

2 **A**cknowledge mistakes when they occur without placing blame or making excuses

3 **A**pologize sincerely for the mistake even if you are not at fault

4 Make **A**mends for the mistake by taking corrective action and following up to make sure the problem is resolved.

Guarantees provide a way of communicating to customers and employees specific benefits and expectations, and amends for service failures. A *service guarantee* specifies a tangible service performance target or outcome, e.g. a maximum wait time for a service, and provides compensation in case of failure. The Toronto Dominion Bank offered a service guarantee when it began offering customers a $5 bill if they had to queue for more than 5 minutes. Service guarantees also makes it easier to quantify the effects of quality failures, and provide the basis for continuous improvement.

As well as guarantees, organizations can also take steps to make sure that potential causes of service failures are identified and eliminated through process redesign. *Service fail-safing* is an idea that has been adapted from just-in-time (JIT) operations to services by Professor

Dick Chase of the University of Southern California. This takes the idea of the *pokayoke* from JIT management and applies it to services.

Service recovery can only take place when service failures are identified so that they can be acted upon. Organizations can identify service failures through *customer complaints*. These can be gathered through complaints made to front-line personnel or management, via customer complaint cards or hotlines, and so on. Effective complaints gathering and resolution is a hallmark of high-quality organizations.

Customers who are dissatisfied with products or services have a new weapon – the Internet – to publicize unresolved complaints (Oger, 2000). This 'word of mouth' approach to complaining has led to the emergence of thousands of protest sites, targeting nearly every large corporation. Some sites are even put up by disgruntled employees.

However, customers have unclear expectations about many services and may not complain when they are dissatisfied. As Levitt (1980) remarked about services versus tangible goods, 'You don't know what you aren't going to get until you don't get it'. Good service providers systematically listen to the 'voice of the customer' besides just listening to complaining customers (Berry and Parasuraman, 1991).

First Direct, the telephone banking arm of Midland Bank, surveys every new customer 3 months after opening an account. In addition it surveys 15 000 customers quarterly, conducts focus groups with 1000 customers annually, and sponsors independent research by MORI and NOP. In addition, comments, suggestions and queries are logged after each call. This was used to identify customer demand for PC banking (*Management Today*, 1998).

Mystery shopping allows service providers to experience their services from the perspective of a customer, either through the use of anonymous professionals or actual customers. Pizza Hut (UK) uses mystery shoppers to gather data each month on each restaurant, as well as using questionnaires, focus groups, market research and complaints. The company has a central contact point for customers in a customer care centre (*Management Today*, 1998, p. 92).

QUALITY AWARDS PROGRAMMES

Quality awards have become popular as a way of recognizing outstanding achievements in quality management, and as a way for organizations to assess their own quality performance. Three important quality awards are the Deming Prize (the most desirable industrial quality award in Japan), the Baldrige Award, and the European Quality Award.

The Deming Prize was established in Japan by the Japanese Union of Scientists and Engineers (JUSE) in 1950 to recognize organizations that have excelled in total quality management. The competition is open to organizations from any country, and is based on 10 criteria. The attention given to the Deming Prize in Japan can be compared with the popularity of the Academy Awards for motion pictures, or the Eurovision Song contest.

The Malcolm Baldrige National Quality Award (MBNQA) has been awarded annually in the USA in 1987 to recognize total quality management excellence in American companies. The Baldrige criteria are a good measure of the company's internal and external excellence, and Baldrige winners receive national (and international) attention. Companies apply in five different categories: manufacturing, service, small businesses, health care and educational institutions. Like the Deming Prize, points are awarded in different categories.

Compared with the Deming and Baldrige Awards, the European Quality Award (established in 1988) is a relative newcomer. It is awarded by the European Foundation for Quality Management, and is presented annually to companies. The EQA framework is shown below in Figure 9.11.

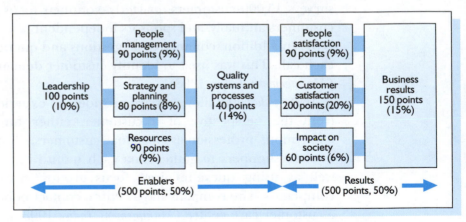

Figure 9.11 The European Quality Award (EQA) framework.

DESIGN QUALITY

The importance of managing the inputs to the transformation process (besides those issues having to do with the supply chain) should be noted. This includes the quality of the design of the product or service in the first place. *Design quality* describes how the marketplace perceives the product. Chapter 3 introduced practices that are associated with quality of design, including:

- Quality Function Deployment (QFD)
- Taguchi Methods
- Failure Mode Evaluation Analysis (FMEA).

The *quality function deployment* approach attempts to integrate customer requirements and needs into the design specifications of the product through 'listening to the voice of the customer'. In his work on QFD, Akao (1990, p. 5) states:

> ... we can define quality function deployment as converting consumers' demands into 'quality characteristics' and developing a design quality for the finished product.

and, speaking of the effect of QFD, Akao (1990, p. 3) observes how:

> ... the use of quality function deployment has cut in half the problems previously encountered at the beginning stages of product development and has reduced development time by one-half to one-third, while helping to ensure user satisfaction.

The QFD process begins with market research to define the customer's needs and preferences for a certain type of product. These are divided into categories known as *customer attributes,* and are weighted by their relative importance to the customer.

The *house of quality* matrix is used to match customer attributes with the organization's design, engineering and marketing capabilities. Figure 9.12 shows how the two major categories of information – information about customer needs and preferences and information about the product's engineering characteristics – are combined to help decide what the target engineering characteristics of the good or service should be.

A technique that is associated with quality management in the design stage is *value analysis/value engineering.* Value analysis is a technique for analysing the specifications for existing products and determining where redesign or respecification can be used to reduce costs without changing the product's performance. Purchasing and engineering departments may together use value analysis to identify and eliminate unnecessary costs.

Value engineering is a similar technique, but it is used *before* production.

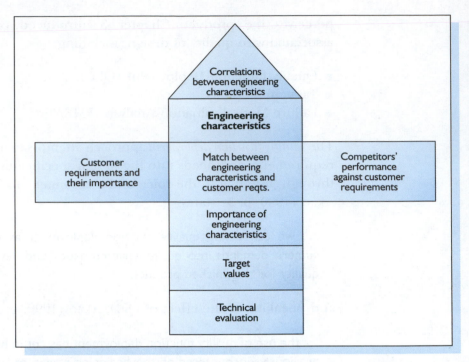

Figure 9.12 The house of quality matrix (based on Hauser and Clausing, 1988).

Both value analysis and value engineering ask similar questions, such as:

- Does the item have any design features that are not necessary?
- Can any parts be eliminated?
- Can two or more parts be combined into one?

The Swedish home furnishings retailer IKEA has developed value analysis and value engineering into a high art in its furniture design.

TOTAL QUALITY MANAGEMENT

Total quality management incorporates a holistic set of ideas about quality that go well beyond operations. TQM goes beyond the idea of quality as conformance to some set of specifications to that of quality as excelling on all dimensions that are important to the customer. TQM describes an organizational culture as well as the sort of tools, techniques and organizational structures that are associated with the conformance-based approaches above.

The development from inspection to TQM reveals the increasing strategic importance of quality over time. As we mentioned earlier, quality used to mean conformance to specification: the nature of this was conforming to process quality criteria (in-house). By the 1980s and 1990s, however, quality became seen in terms of a *total* commitment from all areas including the supply chain. The scope of each stage of developments in quality is shown in Table 9.2.

Although TQM does include statistical process control and other quality tools and techniques, the outermost layer of TQM is often described as being a philosophy. This philosophy has four basic elements:

1 Customer-driven quality
2 Leadership
3 Employee involvement
4 Continuous improvement.

Customer-driven quality. In TQM, customers include both the external customer who purchases the products and services, and the internal customers who receive the output of internal processes. Customer-driven quality means that the organization listens to the 'voice of the customer' in everything that they do. Techniques such as quality function deployment (Chapter 3) support this customer focus.

Table 9.2   Stages of development in quality and related activities (adapted from Brown, 1996, p. 190)

Stage of development	Activities
Inspection	Salvaging, sorting, grading and corrective actions
Quality control	Quality manuals, product testing, basic quality planning, including statistics
Quality assurance	Third party approvals, advanced planning, systems audits, SPC
Company-wide QC	Quality measured in all areas of the firm
TQM	Continuous improvement; involvement of suppliers and customers; employee involvement and teamwork

Leadership. The 'quality gurus', including Deming, Juran and, more recently, Crosby, all agreed that there must be senior management commitment to quality within the firm. Juran (1993, p. 43) mentions how this factor was important to the success of Japanese quality:

> The senior executives of Japanese companies took personal charge of managing for quality. The executives trained their entire managerial hierarchies in how to manage for quality.

In another publication, Juran (1994, p. 46) also states:

> Charting a new course [for TQM] requires extensive personal leadership and participation by managers.

In the same vein, Deming (1986) commented how:

> Actually, most of this book is involved with leadership. Nearly every page heretofore and hereafter states a principle of good leadership.

Employee involvement. However, leadership itself is not enough. Company-wide employee involvement is also central to successful TQM. However, this has proved to be difficult for many firms. In an address to a group of American executives, Mr. Konosuke Matsushita stated the following (Shores, 1990, p. 270):

> We will win, and you will lose . . . Your companies are based on Taylor's principles . . . You firmly believe that good management means executives on one side and workers on the other; on one side men who think, and on the other side men who can only work. For you, management is the art of smoothly transferring the executive's ideas to the workers' hands . . . For us, management is the entire workforce's intellectual commitment at the service of the company.

The scathing attack by Matsushita offers the biggest challenge to many traditional approaches in firms. Resistance to this might include the cost of doing so (training) together with the reluctance to relinquish management power. Often a change of culture has to take place if TQM is to be successful, and such success in quality will depend to a very large degree on employee empowerment.

Continuous improvement. This will be discussed more fully in Chapter 10, and is an attitude that sees improvement as a never-ending process of small gains. Continuous improvement relies on committed and involved employees, who contribute suggestions and ideas for improving products and processes. This is built on the Japanese idea of *kaizen*, which emphasizes providing workers with various tools for improving operations.

The following definition of the role and scope of TQM provided insight (Ahire *et al.*, 1996, p. 9):

TQM is an integrative management philosophy aimed at continuously improving the quality of products and processes to achieve customer satisfaction [by] making quality a concern and responsibility for everyone in the business.

This is a useful definition because it brings out several important, interlinking factors:

- The need to integrate functions
- TQM is a management philosophy
- The importance of continuous improvement
- The need to think in terms of both product and process quality;
- The focus is providing customer satisfaction
- The issue of quality as a company-wide concern.

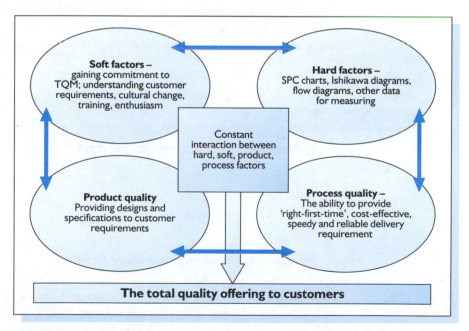

Figure 9.13 The four linkages in the scope of quality (from Brown, 2000, p. 119).

However, the reason for failure of TQM includes the inability to have these and other pertinent areas in place.

QM is a comprehensive term, which must include both *process* and *product* quality and 'hard' and 'soft' factors, as shown in Figure 9.13.

 # SUMMARY

Quality is about providing customer satisfaction. Undoubtedly this is not always easy – customers can be, amongst other things, annoying, fickle and frustrating. Often they may not even know what they want, which adds to the difficulty of the task of trying to provide customer satisfaction. This task is made even more difficult because the customer may not always be the end user, particularly in industrial markets. Quality is a comprehensive term which must include both *process* and *product* quality. A product can be a 'quality' product but, if it is not supported by process enhancements (delivery speed, cost, various configurations, and any other customer requirements), will fail as a total quality offering. Conversely, a quality assurance system may well be in place whereby sophisticated process charts and other tools are being used to ensure process quality, but the product itself may not be perceived as providing satisfaction to the customer. If this is the case, then there is a failure in *product* quality. In order for quality to be in place it is essential that marketing and operations clearly understand the needs and requirements of customers. Operations capabilities then need to be in place so that these needs can be satisfied.

Case study

Quality is more than just the product

Quality is more than just the product. Here, two customers describe their experience of how they were treated when the product they bought failed.

Example 1: Obodex Computers Limited

I bought an Obodex laptop computer and was very pleased with its performance. After a few weeks, however, the screen failed. I rang the company and was put straight through to their service manager, who apologized profusely for the failure and, after a few questions, identified what he thought was the fault. He asked if it was convenient for me to drop the machine into their service centre and said that he would ensure that it was dealt with while I waited. Given the possibility of having my computer up and running again so quickly, I agreed. When I arrived at the centre, I was shown to a waiting area and supplied with a cup of coffee while the laptop was taken away. As I handed it over, the technician asked, 'Would you like me to make a small upgrade on it while I am working on it, at no charge?' This sounded too good an offer to pass up, and so I agreed. Thirty minutes later, I was walking out of the centre with my repaired and upgraded machine. You would not believe the number of people who I knew who then bought Obodex when they heard of the service that I had received.

Example 2: Car dealers

We bought a brand new car for our family business. It was needed to go and visit customers and so reliability was vital to us. If we could not keep appointments with customers, this reflected on our business and customers would buy elsewhere. We had had it for 10 days when the power steering failed. This made the car undriveable. It happened at the weekend and so I rang the dealer where we had bought the car first thing on the Monday morning, asking them to come and get the car at the earliest opportunity, as we needed it for several important trips that week. The response was pathetic. They said that they were far too busy and initially offered to look at the car, if we could get it to them, the following Thursday – 11 days later. I complained, but was told that 'You are not our only customer!'. This made me very angry, and so I called the manufacturer direct. Their customer service people were far more helpful, and eventually agreed to arrange for the car to be collected later that day. It was collected by the same garage that I had called first. I wasted nearly 3 hours on the telephone trying to sort this problem. I will never do business with that dealer again, which probably means we will never buy another car from that company. This is a shame, as it wasn't a bad car.

Discussion questions

1 Compare the two cases in terms of how each firm looked after their customers.
2 What is the influence of apostles (customers who tell others how good your service is) and terrorists (customers who tell others how bad your service is) on a business?
3 How might customer complaints actually be an opportunity for gaining greater loyalty to an organization?

Key questions

1 Why has quality emerged in terms of strategic importance in recent times?
2 How might you apply SPC to service setting?
3 What is meant by the 'cost of quality'?
4 How might you apply the SERVQUAL model to a restaurant?

Key terms

Acceptable quality level
Acceptance sampling
Appraisal
Attributes
External failure
Inspection
Internal failure
ISO 9000
Lot tolerance per cent defective
Prevention costs
Process control charts
Quality assurance
Quality certification
Quality control
Quality management
Quality standards
SERVQUAL
Total quality management
Variables

References

Ahire, S.; Waller, M. and Golhar, D. (1996). Quality management in TQM versus non-TQM firms: an empirical investigation (total quality management). *Int. J. Qual. Reliability Man.*, **13(8)**, 8–28.

Akao, Y. (1990). *Quality Function Deployment*. Productivity Press.

Associated Press (2000). A Rolls by any other name should smell sweet. 7 July, 2000.

Berry, L. L. and Parasuraman, A. (1991). *Marketing Services: Competing Through Quality*. Free Press.

Brown, S. (1996). *Strategic Manufacturing for Competitive Advantage*. Prentice Hall.

Brown, S. (2000). *Manufactuing the Future – Strategic Resonance for Enlightened Manufacturing*. Financial Times Books.

Corrigan, J. P. (1994). Is ISO 9000 the path to TQM? *Quality Progress*, **May**, 33–6.

Crosby, P. (1979). *Quality Is Free*. McGraw Hill.

Deming, W. (1986). *Out of the Crisis*. MIT Center for Advanced Engineering.

Department of Trade and Industry (1993). *BS5750/ISO 9000/EN 29000: 1987, A Positive Contribution to Better Business*.

Feigenbaum, A. (1983). *Total Quality Control*, 3rd edn. McGraw Hill.

Garvin, D. (1983). Quality on the line. *Harvard Bus. Rev.*, **Sep–Oct**, 65–75.

Hauser, J. R. and Clausing, D. (1988). The house of quality. *Harvard Bus. Rev.*, **May–Jun,** 62–73.

Hutchins, D. (1988). *Just in Time*. Gower Books.

Juran, J. (1951). *Quality Control Handbook*, 4th edn 1988. McGraw Hill.

Juran, J. (1993). Made in the USA: a renaissance in quality. *Harvard Bus. Rev.*, **Jul-Aug**, 42–50.

Juran, J. (1994). The quality trilogy: a universal approach for managing for quality. In: *Total Quality Management* (H. Costin, ed.). Dryden.

Levitt, T. (1980). Marketing success through differentiation – of anything. *Har. Bus. Rev.*, **58(1)**, 83–91.

Management Today (1998). **October**, 89.

Maylor, H. (2000). Strategic quality management. In: *Strategic Management in Tourism* (L. Moutinho, ed.), pp.239–56. CABI Press.

Nicholas, J. M. (1998). *Competitive Manufacturing Management*. Irwin McGraw-Hill, p.20.

Oger, G. (2000). Don't get mad, get a web site. Agence France-Press, 19 October 2000.

Parasuraman, A., Zeithaml, V. A. and Berry, L. L. (1985). A conceptual model of service quality and its implications for future research. *J. Marketing*, **49,** 41–50.

Pirsig, R. (1974) *Zen and the Art of Motor Cycle Maintenance*. Bantam.

Reichheld, F. F. (1996). *The Loyalty Effect*. Harvard Business School Press.

Shewart, W. (1931). *The Control of Quality of Manufactured Product*. Van Nostrand.

Shores, A (1990). *A TQM Approach to Achieving Manufacturing Excellence*. ASQC Press.

Voss, C. A. and Blackmon, K. L. (1994). ISO 9000, BS5750, EN2900 and quality performance: the UK experience. In: *Proceedings of the European Foundation for Quality Management Conference*, Barcelona, 26/27 May.

Zeithaml, V. A., Parasuraman, A. and Berry, L. L. (1990). *Delivering Quality Service: Balancing Customer Perceptions and Expectations*. The Free Press.

Further reading

Burn, G. (1990). Quality function deployment. In: *Managing Quality* (B. Dale and J. Plunkett, eds). Philip Allan.

Ciampa, D. (1992). *Total Quality*. Addison-Wesley.

Dale, B. and Plunkett, J. (eds) (1990). *Managing Quality*. Philip Allan.

Dawson, P. (1993). Total quality management. In: *New Wave Manufacturing Strategies* (J. Storey, ed.). Paul Chapman Publishing.

Deming, W. (1982). *Quality, Productivity and Competitive Position*. MIT Center for Advanced Engineering Study.

Garvin, D. A. (1988). *Managing Quality: The Strategic and Competitive Edge*. Free Press.

Garvin, D. A. (1991). 'How the Baldridge Award really works. *Harvard Bus. Rev.*, **Nov–Dec,** 88–93.,

Heskett, J. L., Jones, T. O., Loveman, G. W. *et al.* (1994). *Putting the service–profit chain to work. Harvard Bus. Rev.*, **Mar–Apr,** 164–74.

Heskett, J. L., Sasser, W. E. Jr. and Schlesinger, L. A. (1997). *The Service Profit Chain: How Leading Companies Link Profit and Growth to Loyalty, Satisfaction and Value*. Free Press.

Ishikawa, K. (1985). *What is Total Quality Control: The Japanese Way*. Prentice Hall.

Oakland, J. (1994). *Total Quality Management.* Butterworth-Heinemann.

Terziovski, M., Samson, D. and Dow, D. (1997). The business value of quality management systems certification: Evidence from Australia and New Zealand. *J. Operations Man.,* **15,** 1–18.

CHAPTER 10

Performance measurement and improvement

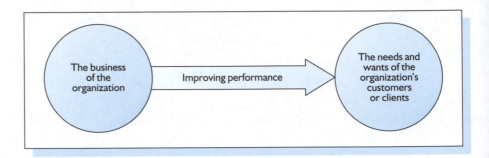

INTRODUCTION

 Case study

In 1989, the staff at the Hollola Roll Finishing plant were given an ultimatum by Valmet Corporation, their parent company: Turn around the plant and make a profit within the next 18 months, or you will be shut down. Just 12 months later, the plant was not only making a profit, it had become Valmet's best-performing unit, and other plant managers – and even management professors – were coming to Hollola, a small city in Finland, to see how it had been done (Blackmon and Boynton, 1994).

Hollola manufactured a critical piece of the equipment for papermaking; the systems that remove finished rolls of paper from the papermaking machines, then wrap, label, and move the rolls to finished goods storage. When Hollola's roll-finishing systems didn't arrive at the customer site on time, or took extra time to start up, or failed to work, then the entire papermaking plant was delayed in starting up.

All 90 of Hollola's staff attended a 2-day survival meeting, at which they completely mapped out the existing processes, including marketing, R&D, production and field service. They then completely transformed the system's design, and figured out a way to use information technology to support the process from beginning to end. The new reference model system (RMS) not only supported the plant in all of the steps in delivering value to customers; it also helped the company dramatically improve its performance in time, inventory, product quality and other important aspects.

You have probably heard the saying 'What gets measured gets done'. People make decisions and do their work at least partly based on how they will be evaluated. As a result they tend to improve in performance aspects that will be measured and rewarded, rather than in unmeasured aspects, even it these do not necessarily support organizational goals or customer satisfaction. As anyone who has called up Directory Inquiries with a tricky request will know, call-centre operators who are evaluated on the number of calls that they handle during a given time period will try to minimize the length of calls rather than search for the right number.

Measurement is not only a way of determining what has already happened, which is like 'driving by looking in the rear-view mirror', but is also a way of getting people to act in ways that will bring about desired future outcomes. Aligning performance measurement with organizational goals can be a significant challenge. This is noticeable when different ways of working are being introduced – for example, total quality management (TQM) and just-in-time (JIT) – if performance is still being measured using standards based on old-fashioned, mass production ideals.

Another problem is that performance measurement in operations has been largely accounting-driven, so that financial goals predominate. Accounting and operations must work together to support long-term organizational competitiveness and world-class performance. The problem is that financial measures are often short term. For example, a firm's financial performance is measured in quarters – a matter of weeks! – by the financial markets such as the Dow on Wall Street in New York and the Stock Exchange in the City of London. Consequently, long-term strategic performance measurements can sometimes be sacrificed in order to satisfy short-term financial targets.

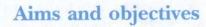

Aims and objectives

This chapter introduces the concepts of performance measurement and performance improvement. The first section reviews the basics of performance measurement for operations management. The second section looks at *kaizen*, and ways to analyse and continuously improve processes. The final section introduces some techniques for more radical improvements in performance, process re-engineering and benchmarking.

After reading this chapter you will be able to:

- Distinguish between measures of economy, efficiency, and effectiveness
- Describe the traditional and enlightened bases of performance standards
- Apply different techniques for improving operations.

PERFORMANCE MEASUREMENT

Performance measurement systems measure the inputs and outputs to an operation in order to determine how well (or poorly) the operation is using them. Performance measurement is important to all functional and strategic areas within an organization, but it is especially critical to operations management because of the direct impact operations has on the business in terms of efficiency (processes), including the acquisition (purchasing) and use (inventory) of materials through the business.

The objectives of any operation must include making the best possible use of resources, which can lead to lower costs and higher profits. As seen in Chapter 1 these resources include *transforming* resources such as facilities, technology and people, and *transformed* resources such as materials, energy and other natural resources, and financial resources.

The value added by operations must also be considered. For operations to be self-sustaining, the economic value of outputs must be higher than the economic value of the inputs. In addition, the organization will want to concentrate on those products that have higher value-added and discontinue those with lower value-added.

Historical performance measurement

The major focus of traditional performance measurement is financial performance. The performance measurement systems used in modern business originated in the systems of double-entry book keeping developed in Venice during the fourteenth century. These formed the basis for the financial measurement systems that developed in the mid-nineteenth century for the American system of manufacture. These accounting systems were appropriate for keeping track of the repetitive production of large quantities of standardized products using standardized parts in mass production.

As businesses grew larger, elaborate management accounting systems were developed for external reporting and internal control. The principles for external accounting and financial reporting were introduced in the 1920s, and have remained largely unchanged since the 1930s. These were developed to standardize reporting performance to external monitoring agencies and shareholders. These systems focused mainly on financial statistics such as sales, cost of sales, profits, assets and liabilities. However, they also became widely accepted for measuring the performance of manufacturing and distribution operations. This led managers to make poor decisions, because these systems measured the wrong things in the wrong way, and motivated people to do the wrong things.

Economy

Going back to the ideas expressed in the transformation model, performance measurement systems for operations management have focused on measuring inputs and output. These translate into operations performance measurements of economy, efficiency and effectiveness.

A primary concern of operations management has been monitoring and/or reducing costs. *Economy* describes the level of use of resources in creating and delivering products and services. Performance measures based on economy are improved by using less of a particular resource. For example, one performance measure for a fleet of buses might be the amount of petrol used during the year, and its cost.

Purchasing managers are often responsible for a number of performance measures based on economy. For example, they may be measured by how much they have reduced the cost of a particular purchased component or module compared to the cost of the previous year. Effective cost management is important, because up to 70 per cent of product or service costs are typically incurred within the operations function.

Efficiency

A more useful measure than economy is efficiency. *Efficiency* describes how well the operation does in transforming inputs into outputs. Measures of efficiency contrast actual product or service output with the standard for that product or service. Typical measures of efficiency focus on the units of product or service produced per employee or per unit of time.

Traditional performance measurement systems often focus on measures of efficiency – that is, the level of outputs produced relative to inputs such as labour and equipment. Traditionally, product costs have been computed by adding together overhead costs and the direct cost of labour and materials. *Overhead costs* are costs that cannot be associated directly with particular processes or outputs, such as administrative costs, sales, research and development, and capital expenditures, which must be allocated across the organization. These are usually calculated as a percentage of direct labour hours, but may also be allocated to machines according to their maximum output capacity. The efficiency ratio is simply:

$$\frac{\text{Input}}{\text{Output}} \text{ measured in individual variables} - \text{e.g. labour, machine hours, and space.}$$

However, there are concerns with the efficiency ratio: it can be made to look artificially strong simply by reducing the number of inputs. For example, if a firm divests part of its operations, then typically its efficiency ratio will appear to be stronger. However, such divestment is not sustainable over the long term, because the firm will go out of business. So we need to be a little careful: if we see that the efficiency ratio is × per cent now and was y per cent last year, it sometimes pays to 'get behind the numbers' to see the reasons for the change.

Standards and variances are based on an accounting approach to performance measurements. In this system, a standard measurement is first developed for each input or output, which focuses on time and/ or cost. For example, the standard output for a process might be determined to be 100 units per hour. If the process actually produces 75 or 125 units, then a negative variance of –25 units or a positive variance of +25 units from the standard occurs, which must be accounted for by the operations manager.

Along with direct labour, performance measurements may also use *equipment usage* as the denominator in performance measures. Two measures of machine utilization are: the actual time a machine is producing output compared with the available time; and the proportion of rated output that a work centre is producing.

As you can see, traditional performance measurement concentrates on direct inputs (especially labour), and thus on keeping people and machines fully occupied, whether or not they are producing the right products at the right time in the right amount. Direct labour costs were a significant part of the costs of producing goods when traditional performance measurement systems were introduced, and are still significant for many service operations. Major criticisms that have been levied against this way of thinking are that it emphasizes internal rather than external measures, focuses on conformance, and is short-term in orientation – in other words, it reflects the time and motion study mentality of the mass production era.

These measures focus on whether people are being kept busy producing output, rather than if they are producing the right things. One operations outcome of this way of thinking has been a focus on reducing direct labour hours, reflected in practices such as downsizing and outsourcing.

Effectiveness

Efficiency is a better measure than economy, but effectiveness is better than either. *Effectiveness* concentrates on whether the right products or services are being produced, rather than on how efficiently they are being produced. Examples of effectiveness measures across the organization include market share, profitability, competitor growth rates, raw materials, direct labour, indirect labour, R&D, overhead costs, capital costs, product features, customer service, product quality, brand image, manufacturing, distribution, sales force, information technology, human resources and finance.

New approaches to performance measurement

Traditional performance measurement systems were useful in the relatively stable competitive environment that persisted through the 1960s, but began to be questioned during the 1980s and 1990s. A particular weakness was its cost focus, which is only one of the key performance criteria that operations supports. In particular, new performance measures are needed to support manufacturing techniques such as TQM and JIT, which emphasize process rather than outcomes. Further, performance measurements must support a change in focus from management to customers.

During the 1980s, accounting and manufacturing groups began working together to develop organization-wide systems that more accurately reflect product variety, quality and customer service. Compared with the financial focus of traditional performance measurement systems, these emphasize clear, commonsense measures that reflect trends and long-term improvements, provide decision-making support, and direct and motivate workers.

Two of the more well-known approaches to performance measures that developed during this period are activity-based costing (ABC) and the balanced scorecard. These two practices are briefly discussed below. Whilst they are not specifically limited to operations management, they have direct relevance.

Activity-based costing

Activity-based accounting (ABC) is an accounting method for realistically estimating costs for products and services, and ultimately for supporting strategic decision-making. As seen above, traditional cost accounting systems measure labour costs, machine costs and materials costs at the unit level (one unit of product or service), and assign common costs among multiple products on the same per-unit basis. Larger quantities of a product are penalized by assignment of a larger share of these common costs, since they are charged a larger share of overhead costs even when they do not actually create higher costs.

Activity-based costing tries to proportion common costs to products based on the resources that the products or services actually consume. Instead of relying on standard cost-accounting procedures, ABC defines activities and cost drivers that accurately reflect resource consumption. Cost drivers are selected based on what actually causes the cost of an activity to increase or decrease, rather than direct labour hours or machine utilization. Furthermore, ABC allows costs to be allocated at the unit, batch, process or plant/organizational level.

The five steps to implementing ABC are:

1 Identifying all activities performed in the operation
2 Categorizing activities as value-added or non-value-added

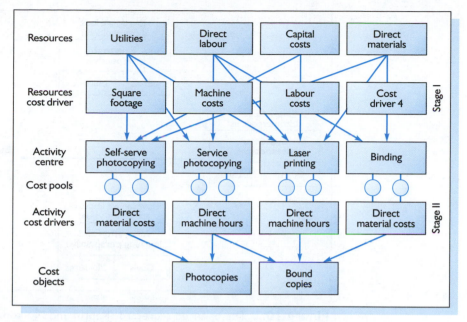

Figure 10.1 The two-stage cost allocation process.

3 Selecting the cost drivers

4 Allocating the total budget to the activities

5 Identifying the relationships between cost drivers and activity centres.

Most ABC systems use a two-stage system for allocating costs to products or services, as shown in Figure 10.1. The cost pools represent the resource costs allocated to a particular activity centre, such as a machine, or a particular function within a service operation.

ABC systems can be used to improve product decisions through more accurate costing, engineering design through life cycle and parts costing, cross-functional decision-making through accurate process costing, and continuous improvement through identifying value- and non-value-added activities. However, ABC systems are not perfect ways of allocating costs, although they fit with operations logic much better than traditional cost-accounting systems.

Balanced scorecard

Another performance measurement tool that has been widely taken up by top management is the balanced scorecard. The *balanced scorecard* was developed by accountants Kaplan and Norton (1996) to

313

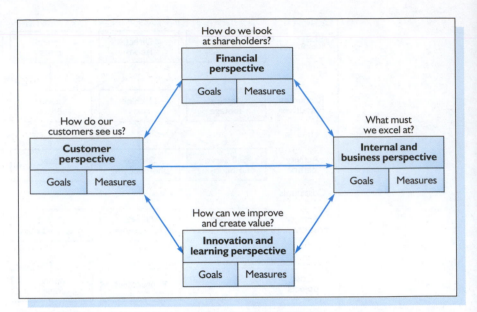

Figure 10.2 The balanced scorecard (Kaplan and Norton, 1993).

represent how well an organization performs with respect to different stakeholder groups. Figure 10.2 shows a generic balanced scorecard. The balanced scorecard is really targeted towards senior management, but operations managers may find themselves responsible for activities that show up on the scorecard.

Designing a performance measurement system

An enlightened performance management system measures the right things rather than things that are easy to measure, in order to change the way people work and to support strategy. Enlightened performance measures must be balanced, dynamic, timely and efficient, measure key processes (including asset utilization, productivity, quality and improvement), and focus on customer satisfaction (Table 10.1).

Whilst enlightened performance measures include financial performance and productivity, they focus more on effectiveness and value-added measures rather than ratios of outputs to inputs. One way of enlightening performance measures is to base them around processes rather than outcomes.

A performance measurement system should support both operations and the overall corporate strategy. At the operations level, performance measures should link processes to strategic objectives, and motivate both workers and managers. They should balance

Table 10.1 Traditional and world-class performance measurement systems compared

	Traditional	Enlightened
Purpose of measurement	External reporting	Information for improvement
Emphasis	Profits	Continuous improvement
Cycle times	Long	Short
Production	Batch	Continuous
Volume	High	Just right
Inventory	Buffers	Eliminated
Waste	Scrap and rework	Eliminated
Design emphasis	Engineering	Manufacturing/customer value
Employee	Deskilling	Involvement
Environment	Stable	Rapid change

financial measures with non-financial measures such as measurements of waste and of customer satisfaction. Over the long run, good performance measures will help support organizational transformation and organizational learning, and sustain competitiveness.

Enlightened performance measurement systems are those that are:

- Relevant
- Integrated
- Balanced
- Strategic
- Improvement-oriented
- Dynamic.

In order to be relevant to operations, performance measures should be primarily non-financial. Process-based performance measures are particularly relevant in operations management, because they relate to a particular process and can be used and maintained by people working in the process. Good process-based measures provide very quick feedback on performance. They can often be visually displayed in the workplace as charts, graphs and other pictures that can be quickly and easily understood. Such visual management is a key element of Japanese practices.

Performance measurement systems should be aligned with strategic priorities (Kaplan and Norton, 1993); in operations, this means being aligned with manufacturing/operations strategy. New performance measurement systems should take into account not only current measures, but also strategic objectives. They should be focused around critical success factors, and take into account trends that might affect the organization.

As you will see later in this chapter, performance measurement systems should support improvement as well as monitoring. To support improvement performance, measures should be simple and easy to use, and provide fast feedback.

They should also be dynamic, rather than static, so that they can monitor and respond to changes in both the internal and external environment (Bititci et al., 2000) through changing over time as needs change. Performance measurement systems can also harness computer and communications technology. Bititci et al. (2000) suggest that corporate Enterprise Resource Planning (ERP) systems can be used to support dynamic performance measurement systems.

Enlightened performance measures in practice

Process measures include those of layout, inventory and throughput, such as manufacturing lead time, customer lead times and supplier lead times, schedule performance and equipment effectiveness.

Enlightened performance measures are related to performance objectives. Enlightened quality measures might include measures of waste and errors, such as failure and error rates, distance travelled and order changes. A final category of enlightened performance measures is measures of improvement and innovation, such as investment in employees, including employment and training.

Process-based measures are more useful in operations than results-based measures, which relate to broader issues or targets for larger organizational units. Results-based measures usually comprise data collected in the workplace that are analysed and presented some-where else. They are still useful, however, as management information, although they are often too detailed to be useful in the workplace.

The new bases of performance measurement for operations are shown in Figure 10.3.

The changes in organizations and their environments have fundamentally altered the relationships between organizations, employees, customers, suppliers and other stakeholders. Performance measurement systems should reflect these changes. However, traditional

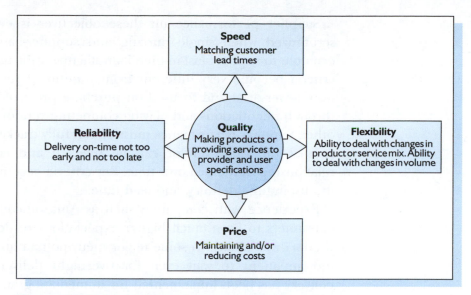

Figure 10.3 Enlightened performance objectives.

managerial accounting systems focus on uniformity rather than utility. Special issues relating to service operations and supply chain management are briefly raised below.

Service operations issues

In designing a performance measurement system for a service operation, special consideration should be given to whether the operation being measured is a front-room or back-room operation. The principles underlying back-room performance measurement are similar to those underlying manufacturing performance measurement systems, but those applied to front-room performance measurement also need to focus on service quality and customer satisfaction.

The service–profit chain emphasizes the role of service quality and customer satisfaction in overall service business performance.

Supply chain issues

Performance measurement in supply chains has been profoundly affected by changes in customer requirements, particularly for reliability, speed and quality. On-time deliveries have become an order-qualifier in many industries. Short-lead times are becoming the norm in many industries, as are six-sigma quality or zero defects in delivered items.

Supplier performance on these objectives is even more closely scrutinized when single-sourcing and supplier-base reduction (for example to support just-in-time manufacturing) is used. Performance criteria become very different from traditional relationships, which were adversarial and focused on purchase price reduction, achieved through negotiations and playing competing vendors off against each other. Supplier performance must be carefully tracked and monitored so that the right vendor can be selected and certified, and the relationship developed over time. Key criteria become quality, reliability, just-in-time delivery, and lead time.

Experience with companies such as Amazon.com is also training consumers to have much higher expectations of delivery speed and product availability. In some major metropolitan areas customers are too impatient to wait even for overnight delivery, and same-day delivery has been implemented for immediate gratification.

CONTINUOUS IMPROVEMENT

An effective performance measurement system must be in place so that the organization can assess how well (or poorly) it is doing, and identify where to target its performance improvement efforts.

There are two different approaches to improving performance:

1 Kaizen (continuous improvement)
2 Radical improvement (big leaps in improvement).

Continuous improvement

Continuous improvement is a management philosophy that sees quality improvement as an ongoing process of incremental improvement rather than once-and-for-all or episodic series of major improvement efforts. A key aspect of continuous improvement is setting demanding but achievable objectives, and feeding back achievements against these objectives.

Kaizen describes the Japanese concept that major improvements come through a series of small, incremental gains (Imai, 1986, p. 3):

The essence of kaizen is simple and straightforward: kaizen means improvement. Moreover, kaizen means ongoing improvement involving everyone, including both managers and workers. The kaizen philosophy assumes that our way of life – be it our working life, our social life, or our home life – deserves to be constantly improved.

Continuous improvement is an essential element of total quality management, which was introduced in Chapter 8. Another aspect of TQM, actively involving employees, is central to continuous improvement. Continuous improvement can take place in any situation, but will often be focused around quality circles (QCs).

Many organizations have adopted continuous improvement, especially for processes, where continuous process improvement is used to improve products and services through improving the inputs and processes used to produce them. This approach is clearly evident at Toyota, who state (Brown, 1996):

> All Toyota employees in their respective functions pledge to:
>
> ● Consider customers first
> ● Master basic ideas of QC; adhere to the cycle of management; plan, do, check and act; judge and act on the basis of concrete facts and data; provide standards to be observed by all concerned; all personnel should contribute to kaizen
> ● Put them [QC ideas] into practice.

The reason for doing so is:

> ... to improve corporate robustness so that Toyota will be able to flexibly meet challenges.

Quality circles can play an important role in achieving and maintaining process and product quality. Although the circles were initially developed in Japan, they have been one of many ideas 'transferable' to the West. It must be kept in mind, though, that quality circles will be successful only if senior managers are prepared to be committed to implementing ideas for change that might come from the quality circles. For example, Huge (1992, p. 71) observes how Japanese companies that are successful global competitors use quality circles to achieve the following:

> ... an astounding 20–100 suggestions per employee with over 90 percent implemented compared to less than one suggestion per employee in UK companies; lower absenteeism – 1 percent compared to 7–11 percent for UK companies.

Toyota refer to quality circles as 'small group improvement activities' (SGIAs). Although quality circles will differ according to the nature of the industry in which they operate, common features tend to include:

1 Identifying a particular problem that a group needs to investigate
2 Forming a group, from a range of levels and across a number of functions within the firm
3 Freedom to suggest improvements from every member within the group
4 Decisions on implementation are left, largely, to the group
5 Disbanding the particular group and the creation of further ad-hoc groups for other quality investigations.

This not only serves as a means of improving process quality; QCs also greatly enhance employee involvement, and feelings of responsibility and morale are heightened. This is spelt out by Toyota (Toyota Motor Corporation Human Resource Division – QCs):

At Toyota we recognize the following three primary aims [for QCs]:

1 To raise morale and create a pleasant working environment that encourages employee involvement
2 To raise the levels of leadership, problem-solving and other abilities; and
3 To raise the level of quality, efficiency and other worksite performance.

The Japanese transplants make extensive use of quality circles. For example, in the Marysville Ohio plant, Honda's QCs are a part of everyday life and are an integral part of their approach to manufacturing.

The amount of enhancement that can be gained from improvement activities varies over time, as shown by the S-curve model (Figure 10.4). This shows how large gains (relative to effort) can be achieved early on in the improvement cycle, whilst later on much higher levels of effort are required to achieve improvements.

Many tools have been developed to help work teams and quality improvement teams take a structured approach to improvement. The PDCA (planning, doing, checking and analysing) cycle describes an overall approach to continuous improvement, whilst the five-why process, the fishbone diagram and Pareto analysis are associated with process improvement.

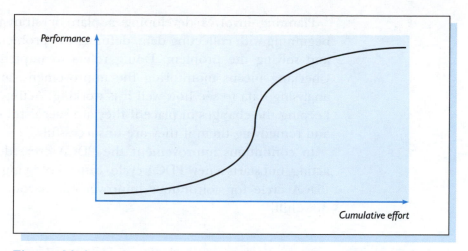

Figure 10.4 The S-curve model for incremental improvement.

The PDCA cycle

A tool called the PDCA cycle (Figure 10.5) is often associated with continuous improvement. The PDCA cycle was popularized by W. E. Deming, the quality expert, although Walter Shewart was actually its originator.

PDCA stands for the continuous improvement steps: planning, doing, checking and analysing. The PDCA cycle is sometimes called the Deming cycle. The PDCA was developed in the USA by A. W. Shewhart, and introduced to Japan by W. E. Deming, and reintroduced to the USA by Shigeo Shingo.

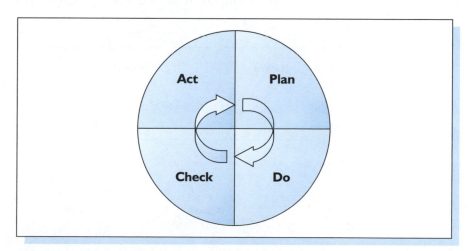

Figure 10.5 The PDCA cycle.

Planning involves developing a plan or strategy for improving, beginning with collecting data, defining the problem, stating the goal and solving the problem. Doing refers to implementing the plan. Checking means monitoring the improvement, and collecting and analysing data to see how well it is working. Acting follows checking, keeping the changes in place if they are successful or analysing them and remedying them if they are unsuccessful.

In continuous improvement the PDCA cycle does not stop with acting, but starts a new PDCA cycle. Instead of being a static wheel, the PDCA cycle for continuous improvement becomes a wheel rolling downhill!

The fishbone diagram

Another type of cause–effect diagram (besides the five-why) is the fishbone, which was developed by Ishikawa. Ishikawa is chiefly remembered as the founder of quality circles. The Ishikawa (or cause and effect) diagram is one of a number of tools and techniques that can be used within these groups and can be a valid discipline in the pursuit of ongoing process quality improvements. Continuous improvement groups will brainstorm for ideas and divide problem awareness into basic categories, using these as the basis for the Ishikawa diagram (as shown in Figure 10.6.

The diagram is important in focusing efforts to improve upon specific areas. Often firms' continuous improvement groups will rank problems in order of importance, or award a percentage value to the problem. For example, in the above diagram it may emerge in an actual group session that material problems account for 50 per

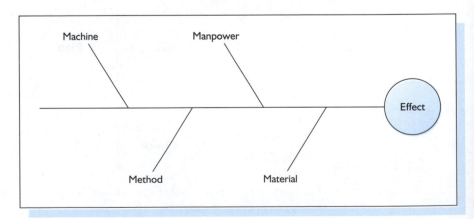

Figure 10.6 An Ishikawa (fishbone) diagram.

cent of the whole problem, with methods accounting for 10 per cent, machines 20 per cent and humans 20 per cent. The allocation of weightings to the diagram creates a sense of urgency for dealing with specific problems. Tasks will then be allocated and staff made responsible for rectifying the problem. The group will then agree to meet at another time to track process in improvements.

Pareto diagrams (histograms)

In Chapter 7, we saw how a Pareto analysis can be used to determine the importance of specific inventory items. The Pareto analysis (the 20:80 rule) has many applications, and an important one is in analysing and classifying problems. Class 'A' items will be those where 80 per cent of the numbers of occurring defects will be centred round the same 20 per cent grouping of causes.

This analysis is important because unless all items are identified and dealt with, particularly the Class A causes, competitive factors such as cost and delivery may be threatened. Pareto analysis is best

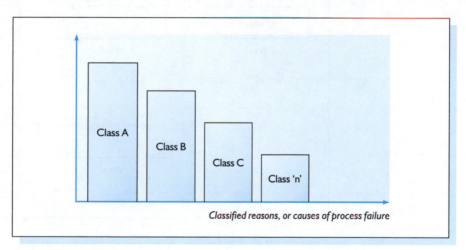

Classified reasons, or causes of process failure

Figure 10.7 The Pareto process applied to types of problems.

undertaken in quality circles – groups can identify major causes themselves, and then take responsibility for changing processes in order to make improvements. A simple Pareto analysis is shown in Figure 10.7.

Class A are the 20 per cent of recurring causes resulting in the greatest overall number of problems. These are critical, and must be rectified.

The five-why process

Most improvement opportunities require getting beyond apparent problems and superficial problem symptoms to identify real problems and their causes. The 'why-why' process, developed at Toyota, can be used by work teams and quality improvement teams to identify the root cause of problems. It is called the 'five-why' process at Toyota, because it usually takes five rounds of questioning why to get to the real problem. A diagram of the process is provided in Figure 10.8.

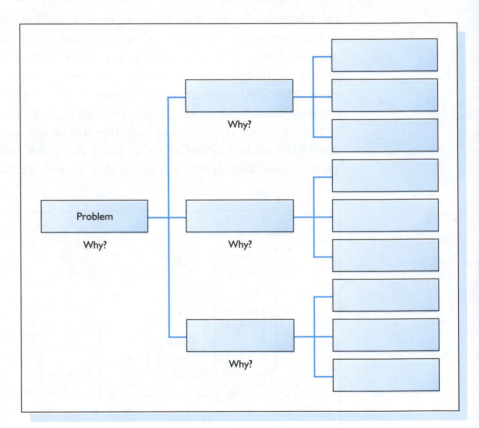

Figure 10.8 The five-why approach to process analysis.

The following is a transcript of an interview undertaken by one of the authors in 1996. It has not been published, but is provided here to offer insight into the use of the five-why process from a supplier to Toyota in the UK:

It was the most incredible thing I've experienced – I would be asked, why I did something in particular way. I would then explain it and the Toyota engineer would ask: 'why?' Everything we said was met with one of the engineers asking, 'why'. It drove me crazy to begin with – a series of 'why, why, why' all the time. But when we realized that they were here for our benefit as well as theirs we were willing to change the way we did things. In less than 6 months we had reduced costs by 20 per cent without hurting our business. They [Toyota] benefit but so do we. Now we always ask the question 'why?' before we do anything new in this plant. We also ask it of everything we do anyway, new or not. What a difference . . .

Although all of these techniques are useful and can have a powerful impact on performance, there are occasions when an organization has to reorganize itself fundamentally. The following section discusses the more radical approaches to improvement that have emerged recently.

RADICAL PERFORMANCE IMPROVEMENT

Sometimes continuous improvement is not enough for the organization to reach its goals, and more drastic performance improvements are needed. Two practices often associated with the step-changes in operations improvement are:

- Business process re-engineering (BPR)
- Benchmarking.

Business process re-engineering

Business process re-engineering (BPR) is an approach used in fundamental, radical, dramatic process change, over short time horizons. BPR involves rethinking all aspects of a business process, including its purpose, tasks, structure, technology and outputs, then redesigning them from scratch to deliver value-added process outputs more efficiently and effectively. As explained by Hammer and Champy in 1990 (Hammer, 1990; Hammer and Champy, 1993), the four general themes of BPR are process orientation, the creative use of information technology (IT), ambition, and rule-breaking.

Process orientation refers to BPR's strong focus on the process, including jobs, tasks, precedence constraints, resources and flow management protocols. The focus on the use of IT includes the use of automation to facilitate processes (see, for example Davenport and Short, 1990; Davenport, 1993).

The five phases of process re-engineering are:

1 Planning
2 Internal learning
3 External learning
4 Redesign
5 Implementation.

BPR provides answers regarding where to go and how to get there.

Process mapping

BPR makes use of a core operations tool, process mapping. Process maps are pictures of the way that work, information, customers and materials flow through an organization. BPR is a technique for mapping, analysing and improving processes, because processes link the customer's or client's requirements and the delivery of products or services (Jones, 1994, p. 25).

Key business processes include delivery (customer-facing processes) and support (those required to sustain the delivery functions) (Jones, 1994). Delivery processes include product/service development, customer order processes,and product (service) maintenance processes. Support processes include human resource acquisition processes, material acquisition processes, cash acquisition processes, business management processes, and business acquisition processes.

The stages in process mapping are as follows:

1 Define the boundaries of the activity and clarify customer and currency
2 Clarify the desired outcome of the activity
3 Map the process elements undertaken now
4 Confirm functional responsibility for each element
5 Identify failure points – a key failure may be that the current practice fails to achieve the desired outcome
6 Decide if failure points can simply be corrected, or require search for best practice or more detailed mapping.

Processes can be measured and controlled:

- At each internal supplier/customer (user) interface
- At each interface with the external customer
- By the process owner.

Processes can be either internally or externally focused. They have measurable inputs, measurable outputs, added value and repeatable activity. Because process maps represent both sequences of events and the relationships between them, they are an effective way to understand operations processes and to begin to improve them.

BPR is often confused with, and is sometimes used as a euphemism for, downsizing. It is true that BPR often identifies inefficiencies in processes that, once identified, reduce the number of people required to carry out a particular process, especially when IT systems are used to automate specific elements or entire processes. However, the decision as to whether to retain or downsize the workforce is independent of the BPR process.

Benchmarking

Benchmarking is a technique for operations improvement through setting goals based on best performance, whether in industry, in class or in the world. Benchmarking is the practice of comparing one's own organization's practices and performance against other organizations in order to identify and implement better ways of doing things. Along with BPR, benchmarking is one of the most used tools in operations improvement.

Table 10.2   The evolution of benchmarking in the USA (based on Watson, 1992)

Dates	Major method	Description
1950–1975	Reverse engineering	Taking apart a product to find technical improvements that can be copied
1976–1986	Competitive benchmarking	Analysing competitors to find out best practices
1982–1988	Process benchmarking	Searching out best practice examples from unrelated industries as well as competitors
1988+	Strategic benchmarking	Focuses on change at the business level as well as the process level
1993+	Global benchmarking	Benchmarking that crosses national boundaries

Over time, benchmarking has evolved from identifying perform-ance measures and setting targets to learning about best practices and linking them to an organization's strategy through the five phases seen in Table 10.2.

Robert Camp (1989) of Xerox, one of the best-known champions of benchmarking, defined the practice as 'the search for industry best practices that lead to superior performance'. Other definitions include:

- The overall process by which a company compares its performance with that of other companies, then learns how the strongest performing companies achieve their results
- Looking at what you do, identifying areas for improvement, examining ideas or best practices and implementing changes
- A formally structured process of measuring products, services or practices against the recognized leaders in these areas
- A process-driven activity that requires an organization to have a fundamental understanding of its 'as is' process and the superior performing benchmark process, both outputs and processes, in order to incorporate transferable practices into the organization's inferior performing practice and achieve a dramatic improvement in process performance
- Learning from and with others to achieve a level of performance better than the rest.

Although benchmarking was originally used in surveying to refer to a fixed reference point, the American company Xerox is generally given credit for introducing and popularizing benchmarking as a management tool for a 'continuous process of measuring our products, services and practices against our toughest competition or those companies recognized as world leaders'. Xerox used bench-marking as one of its major weapons in fighting off a serious challenge in photocopying from Canon in 1979 (Zairi and Hutton, 1995, p. 35).

In the UK, benchmarking was first used by affiliates of American firms such as Rank Xerox, Digital Equipment and Milliken, whilst British Steel, British Telecom, ICI, Shell and Rover followed. The DTI published Best Practice Benchmarking in 1989 (DTI, 1989), and the British Quality Associate organized a benchmarking seminar in 1991. By 1993, a survey by Coopers & Lybrand for the Confederation of British Industry found that 67 per cent of respondents claimed to be undertaking some form of benchmarking.

Many benefits have been claimed for benchmarking. The Cardiff Business School and Andersen Consulting (Andersen Consulting, 1993) described benchmarking as 'the most powerful tool for assessing industrial competitiveness and for triggering the change process in companies striving for world class performance'. Similarly, Voss et al. (1997) found that benchmarking and a learning orientation were powerful tools in performance improvement. However, it is an indication of the volatile competitive environment that even when firms do employ benchmarking this is no guarantee of success. At the beginning of the new millennium, Xerox's financial performance was poor and Rover's very future remained in doubt.

Types of benchmarking

The two major distinctions between types of benchmarking are between internal benchmarking, in which units within a firm are compared with other units in the same firm, and external benchmarking, in which the organization compares itself with other organizations. Companies usually begin with internal benchmarking before external benchmarking, which includes comparisons against organizations in the same industry (competitive benchmarking), non-competing firms in another industry (generic benchmarking), and the best firms in the world (world-class benchmarking). For example, the Bradford Health Trust in the UK deliberately looked outside and benchmarked against an airline company. In terms of their core business, the two have little in common. However, the Health Trust was able to learn a great deal about how the airline was managing the movement of people, which is a key feature of some of the processes within health care.

Objectives of benchmarking

The objectives of benchmarking are to:

- Assess current performance relative to other companies
- Discover and understand new ideas and methods to improve business processes and practices
- Identify aggressive, yet achievable, future performance targets.

Bullivant (1994, p. 4) lays out four conditions for using benchmarking:

1 It must be key to business survival or development
2 There must be a high value area of concern

329

3 It must present a high opportunity for improvement
4 It must be unable to be solved by other means.

Stages of the benchmarking process

As well as many definitions of benchmarking, there are many different models of the benchmarking process. Many authors see benchmarking as following the PDCA cycle (e.g. Pulat, 1994; Zairi and Hutton, 1995), which was described above. One of the most widely used models was developed by Camp (1989), and is presented in Figure 10.9.

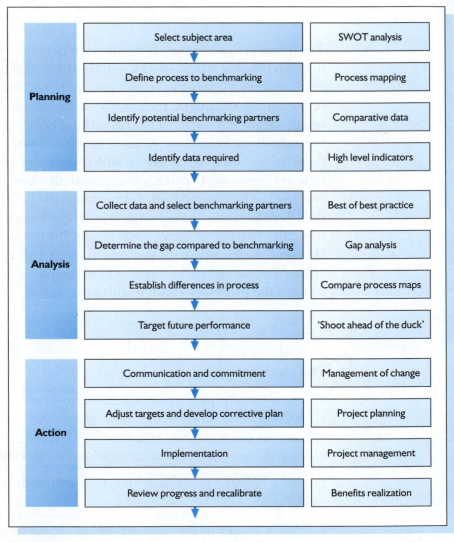

Figure 10.9 The twelve steps to successful benchmarking (Camp, 1989).

Key issues vary between phases, including who should participate.

Finding out what to benchmark. Sources of information about what areas should be addressed include suppliers, customers, employees, and competitors or others in a similar field (Webster and Lu, 1995). SWOT analysis, internal or external reviews or audits and/or customer feedback are useful tools for selecting the subject area. Setting out a simple process map may help identify the area concerned.

Selecting one area for benchmarking. The team may best be composed of process owners and results. Typical criteria include benefits, feasibility and expense (Webster and Lu, 1995).

Exploring key features of the area. Good tools include brainstorming, Ishikawa diagrams and systematic diagrams (Webster and Lu, 1995) in order to generate a range of possible solutions. The problem-solving team will normally be multidisciplinary, and may include both internal and external members.

Analysing solutions. Experts should be used to evaluate the ideas, based on their expert knowledge and experience.

Specify a solution. Figuring out the way forward may consist of ignoring the findings, following them exactly, or interpreting them.

Once the area has been selected, the next step is to define the process to benchmark.

Gathering information about other company's practices can be done through telephone discussions and on-site visits with selected partners. Other sources of benchmarking information include benchmarking clubs, common interest groups and published data. Some questions that often come up during benchmarking are:

- Which companies should we talk with and/or visit?
- Who else should be involved in benchmarking?
- Who else has important information about (or access to) a company not available elsewhere?
- What issues that relate to acceptance of benchmarking can be addressed?
- Whose ideas should be voiced?

Benchmarking succeeds when it results in the implementation of real, meaningful change that shows up in the company's financial performance (Goldwasser, 1995). Bullivant (1994, p. 3) describes the keys to successful benchmarking as:

1 Senior management commitment
2 Process mapping

3 Process measurement
4 Identification of high performance partners
5 Goodwill from benchmarking partners
6 Effective project management.

There is nothing new or unique in the components of benchmarking; rather, it is a framework for focusing attention on issues significant to business survival and development (Bullivant, 1994, p. 2; Mann et al., 1998). It shares many elements with competitive analysis, competitive information gathering, total quality management (TQM) and business process re-engineering (BPR). Perhaps the best way to understand how these all link is to see benchmarking as a process for identifying problems and potential solutions, whilst the others are the tools for actually accomplishing the implementation of solutions. If the problems and solutions are relatively well known, problem-solving teams and quality teams may be more applicable.

Goal setting is one of the key components of benchmarking (Camp, 1989; Watson, 1992), and may account for a significant portion of its effects as compared to other factors such as information about best practices, etc. (Mann et al., 1998).

SUMMARY

In the modern era where many markets are highly competitive, organizations have to improve all aspects of their business on a continuous basis. The temptation for firms if they achieve recognition – in the forms of awards or prizes, for quality, or services to industry – is to relax. This is understandable but is not acceptable. However, it's not just organizations within the private sector that have to improve their performance. Organizations in the public sector have to make better use of resources than before simply because there are less resources available. This means that techniques and tools employed in large privately owned firms can be transferred and utilized within organizations in all types of sectors.

Improvements can come from a regular ongoing pursuit, via kaizen. On occasions, though, an organization may have to embark upon more fundamental improvements, and these can include business process re-engineering (PBR) and benchmarking. All of these techniques are aimed at dealing with the core issue of this chapter – performance measurement and improvement.

The European aerospace manufacturer

In the late 1990s, a large aerospace manufacturer undertook a strategic review of its business and, in particular, the way it measured its performance both internally and externally (suppliers). This process was part of a much wider initiative aimed at improving the overall levels of profitability of the firm. All the signs were that the company was doing very well. The aerospace market, which had been in a downturn, was now booming. Commercial and military orders were up, and the entire market was in a buoyant mood. It was clear from the firm's position that they were doing very well; Sales targets were well in excess of what they had anticipated a few years ago. As a singe measure of performance, this put the company in a very good light. Indeed, managers and employees throughout the business often remarked on the high levels of orders – phrases such as 'this will put us in good stead for the next 10 years', were often heard. However, on further analysis it was clear that if a profitability measure was used, the firm was hardly making any profit on its sales and in some cases was actually making a loss. The logic often used was that they could reverse the problem with profits by selling spares to the customer. However, the spares business, due to new trade laws, was now in danger of becoming deregulated and losing its once lucrative monopoly status.

In addition to the confusion with the overall measurement system, several other key issues arose from the review process. First, the firm used only one method for assessing its suppliers, so no matter what was bought the focus was essentially on price. Whilst this is appropriate for high-volume/low-value items, it was inappropriate for the complex procurement tasks where innovation was required. Secondly, the firm measured each business function individually. For example, Purchasing would be measured on how cheaply it bought things, and Engineering on the quality of its designs. The problem with this method was that these measurements were often directly opposed to each other. For example, Engineering would be encouraged to over-design to exceed its measures, but Purchasing could now not purchase a standard part due to all the (often unnecessary) design additions (as seen in Chapter 3, this concept is often known as over design).

In order to make the firm competitive, it was decided that a new way of working was required. The firm adopted the balanced score card approach to focus the strategic development across a range of issues. This led to changes throughout the organization. The internal structure was changed to cross-functional teams, thus placing an emphasis away from function to that of process. In order to achieve this change it was necessary to refocus the measurements from a function- to a team-orientated approach. This meant that each project team would work together to find the best solution possible and not focus on maximizing their individual functional goals and objectives. The vendor assessment scheme was also changed to reflect the variety of goods and services bought. For the straightforward items – low-value, low complexity 'standard' components – efficiency-based measures were used. For the more complex 'critical' components, effectiveness measures, including innovation development, and cost transparency were used.

The combination of the overall strategic focus and the alignment of the measures throughout the organization has allowed this firm to achieve its goals of maintaining a competitive market position whilst focusing on improving its internal efficiencies.

Key questions

1 In the modern era, why is it important for all firms to measure and improve upon their performance?
2 What type of performance measures and improvements might you see within operations management in the following settings?
   a. Higher education
   b. Provision of health care
   c. Provision of social services
   d. A high street bank
   e. A fast-food outlet
   f. A large manufacturing firm.
3 What are the key differences between continuous improvement and business process engineering?
4 What are the major differences between effectiveness and efficiency? How can the balanced score card align these measurement issues?

Key terms

Activity-based costing
Balanced scorecard
Benchmarking
Business process re-engineering
Direct labour
Economy
Effectiveness
Efficiency
Fishbone diagram
Histogram
Indirect labour
Kaizen (continuous improvement)
PDCA cycle
Performance measurement
Standards and variances

References

Andersen Consulting. (1993). *The Lean Enterprise Benchmarking Project:* Report, London: Andersen Consulting.

Bititci, U. S., Turner, T. and Begemann, C. (2000). Dynamics of performance measurement systems. *Int. J. Operations Product. Man.,* **20**(6), 692–704.

Blackmon, K. and Boynton, A. C. (1994). *Valmet: Dynamic Stability in Action.* IMD Management 2000 Business Briefing No. 2 (Spring).

Brown, S. (1996). *Strategic Manufacturing for Competitive Advantage.* Prentice Hall.

Bullivant, J. R. N. (1994). *Benchmarking for Continuous Improvement in the Public Sector.* Longman.

Camp, R. C. (1989). *Benchmarking: The Search for Best Practices that Lead to Superior Performance.* ASQC Quality Press.

Davenport, T. H. (1993). *Process Innovation: Re-engineering Work through Information Technology.* Harvard Business School Press.

Davenport, T. H. and Short, J. E. (1990). The new industrial engineering: information technology and business process redesign. *Sloan Man. Rev.,* Summer, **31**(4): 11–27.

Department of Trade and Industry (1989). *Best Practice Benchmarking.* DTI.

Goldwasser, C. (1995). Benchmarking: people make the process. *Man. Rev.*, June, 39–43.

Hammer, M. (1990). Re-engineering work: don't automate, obliterate. *Harvard Bus. Rev.*, Jul–Aug, 104–12.

Hammer, M. and Champy, J. (1993). *Re-engineering the Corporation: A Manifesto for Business Revolution*. Harper Business.

Huge (1992). *Personnel Management Plus*, Sep., 62–3.

Imai, M. (1986). *Kaizen: The Key to Japan's Competitive Success*. McGraw-Hill.

Jones, C. R. (1994). Improving your key business processes. *TQM Magazine*, **6**(2), 25–9.

Kaplan, R. S. and Norton, D. P. (1993). Putting the balanced score card to work. *Harvard Bus. Rev.*, Sep–Oct.

Kaplan, R. S. and Norton, D. P. (1996). *The Balanced Scorecard*. Harvard Business School Press.

Mann, L., Samson, D. and Dow, D. (1998). A field experiment on the effects of benchmarking and goal setting on company sales performance. *J. Man.*, **24**(1): 73–96.

Pulat, B. M. (1994). Process improvements through benchmarking. *TQM Magazine*, **6**(2), 37–40.

Voss, C. A., Ahlstrom, P. and Blackmon, K. (1997). Benchmarking and operational performance: some empirical results. *Int. J. Operations Man.*, **17**(9/10), 1046–58.

Watson, G. H. (1992). *The Benchmarking Workbook*. Productivity Press.

Webster, C. and Lu, Y.-C. (1995). Using IDEAS to get started on benchmarking. *Managing Service Qual.*, **5**(4), 49–56.

Zairi, M. and Hutton, R. (1995). Benchmarking: a process-driven tool for quality improvement. *TQM Magazine*, **7**(3), 35–40.

Further reading

Atkinson, A. A., Waterhouse, J. H. and Wells, R. B. (1997). A stakeholder approach to strategic performance measurement. *Sloan Man. Rev.*, Spring, 25–37.

Reichheld, F. F. (1996). *The Loyalty Effect*. Harvard Business School Press.

World-class operations

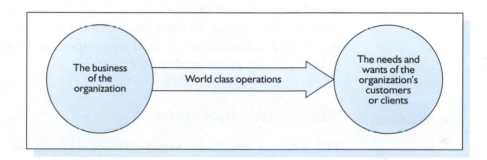

INTRODUCTION

The national origins of the *Fortune* Global 500 companies have changed dramatically over the past few years. The list is now more international in scope, with Russia and China among the countries now represented that would not have been included a few years ago. Although certain countries continue to be associated with certain industries (Italy with fashion and design, for example), other countries have emerged as leaders in industries or industry segments. For example, India has become a leader in technology, specifically software development. India's movie industry, 'Bollywood', even competes with American productions in some markets. Another new star is Brazil, as *Industry Week* (1998a, p. 48) pointed out:

> In South America, Sao Paulo, Brazil, unmistakably is the industrial standout community, a place that really matters for manufacturing. But the rest of South America, or Central America, or the Caribbean cannot be cavalierly dismissed. In Argentina, Chile, Costa Rica, and elsewhere in Brazil, there are pockets with the potential to be world-class manufacturing communities.

Existing companies must continuously improve in order to compete with these emerging new competitors, as having been in business many years counts for nothing in highly competitive industries.

Harvard Professor Michael Porter (1980) suggested that firms could compete either on cost leadership or differentiated capabilities, but this is no longer enough. The key responsibility for operations managers today is ensuring that the operation can compete in a globally competitive environment, through managing all of the key competitive factors (such as low cost, quality and delivery) simultaneously.

Being world class in operations capabilities is thus crucial to survival. When Richard Schonberger wrote *World Class Manufacturing* in 1986, 'world class' implied being better than other competitors. However, by 1996 Rosabeth Moss Kanter's book *World Class* defined world class as the level of capabilities required to compete at all today: world class has become an order-qualifying criterion.

Aims and objectives

This chapter explores world-class operations. After reading this chapter you will be able to:

- Explain what world-class operations means today
- Describe the importance and limitations of lean production
- Identify the role of human resource management, innovation and quality in world-class operations
- Describe how firms have reconfigured themselves to enhance operations capabilities
- Explain how linkages with other firms contribute to world-class operations
- Identify the importance of ethical and environmental considerations in operations.

IS LEAN PRODUCTION THE SAME AS WORLD CLASS?

Chapter 2 introduced mass customization, flexible specialization, lean production, agile manufacturing and strategic operations as terms that have been proposed for the era of operations that has succeeded mass production.

Lean production, one of the most popular terms, was introduced by Krafcik in 1988, and popularized in *The Machine that Changed the World*

(Womack *et al.*, 1990) and *Lean Thinking* (Womack and Jones, 1996). The authors claim that lean practices will ultimately spread to all types of manufacturing (Womack *et al.*, 1990, p. 12):

> ... the adoption of lean production, as it inevitably spreads beyond the auto industry, will change everything in almost every industry – choices for consumers, the nature of work, the fortune of companies, and, ultimately, the fate of nations

and further that (p. 278):

> ... lean production will supplant both mass production and the remaining outposts of craft production in all areas of industrial endeavor to become the standard global production system of the twenty-first century.

The lean producers studied in *The Machine that Changed the World* achieved a 2 : 1 advantage over non-lean producers. Lean producers are said to use half the time to develop new automobile models, and lean plants to be twice as productive as non-lean plants. Lean working practice, explains Dankbaar (1997, p. 567):

> makes optimal use of the skills of the workforce, by giving workers more than one task (multiskilling), by integrating direct and indirect work, and by encouraging continuous improvement activities (quality circles). As a result, lean production is able to manufacture a larger variety of products, at lower costs and higher quality, with less of every input, compared to traditional mass production: less human effort, less space, less investment, and less development time.

Lowe *et al.* (1997, p. 785) emphasized the lean production's link between the worker, quality, and productivity in lean production, saying that (emphasis added):

> A central claim made by 'lean' proponents is that manufacturing performance in the form of labour productivity and product quality is dramatically improved by the synergistic pursuit of these 'lean' production practices in conjunction with flexible multiskilling work systems and high commitment human resource policies ... Furthermore, lean production management practices are advanced as a universal set of best practices which yield performance benefits at the establishment level, *regardless of context and environment*

Whether lean production can be transferred from the automotive industry to other industry sectors needs further exploration. Cook (1999, p. 15) suggests that the aerospace industry is one such possibility:

> Lean aircraft designers consider that a new 'right first time' culture in aerospace manufacturing will do for aircraft what it did for the car industry a decade ago. Under the new regime, panels and components damaged in operation can be quickly replaced at the front line without special customization in much the same way that car parts are ordered up and fitted in the commercial world. Employees involved in all aspects of Eurofighter production – from the design stage through to logistic support – are grouped in integrated product teams (IPTs). Each IPT is responsible for its own budget and accountable for its particular section of the aircraft.

In the USA, Lockheed Martin's Aeronautics sector declared 1999 'the year of lean', applying lean practices to the F-16 and F-22 fighter programmes and the C-130J military transport aircraft. Lockheed's executives have declared their commitment to lean (*Industry Week*, 1998b, p. 43):

> 'Lean manufacturing is not a one-time event', notes an executive at Lockheed Martin Corp.'s 11 000-employee Ft. Worth plant that builds military fighter aircraft. 'It is a systematic and continual refinement of processes over an extended period of time'.

In the USA and the UK, it is said (*Flight International*, 1999, p. 10):

> The aerospace industry is in the grip of a revolution. Its name is 'lean' and its guiding principle is the elimination of waste from the production cycle. The revolution is moving out of the prototyping shops and on to the assembly lines, with dramatic results – and none too soon. The automotive industry has been lean for years. In aerospace, avionics and engine manufacturers embraced lean thinking long before the airframe makers. Now airframers are moving fast to catch up. Their motivation is the promise of faster development, better quality and lower cost.

Are world-class operations and lean production synonymous? Critics of lean production point to its effects on the workforce. For example, Delbridge (1998), in *Life on the Line in Contemporary Manufacturing*, argues that the benefits of team working and empowerment are largely mythical. Similarly, Niepce and Molleman (1998, p. 260) suggest that:

> In our view, the leading coordination mechanism in LP is the standardization of work processes ... Instead of having freedom as to when to work, workers have to adhere to the fixed pace as the reduction of inventory buffers makes workers increasingly dependent on work-flow time-sequencing that is governed by the technology employed ... Teams are not autonomous but are built around the supervisor, a strong hierarchical leader who commands the team and carries the responsibility for the team's activities.

Similar criticisms have been made of Lockheed's lean initiatives (*Manufacturing News*, 2000, p. 3):

> 'Lockheed's version of lean manufacturing isn't with employee empowerment,' says Terry Smith, a business representative with the International Association of Machinists and Aerospace Workers (LAM) at the Ft. Worth plant. 'Their version of lean manufacturing is more top down where they say, "We want you to do it this way so we can figure out how to do it cheaper and with less people."'

Brown (1996, 1998) suggests that lean production ignores four critical operations areas:

1 *Manufacturing's strategic role.* Manufacturing's explicit contribution to corporate planning is ignored within lean production. In Japanese plants this role is both central and explicit, which creates strategic resonance (Chapter 2).

2 *Manufacturing strategy.* Lean production ignores manufacturing strategy itself, which links corporate planning and operations strategy. In Japanese firms, manufacturing strategy feeds into and forms an essential part of corporate strategy.

3 *The seniority of production/operations staff.* Lean production ignores the link between operational performance and operations involvement at senior levels within the firm. In Japanese and, to some extent, German organizations, senior production/operations managers help set the agenda at the board level for key internal and external factors. These factors include the nature, scope and extent of horizontal strategic alliances; strategic partnerships with suppliers; commitment to training; ongoing, lifetime commitment to quality; and investment in process technology.

4 *Horizontal alliances.* The major role of horizontal partnerships is ignored within lean production, although the importance of vertical relationships in achieving lean supply is discussed.

So, whilst lean practices are important, they are only part of world-class operations. In particular, lean production neglects a key input into world-class operations – human resources.

THE IMPORTANCE OF HUMAN RESOURCES, QUALITY, AND INNOVATION IN WORLD-CLASS OPERATIONS

The operations manager's responsibilities, as shown in Chapter 1, include managing people. Firms must get the very best out of their workforces, because passion, commitment, vision and new ideas come from people, not technology. However, this is difficult today because of the increased uncertainty about jobs in both manufacturing and service organizations. The era of the 'job for life' is past, due to mergers, acquisitions, and downsizing within firms. The old message of 'join us and have a job for life' has been replaced by 'we can't offer you a job for life, but we can train you so that you are a lot more employable as a result of working for us'. Workers must continuously enhance their skills to stay employable, or be left behind, as Davis and Meyer (2000, p. 12) propose in their book *FutureWealth*:

> You must realize that how you invest your human capital matters as much as how you invest your financial capital. Its rate of return determines your future options. Take a job for what it teaches you, not for what it pays. Instead of a potential employer asking, 'Where do you see yourself in 5 years?' you'll ask, 'If I invest my mental assets with you for 5 years, how much will they appreciate? How much will my portfolio of career options grow?'

During the mass production era machine operators received little or no training, since work was very repetitive and required little or no skill under the 'machine-type' approach to work. Today, workers are exhorted to be flexible, multiskilled and highly trained.

Peter Drucker, the influential management writer, has commented that (*Business 2.0*, 2000):

Knowledge becomes obsolete incredibly fast. The continuing professional education of adults is the No. 1 industry in the next 30 years . . . mostly on line.

The consequences on a national level are described by Richard Rosecrance in *The Rise of the Virtual State* (1999, p. 22):

At the ultimate stage, competition among nations will be competition among educational systems, for the most productive and richest countries will be those with the best education and training.

However, corporate initiatives such as 'right-sizing', 'downsizing' and 'focus' have shed operations workers, often in large numbers. It has been argued that this can result in a 'corporate lobotomy', where the essential expertise and know-how on which core competences depend are lost with these workers. The *Economist* (1995, p. 6) stated that:

In the end, even the re-engineers are re-engineered. At a recent conference held by Arthur D. Little, a consultancy, representatives from 20 of America's most successful companies all agreed that re-engineering, which has been tried by two-thirds of America's biggest companies and most of Europe's, needs a little re-engineering of its own . . . As well as destroying morale, this approach leads to 'corporate anorexia', with firms too thin to take advantage of economic upturns.

Downsizing in recent years has been dramatic. In 1995 AT&T announced that it was reducing the workforce by 40 000 employees, adding to the 140 000 it shed during the decade following deregulation in 1984. Wall Street responded to the announcement by boosting the company's shares. For employees, though, the 1995 announcement was painful, because AT&T was prospering and the salary of AT&T's CEO, Bob Allen, had just been increased to $5 million per year. Other dramatic reductions during the 1990s included 50 000 at Sears, 10 000 at Xerox, 18 000 at Delta, 16 800 at Eastman Kodak and 35 000 at IBM. IBM alone shed 100 000 jobs between 1990 and 1995. In 1998, General Motors announced that it would close a number of domestic factories, shed jobs and eliminate models in an effort to become more competitive. GM's North American sales and marketing operations would be reduced to a single division, thereby reducing bureaucracy, costs and jobs. The downsizing phenomenon has become evident in the new millennium, with horrific headlines such as the following appearing (*New York Times*, 2000, p. 3):

> Bank of America to Cut ... 10 000 Jobs... Middle-level and senior managers are expected to be the principal targets of the job cutbacks.

Lean approaches have been misunderstood as getting rid of staff in order to make the organization lean, which instead results in it not being able to function properly. Driving down costs, a key ingredient of lean production, does not mean simply getting rid of people. Drastic downsizing can result in corporate amnesia, where a great deal of knowledge goes with the staff and can't be replaced. Some large firms have had to rehire staff on a consultant or contractor basis, often at an increased salary!

Sometimes companies have little choice but to downsize, but downsizing takes little or no skill and is at best a short-term solution. As Kanter (1996) pointed out, the real skill in downsizing lies in managing the process so that the remaining staff are committed to operations, including quality and innovation. World-class operations can reduce costs through reducing throughput time, improving layout, and enhancing quality through 'right first time, every time' approaches.

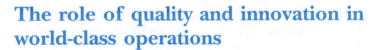

The role of quality and innovation in world-class operations

Why did quality emerge as a strategic factor in Western firms during the 1980s and 1990s? Two key factors are:

1 The number (and capabilities) of new entrants, which increased competition between new and existing companies, all of whom must compete to 'world-class' standards
2 The increasing choice available to customers, again largely due to new entrants.

Many firms have become blasé about quality, as Hamel (1998, p. 23) notes:

> The challenge is no longer quality; nor is it globalization. You've been there, done that, got the ISO 9001.

However, firms cannot afford to give up on quality, since continuous improvement is an integral feature of world-class quality. Quality is important for any firm in the public or private sector, and achieving quality certification or implementing a quality initiative does not mean that the firm can relax.

World-class quality makes no distinctions between 'high' and 'low' quality – quality is no longer associated with 'high-end' market tastes, but is measured by each particular customer segment within the overall market. Each segment may differ in its needs and requirements, and the firm must identify these requirements and then provide customer satisfaction through world-class operations capabilities. Meeting customer requirements may mean competing on cost or any other competitive variable. In some industries customer satisfaction may be the minimum requirement, and the firm may need to 'delight' the customer instead. Tom Peters (1991, 1992) has described this as going beyond customer satisfaction to 'customer success', quoting Bob Nardelli of GE Power Systems as saying:

> We're getting better at [Six Sigma] every day. But we really need to think about the customer's profitability. Are customers' bottom lines really benefiting from what we provide them?

World-class firms pay attention to quality areas that other firms either neglect or consider unimportant. Such attention to detail can provide advantages. For example, Federal Express transports parcels and other packages around the world, making its top objective on-time delivery. However, Federal Express goes beyond this to being obsessive about customer response times. Their ability to answer incoming telephone calls has become legendary. Good service is usually considered answering the telephone within three rings: Federal Express can actually answer before the first ring, although it has installed a cosmetic first ring to reassure customers who found this un-nerving.

Another example is Walt Disney Corp., which is highly successful in operating theme parks. A not-so-obvious quality issue is, as Tom Peters described in one of his seminars in 1990:

> Everybody can copy Disney's technology in theme parks; nobody else can figure out how to keep the damn park clean!

Keeping the park clean, Peters suggests, is fundamental to Disney's success. Other important factors in world-class quality (Brown, 2000) include never giving up on quality, instead of saying 'we have done quality' after being certified under ISO 9000 or receiving a quality award. World-class operations is also about getting better in those areas

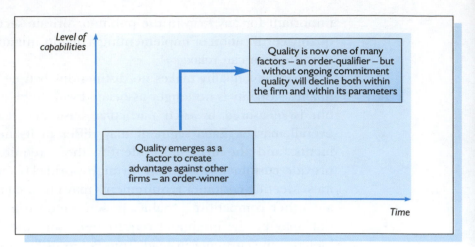

Figure 11.1 World-class operations and quality

where the organization already excels, as well as actively seeking out new and non-obvious areas of improvement, as at Federal Express and Disney.

Figure 11.1 illustrates world-class quality.

For world-class quality, the following factors need to be in place.

Top management commitment, both in terms of 'setting an example' and in terms of their willingness to invest in training and other important features of TQM. Juran's (1993) account of his contribution to the Japanese quality revolution provides important insight into the process of spreading the quality message throughout Japanese firms:

> The senior executives of Japanese companies took personal charge of managing for quality. The executives trained their entire managerial hierarchies in how to manage for quality.

However, as seen in Chapter 2 and previously pointed out in the discussion on lean production, this may prove a problem for firms that have no senior-level operations managers in place who might help to champion the cause of quality within the organization.

Continuous improvement. Deming, Juran, Crosby and other quality 'gurus' may have different views in their actual approaches to and prescriptions for quality. However, what becomes a common denominator, both for the 'quality gurus' and for firms involved in quality, is that quality is a 'moving target', and therefore a firm must have a strategic commitment to always improve performance. 'Signposts', in terms of amounts of rejects and scrap, act as guidelines rather than as a completed goal. A firm must continuously improve and go from, for example, percentage defects to parts per thousand, then parts per hundred thousand and so on, committed to reducing defects, as a way of life. As seen in Chapters 7 and 8, any organization has to strive to improve its performance in operations.

Quality in all aspects of the business. Quality relates to all personnel within the firm and also outside, including all aspects of the supply chain and other strategic partnerships. One of Deming's statements was that managers should 'drive out fear' from the workplace. In the current age of electronic commerce and virtual organizations, the same rule applies. Quality has to pervade all relationships within various networks in which the organization is involved.

Long-term commitment. Total quality management is not a 'quick-fix' solution. Rather, it is an everlasting approach to managing quality. This long-term commitment is probably the most difficult challenge for many organizations. There can often be a tendency to 'wear the T-shirt' or display an award or accreditation in quality. Once an achievement in quality has been made, the temptation is to relax. However, in the conditions of hyper-competition in which many markets now operate, ongoing commitment to continuous improvement is a key requirement in order to compete.

World-class operations and innovation

As Professor John Kay stated in *The Foundations of Corporate Success*, innovation is one of the very foundations of corporate success. Tom Peters (1991) says this more succinctly: 'Get innovative or get dead'. A survey of global manufacturing executives by consultants Deloitte and Touche found that product innovation was seen as driving growth and customer retention (*Industry Week*, 1998c). Gary Hamel (1998) points out that today we fly with Virgin Atlantic (founded in 1984), purchase computers from Dell (founded in 1984), and buy insurance from Direct Line (founded in 1985), none of which existed 20 years ago, concluding that:

> Never has the world been a better place for industry revolutionaries; and never has it been a more dangerous place for complacent incumbents.

It has also never been more important to have world-class innovation capabilities. Being first to market does not necessarily sustain success, because in many cases 'followers' have outperformed first entrants.

For example, whilst Pilkington (float glass), Polaroid (instant cameras), Corning (fibre optic cable) and Procter and Gamble (disposable diapers) have stayed market leaders, EMI (X-ray scanner), Ampex (VCRs), Bowmar (pocket calculators) and Xerox (with both PCs and plain paper copiers) have been outperformed by 'market followers' who had world-class innovation capabilities.

Likewise, the inability to innovate has major repercussions. Over 50 per cent of the firms listed in the Fortune 500 in 1985 have now disappeared. As the Austrian economist Joseph Schumpeter (1939) first noted, innovation can lead to *creative destruction* of entire industry sectors, in which existing firms are replaced by new entrants due to changes in products, technology, supply or organization.

The rate of innovation has also had an impact on everyday life. As the *British Medical Journal* (1999) puts it:

> Medicine looks likely to change more in the next 20 years than it has in the last 200.

World-class innovation requires capabilities beyond operations. Innovation is a difficult and uncertain process, whose success is only known after the event, as can be seen from the following (Yates and Skarzynski, 1999, p. 16):

> 'Who the hell wants to hear actors talk?' said Hollywood mogul H. M. Warner in 1927. Equally notorious was Ross Perot's retort when colleagues suggested in 1980 that EDS buy an upstart company named Microsoft: 'What do 13 people in Seattle know that we don't know?' complained Perot.

However, world-class operations are necessary for successful innovation. Some firms have put world-class operations in place and then forgotten the reasons behind their success. Breakthrough innovation often comes not from large, incumbent organizations, but from new entrants pioneering innovations that may be related but are not necessarily specific to an existing industrial sector. As Chandy and Tellis (2000, p. 21) state:

> One lesson from stories of corporate innovation is that it's rare for incumbent firms in an industry to reinvent that industry. Leadership in the typewriter industry, for example, changed hands from Remington to Underwood to IBM (with the 'golf-ball' typewriter) to Wang (with the advent of word-processing) and now to Microsoft. Never once did the leader at a particular stage pioneer the next stage.

This incumbent's curse, the authors argue, results when incumbents in a particular product generation are so enamoured by their past success or so restricted by their bureaucracy that they fail to develop the next generation of new products. Hamel (1998, p. 22) states:

> Of course, there are examples of incumbents like Coca-Cola and Procter & Gamble that are able to continually reinvent themselves and their industry, but all too often, industry incumbents fail to challenge their own orthodoxies and succumb to unconventional rivals.

Small- and medium-sized companies can seize major opportunities when this happens, because companies tend to develop inertia as they age and grow in size. 'Bureaucratic inertia' (Tornatzky and Fleisher, 1990) results from more levels of screening and group decision-making, diluting individual contributions, so that innovators are less likely to see their efforts resulting in actual innovations. Large firms must ensure that their operations capabilities fully support the innovation process from the very early, concept development stages. This is often hard, because success can create arrogance. At one time IBM lost its ability to translate patents into final products via operations capabilities. This had significant repercussions (Hamel, 1998, p. 16):

> When, in the late 1980s and early 1990s, IBM unwittingly surrendered its historic role as the architect of industry transformation, it also surrendered billions of dollars in future wealth creation.

So the key issue for large firms is to ensure that their operations capabilities fully support, and are involved in, the innovation process from the very early, conceptual stages. This is often harder to do than first appears, because successes can be the cause of arrogance (Markides, 1998. p. 31):

> Successful companies 'know' that the way they play the game is the right way. After all, they have all those profits to prove it. Not only do they find it difficult to question their way of doing business, but also their natural reaction is to dismiss alternative ways even when they see competitors trying something new. For example, it took Xerox at least twenty years to recognize Canon as a serious threat and respond. It took Caterpillar even longer to face up to Komatsu.

As Geoff Yang from Institutional Venture Partners (IVP) points out, in-house innovation prioritizes speed:

It used to be that the big ate the small. Now the fast eat the slow.

(quoted in Tom Peters Seminar, 2000).

GEO's Chief Executive Officer, Jack Welch, echoed this sentiment in *Forbes* (2000, p. 28):

> One cannot be tentative about this. Excuses like 'channel conflict' or 'marketing and sales aren't ready' cannot be allowed. Delay and you risk being cut out of your own market, perhaps not by traditional competitors but by companies you never heard of 24 months ago.

Chapter 3 showed how firms have introduced a range of techniques to improve the innovation process. Many firms also outsource some of the innovation process. Quinn (2000, p. 13) discusses the benefits of outsourcing:

> Leading companies have lowered innovation costs and risks 60% to 90% while similarly decreasing cycle times and leveraging the impact of their internal investments by tens to hundreds of times. Strategic management of outsourcing is perhaps the most powerful tool in management, and outsourcing of innovation is its frontier.

World-class operations must choose partners and manage the relationships with these partners. Chapter 5, discussing strategic supply, explains why this can be difficult. Where firms have retained much of their innovation process in-house, they have had to reconfigure the organization to enable world-class innovation.

An important breakthrough strategy for solving the design/operations gap in mass production is the development of product platforms, to ensure communication and cooperation from the concept development stage of product development. Platforms link various functions in the innovation process, but sometimes this needs to be supported by organizational change. For example, in 1991 Ford created the Design Institute, whose charter was to 'change the fundamental way of doing our design, development, and manufacturing'. Although the Ford Taurus had been the best-selling car in the USA between 1992 and 1997, Ford had to change its approach radically at the end of the 1990s. Former CEO Alex Trotman argued that (*Ward's Automotive Year Book*, 1998, p. 66):

> The economies of scale that come from purchasing materials from a simplified buying list, the single manufacturing system, the benefits of

using best practice worldwide, all those things hold true [but] what is a big issue is the number of platforms you have, how many drivelines, and how many people you have designing those products.

Ford has responded to increasing pressures for globalization by introducing 'world cars' designed around a single (or very small number of) platforms that can be sold in multiple regions. The idea of the world car is to share best practice among various divisions and plants, as well as trying to gain scale economies. Thus far, Ford's world cars have not been successful. In the early 1980s, the Ford Escort's American and European platforms did not share enough common components, and Ford lost money on the Escort. The more recent Mondeo/Contour/Mystique world car also lost money, even with 70 per cent common components. As *Standard and Poor's Industry Survey* (1999, p. 56) stated:

> ... while the rationale for building a world car is straightforward, the ability to do so successfully is not. For example, local tastes, infrastructure, government regulations, and other factors may make it difficult for a manufacturer to keep variations to a minimum.

Similarly, Renault fundamentally reorganized its development process, bringing together in the Renault Technocentre 7500 engineers, designers and supplier staff who had been formerly split between different Parisian locations. Renault intended to reduce its R&D spending by FFr1 billion per year, and to reduce product development times to 24 months (Brown, 2000).

Prior to the merger between Daimler and Chrysler, Daimler's design centre brought together personnel previously housed in 19 different sites. Helmut Petre, the group head of passenger car development, explained the rationale (*Financial Times*, 1998, p. 6):

> We will become much faster in processes – although speed for itself was not our first aim ... Product development has already got 30 per cent faster, but we see scope to do more.

Japanese auto firms had been held up as exemplars of fast innovation in the 1980s, but fell behind in the early 1990s. Honda in particular struggled, but has made a major turnaround (*Fortune*, 1996, p. 33):

> Honda, the fairy-tale come-from-nowhere auto success of the Eighties, suddenly started falling apart in the early Nineties when the Japanese

economy sank back to reality. Business dried up ... The sport-utility boom? Honda missed it – completely. The company lost its famous sense of Japanese tastes. Honda's car sales fell in 1993 and again in 1994. Yet now, just two years later, Honda is zooming ahead of competitors to enjoy the greatest success of its 48-year history. [CEO] Kawamoto says that before the bubble burst, 'Honda was in tune with the times. Everything it did was a roaring success. Then the environment changed, and we had to change the organization'.[qr] (*Fortune*, Sep 9, 1996: p33).

Honda's success was based not only on a particular product development but also on organization-wide change and redevelopment – organizational reconfiguration. This brought benefits in resources and speed. Honda has not yet matched Toyota, though (*Fortune*, 1997, p. 25):

Like everything else at Toyota, product development is changing too ... Two years ago Toyota reorganized its engineers into three groups – front-wheel-drive cars, rear-wheel-drive cars, and trucks ... In the past two years it has introduced 18 new or redesigned models, including the new Corolla, which is made in different versions for Japan, Europe, and the US. Several Japanese models, like the Picnic and the Corolla Spacio, went into production as little as $14\frac{1}{2}$ months after their designs were approved – probably an industry record. Toyota also caught the auto world napping by announcing a breakthrough in engine design. The 120-horsepower engine in the 1998 Corolla uses 25% fewer parts than its predecessor, making it 10% lighter, 10% more fuel-efficient, and significantly cheaper.

At Toyota, innovation is not only evident in the surge of new models (18 in two years), but also in the complete redesign of engines and other major components. The deliberate redesign of the organization to support innovation challenges firms who think that a radical cultural change will take place around a particular new product.

Toyota's innovation capabilities rely on the company's engineers. As Sobek *et al.* (1998, p. 39) observe, at Toyota manufacturing personnel are pivotal to the innovation process (emphasis added):

Some of the remaining integration problems at US companies may in fact stem from a lack of precisely this kind of system design. Even companies with able heavyweight product managers tend to jump directly from product concept to the technical details of engineering design. They bypass, without going through, the very difficult but important task of designing the overall vehicle system: planning how all the parts will work together as a cohesive whole before sweating the fine details. *At Toyota, the chief engineer provides the glue that binds the whole process together.*

For some firms, the idea that senior staff members should be involved in strategic areas such as innovation is a problem that needs to be overcome if they are to attain success in world-class operations. The role of world-class operations in innovation is shown in Figure 11.2.

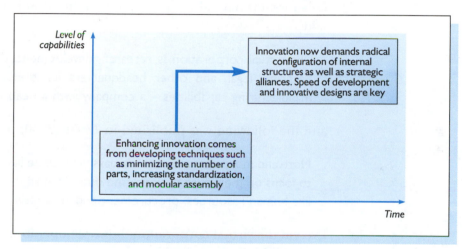

Figure 11.2 World-class operations and innovation.

HOW FIRMS RECONFIGURE THEMSELVES TO BECOME WORLD-CLASS

A highly qualified and dedicated workforce is only one facet of world-class operations, whether a firm competes in premium markets where high prices can be charged or in price-sensitive markets, since organizations depend on operations capabilities to drive down costs.

Mass production did not permit world-class operations capabilities to emerge. Under mass production, many corporations adopted the multidivisional form identified by Chandler (1962), with the firm arranged by divisions around functional groupings. Under this arrangement the manufacturing division might be in one place and the sales division in another, often far apart. Innovation became a protracted process. The cross-functional teams described in Chapter 3 are one way of partly overcoming this.

Many firms have had to reorganize themselves fundamentally in order to become world-class in a range of operations capabilities. This sometimes, but not always, entails downsizing. The 'virtual organization' is an example of radical reconfiguration.

Drucker suggests that profound changes are taking place (*Business 2.0*, 2000, p. 13):

> The corporation as we know it, which is now 120 years old, is not likely to survive the next 25 years. Legally and financially, yes, but not structurally and economically.

Other writers have also commented on this. Rosencrance (1999, p. 35) said:

> The virtual corporation is research, development, design, marketing, financing, legal, and other headquarters functions with few or no manufacturing capabilities – a company with a head but no body

and the following was published in *Forbes* (2000, p. 67):

> More and more companies these days want to be like Cisco. They want to focus on their core business and outsource all the superfluous stuff, like human resources, procurement and accounting.

Even in the virtual corporation, however, operations managers are still responsible for coordinating the remaining 'core' activities so that world-class operations are in place.

WORLD-CLASS OPERATIONS, MERGERS AND ALLIANCES

Chapter 2 mentioned strategy's military origins. It makes sense to ensure that 'enemies' become 'friends' or 'allies' in world-class operations, as in the relationships and alliances that have happened in many industries. This only confirms the military analogy – one group clusters together against other, competing alliances (or clusters), all of which are seeking to position themselves and gain some sort of defensive cover or competitive advantage.

As Brown (2000, p. 34) explains, forming alliances is directly relevant to world-class operations:

> In order to be a contender as a player within these alliances, a would-be partner has to demonstrate some unique or outstanding operations

capability that another partner does not have. Clearly, world-class performance in operations has profound, strategic importance for firms in terms of alliances. Such alliances will be formed between world-class firms, who possess outstanding, and complementary, capabilities.

Alliances are common in many industries, due to a large extent to two factors:

1 Fewer companies have the resources to enter into mergers and acquisitions than in the relatively cash-rich 1960s and 1970s. Many firms cannot 'go it alone' in R&D, and alliances let them collaborate with others, as Dussauge *et al.* (1992, p. 127) observe:

> Not all alliances are technology-based but in a majority of cases, technology is a key element ... About two-thirds of all strategic alliances can be considered as technology-based.

2 Mergers and alliances have not proved successful for many companies, and alliances are an alternative, as are forming strong buyer–supplier relationships throughout the supply chain.

For manufacturing firms, the benefits of alliances are first allowing the firm to concentrate on core manufacturing activities, and second becoming a means of organizational learning. Types of alliances include:

- Licensing agreements
- Joint ventures
- Franchising
- Marketing agreements/dual marketing
- Buyer–seller relationships (particularly in JIT production)
- Consortia
- Research and development alliances
- Joint access to technology and markets.

Firms enter alliances for two purposes:

1 To create advantage for the firms involved in the alliance
2 To act as a defensive mechanism against firms who have entered competing agreements.

Such alliances have become commonplace in the auto industry. As seen in Chapter 6, a key issue for the industry is over-capacity; another 20 million more cars and trucks could be produced per year with current resources. The Asia-Pacific region alone will add capacity for 6 million cars by 2005. One forecast is that by the year 2010 the current 40 carmakers will have been reduced to a 'Big Six' (*Business Week*, 1999):

> By 2010, the thinking goes, each major auto market will be left with two large, home-based companies – GM and Ford in the US, Daimler–Chrysler and Volkswagen in Europe, and Toyota and Honda in Japan. Players such as Nissan or Volvo may keep their brand names, but someone else will be running the show.

In telecommunications, a number of alliances were put in place essentially to deal with major technological uncertainties. These alliances have included Concert, involving BT and MCI; Global One, which consisted of Deutsche Telekom, France Telecom, Sprint and partners; and WorldPartners/Unisource, made up of AT&T, Telecom Italia, KPN of the Netherlands, the Swiss PTT, Telia of Sweden, Telstra of Australia, and Singapore Telecom. Such alliances have major consequences on operations because they are often designed to result in end products, the speed, volumes and mix of which are ultimately determined by operations capabilities.

Thus world-class operations are important in alliances and merger activities for at least two reasons. First, being world-class means that firms have the potential to be linked with other world-class firms to form important, powerful alliances. Second, world-class operations capabilities may be threatened if the supposed benefits of the alliance or merger do not create strategic fit between two or more firms' operations capabilities Mergers and acquisitions do not always enhance operations and supply capabilities. For example, the 1999 Daimler–Chrysler merger created the world's fifth-largest car company, but the strategic fit is difficult. Chrysler purchases 70 per cent of its added value from mainly American suppliers, and came closer than GM or Ford to lean production standards. By contrast, Daimler is a fully integrated German luxury car producer. After the merger, Daimler–Chrysler reviewed the entire component supply chain in Europe and North America to improve strategic fit, but this may well threaten Chrysler's strategic relationships with suppliers.

THE ROLE OF ETHICS IN WORLD-CLASS OPERATIONS

Ethics should be considered in world-class operations, as well as being discussed in business ethics and corporate responsibility areas. First, ethical issues are often created at the operations level, particularly in the transformation process – 'on the production line'. Second, outsourcing and 'virtual organizations' are often pursued to gain cost advantages, but have ethical consequences.

Ethics and operations management

In the USA, manufacture and distribution of firearms has created heated debate at various government levels. When Smith & Wesson, the nation's largest handgun manufacturer, agreed with federal, state and local governments to restrict the sale of handguns (Singer, 2000):

> The National Rifle Association and the National Shooting Sports Foundation (NSSF) denounced Smith & Wesson for 'selling out' the industry and called for an immediate boycott of the company's products.

Quality has emerged as the operations topic most closely related to ethical issues. For example, when a high rate of accidents with Ford sports utility vehicles (SUVs) equipped with Firestone tyres was revealed, Ford released its first-ever 'corporate citizenship' report, a 98-page document called *Connecting with Society*. The report highlighted two serious problems with SUVs: first, SUVs pollute the air and consume petrol at rates far higher than conventional automobiles; and second, SUVs are hazardous to other vehicles!

Roger Cowe's article 'The rise of the virtuous company' mentions how (Cowe, 2000):

> There is a tension between profits and responsibilities, between marketing or cost-cutting and exploitation. But selling one Hawk jet to Indonesia instead of ten does not make it responsible. Nor does it become acceptable to employ children if you double their pay. The tension does not really stem from how much profit is enough (whether you are a bank, and oil company or a supermarket chain). It is about how the profit is made, rather than how much profit piles up or how

Table 11.1   Examples of ethical issues in operations management (source: *Business Week,* 2000)

US company/product	Factory/town	Labour problems
Huffy bicycles	Baoan Bicycle, Shenzhen, Guangdong	15-hour shifts, 7 days a week. No overtime pay
Wal-Mart	Qin Shi Handbag	Guards beat workers for being late
Kathie Lee Handbags	Zhongshan, Guangdong	Excessive charges for food and lodging mean some workers earn less than 1 cent an hour
Stride Rite	Kunshan Sun Hwa Footwear	16-year-old girls apply toxic glues with bare hands and toothbrushes
Keds Sneakers	Kunshan, Jiangsu	Workers locked in factory behind 15-ft walls
New Balance Shoes	Lizhan Footwear, Dongguan, Guangdong	Lax safety standards, no overtime pay as required by Chinese law

much is given away. This gets to the heart of what responsible business is about – issues such as child labour, human rights, animal welfare, armaments, genetic engineering and pollution.

In May 2000, the New York-based National Labor Committee reported findings of abusive conditions in 16 Chinese factories randomly selected from those to whom American factories had outsourced manufacturing operations. A summary of these is found in Table 11.1.

Such working conditions are clearly not acceptable. However, some firms seek out every means of competitive advantage, including outsourcing activities and then abdicating responsibility for monitoring labour conditions in low-wage countries. *Business Week* (2000, p. 4) highlights this ethical issue:

Investigators for US labor and human-rights groups estimate that Asia and Latin America have thousands of sweatshops, which do everything from force employees to work 16-hour days to cheat them out of already meager wages, that make products for US and European companies. 'It would be extremely generous to say that even 10% of [Western companies charged with abuses] have done anything meaningful about labor conditions,' says S. Prakash Sethi, a Baruch College business professor who helped set up a monitoring system for Mattel at its dozen factories in China, Indonesia, Mexico, and elsewhere.

Business ethics encompasses more than exploitation of workers; it also concerns the means of exchange between buyer or consumer and suppliers of particular products. For example, H. B. Fuller enjoyed a reputation as one of the USA's most socially responsible companies, endowing a Chair in Business Ethics at the University of Minnesota and 'establishing a charitable foundation dedicated to the environment, the arts, and social programs' (Singer, 2000). However:

> . . . beginning in the late '80s, the company was dogged by reports that one of its adhesives, Resistol, had become the drug of choice for glue-sniffing street kids in Central America . . . H. B. Fuller seemed unprepared for the furore that arose over the abuse of one of its products. 'It's a social problem. It's not a product problem,' the company argued. Still, it pulled the product off retail shelves in Guatemala and Honduras.

Organizations that claim to be ethical can set themselves up for criticism. The Body Shop shows how firms can change working practices and deal with a range of ethical issues. However, the company has been criticized in the media for its practices. In the UK, for example, an hour-long television programme on Channel 4 questioned the Body Shop's practices on animal testing, as well as probing investments in projects in underdeveloped areas. Professor Norman Bowie, of the London Business School warns (Singer, 2000):

> If you do something ethical, and then market it, and there's a little failure, you get hammered.

Michael G. Daigneault, president of the non-profit Ethics Resource Center in Washington, D.C., adds that (Singer, 2000):

> The irony . . . is that a lot of these organizations have the best intentions, and many actually walk the talk – 99 percent of the time. But the 1 percent of the time that they slip up, someone will be waiting for them.

Environmental responsibility and operations management

Whether environmental systems and environmental performance lead to higher corporate performance is far from clear. The quality saying 'do things right first time, every time' does imply less waste.

Some authors (for example, Makower, 1993, 1994; Porter and Van der Linde, 1995) suggest that becoming more environmentally responsible means that firms uncover new sources of waste and so enhance their productivity, so that enhanced environmental responsibility leads to improved business performance. Other writers (such as Walley and Whitehead, 1994) argue that in most cases improved environmental performance actually reduces profits and shareholder value.

However, this is not the whole of ethical issues. The need to document business responsibility has become important. ISO 14000 was introduced in 1996, in response to demand for a single international environmental standard. It was developed by an international technical advisory committee of industry, government, consumer interest groups and the general public. The scope of environmental issues is defined in the standard as:

Surroundings in which an organization operates, including air, water, land, natural resources, flora, fauna, humans and their interrelation. The environment in this context extends from within an organization to the global system.

ISO 14000 sets standards in seven general areas:

1 Environmental management systems
2 Environmental auditing
3 Environmental performance evaluation
4 Environmental labelling
5 Life cycle assessment
6 Environmental aspects of product standards
7 Terms and definitions.

Just as ISO 9000 certifies that a quality documentation system is in place and being adhered to, ISO 14000 certifies that an environmental management system is there. ISO 14000 combines the quality certification aspects of ISO 9000 with preventive environmental management. Many companies objected to the paperwork associated with ISO 9000, and ISO 14000 requires written documentation of policies and procedures for only four or five instances. In addition, ISO 14000 builds on the administrative elements of ISO 9000 where that system is already in place (such as in document control and record keeping systems).

Montabon *et al.* (2000, p. 15) suggest that being environmentally responsible should pervade the supply chain:

> Being environmentally responsible is increasingly viewed as a requirement of doing business. For manufacturing managers, this has meant re-examining their products and processes, with an eye toward the reduction or elimination (if possible) of any resulting waste streams. For the purchasing profession, the corresponding challenge has been to identify suppliers who can provide environmentally responsible goods and services without sacrificing cost, quality, flexibility, or lead-time. It has also meant identifying and evaluating any initiative consistent with these new expanded objectives. One such initiative is ISO 14000.

ISO 14000 has had a global impact. In Malaysia, for example, 96 companies from the manufacturing sector registered with Sirim Bhd for ISO 14000 certification, and although this is only a few of the more than 700 manufacturing companies in Malaysia, more are expected to attempt certification (*Business Times (Malaysia)*, 1999, p. 23). In Brazil, Cosipa, a major iron and steel producer, has been certified, and has signed a letter of intent with the Sao Paulo environmental agency SMA to deal with its pollution problems.

There are many valid reasons why firms register for ISO 14000 certification. First, customers are increasingly demanding environmental management systems be in place, as Xerox Corp. found. A 1995 survey of 99 US businesses considering ISO 14000 implementation found that 50 per cent reported customer demand or competitive advantage as reasons to pursue certification (Graff, 1997). Companies in European and Asian countries are demanding ISO 14000 registration. For example, China has adopted ISO 14000 as state policy. Major US automobile manufacturers expect first-tier suppliers to have environmental management systems. Other global corporations are making similar demands on suppliers, including in the pulp and paper industry (Graff, 1997). Just as ISO 9000 became important in industries from health care to the military, ISO 14000 will become an important order-qualifier for organizations.

Tibor and Feldman (1996) suggest that the following situations lead to ISO 1400 registration:

- A customer requires certification as a condition to sign a contract

- An organization supplies to a customer who strongly suggests you become registered
- A government provides benefits to registered organizations
- A firm has a site in the European Union, where market pressure or the regulatory environment forces you to obtain registration or certification
- A single international environmental standard can reduce the number of environmental audits conducted by customers, regulators, or registrars.
- A firm exports to markets where EMS registration is a *de facto* requirement for entering the market.
- A firm expects to gain a competitive advantage through EMS registration.
- The organization's stakeholders (local community shareholders, unions etc.) expect environmental excellence, and an EMS registration is the way to demonstrate it.

SUMMARY

Being world-class in operations capabilities is crucial to survival, because world-class has become an order-qualifier rather than an order-winner. Lean production is not synonymous with world class (although lean practices are part of world-class operations), because it neglects a key input into world-class operations – human resources. All the things that make business exciting come from people, not machines, and downsizing can lead to a 'corporate lobotomy' or 'corporate amnesia'.

Firms have fundamentally reorganized themselves to become world class in a range of operations capabilities. Quality in world-class firms is about never giving up on quality, getting better in the areas where the firm already excels, and actively seeking out areas of improvement that do not appear to be important on the surface. Innovation is also a major requirement for firms, although being first to market does not necessarily bring sustained success. World-class firms must also chose partners in a range of areas, and manage relationships with them. Enemies must become friends or allies as part of world-class operations.

Finally, business ethics and corporate responsibility are part of world-class operations. This responsibility is likely to increase, as awareness in major ethical and environmental issues becomes greater.

Japan Inc.

Introduction

The case study in Chapter 1 looked briefly at Toyota. This chapter ends with an overview of Japan's successes via its operations management capabilities, which enabled many companies within Japan to become world class.

In 1945 many of Japan's cities and factories were reduced to little more than rubble. Goods of all kinds, including food, were scarce. Inflation was running at around 100 per cent per year. The major economic transformation began in about 1949, and was greatly dependent upon a range of operations capabilities that were performed simultaneously to very high standards. The term 'economic miracle' is one that best describes the remarkable attainments in manufacturing and trade that the Japanese people achieved in the decades after World War II..

When the American market was opened to Japan in the 1950s, very few people could have anticipated Japan's extraordinary economic growth, via the high quality of its products, or the competition it would pose to American manufacturers. Indeed, the danger to Japan, as Americans became concerned about an imbalance of trade, was over-dependence on the USA as a market for its goods. Many Japanese companies have become household names: Sony, Panasonic, Toshiba, Toyota, Honda, Nissan, Fujitsu, Mitsubishi, Canon, Hitachi and many others.

The manufacturing focus

In 2000, slightly less than 25 per cent of Japan's labour force was employed in manufacturing. Most Japanese manufacturing units comprise small workshops, often family-owned and employing only very few workers. Factories employing more than 300 workers – which are less than 1 per cent of the total number – account for about 50 per cent of Japan's industrial production. Conversely, about 60 per cent of the workers are in firms that employ fewer than 100 people.

The Japanese became the leading makers of electronic equipment, such as radios and television sets, calculators, microwave ovens, watches and photocopiers. Japan is also a leading producer of industrial chemicals, pharmaceuticals, chemical fertilizers, and petrochemical products, such as plastics, synthetic fibres and synthetic rubber. Japanese oil-refining capacity has grown to the third largest in the world. Japan is also a major world producer of cement. Large amounts of Japanese-made plate glass, firebrick, asbestos products, fibreboard and other construction materials find application within the nation's fast-growing cities.

The Japanese iron and steel industry, vital to the development of all manufacturing, grew spectacularly in the 1950s. By the mid-1950s, Japan was building 50 per cent of the world's new shipping. This industry went into a slump from the 1970s, and has never made a full comeback. South Korea proved to be a strong competitor, and shipping suffered from over-capacity around the world. Five corporations accounted for more than 80 per cent of Japan's steel output.

Japan's abilities in manufacturing were based upon a range of capabilities described in previous chapters.

Making best use of limited resources

This is a recurring theme in this book, and has been used largely within the focus of a single organization. In Japan's case it was a *whole nation* that had limited resources! However, Japan's short supply of natural resources did not prove to be a limiting factor on productivity. The country lacks oil, which is the basic mineral for modern industry, and most of its petroleum comes from the Middle East. Its coal is of poor quality and the supply of iron is small, while lead, zinc, potassium and phosphates must be imported. A large amount of food is also imported.

All of these factors were against Japan. However, the ability to add value to its raw materials as they are turned into finished products meant that Japan's economy grew despite natural shortages. What made the difference were world-class capabilities in managing supply (Chapter 5) and quality (Chapter 8), and extraordinary capabilities in managing and implementing strategy, which resulted in synchronization between customer demand and operations output – through just-in-time (Chapter 7).

Strategy

The main strategy behind the Japanese miracle has been aggressive exporting of manufactured goods to gain market share around the world. For many Japanese manufacturers, the strategy was to expand market share at the expense of immediate profit. They were often willing to let profits be minimal for some time – even to post a loss – in order to gain customers. The shareholders, being mainly banks, were not concerned with receiving dividends from profits.

A powerful strategy for dealing with fears over exports was in the creation of transplants in key foreign sites in the USA, Europe and Latin America. Another reason for this practice was a diminished supply of manual labour within Japan. Developing countries, such as Indonesia and Thailand, had large numbers of manual labourers available. By 1991, Japan had direct foreign investment of more than 81 billion dollars. Clearly, such investment is not restricted to Japan. However, it is Japan that has made the most dramatic use of this strategy.

Alliances

Many large manufacturing firms formed enterprise groups called *keiretsu*, which are bound together through mutual stockholding and interlocking directorates. These close relationships involve manufacturing firms and the banks that are their major sources of funds. This means that ownership of corporations is much more concentrated in Japan than in the USA, since banks hold most of the shares of a company. The *keiretsu* also maintain relationships with smaller firms. The large manufacturers of machinery, for example, have ties to specific small workshops. These workshops receive subcontracts for work and parts from the big firms. The *keiretsu* are basically oligopolies – a few large firms and their associated subcontractors.

Innovation

The success of Japanese manufacturing owes much to the willingness of their businesses to innovate. In the 30 years after 1950, Japanese corporations made more than 30 000 licensing and other technology agreements with other nations. A famous example was in 1952 when Akio Morita and Masaru Ibuka, who had started a company named Tokyo Telecommunications and Engineering, heard of an American invention called the transistor. Bell Laboratories in the USA had invented this electronic device in 1947, but American manufacturers saw little immediate potential for it. The two Japanese businessmen paid $25 000 for a licence to use the transistor and within 2 years were producing transistor radios. They named the little radios Sony, and soon that became the corporate name.

The changes from the 1990s

By the early 1990s, the Japanese economy, especially manufacturing, found itself in a new global environment. By the 1980s, industrialization had expanded in previously underdeveloped areas, notably in Far Eastern countries. These were providing competition for Japan in its export trade, and labour costs in these countries were much less than in Japan.

The partial breakdown of the *keiretsu* system provided the basis for another trend in the economy – entrepreneurship, the starting up of new privately owned business ventures. The notion of entrepreneurship – starting a new business – had not been nearly as common in Japan as it has long been in the USA. In the 1990s, however, a number of universities started teaching courses on how to operate one's own business. Numerous ventures were started and met with great success.

Japan is no longer the only economic powerhouse in Asia. South Korea, Taiwan, Hong Kong and Singapore (collectively called the Four Little Tigers) have very robust economies. South China was experiencing astounding growth, and there were predictions that it would become the world's largest economy by 2010.

Undoubtedly there have been major mistakes made on a financial level in Japan. However, nobody can assume that all of the world-class operations capabilities that many Japanese firms have accrued over time are now worthless. Indeed, the very foundations on which Japan's future rests will depend upon these world-class capabilities in operations management.

Key questions

1 Why has the term 'world-class' changed in meaning over time?
2 Why is managing human resources a particularly difficult task in the modern era?
3 In what ways can operations managers play an important role in 'ethical' factors within an organization?

Key terms

Business ethics
ISO 1400
World-class operations

References

British Medical Journal (1999). **11 November**, p.12.

Brown, S. (1996). *Strategic Manufacturing for Competitive Advantage – Transforming Operations from Shop Floor to Strategy.* Prentice Hall.

Brown, S. (1998). Manufacturing strategy, manufacturing seniority and plant performance in quality. *Int. J. Operations Product. Man.,* **18(6),** 565–87.

Brown, S. (2000). *Manufacturing the Future – Strategic Resonance for Enlightened Manufacturing.* Financial Times Books.

Business 2.0 (2000). 22 August.

Business Week (1999). 25 January.

Business Times (*Malaysia*) (1999). 2 November.

Business Week (2000). 6 November.

Chandler, A. (1962). *Strategy and Structure: Chapters in the History of the American Industrial Enterprise.* Irwin.

Chandy, R. and Tellis, G. (2000). The incumbent's curse? Incumbency, size, and radical product innovation. *J. Marketing,* **64(3),** 1–12.

Cook, N. I. (1999). The race is on in lean production. *Interavia Bus. Technol.,* **54,** 15–20.

Cowe, R. (2000). The rise of the virtuous company. *The New Statesman,* 6 November.

Dankbaar, B. (1997). Lean production: denial, confirmation or extension of sociotechnical systems design? (Special issue: Organizational Innovation and the Sociotechnical Systems Tradition). *Human Relations,* **50(5),** 567–84.

Davis, S. and Meyer, C. (2000). *FutureWealth.* Harvard Business School Press.

Delbridge, R. (1998). *Life on the Line in Contemporary Manufacturing.* Oxford University Press.

Dussauge, P., Hart, S. and Ramanantsoa, B. (1992). *Strategic Technology Management.* Wiley.

Economist (1995). 9 September.

Financial Times (1998). 3 December.

Flight International (1999). September.

Forbes (2000). 27 July.

Fortune (1996). 9 September.

Fortune (1997). 8 December.

Graff, S. (1997). ISO 14000: should your company develop an environmental management system? *Industrial Man.*, **39(6),** 19–33.

Hamel, G. (1998). The challenge today: changing the rules of the game (importance of non-linear innovation). *Bus. Strategy Rev.*, **Summer,** 18–29.

Industry Week (1998a). 6 April.

Industry Week (1998b). 21 September.

Industry Week (1998c). 6 July.

Juran, J. (1993). Made in the USA: a renaissance in quality. *Harvard Bus. Rev.*, **Jul–Aug,** 42–50.

Kanter, R. (1996) *World Class.* Simon and Schuster

Kay, J. (1993). *Foundations of Corporate Success.* Oxford University Press.

Krafcik, J. F. (1988). Triumph of the lean production system. *Sloan Man. Rev.*, **30(1)**, 12–25.

Lowe, J., Delbridge, R. and Oliver, N. (1997). High-performance manufacturing: evidence from the automotive components industry. (Special Issue on Organizing Employment for High Performance). *Organization Studies*, **18(5),** 783–99.

Manufacturing News (2000). 10 April.

Makower, J. (1993). *The Bottom Line Approach to Environmentally Responsible Business.* Times Books.

Makower, J. (1994). *Beyond the Bottom Line.* Simon & Schuster.

Markides, C. (1998). Strategic innovation in established companies. *Sloan Man. Rev.*, **39(3),** 31–43.

Montabon, F., Melnyk, S., Sroufe, R. and Calantone, R. (2000). ISO 14000: assessing its perceived impact on corporate performance. *J. Supply Chain Man.*, **36(2),** 14–23.

Niepce, W. and Molleman, E. (1998). Work design issues in lean production from a sociotechnical systems perspective: neo-Taylorism or the next step in sociotechnical design? *Human Relations*, **51(3),** 259–88.

New York Times (2000). 29 July.

Peters, T. (1991). Get innovative or get dead (part 1). *Eng. Man. Rev.*, **19(4),** 4–11.

Peters, T. (1992). Get innovative or get dead (part 2). *Eng. Man. Rev.*, **19(5)**.

Porter, M. (1980). *Competitive Strategy.* Free Press.

Porter, M. E. and Van der Linde, C. (1995). Green and competitive – ending the statement. *Harvard Bus. Rev.*, **Sep–Oct,** 120–34.

Quinn, J. B. (2000). Outsourcing innovation: the new engine of growth. *Sloan Man. Rev.*, **41(4),** 13–28.

Rosecrance, R. (1999). *The Rise of the Virtual State.* Basic Books.

Schonberger, R. (1986). *World Class Manufacturing.* Free Press.

Schumpeter, J. (1939). *Business Cycles: A Theoretical, Historical and Statistical Analysis of the Capitalist Process.* McGraw-Hill.

Singer, A. (2000). The perils of doing the right thing. *Across the Board,* **37(9),** 14–19.

Sobek, D. K., Liker, J. K. and Ward, A. (1998). Another look at how Toyota integrates product development. *Harvard Bus. Rev.*, **76(4),** 36–48.

Standard and Poor's Industry Survey: Automobiles (June) (1999). McGraw-Hill.

Tibor, T. and Feldman, I. (1996). *ISO 14000: A Guide to the New Environmental Management Standards.* Irwin Professional Publishing.

Tornatzky, L. G. and Fleisher, M. (1990). *The Process of Technological Innovation.* Lexington Books.

Walley, N. and Whitehead, B. (1994). It's not easy being green. *Harvard Bus. Rev.*, **May–Jun,** 46–52.

Ward's Automotive Year Book (1998). Intertec Publishing Group.

Womack, J. and Jones, D. (1996). *Lean Thinking.* Simon and Schuster.

Womack, J., Jones, D. and Roos, D. (1990). *The Machine That Changed the World.* Rawson Associates.

Yates, L. and Skarzynski, P. (1999). How do companies get to the future first? *Man. Rev.*, **Jan,** 16–29.

Analysing manufacturing operations: quantitative methods

> ## INTRODUCTION

The purpose of this and the subsequent chapter is to give an insight into some basic numerical techniques that can be used to help solve simple problems that we often encounter within firms. These chapters are not designed to turn you into a statistician or an operational researcher. The chapters are designed to take you through some basic statistical tools and techniques.

This chapter will concentrate on several key techniques that will allow you to assess a range of situations quickly. These are basic mathematical techniques that you will have covered on a quantitative methods course. However, we will demonstrate how they can be used and applied in practice. In business there will be occasions when it important for you to be able to produce graphs, identify relationships in data quickly and be able to see trends. This is why we offer some techniques in this chapter. In addition, we have added an Operational Research section because firms often want to know how to assign resources and work out the best allocation of these key assets. As stated throughout the book, one of the central tasks for operations managers is in making the best use of these resources.

We have tried to take a step-by-step approach that should help you understand how to operate the techniques (even if you don't understand what they are doing!).

Aims and objectives

This chapter will provide you with experience in analysing manufacturing operations, and practice with some tools and techniques for that purpose.

After reading this chapter you will be able to understand the application of the following techniques:

1 Statistical approaches:
- Linear functions
- Regression and correlation analysis (linear)
- Time series analysis (bi-variate)
- Index numbers.
2 Operations research approaches:
- Assignment modelling.

Whilst these may sound a bit complicated, don't worry – they are actually quite easy to do and useful for being able to produce a quick analysis. It is also worth pointing out that Excel spreadsheets are able to do all of the above techniques very quickly for you.

STATISTICAL APPROACHES

This section will look at the statistical tools and techniques highlighted in the introduction. We will learn to do four key techniques. Table S1.1 should help you decide what techniques you should use and when.

Table S1.1 can be used as a quick reference guide to the techniques and how they are applied to a given problem or set of data. Before going through the techniques, it is worth spending a few minutes to discuss the various data types.

There are basically two types of data that you will come across; bi-variate and multi-variate. Although these sound technical, they are actually quite simple; bi- (means two) variate data simply means that you are comparing one variable with another (e.g. sales over time, production output in a given period, the relationship between use of birth control devices and birth rates). A variable is something that you are comparing – i.e. the thing itself. For example, sales will be a variable, and time will be a variable. Often we will put a letter to indicate these variables. Don't get confused by this, you can use the full names or letters as you wish – for example, y = sales and x = time (useful tip: time is always shown on the x axis). Sometimes these relationships will be positive (for example, more time results in greater

Table S1.1   Statistical tools and techniques

Technique	Purpose/Focus	When Used
Linear functions	Plotting a straight line. Working out the points of a line, calculating the gradient of a line	Plotting simple data to understand trends, i.e. growth or declines in sales, deliveries etc. Easy to do on Excel, or just with a paper and pencil!
Regressions and correlation	Allows you to make sense of clusters of data. Will allow you to predict (extrapolate) the data and see just how the data is clustered. This technique will also tell you how accurate your prediction is.	Very useful method, used constantly in industry for predicting trends in data – e.g. sales increases and decreases
Time series modelling	Builds on regressions and correlation techniques. Focus is on how data varies over time and the types of variations that are basically split into two: seasonal versus cyclical	Anywhere where you want to see a time effect or know a time effect – e.g. in marketing for promotions, in purchasing to understand commodity price variation etc.
Index numbers	Allows you to be able to scale a range of numbers and then to tell the differences between these numbers	Purchasing will use the technique to track spends and inflation targets. It will help you make sense of ranges of numbers and to build your own index to track the number changes
Assignment modelling	A useful technique that helps with scheduling complex problems. Based on operational research, it will allow you to minimize or maximize a range of constraints	Used for scheduling. Originally developed for assigning workers to machines, but the use has been extended to a variety of scheduling problems

numbers of sales); sometimes they may be negative (for example, the greater the use of birth control methods, the less births!). The positive and negative relationships are generally reflected in the slope or gradient of the line (linear relationship), i.e. if positive the line slopes up, if negative the line slopes down.

Multi-variate data involve more than two variables – e.g. birth control, birth rates and time. This requires more complex techniques, but uses basically the same principles. This chapter will concentrate on only bi-variate (two variables) techniques.

Linear functions

Basically, a linear function represents a straight line. We often express a straight line in algebraic form. Don't get confused when you see an equation; it is merely a shorthand form. The longhand version of the equation is:

> A straight line is described as the start point (known as the *intercept*), plus a level of increase or decrease (known as the *gradient*).

In algebraic terms, the following equation is used:

$$y = a + b(x)$$

Where the intercept and $b(x)$ is the gradient, this could be positive (i.e. going up) or negative (i.e. going down). You will often see an equation for a line written like this: $y = 4x + 6$. Immediately you should realize that this is a positive line (i.e. going up), because it has a plus sign. Remember, y means the axis. Plotting a straight line is actually quite easy. First, you only need two points (although you should really go for three to double check). Let's take the equation $y = 4x + 6$. The easiest way to draw the line is to put in values for x, so for simplicity start with $x = 1$. The value of y can be found by substituting x into the equation, i.e. $y = 4(1) + 6$, which will give you 10. This is one point on a line. If you put any other values for x into the equation you will get other points on the line; the logical ones to use are 2 and 3!

Try a few with different numbers and see what results you obtain.

Now let's just summarize how you might do this on a step-by-step approach:

- *Step 1.* Select a few convenient values for x (three points are better than two)
- *Step 2.* For each x value calculate the corresponding y value, using the formula:

$$y = a + b(x)$$

- *Step 3.* Draw a graph with y (vertical axis) and x (horizontal) axes – always remember x as 'x marks the spot and therefore it must be on the ground', and so the vertical axis is the y one!).
- *Step 4.* Plot the pairs of x and y values on the graph.
- *Step 5.* Join up the points to see the line.

That's all there is to it!

Example

Here is a worked example to help you. Plot the straight line corresponding to the function $y = 4(x) + 6$. Choosing the values $x = 1$, 2 and 3, the following calculations are made:

For $x = 1$, $y = 4(1) + 6 = 10$

For $x = 2$, $y = 4(2) + 6 = 14$

For $x = 3$, $y = 4(3) + 6 = 18$

Now all we have to do is to plot this onto a graph and join up the dots to make a straight line (Figure S1.1).

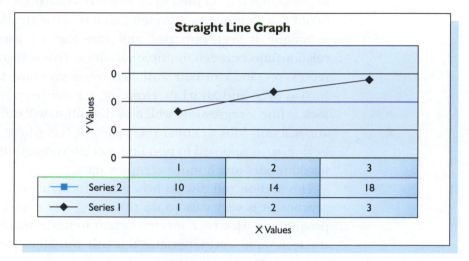

Figure S1.1 Straight-line graph.

There are a couple other little tricks that you might want to think about. First, you are not always given the equation in a straightforward form and so you may need to work out the gradient of the line for yourself. Second, you might need to work out the equation for the line. Let's now work through how you would do each of these things – if you have understood things so far, this next bit will be easy!

Determining the value of a gradient of a given line

First, if a line is given (without its equation), the procedure for calculating the gradient is quite easy:

● *Step 1.* Identify any two points on the line (just read off the x and y coordinates).

- *Step 2.* Calculate the vertical numerical difference between the points, and the horizontal differences between the points.
- *Step 3.* Gradient = vertical numerical differences/horizontal numerical differences.

Having looked at straight-line functions, let's now move on to something a little more detailed.

Regression analysis

Regression is a term used to describe relationships between variables – in our case between two variables, as it is bi-variate data. The regression technique is very powerful and can also be used to look at the relationships between multiple variables. This is known as multi-variate regression, and can be conducted using standard statistical packages such as SPSS and MiniTab. However, for our purposes we are going to look at linear regression, which by definition will only use two variables and will only look at linear relationships (i.e. where a straight line can be drawn) as opposed to non-linear or polynomial relationships, which would model much more complex data.

This section will discuss how you can calculate a regression line. In practice, it is very easy to do this using any mainstream spreadsheet programme. However, it is important to understand the basics of how the technique works, because this will also allow you to understand if you have done anything wrong!

Regression and its uses

Imagine you are a consultant working in a purchasing department whose input into business decision-making process is welcomed within the firm. The Purchasing Manager believes that by working more closely with suppliers, subsequent delivery performance will improve. His idea of working more closely means visiting suppliers on a regular basis to discuss business issues, and also to show an interest in the firm. As a consultant you want to know if his assumption is true (as it will obviously have a cost and possibly a benefit, i.e. the cost of visiting vs. the benefit of improved delivery performance). You need to understand if there is a relationship between the amount of visits and delivery performance. If a relationship between these two variables were found, you might expect to find that the more visits that you make to a supplier the better the delivery performance. We could also go further than this and ask, if we made 10 visits, by how much more would delivery performance improve?

This question can be answered, and demonstrates one of the most useful aspects of regression, which is being able to predict (or extrapolate) the trend of the data based on previous data. In effect, it is the ability to estimate the value of one of the variables, given the value of the other. Regression relationships are also useful for comparing against other firms – e.g. advertising expenditure vs. turnover could be compared against other firms. Consultants refer to this cross comparison as 'benchmarking', which was discussed in Chapter 10.

Standard methods of obtaining a regression line

The regression line (which is also known as the line of 'best fit') is a straight line that has the closest fit to the data points you have gathered from your data set. This means it is the line that cuts through the middle of the data points (this will become clearer shortly). This line can be calculated in three ways:

1   *Inspection*: This method is the simplest, and consists of plotting a scatter diagram and drawing the line that most suitably fits the data points. The main disadvantage of this method is that different people would probably draw different lines using the same data, just because they would see the data differently! To make it a little more scientific you could plot the average, or mean, point of the data and ensure that the line passes directly through it.

2   *Semi-averages*: This technique consists of splitting the data into two equal groups, plotting the mean points for each group and then joining them together to get a straight line. This again is quite quick and easy, but because of the averaging effect it may mean that the line is not an accurate fit. The problem then comes when you attempt to predict with the line (or extrapolate) – any errors in the line fitting will be exaggerated as the line is extended, which will mean that your predictions become difficult to substantiate.

3   *Method of least squares*. This method is considered as the standard method for obtaining a regression line. Your calculator or spreadsheet will use this method to obtain the 'line of best fit'. This method will calculate the route of the line by squaring the points along the line to find the narrowest path through the data points. Think of it this way; as you square a number it becomes bigger, which means that the distance between the points becomes smaller,

and the line can then be fitted through the space much more accurately. The general rule is:

> ... the least squares regression line of y on $\times$ is that line for which the sum of squares of the vertical deviations of all the points from the line is least.

The next section will concentrate on the method of least squares, as this is the most common method used in practice. We will have a look at some of the mathematics that sits behind it. Try not to worry too much about the complex looking formulae; simply think of them as a list of instructions. All you have to do is put the relevant numbers into the equation to read off the results.

There is one other main point to note before we look at the equation. Because we are dealing with bi-variate data, the line is referred to as a y on x regression line. This means that y is the *dependent* variable and x is the *independent* variable. This might sound a bit confusing. So think of it like this – the y (vertical) axis is always the thing that you are trying to predict, and x is the variable that will always be there.

Formulation for obtaining the y on x least squares regression line

The line that you are deriving is basically the straight line that we discussed in the first section – in other words, $y = a + b(x)$. However, to find the values of a and b you will need to use the following formulae (or lists of instructions). This first formula will give you the value for b within the $y = a + b(x)$ equation; n is the number of observations.

$$b = \frac{n.\Sigma xy - (\Sigma x)\,(\Sigma y)}{n.\Sigma x^2 - (\Sigma x)^2}$$

At first glance this may look complicated, but when we go through the example the application of the formula will become clear. This next formula will give you the value for 'a'. Note that you must work out 'b' first, as you need the result to put into the next equation.

The value for a is calculated as follows:

$$a = \frac{\Sigma y}{n} - b.\frac{\Sigma x}{n}$$

Now all you have to do is to work out the values for each, put them into the equation and work them through. Let's work through an example to see how to do it.

Example

Assume that you are a consultant and have been commissioned by the Director of Production to help her with a small problem. She is concerned about the cost of maintaining her machines, and she also worried about their age. She wants to know if there is a relationship between the cost and age of the machines. Furthermore, she would also like to know what would be the predicted maintenance costs of a machine that is 40 months old. (Remember that regression lines can be positive and negative, although this one is very likely to be positive – i.e. the older the machine, the more it will cost).

You set off and look at 10 machines, and collect cost and maintenance data for each. Now remember, you must first think about what you are trying to predict – i.e. dependent (y) vs. independent (x) variables. In this case, as in most, time is independent (i.e. it is marching on regardless) and therefore that must be the (x) variable. Consequently, cost must by the y axis! You could also think, 'what am I trying to predict – time or cost?' The answer is cost; therefore y is cost as this is dependent. The data from your observations are as follows:

Machine (n)	1	2	3	4	5	6	7	8	9	10
Age (x)	5	10	15	20	30	30	30	50	50	60
Cost (y)	190	240	250	300	310	335	300	300	350	395

(**Note**: The number of observations (in our example, machines) is always referred to as 'n').

Having decided on the x and y variables, you now need to construct a table to conduct the calculations (note a spreadsheet will do all this for you). You then simply take the elements for the formula and do the calculations, making sure you don't rush this bit!

x	y	xy	x^2
5	190	950	25
10	240	2400	100
15	250	3750	225
20	300	6000	400
30	310	9300	900
30	335	10050	900
30	300	9000	900
50	300	15000	2500
50	350	17500	2500
60	395	23700	3600

Now you need to total them all up. Remember that Σ means summation, or 'sum of', which simply means add it all up. So anytime you see this sign in front of anything, it means you must add all the values to give a total. The totals for the above are:

Totals

x	y	xy	x^2
300	2970	97650	12050

Now simply list the elements so that you can see which bits go into which parts of the equation:

Σx = 300

Σy = 2970

Σxy = 97650

Σx^2 = 12050

All you then have to do is put these numbers back into the formula:

$$b = \frac{n.\Sigma xy - (\Sigma x)\ (\Sigma y)}{n.\Sigma x^2 - (\Sigma x)^2}$$

which will give you:

$$b = \frac{10(97650) - (300)(2970)}{10(12050) - (300)^2}.$$

This will give you

$$b = \frac{85500}{30500} = 2.8033$$

You then need to do the same for 'a', using the formula:

$$a = \frac{\Sigma y}{n} - b.\frac{\Sigma x}{n}$$

which will give you:

$$a = \frac{2970}{10} - (2.8033)* \frac{300}{10}.$$

This will give you:

$$a = 297 - 30(2.8033) = 212.90$$

Therefore, the least squares regression line on age is $y = 212.90 + 2.8033(x)$. You can now use this equation to calculate your predicted maintenance cost by inserting the figure 40 (for time) instead of the 'x' and multiply through. This will give you the total of £325. In other words, it will cost £325 to maintain the machine after 40 months.

As you can see, this is relatively mechanical. You should try this by longhand, and then using a spreadsheet programme. You could also try plotting the data in a scatter diagram; substitute two figures for x and then draw the regression line through the data.

Here is an example for you to work through:

A large company's Sales Manager has tabulated the price (£) against engine capacity (cc) for 10 models of car available for salesmen as follows:

| Price | 4900 | 5200 | 6160 | 7980 | 7930 | 3190 | 3190 | 5160 | 4050 | 7150 |
| Capacity | 1000 | 1270 | 1750 | 2230 | 1990 | 600 | 650 | 1500 | 1450 | 1650 |

Obtain the least squares regression line of price on engine capacity. Discuss how you might use the regression line to help you in making management decisions. What are the advantages and disadvantages of your model?

Correlation techniques

Correlation is a technique that is used to measure the strength between two variables. It is often used in partnership with regression, as it will allow you to understand how well your line fits, plus how much of the data your line explains. This is very important for understanding the accuracy of the prediction. There are two well-known techniques for conducting correlation analysis; these are Rank correlation and the Product moment correlation. There are also other correlation methods, such as the coefficient of determination and various measures of dispersion. For our purposes, we will concentrate on the Product moment correlation. You should refer to a statistics textbook for some of the more complex methods.

The purpose of regression is to identify a relationship for a given set of bi-variate data; however it does not give any indication of how good this relationship might be – i.e. how well the line fits the data. This is where correlation analysis steps in. The better the correlation the closer the data points are to the line, and the more accurate the predictions. Correlations are given from +1 to –1; i.e. the closer to 1 you get the better the fit, and therefore the more accurate your line. A positive correlation of +1 would indicate a line sloping upwards where the data and the line fit exactly, a correlation of –1 would indicate the same thing, although the line would be pointing downwards – e.g. in the relationship between birth rate and use of condoms, the more condoms used, the lower the birth rate! Remember that a correlation of 0 would signify no relationship. To give you an idea:

> ... correlation is concerned with describing the strength of the relationship between two variables by measuring the degree of 'scatter' of the data values.

The basic rule is that the less scattered the data, the stronger the correlation. Again, don't be put off by the formula; it is quite easy when you start substituting variables into the equation.

The Product moment coefficient is known as r, and it is derived by using the following formula:

$$r = \frac{n.\Sigma xy - (\Sigma x)(\Sigma y)}{\sqrt{[n.\Sigma x^2 - (\Sigma x)^2]} \sqrt{[n.\Sigma y^2 - (\Sigma y)^2]}}$$

Using the example from the regression section, let's look at the correlation coefficient for machines to see how accurate our forecast was. The data are as follows:

Machine (n)	1	2	3	4	5	6	7	8	9	10
Age (x)	5	10	15	20	30	30	30	50	50	60
Cost (y)	190	240	250	300	310	335	300	300	350	395

We calculate the data in the normal way, using a similar tabular approach to that used above; however, notice that we have a new column in this table, y^2.

x	y	xy	x^2	y^2
5	190	950	25	36100
10	240	2400	100	57600
15	250	3750	225	62500
20	300	6000	400	90000
30	310	9300	900	96100
30	335	10050	900	112225
30	300	9000	900	90000
50	300	15000	2500	9000
50	350	17500	2500	122500
60	395	23700	3600	156025

This table gives the following output when the columns are totalled:

Σx = 300

Σy = 2970

Σxy = 97650

Σx^2 = 12050

Σy^2 = 913050

Now all we do is substitute it into the equation as before:

$$r = \frac{n.\sum xy - (\sum x)(\sum y)}{\sqrt{[n.\sum x^2 - (\sum x)^2]}\ \sqrt{[n.\sum y^2 - (\sum y)^2]}}$$

(**Note**: when a squared sign is outside of the brackets you have to square the numbers inside – i.e. $(\sum y)^2$ is the sum of all the y values squared, as opposed to y^2, which has already been calculated.)

So, substituting the values above into the equation will give you the following:

$$r = \frac{10(97650) - (300)(2070)}{\sqrt{[10(12050) - (300)^2]}\ \sqrt{[10(913050) - (2970)^2}}$$

When you work this through, you will get:

$$r = \frac{85500}{\sqrt{[30500]}\ \sqrt{[309600]}} \ = \ > r = 0.880$$

The final correlation is 0.88, which would indicate a good fit with the data. As a rule of thumb, anything above 0.75 (plus or minus) would indicate a good fit.

Having taken you through the basics of correlation and regression, we will now move on to look at some other statistical techniques that take this work as their basis.

Time series modelling

A time series looks at the movement of data of over time and attempts to find a trend within the data. This trend can then be used to predict future events. Time series is a very useful technique, and is employed regularly as part of general business practice. Time series models range from the very simplistic to the very complex. On the simple end of the scale, the models will look at extrapolating a data range (for example using multiple regression); this can be achieved by extending a line of best fit through the data. Other methods included calculating semi-averages and moving averages. These methods are relatively simple, and we will explore them briefly.

As mentioned, the basis of time series is to identify trends; the power of time series is being able to model these trends. In the basic form we can categorize these trends into two distinct types: seasonal (within a year) and cycle (yearly or greater than a year). This section will explore how to identify and calculate these types of models. These trends can also move in two ways; they are said to be either additive or multiplicative (these terms will be explained later). The more complex time series models will be multi-variate, and will combine seasonal and cycle as well as error movements, these are known as Arithmetic Integrated Moving Average (AriMA) models. This technique combines multi-variate regression analysis with time series models. However, this is too complicated for us, so we will concentrate on the more simple approaches. If you are interested in developing your skills in time series modelling you should refer to some specialist textbooks on the subject.

Techniques for finding the trend

There are three techniques for finding the trend within data:

1 *Least squares regression.* This method was introduced in the last section, and looked at ways of extending (extrapolating) a line through a series of data.
2 *Semi-averages.* This is a very simple technique which, as its name suggests, involves calculating two averages through the data and plotting a line.
3 *Moving averages.* This is the most commonly used method for identifying a trend, and involves the calculation of sets of averages.

Each method will be discussed in turn, with an example.

The method of least squares regression

This technique will only work if the data is bi-variate (two variables), i.e. something against time. Remember the rule of dependent and independent variables, therefore time will be independent (x) versus something that you want to predict (y). To develop this model, the steps are as follows:

1 Take the physical time points as values (you could code them 1, 2, 3, . . . 10 etc.); remember these will be independent (x).
2 Take the data values themselves as values of the dependent variable (y) and match them to the time points.
3 Calculate the least squares regression line of y on x, $y = a + b(x)$.
4 Translate the regression line as $t = a + b(x)$, where any given value for the time point x will give a corresponding value for t.

This process for developing t is exactly the same procedure that we carried out in the last section. The only difference is that once you have got your y on x line, you substitute in all the time values to get your trend line. In other words, you put the coded time points into the x bit of the equation.

Example

You have been asked to calculate a trend for the distribution of airline passengers against time. The airline has calculated data of 12 equal time points (x) and the number of passengers that have travelled (y). The time slots refer to quarters, i.e. 1 = year 1 quarter 1; 10 = year 3 quarter 2).

The data are shown in the following table.

x	y	xy	x^2	Trend (t)
1	2.2	2.2	1	4.11
2	5.0	10	4	4.28
3	7.9	23.7	9	4.45
4	3.2	12.8	16	4.62
5	2.9	14.5	25	4.79
6	5.2	31.2	36	4.96
7	8.2	57.4	49	5.13
8	3.8	30.4	64	5.30
9	3.2	28.8	81	5.47
10	5.8	58	100	5.64
11	9.1	100.1	121	5.81
12	4.1	49.2	144	5.98
Total				
78	60.6	418.3	650	

Putting the regression line together you will have $b = 0.17$ with $a = 3.94$. Therefore the regression line for the trend is $t = 3.94 + 0.17(x)$. The time points can now be substituted into the regression line to give the trend line. This has already been calculated in the above table; now all you have to do is to plot the trend line on a scatter diagram.

The method of semi-averages

This is a very simple method of obtaining a line and, although it is not as accurate as the least squares method, it will provide you with a quick result. It simply involves calculating two averages, which will give you two points on a graph; you then draw a line through these two points to produce your trend line. (Remember, with these two points you could work backwards and construct the equation for the line using the work on linear functions; this would then give you a more accurate predictor.)

This method will be demonstrated by using an example. Suppose you were asked to work for a gallery and to estimate the trend of customers through the exhibition based on the first 2 weeks. The following data set has been recorded:

Gallery attendance data

Days (x)	Mon	Tue	Wed	Thur	Fri	Mon	Tue	Wed	Thur	Fri
Sales (y)	250	320	340	520	410	260	380	410	670	420

You are required to obtain the semi-average trend line for this data. (Note that the data is time ordered, which is what you need for time series data. If it is not given to you in this form, then just simply order it so that it makes sense).

- *Step 1*. Split the data into two groups, an upper and a lower group. The easiest way to do this is to split it into weeks 1 and 2.
- *Step 2*. Find the mean of each group (add them up and divide by n – in this case 5).

   The mean of the lower group (L) is $1840/5 = 368$
   The mean of the upper group (U) is $2140/5 = 428$

- *Step 3*. Plot, on a graph, each mean against an appropriate time point. (Note that you could also code the time points 1 to 10 if you wanted.) An appropriate time point would be the mean of the time points that you are looking at i.e., L against Wednesday of week 1 and U against Wednesday of week 2.
- *Step 4*. Now all you do is draw a line that connects these two points. This gives a trend line through the data, and you can now read off of the points and extend the line for future predictions.

Example

Now attempt this example – the data set is from the least squares method, so you should be able to double check your calculations!

Using the method of semi-averages, calculate the trend line for this data set.

You work for a large airline company and have been asked to examine the trends in flying so that the airline can predict the impact on its operations and see if it needs to increase (or indeed decrease) capacity in any area. The following data have been obtained regarding UK outward airline passengers.

Year		1				2				3		
Quarter	1	2	3	4	1	2	3	4	1	2	3	4
No. of passengers (millions)	2.2	5.0	7.9	3.2	2.9	5.2	8.2	3.8	3.2	5.8	9.1	4.1

When you are confident with this technique, move on to the next section.

The moving average

This is the most common method of calculating a time series trend, and involves calculating a set of averages, each one corresponding to a trend (t) value for a time point of the series. These are known as moving averages, since each average is calculated by moving from one overlapping set of values to the next. The number of values in each set is always the same, and is known at the *period* of the moving average. The period is simply the time period over which the averages are obtained, and will depend on the data. For example, the following data set has been calculated for moving averages of period 5. There are a few things to notice here. First, you will not obtain a moving average for the first or last data point (this is a weakness of the technique). This is because these points are needed for the calculation of the average, which by definition will be in the middle of the data points. Have a look at the following table.

Time point	1	2	3	4	5	6	7	8	9	10
Original values	12	10	11	11	9	11	10	10	11	10
Moving totals			53	52	52	51	51	52		
Moving averages			10.6	10.4	10.4	10.2	10.2	10.4		

The first total, 53, is formed from adding the first five items (time points 1–5). That is, 12 + 10 + 11 + 11 + 9 = 53. Similarly the second total is derived from adding the next five time point values (2–6), and then time points 3–7 and so on. This process will give you the moving totals of the data points. The averages are then obtained by dividing each moving total by 5, because you are working on a 5-period average. This will give you the moving average total for the data. You can then plot this on a graph; remember time (x) against y data (predictor). A simple definition is:

> Moving averages (of period n) for the values of a time series are arithmetic means of successive and overlapping values, taken n at a time.

There are two rules for you to remember when working with moving average data:

1 The period of the moving average MUST coincide with the natural cycle of the series – e.g. if the data were in quarters then the period would be 4, if you were looking at monthly sales then the period would be 12. If a supermarket were open 7 days a week and you were looking at the trend over 2 weeks, what would be the period? The answer is 7, as you are looking at the average of the week's takings over 2 weeks. 7s will give you the average.

2 Each moving average trend must correspond with a relevant time point for the values being averaged. These can always be determined as the median of the time points of the values being averaged. For moving averages with an odd numbered period (3, 5, 7, etc.) the relevant time point is that corresponding to the second, third, fourth value etc. However, if the time points are even there is no obvious point to place the average. Therefore we have to employ another technique, which is known as *centring*, and we'll guide you on this.

Centring a moving average series

Remember, this technique only applies when calculating moving averages of data that have an even period point (i.e. 4, 6, 8 etc.); this is because the resulting moving average has to be placed in between two corresponding time points. As an example, the following data set has a 4-period moving average calculated, and shows where the calculated average should be placed.

Time point	1	2	3	4	5	6	7	8	9	10
Data values	9	14	17	12	10	14	19	15	10	16

Totals (4)		52	53	53	55	58	58	60	
Averages (4)		13	13.25	13.25	13.75	14.50	14.50	15.00	

As you can see from the data, the averages are placed between the time points – e.g. 52 is placed between 2 and 3 and so on. The placing of these averages in the mid-time points will make it very difficult for plotting trend lines. We will need to align these averages to the time points so that they can be plotted, and this is the concept of centring. This a simple process, where the calculated averages are themselves averaged in successive overlapping pairs; hence the term centred moving averages. Taking the above data set, centring the averages will give the following:

Time Point	1	2	3	4	5	6	7	8	9	10
Averages (4)			13	13.25	13.25	13.75	14.50	14.50	15.00	
Average (2)			13.125	13.250	13.5	14.125	14.50	14.750		

You can see that by averaging the mid-data points we have centred each data point against a time value – i.e. 2, 4, 5, etc. You can now easily plot this line on a graph.

Example

Now it is your turn. Try to create a centred moving average trend line using the following data set for aircraft passengers.

Year		1				2				3		
Quarter	1	2	3	4	1	2	3	4	1	2	3	4
No. of passengers (millions)	2.2	5.0	7.9	3.2	2.9	5.2	8.2	3.8	3.2	5.8	9.1	4.1

Comparison of techniques

Having completed the examples, you will see that each technique gives a slightly different result. This demonstrates that there is no unique trend for a set of data values; the trend will depend on the sophistication of the technique that you are using. Semi-averages, although very simple to apply, is probably the weakest of the techniques, due to the fact that only using two data points to plot a line can lead to ambiguity. In addition, it assumes a strictly linear function! The least squares method, whilst more sophisticated and accurate, still assumes a linear relationship – i.e. it will ignore any seasonality within the data set. Finally, the method of moving averages is the most widely used technique for obtaining a trend line. If the period of the averages is chosen appropriately it will show the true nature of the trend, whether linear or non-linear. The disadvantage of this technique is that there are no beginning and end values obtained for the trend cycle.

Seasonal variation and forecasting techniques

This concept is the basis of time series modelling. Seasonal (or short-term cyclical) variations are present in many time series. For example, you could be looking at trends in fashion, sportswear, buying behaviour, price movements, consumer numbers, sales figures etc.

Seasonal values or factors are generally expressed as deviations, i.e. plus or minus from the underlying trend – for example, inflation has risen by 1 per cent above the trend, or oil prices have fallen 5 per cent below the trend, etc. We can therefore define seasonal as:

> A seasonal variation gives an average effect on the trend that is solely attributable to the 'season' itself. They are expressed in terms of deviations from the trend.

Having established the need for this type of work, let's go onto examine how we can calculate the seasonal variation component.

Techniques for calculating seasonal variation

Remember, we started with $y = a + b(x)$ for our straight line. We then refined it to read $t = a + b(x)$ in order to give us a trend line. We will now need to add a few more components to give us the seasonal variation. The new model will take the form:

$$y = t + s + r$$

where t is the trend, s is the seasonal variation and r is the residual or error (the bit we can't explain). In the more complex models the residual factor is also modelled; this is something we will not worry about! Here is how you calculate the seasonal variation:

- *Step 1.* Calculate, for each time point, the value of $y - t$ (i.e. difference between the value and the trend – note, this could be plus or minus).
- *Step 2.* For each season in turn, find the average of all the $y - t$ values.
- *Step 3.* If the total of the averages differs from zero, adjust one or more of them so that their total is zero (you'll see how to do this in the example, although it is generally a matter of common sense).

Example

Let's work through an example so that you can see step-by-step what you have to do. Assume that you have been given a set of production figures and are trying to see the trend in seasonal variations. The following data set has been collected.

Step 1: Calculate $y - t$, i.e. the trend differential. Do this and put it in a row below.

Year		1				2		
Quarter (x)		1	2	3	4	1	2	3	4
Production output (y) (000s)		20	15	60	30	35	25	100	50
Trend (t)		23	29	34	39	45	50	55	61
Deviations ($y - t$)		–3	–14	26	–9	–10	–25	45	–11

Step 2: for each season in turn you now need to calculate the $(y - t)$ averages.

Quarter	1	2	3	4
Year 1	–3	–14	26	–9
Year 2	–10	–25	45	–11
Totals	–13	–39	71	–20
Averages	–6.5	–19.5	35.5	–10.0

Step 3: you now need to sum the averages and see if they add up to zero. In this case they do not. They come to –0.5, and therefore we will need to add on an extra 0.5 to one of the values. In order to minimize the amount of error, add 0.5 on to the largest value (which will give proportionately the smallest change). Therefore readjust 35.5 to read 36, so that they now sum to zero. This will give us the following amended table.

| Averages | –6.5 | –19.5 | 36.0 | –10.0 |

The interpretation of the figures is that the average seasonal effect for quarter 1, for instance, is to deflate the trend by 6.5 (000s) units, and that for quarter 3 it is to inflate the trend by 36 (000s) units.

Seasonally adjusted time series

Once we have these data we can use them to adjust the actual trend itself, in the light of seasonal variations. This is achieved by subtracting the appropriate seasonal figure from each of the original time series values. This can be shown in the model $y - s$. The effect of this operation will be to smooth away seasonal fluctuation, leaving a clear view of what might be expected had seasons not existed. This effect is shown in the following data table.

Year		1				2			
Quarter (x)		1	2	3	4	1	2	3	4
Production output (y) (000s)		20	15	60	30	35	25	100	50
Season (s)		–6.5	–19.5	36	–10	–6.5	–19.5	36	–10
Adjusted ($y - s$)		26.5	34.5	24	40	41.5	44.5	64	60

Now we can see the trend without the seasonal component. It is common practice to adjust trends seasonally. You will often read in the newspaper or see on the TV examples of this technique, such as inflation referred to as actual and seasonally adjusted.

Seasonally adjusted time series values are obtained by subtracting the appropriate seasonal variations from each of the original time series values $(y - s)$.

Example

Now it's time for you to attempt a problem! Use the data regarding UK outward airline passengers given below, find the seasonal variations, and then plot the time series on a graph and adjust for any seasonal variance. Plot the new seasonally adjust trend line and comment on the differences.

Year		1				2				3		
Quarter	1	2	3	4	1	2	3	4	1	2	3	4
No. of passengers (millions)	2.2	5.0	7.9	3.2	2.9	5.2	8.2	3.8	3.2	5.8	9.1	4.1

TECHNIQUES FOR FORECASTING

One of the main uses of time series is to develop forecasts from the data series, and this is sometimes referred to as 'projecting the series'. This projection of the series is, however, only as good as the historical data on which it is based, and also on the accuracy and complexity of the model that has been created – no one can predict the future, but we can (under certain assumptions) make a guess regarding what might happen based on past events.

Forecasting models can be generalized into two approaches; additive and multiplicative. We will concentrate on the simpler of the two, the additive model, which is given by the following:

Time series forecasting can be attempted using the simple additive model:

$$y_{est} = t_{est} + s$$

where:
y_{est} = Estimated data value
t_{est} = Estimated (projected) trend value
s = Appropriate seasonal variation value.

This model does not make a provision for residual 'r', because residual values are assumed to average out at zero.

In order to see how this works, let's try an example.

Example

Forecast the values for the four quarters of year 4, given the following information calculated from a time series. Assume that the trend in year 4 will follow the same pattern as in years 1 to 3.

Year	1				2				3			
Quarter (x)	1	2	3	4	1	2	3	4	1	2	3	4
Trend (t)	42	44	46	48	50	52	54	56	58	60	62	64

S1 = seasonal factors for quarter 1 = –15; S2 = –8; S3 = +6; S4 = +17.

- *Step 1.* Estimate trend values for the relevant time points. Trend for year 4, Q1 = t4,1 = 66 Similarly, t4, Q2 = 68, t4, Q3 = 70 and t4, Q4 = 72.
- *Step 2.* Identify the appropriate seasonal factors. The seasonal factors for year 4 are taken as the given seasonal factors – that is, seasonal factor for year 4, Q1 = S1 = –15 etc.
- *Step 3.* Add the trend estimates for the seasonal factors, giving the required forecasts.

Forecast for year 4, Q1 = t4,1 + S1 = 66 – 15 = 51;
Forecast for year 4, Q2 = t4,2 + S2 = 68 – 8 = 60;
Forecast for year 4, Q3 = t4,3 + S3 = 70 + 6 = 76;
Forecast for year 4, Q4 = t4,4 + S4 = 72 + 17 = 89.

Forecasting the trend line is relatively straightforward given a linear trend; if linearity does not exist, you could use a moving averages trend line to extend the series.

INDEX NUMBERS

Index numbers are constantly used by a variety of people in organizations to make decisions. These numbers allow us to make comparisons of trends over a period of time. They convert series of numbers to linear scales, which can be extremely useful in helping us to make quick and accurate comparisons of data sets.

Definition of an index number

An index number measures the percentage change in the value of something (for example, an economic commodity such as oil or sugar etc.) *over a period of time.* It is always expressed in terms of base 100.

Examples of index numbers

In order to understand index numbers, let's work through a few simple examples. First, we will look at a price increase index. Suppose that the price of a standard box of ballpoint pens was 60p in January and rose to 63p in April. What is the percentage increase?

You would calculate this by taking the second number (N2) and subtracting the first number (N1); then divide by N1 and multiply by 100 to give you a percentage.

The equation to give percentage change is:

$$\left(\frac{N2 - N1}{N1}\right) * \frac{100}{1} = X\%$$

In other words, the price of ballpoint pens rose by 5 per cent from January to April. To put this into an index number form, the 5 per cent increase is added to the base of 100, giving 105. This is then described as follows:

The price index of ballpoint pens in April was 105 (January + 100)

which:

- Gives the starting point (January) over which the increase in price is being measured.
- Emphasizes the basis value (100) of the index starting point.

Having seen that this is quite an easy process, let's look at an example of a decreasing index. If the productivity of a firm (measured in units of production per man day) decreased by 3 per cent over the period 1998–2000, how would this be shown using the index number method?

First, take the percentage decrease of 3 per cent (which has already been calculated for you) and then subtract this from the base index 100 (i.e. 100 – 3); this will give you an index number of 97. If you were asked to describe this index shift, you would say:

The productivity index for the company in 2000 was 97 (1998 = 100).

Again, this statement gives the year of the index plus the base year. The base year is the year in which the index started, or the year from which conversions are currently being made. This is because sometimes indexes are re-indexed to a new base year, especially when there has been a massive movement in the index itself.

Notation

In order to be able to describe some of the more complicated index processes it is necessary to use some 'shorthand', and this is referred to as notation. It is convenient, particularly when giving formulae for certain types of index numbers, to be able to refer to an economic commodity at some general time point. Price and quantities (since they are commonly quoted indices) have their own special letters, p and q respectively. In order to bring in time, the following standard convention is used:

$P0$ = Price at base time point
Pn = Price at some other time point
$Q0$ = Quantity at base time point
Qn = Quantity at some other time point.

Using the ballpoint pen example, the time period '0' was January, and the time period 'n' was April; $P0 = 60$ and $Pn = 63$. It is just a matter of substituting the words for letters.

Index relatives

As well as index numbers, there are also index relatives. These are sometimes just called 'relatives', and this is the name given to an index number that measures the change in a simple distinct commodity. A *price* relative was calculated in the ballpoint pen example, and a *productivity* relative was calculated in the second example. There is, however, a more direct way of calculating relatives, and this is given by the following formulae.

Price relative index. You should use this formula to calculate the relative *price* movement of an index from its base starting point:

$$1 = \frac{Pn}{P0}$$

Quantity relative index. You should use this formula to calculate the relative *quantity* movement of an index from its base starting point:

$$1 = \frac{Qn}{Q0}$$

Time series of relatives

It is often necessary to see how the values of an index relative change over time. Given the values of some commodity over time (i.e. a time series), there are two distinct ways in which relatives can be calculated: fixed- and chain-based relatives.

Fixed-based relatives

Here, each relative is calculated based on the *same fixed* time point. This approach can only be used when the basic nature of the commodity is unchanged over the whole period. Fixed based relatives are used for comparing 'like with like'.

Chain-based relatives

In this case, each relative is calculated with respect to the immediately preceding time point. This approach can be used with any set of commodity values, but must be used with the basic nature of the commodity changes over the whole time period.

OPERATIONAL RESEARCH TECHNIQUES

Assignment modelling

The use of assignment modelling is widespread within, business. Although it is often performed using computer software, it is also very easy and quick to do manually. Assignment modelling has its routes in linear programming, and it therefore has the aim of finding 'optimal solutions' to problems that either *maximize* or *minimize*. Assignment models generally focus on minimizing cost or, to put it another way, maximizing value. They can come in all shapes and sizes, and there are some exercises later in the book for you to practise. The trick with learning this technique is simply to be methodical. You do not need to have an advanced understanding of mathematics, but you do need to follow the method.

Matrix 1

Men/jobs	M1	M2	M3	M4
J1	8	7	9	9
J2	5	2	7	8
J3	6	1	4	9
J4	2	3	2	6

Now simply follow this methodology:

Step 1: In the first row of numbers, find the *smallest* number in the row, and write it at the right of the row; repeat this for all the other rows. Matrix 1 should now look like this:

Men/jobs	M1	M2	M3	M4	Smallest No
J1	8	7	9	9	7
J2	5	2	7	8	2
J3	6	1	4	9	1
J4	2	3	2	6	2

Step 2: Make a new matrix from Matrix 1 and call it Matrix 2. Create the new matrix by subtracting the row minimum (i.e. 7 for row 1) from each number in that row. You should then do the same row for row. So, in row number 2, you will subtract the number 2 from everything, for row 3 it will be the number 1, and for row four it will be? (Yes, that's correct; 2 from everything).

This will give you Matrix 2, which will look like this.

Matrix 2

Men/jobs	M1	M2	M3	M4
J1	(8 − 7) 1	(7 − 7) 0	2	2
J2	3	0	(7 − 2) 5	6
J3	5	0	3	8
J4	0	1	0	(6 − 2) 4

Step 3: Find whether the matrix will give a complete basis for making the optimum assignment of men to jobs by first picking out a pattern of zeros in Matrix 2 in such as way that *no row or column (in the pattern) contains more than ONE zero.* In order to help you, identify this pattern by putting a square around or highlighting each zero selected. In many cases, including this one, there is more than one pattern of 'squared' zeros. Any one of these patterns is acceptable for this step. In this particular case, the pattern of zeros is easily found by a case of trial and error. Here is an example of trying to find the pattern:

Men/jobs	M1	M2	M3	M4
J1	1	*0*	2	2
J2	3	X	5	6
J3	5	X	3	8
J4	*0*	1	X	4

(**Note**: J4 row has two zeros, so just choose one – in this case, M1.)

Step 4: Starting with the matrix constructed in Step 3 (Matrix 2), examine each row until one is found that only has *one* zero. Make a square or highlight that zero. If there are any other zeros in the same column, put an X through them. Then repeat this process until every row has just one zero highlighted.

Step 5: Now examine the columns until one is found that has only one unmarked zero. Make a square or highlight it, and put an X through any other zeros in the same row. Repeat until all the columns have been examined. In this example, the first column is the only one with just one zero in it (M3 has been crossed out!). If the result of Step 3 is a pattern of zeros with exactly one highlighted zero in every row and column, then the matrix is an optimal solution. In this particular case, Matrix 2 is not optimal. If it were optimal, you could skip steps 5 to 10.

Step 6: In Matrix 2, write the smallest number in each column *under* the column (note that a minimum number can be a zero as well as any other number).

Men/jobs	M1	M2	M3	M4
J1	1	0	2	2
J2	3	X	5	6
J3	5	X	3	8
J4	0	1	X	4
Smallest no.	0	0	0	2

Step 7: Perform the same operations on the columns that you performed on the rows in Step 2. This will form a new Matrix 3. Check Matrix 3 for the same rule: there is at least one zero in each column, which is as it should be!

Matrix 3

Men/jobs	M1	M2	M3	M4
J1	(1 – 0) 1	0	2	(2 – 2) 0
J2	3	X	5	(6 – 2) 4
J3	5	X	3	6
J4	0	1	X	2

Step 8: Repeat Steps 3 to 7 to see if Matrix 3 is optimal; here it is not!

Step 9: Now put a tick against each *row* that *has no* highlighted zero in it – in this case, row 3. Now do the same process for the *column* that *has* a zero in a ticked row. The matrix should now look like this:

Men/jobs	M1	M2	M3	M4	
J1	(1 – 0) 1	0	2	(2 – 2) 0	
J2	3	X	5	(6 – 2) 4	X
J3	5	X	3	6	X
J4	0	1	X	2	
		X			

Step 10: Make a tick mark at the right of each row that has a highlighted zero in a ticked column.

Step 11: Draw line through all *un*-ticked rows and all *ticked* columns (**tip:** the number of lines should be the same as the number of highlighted zeros).

Men/jobs	M1	M2	M3	M4
~~J1~~	~~(1 – 0) 1~~	~~0~~	2	~~(2 – 2) 0~~
J2	3	X	5	(6 – 2) 4
J3	5	X	3	6
~~J4~~	~~0~~	~~1~~	X	~~2~~

Step 12: Start to form a new Matrix 4. If a number in the previous matrix has only *one* line through it, copy it onto the same position in Matrix 4. Repeat every number in Matrix 3 that has just one line through it.

Step 13: Find the smallest number in Matrix 3 with no line through it (in our example, this is the number 3).

Step 14: For each number in Matrix 3 with no line through it, subtract 3 (the number derived from Step 13) from it. Enter the result in the same position in Matrix 4.

Step 15: To each number in Matrix 3 that is at the intersection of two lines, add 3 (the number derived from Step 13). Enter the result in the same position in Matrix 4.
    This will give Matrix 4.

Matrix 4

Men/jobs	M1	M2	M3	M4
J1	1	(0 + 3) 3	2	0
J2	(3 – 3) 0	0	2	1
J3	(5 – 3) 2	0	0	3
J4	3	(1 + 3) 4	0	2

Now we need to apply the test from Step 3 to Matrix 4: no row or column (in the pattern) contains more than *one* zero.

Men/jobs	M1	M2	M3	M4
J1	1	3	2	*0*
J2	*0*	*0*	2	1
J3	2	*0*	*0*	3
J4	3	4	*0*	2

Step 16: Go back to Matrix 1. The squared numbers in Matrix 4 show which ones to pull out of Matrix 1. Put these numbers into a new Matrix 5 by themselves. This new Matrix 5 indicates that one optimal solution for the problem is to assign job 1 to man 4; job 2 to man 2; job 3 to man 2 and job 4 to man 3. The number in Matrix 5 shows the cost per unit for each assignment indicated. The sum of these numbers (£17) is the minimum total cost. This sum will be the same for any of the optimal solutions, if there is more than one – i.e. 9 + 5 + 1 + 2 = £17 per hour.

Matrix 5

Men/jobs	M1	M2	M3	M4
J1	–	–	–	9
J2	5	–	–	–
J3	–	1	–	–
J4	–	–	2	–

SUMMARY

This chapter has introduced you to a range of processes for analysing manufacturing operations. Care must be taken to ensure that data are valid and that the right technique is used. Some of these techniques can also be used in service operations. However, there are additional techniques that are better suited to service operations, and these are provided in the following chapter.

Key terms

Assignment modelling
Bi-variate formula
Correlation analysis
Index numbers
Linear functions
Regression
Time series analysis

S2

Analysing service operations: service delivery, queuing and shift scheduling

INTRODUCTION

Chapter S1 guided you through the analysis of a manufacturing operation. In this chapter, we will apply a similar approach to analysing some common situations that occur in service operations. A typical case, the Tampopo Noodle Bar, is presented for you to analyse, using a step-by-step model to analyse the service management system, the service delivery system and the queuing system.

Aims and objectives

This chapter will provide you with experience in analysing service operations in a structured fashion, and provide practice with some commonly used tools and techniques.

After reading this chapter you will be able to:

- Use Normann's model to analyse the elements of an organization's service management system
- Blueprint the service delivery system and identify actual or potential failure points
- Apply mathematical techniques for analysing queuing, shift scheduling, and Monte Carlo simulation.

405

Case study

The Tampopo Noodle Bar

In the Japanese movie *Tampopo*, a lighthearted ode to the joys of food and dining out, truck driver Goro searches for the perfect noodle restaurant. Goro searches unsuccessfully until he meets Tampopo. A sweet young widow but a hopeless cook, she can't attract customers to the restaurant left her by her late husband. With Goro's help, Tampopo researches the perfect noodle, and sets up the perfect noodle restaurant.

Ramen shops have been popular in Japan for over 200 years, providing food that is simple, cheap and fresh tasting. Noodles have an extended history in Japan, and even today they are probably the most consumed food in the country. Near the beginning of *Tampopo*, a noodle master explains the correct ritual for eating a bowl of noodle soup. He explains every ingredient: how to cut it, how to cook it, how to address it, how to think of it, how to regard it, how to approach it, how to smell it, how to eat it, how to thank it, how to remember it.

The four common types of noodles are:

1 *Ramen* – thin Chinese-style thread noodles
2 *Udon* – whitish, much thicker wheat noodles, generally served in a soup base or added to *nabe* dishes
3 *Sobu* – thin, tan, buckwheat noodles (similar in colour and texture to wholewheat pasta)
4 *Hiyamugi* and *somen* – very thin noodles, usually eaten cold and argued by their adherents to be vastly superior to the rest.

The first three types are eaten as a kind of fast food – even the noodles served in hot soup are usually *al dente*, and devoured quickly before they can go limp in the broth. Typical ingredients besides noodles include Japanese soup stock, pork, beef, chicken, fish, shellfish, vegetables and various sauces. *Yaki-soba* are fried soba noodles and vegetables, *yaki-udon* are thick fried noodles and vegetables.

The noodle bar concept

The Japanese obsession with noodles has now spread to the West, where noodle bars have successfully capitalized on a growing

Western taste for Japanese noodles served in soups, with various toppings, or pan-fried.

The opening of the first Wagamama noodle bar in London revolutionized oriental dining in the UK. Wagamama reinvented the Japanese noodle bar for Londoners, who have queued time and time again over the last few years. The first Wagamama was located in an obscure alley in Bloomsbury, near the British Museum, but Wagamama has since expanded to higher-profile sites in London (including Selfridges and Harvey Nichols), Manchester, Dublin and Amsterdam.

The rise of noodle bars shows that Asian food isn't just about stir-fries and *dim sum.* These restaurants draw their inspiration from the simple everyday diet of Japan or Northern China, which is dominated by rice, dumpling and noodle dishes, rather than the familiar dishes offered by Chinese restaurants and takeaways. These new-style noodle bars may not provide gastronomic thrills, but are fine for an everyday lunch that feels healthy (MSG and artificial additives are banished from the dishes). They are inexpensive, and don't leave you comatose all afternoon. They also provide a grown-up way to eat Pot Noodles!

What makes noodle bars a vastly preferable alternative to other 'fast-food' joints is the simplicity of their design. With a 100-g helping costing less than 50p, noodles offer a low cost per serving and give a wide range of 'big-bowl' presentations that are visually impressive and carry a high perceived value. Noodles are quicker to cook than pasta, suiting high-throughput dining service, and are widely perceived as good-value, fun food.

DESIGNING AND ANALYSING SERVICE SYSTEMS

Suppose that you have been hired as a consultant by a recent lottery winner who is considering investing his winnings in setting up a local Japanese noodle bar. Your job is to analyse the operations of Wagamama and its closest competitors, and to see if the noodle bar concept could be successfully replicated in your local area. After visiting the restaurant and its competitors, and doing research over the Internet, you have gathered a lot of data on Japanese restaurants.

Your first step has been to check out the competition. With the aid of a *Time Out* guide to London restaurants, a visit to London's Japanese shopping mall Yaohan Plaza and its Japanese supermarket, and lots of back issues of *Caterer and Hotelkeeper* magazine, you have identified the main competitors: Wagamama, Wok-Wok, and Yo! Sushi.

Competitive analysis summary

Wagamama

Wagamama's philosophy is 'to serve great, fresh and nutritious food in an elegant, yet simple environment, and to provide helpful, friendly service and value for money'. According to the company's web site, Wagamama means 'wilfulness or selfishness: selfishness in terms of looking after oneself, looking after oneself in terms of positive eating and positive living'. The restaurant's slogan is 'positive eating', which is 'consciously feeding the body the nourishment it needs to build and maintain a peak physiological state, selecting foods that cleanse and nurture; controlled, balanced consumption'.

The menu specifically points out that 'destinational eating' is not part of Wagamama's policy – a policy supported by the décor, which is a brightly lit, minimalist's dream.

Because of Wagamama's popularity, only those customers who arrive when the restaurant opens don't have to queue for a seat. As the evening progresses, a queue of people stretches along the stairs or corridor just inside the exit. The no-booking policy means that couples are usually seated quickly, but it is difficult to find space for larger groups. Customers queuing to be seated are offered a fascinating view of the food being prepared in a high-tech open kitchen (where dozens of cooks are preparing noodle dishes of all kinds), and the bustling dining area (where the wait staff are constantly busy inside taking customer orders). In the kitchen, a courtesy cloak check is provided, as there is no room for hats and coats downstairs.

Customers enter the huge dining area, where they are seated refectory style, at long rows of tables with bench-style seating. As soon as diners are seated they're handed menus, which describe not only the food and drinks on offer, but also Wagamama's philosophy of balanced eating and healthy living. The menu extols a world view: 'positive meal suggestions for positive value'; 'to cleanse and nurture – the excellent natural synergy of nutrients'; 'helps to cleanse the body of toxins'. Both freshly-squeezed juices and Chinese tea are on offer to support this, but beer and wine are available for the hungry hedonist. If this all seems a bit too serious, then the menu's advice is less so: 'the way of the noodle is to make slurping noises while eating – the extra oxygen adds to the taste!'.

Once customers have made their choice, waiting staff take the order and punch it into hand-held, electronic order pads, which then transmit the order to the appropriate station in the kitchen. (Customers too shy to attempt the Japanese pronunciation can order by number.) To make sure that each customer receives the right order, the wait staff also write the numbers of each dish directly onto each person's paper mat. Each dish is cooked to order and then served immediately, so even though main courses, side orders and drinks are ordered together, each is delivered to the table as soon as it has been prepared. Service is furiously paced – Wagamama is no place to linger! – but customers aren't overly pressured to finish up and leave.

Wagamama offers a variety of drinks, noodle dishes (superb bowls of *ramen*, *soba* and *udon*) and specialty meals such as *yakitori* (grilled skewers of chicken), *teriyaki*, and tempura-based dishes. Most dishes cost just over £5, with many of the side dishes considerably less. The minimal decor is not reflected in the generosity of the food – most people have trouble finishing one of the giant bowls of soup or generous helpings of pan-fried noodles. A surprise hit is the *edamame*, lightly salted fresh green soya beans which you pop from their pods, a side dish which is incredibly addictive – the Japanese equivalent of crisps or popcorn. Each restaurant serves more than 125 kg of noodles daily to over 1000 customers.

Wok-Wok

Like Wagamama, at Wok Wok the ambience is minimalist and comfortable. Wok-Wok is bright and attractive, with simple wooden tables and large windows looking out on to the main road. Frosted glass and gleaming metal are offset by earthy tones and textures to create a warm, inviting and stylish atmosphere. Central to the Wok Wok concept are the restaurants' open kitchens, which create a focal point.

Wok-Wok is laid out and operated much like any other restaurant. Waiting staff are young and funky. Customers defy categorization: family groups with small children, lone diners, twenty- and thirty-somethings and smartly dressed middle-aged couples. Dining can be inexpensive, quick and functional, or you can hang around for a chat.

Brand Director Tania Webb developed the Wok-Wok concept based on a childhood spent in South East Asia and time spent as a restaurateur in Hong Kong, both of which are reflected in Wok-Wok's eclectic menu. Wok-Wok offers a choice of noodle- or rice-based dishes with Chinese,

409

Japanese, Korean and Thai influences, the independent but complementary cuisines of South East Asia. Wok-Wok offers soup noodles and pan-fried noodles as well as rice dishes. Using only the freshest ingredients, which are prepared and cooked to order in the restaurant, the style of food is simple, healthy and bursting with natural flavours.

Yo! Sushi

Not surprisingly, Yo! Sushi concentrates on sushi. The flagship Yo! Sushi opened in Soho in January 1998, featuring the world's longest sushi conveyor belt. Founder (and rock-concert promoter) Simon Woodroffe borrowed the idea of a self-service, conveyor-belt sushi bar (known in Japan as *kaiten*) and situated it in a groovy, upbeat, hi-tech environment combining the modern world of high tech robotics and animated theatre. At Yo! Sushi, customers sit around a long U-shaped counter bar. Colour-coded plates travel around the conveyor belt, each with two pieces of sushi, with a different price assigned to each of the five colours.

Drinks, including cold Japanese beers, hot and cold sake, wine and sodas, are provided by talking robot trolleys that make their way around the restaurant, avoiding collision by the use of highly tuned sensors, and talking to the customers when they get in their way! Still and fizzy mineral water are available in unlimited quantities from pumps at each seating unit for a one-off price of £1.

At the end of the meal, staff add up the value of the plates and glasses to determine the price of the meal. Help is always available from the restaurant staff, who can be called by use of help buttons at every seating station.

There is also a list with specials behind the counter, where you can order from the chefs. Diners enjoy both gourmet and vegetarian sushi while watching sushi being made in the raw, plus live footage from Japan on Sony widescreen televisions – giant TV screens show sumo wrestling matches; and the funky music of Prince comes thumping out of loudspeakers. If you like the food (or just the concept), you can get Yo! Sushi clothing and even Yo! Sushi delivery scooters!

The Service management system

Your employer has visited Wagamama, and was impressed by the speed and throughput of the restaurant. However, he feels that the refectory-style seating and industrial feel of Wagamama is starting to get a bit dated, and has asked you to take a look at alternate ways of setting up and running the restaurant, based on the ones that you have visited. Your first task is to recommend either Wagamama's service delivery system or an entirely new one for the new restaurant chain.

A first step that you might take in analysing a service operation is to analyse the organization's service management system using the model developed by Professor Richard Normann (1991). This model ties together five important aspects of the service management system, as shown in Figure S2.1. These five aspects – culture and philosophy, market segment, service image, service concept and service delivery system – are described further below.

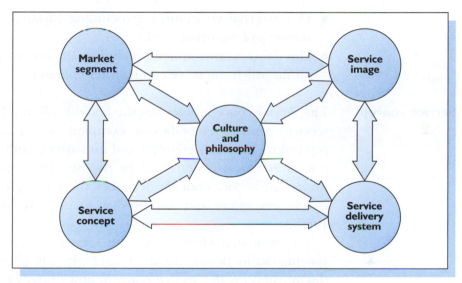

Figure S2.1 The service management system (based on Normann, 1991).

Culture and philosophy

The organization's culture and philosophy are central to the service management system. This describes the overall values and principles guiding the organization, including values about human dignity and worth. It has also been called the organization's service vision.

Market segment

The market segment describes the particular types of clients for whom the service management system was designed. Some different ways of deciding on a market segment are:

- Customer-orientation – a wide range of services to a limited range of customers, using a customer-centred database and developing new offerings to existing customers (e.g. Rentokil)

- Service-orientation – a focused, 'limited menu' of services to a wide range of customers, usually through specialization in a narrow range of services (e.g. Kwik-Fit, Supasnaps)
- Customer- and service-orientation – providing a limited range of services to a highly targeted set of customers (e.g. McDonald's).

Service image

The service image is an information system for influencing clients and customers. An important part of the service image is the physical environment in which the service is produced, because customers are physically present during the production of a service as well as its consumption. The physical environment comprises:

- The external environment, including location, premises, ease of access, and ambiance
- The internal environment, including the atmosphere and structure within which the service personnel operate.

Service concept

The service concept describes the benefits offered by the service. The service concept embodies a complex set of values – physical, psychological and emotional – and thus affects both what the company does and how it is perceived by its customers and clients. In other words, the service concept describes the way the organization would like its employees and stakeholders to perceive its service (Heskett, 1986).

The structural elements of the service concept are the delivery system, facility design, location, and capacity planning. The service design supports the service concept and strategy to provide a service with features that differentiate it from the competition. Major considerations in the design process are:

- Degree of complexity and degree of divergence
- Identifying customer requirements
- Designing supporting facilities and facilitating goods
- Queuing.

The managerial elements of the service concept are the service encounter, quality, managing capacity and demand, and information.

The service delivery system

The service delivery system is the way in which the service concept and service package are provided to the consumer. It is the process in which consumers participate and through which the product is created and delivered to customers, including personnel, clients, technology and physical support. The service delivery system is dictated by and defined by the service concept. Some of the key aspects you might want to consider are the core service, the supporting goods and services, the facilitating goods and services, the role of staff, and the entertainment provided.

The *service package* is the embodiment of the service concept, and includes both the physical and tangible elements of the service offering and its intellectual/intangible elements. The total service package – the bundle of goods and services (Sasser *et al.*, 1978) – includes:

- Physical items – the physical goods that are changing hands, if any (often called facilitating goods in services)
- Sensual benefits – aspects that can be experienced through the sensory system (explicit intangibles)
- Psychological benefits – emotional or other aspects (implicit intangibles).

Task 1: Analyse the service management system

Using Normann's model as described in this section, analyse the three service management systems described above. You might find it helpful to use a grid similar to the one below to organize your analysis, or to fill in your thoughts about each element on a chart like Figure S2.1.

Service element	Traditional restaurant	Wagamama
Culture and philosophy		
Market segment		
Service image		
Service concept		
Service delivery system		

Once you have identified the five service management system elements, a good question to ask is whether the different elements fit together.

Service blueprinting

Your employer is pleased with the quality of your first consulting report, and decides that he will go ahead with the investigation into starting up his own noodle bar. As part of your report, your employer has asked you to prepare a service blueprint for the Tampopo Noodle Bar, based on your first consulting report.

Service blueprinting, developed by G. Lynn Shostack (1984), is a useful way of mapping the service process. A service blueprint can identify all the points where a customer is in contact with the service provider or the organization, and thus those points where things are likely to go wrong. A service blueprint can also be used to identify areas for process improvement. Finally, it can be a useful tool for organizations who want to replicate their service, since it identifies the critical resources and processes in use.

To draw a service blueprint, it is useful to begin by drawing a flowchart for how a customer interacts with the service operation. Three elements included in a service blueprint that make it different from the flow charts commonly used in manufacturing are:

1 Line of visibility
2 Line of internal interaction
3 Failure points.

The example shown in Figure S2.2 develops a service blueprint for a generic restaurant. After you have been through the example, you might find it useful to develop a service blueprint for the service management systems and service delivery system that you developed as Task 1.

Step 1. Identify the main processes that a customer goes through, from his or her initial contact with the restaurant until he or she leaves the restaurant. Figure S2.2 shows the most important steps in this process, although each step could be broken down into more detail.

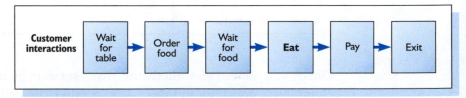

Figure S2.2 Customer interactions with the service system.

Step 2. Identify the interactions between the customer and the front-line staff in the restaurant – the activities that go on within the line of visibility. This identifies the interactions between the customer and the front-office staff, as shown in Figure S2.3.

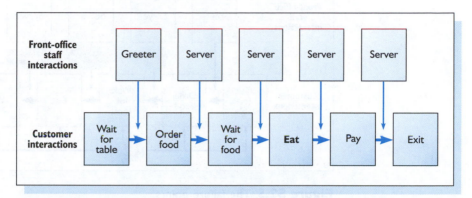

Figure S2.3 Customer interactions with front-line staff.

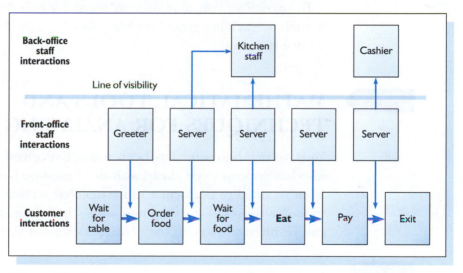

Figure S2.4 Interaction between front-office and back-office staff.

Step 3. Identify the interactions between the front-line staff and other staff that work beyond the line of visibility (Figure S2.4).

Step 4. Identify the failure points in the system, and wherever possible redesign the service system to minimize or eliminate the causes of failures (Figure S2.5).

415

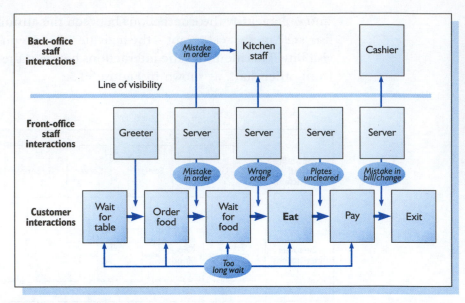

Figure S2.5 The failure points.

In particular, you may wish to focus on how Wagamama and Yo! Sushi have each integrated service *pokayokes*, fail-safe devices, into their service systems.

MATHEMATICAL TOOLS AND TECHNIQUES FOR ANALYSING SERVICES

Your service blueprint has been warmly received by your employer, who has decided to go ahead with the Tampopo Noodle Bar. You have been retained to perform a more detailed service design, specifically to look at issues of queuing and shift scheduling, so that an architect can be hired to start on the physical design of the noodle bar.

Queuing

The importance of analysing queuing systems

Authentic noodle bars don't take reservations, so customers must queue once the available seats have been filled. Although customers often find slow service or long waiting times a reason to complain, organizations want to trade off customer queuing time against the cost of providing additional resources. Customers would like never to wait, and organizations would like facilities and personnel to be utilized 100 per cent of the time.

This section will help you answer the following questions:

1 How should the Clifton Noodle Bar organize its queuing system to maximize efficiency?
2 What is the best priority system to use for allocating customers to tables?
3 What effect does increasing the speed with which customers are serviced have on queues?

Mathematically analysing queuing

The five essential features of queuing systems are the calling population, the arrival process, the queue configuration, the queue discipline and the service process. Any queuing system can be represented using these five elements, as shown in Figure S2.6.

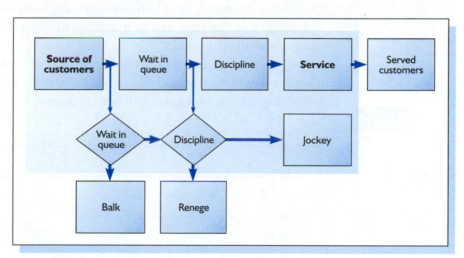

Figure S2.6 A basic model of a service system with queuing.

Let's examine these in more detail.

Calling population

This is the *source of customers*, which consists of the potential customers for the service. This population may be finite or infinite. A finite calling population consists of a countable number of customers, such as a company's mobile phone customers – normally only Orange's customers will call the Orange call centre, only Vodaphone customers will call its centre, etc. An infinite calling population, on the other hand, consists of an uncountable number of customers, such as the number of people who might drop into a news stand on the high street. Generally, finite and infinite calling populations can be treated similarly, unless a finite population consists of only a few people, where the behaviour of one person can conceivably affect the others.

The calling population may also be homogenous or heterogeneous. A homogenous customer set consists of customers with the same requirements; a heterogeneous customer set consists of customers who have different requirements.

Arrival process

This is how customers arrive at the service in time and space, and can be described as a probability distribution of either the number of arrivals per unit of time or the time between successive arrivals. The time between customer arrivals (inter-arrival time) generally follows an exponential distribution (Figure S2.7). The exponential distribution is characterized by most observations falling near the origin, and a long tail of decreasing numbers of observations at higher inter-arrival times. If we know the mean time between arrivals, then we can compute the probability that the time between arrivals will be time t or less using the exponential distribution.

The number of customer arrivals per unit of time can be described using a related distribution, the Poisson distribution, which gives the probability that n customers will arrive during time period t.

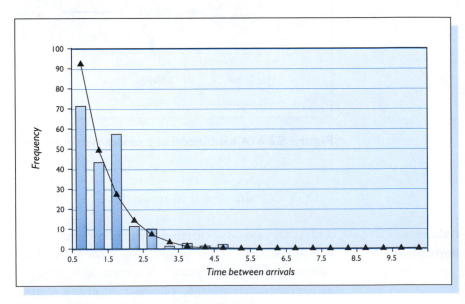

Figure S2.7 The exponential distribution.

Both the exponential distribution and the Poisson distribution are discrete distributions; that is, the probabilities are calculated for a specific inter-arrival time or number of arrivals rather than being continuous.

Queue configuration

This describes how many queues there are, how they are arranged, and how customers behave in them.

A service system can be designed to have either a single or multiple queues, as shown in Figure S2.8. If there are multiple servers, a service can have either one (single) or many (multiple) queues feeding these servers. On the other hand, services such as supermarkets may use single queues, but create special queues for customers with only a few items, paying cash and so on.

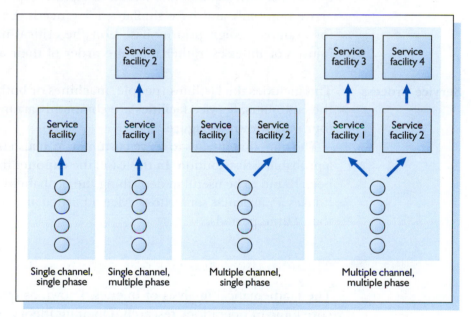

Figure S2.8 Different possible queuing arrangements.

As mentioned in Chapter 7, queues are not always physical lines, but we can think of these situations in the same way.

Another characteristic of interest is customer behavioural tendencies. A patient customer is one who enters the system and remains there until served. This is characteristic of queues where service is mandatory or important. Customers may also be impatient, which leads them to behave in one or more of the following ways:

- Balking – customers may refuse to join a queue if it looks as though they will have to wait too long before being served

- Reneging – customers may join the queue, but get tired of queuing and leave before they are served
- Jockeying – customers may switch between queues if there are multiple queues moving at different speeds.

Queues can also be affected by size constraints. If the physical space for the queue is large enough to hold all customers desiring service, then the queue can be described as an *infinite* queue; if the space is limited, it is called a *finite* queue. Size constraints are not always physical, of course. If you have ever tried to reach a busy call centre or a busy web site, you will have experienced a finite queue.

Queue discipline

This describes how the next customer to be served is selected. Many queues use a first-come, first-served discipline, especially when people arrive randomly and have similar service needs. Emergency services, for example, assign priority based on the critical nature of patients' injuries or illnesses, rather than the order of their arrival.

Service process

This includes the facilities (people, machines or both) that will service the customers. Service facilities are commonly arranged in one of the four ways shown in Figure S2.8.

The time that it takes to serve customers can also be described using a probability distribution. In this case, the exponential distribution has been found to be useful in describing the probability that the time that it takes a particular server to service a particular customer is no more than *t* time periods.

Mathematical analysis of queuing systems

The mathematical analysis of queues, known as queuing theory, is a core topic in operations research. Queuing theory provides managers with a way of analysing both customer waiting time and server utilization, in order to minimize the total costs of customer waiting time and idle server capacity.

This section introduces you to the basic elements of mathematical queuing analysis, which you can use to analyse the relationship between customer queuing systems and waiting times. To analyse a queuing system, you will need to estimate or observe the following information:

- The rate of customer arrivals
- The number of service facilities
- The number of phases

- The number of servers per facility
- The efficiency of servers
- The discipline used
- The queue arrangement.

Once you know this information, you can study the following variables:

- Queue length
- Number of customers in the system
- Waiting time in the queue
- Total time in the system
- Service facility utilization.

Example

Suppose that for the Tampopo Noodle Bar you have been asked to analyse the queue of people waiting to be seated, and that you have decided to use a single-server queue for such customers. The assumptions for the single-server model are:

- Infinite input source
- No balking or reneging
- Arrival distribution – Poisson
- Service distribution – exponential
- Queue – unlimited length
- Priority discipline – first-come, first-served.

Based on obervations of similar restaurants, we have estimated that 75 customers will arrive per hour. This figure gives us 1.25 customers arriving per minute, which is an average of 0.8 minutes between customer arrivals. If you observed a queuing system for 200 customer arrivals, you might expect to observe arrival times something like those seen in Figure S2.7.

We also estimate that the customers can be seated at a rate of 80 per hour.

We use the following notation for queuing models:

S = mean service rate per server
A = mean arrival rate
Q = average number in the queue
U = utilization of the service facility
N = number of customers
W = average time spend in the system

The average utilization of the restaurant is:

$$U = A/S = 75/80 = 93.75\%.$$

The average number of customers in the system is:

$$N = A/(S - A) = 75/(80 - 75) = 75/5 = 15 \text{ people.}$$

The average number of customers in the queue is:

$$Q = U(S - A) = 93.75 * 5 = 14.06.$$

The average time spent in the system is:

$$W = 1/S - A = 1/(80 - 75) = 1/5 = 12 \text{ minutes.}$$

Given these initial calculations, you can then explore the implications of different queuing parameters for the queuing system. For example, if you decide that the average time spent in the queue can be as much as 15 minutes, then you can work back through the calculations to see what changes to the service time or number of customers you could make. Similarly, if you decided that the utilization was too high for staff to maintain, you could see the effects of lowering it to 80 per cent.

Monte Carlo simulation

When you solved the queuing model above, you used equations that you could solve exactly. In queuing, as we depart from the single-server, single-phase model, or from looking at averages, the equations get more and more difficult.

Simulation is the process of reproducing the behaviour of a system using a model and manipulating certain variables to see their effect on the operation. Simulation models, unlike the models in Chapter S1, are descriptive rather than analytical.

Monte Carlo simulation allows us to simulate probabilistic events, such as the arrival of customers at the restaurant. The simplest form of Monte Carlo simulation is to determine what value a probabilistic variable will take by flipping a coin or other chance process. For example, the number of people arriving together in a party could be determined by rolling a die, and using that outcome to assign a value from 1 to 6.

A more common method of selecting values is using random numbers generated by either a random number table or a computer program. A cumulative probability distribution is used to convert the random number to a value.

Example

The cumulative probability distribution for a variable that is normally distributed with a mean of 5 and a standard deviation of 2 is shown in the second column of Table S2.1. For each of 10 trials, the random number in the fourth column is used to look up the number based on the cumulative probability distribution. Thus in the first trial the value of the random number is 0.862, which falls in the range for the cumulative probability distribution for at least 7 but less than 8, from 0.841 to 0.933.

Table S2.1 Monte Carlo simulation for a normal distribution with mean 5 and standard

Value	Cumulative probability	Trial	Random number	Value
1	0.022750	1	0.861997	7
2	0.066807	2	0.183346	3
3	0.158655	3	0.441703	4
4	0.308538	4	0.562898	5
5	0.500000	5	0.072431	2
6	0.691462	6	0.416745	4
7	0.841345	7	0.217615	3
8	0.933193	8	0.933714	8
9	0.977250	9	0.043755	1
10	0.993790	10	0.069527	2

Using a Monte Carlo approach, we can simulate the arrivals and service times for the noodle bar in a much more realistic fashion than in the queuing example before.

Example

Suppose that your employer would like to look at a more detailed picture of the proposed restaurant operation, down at the individual table level. The following assumptions have been made:

● Each table can seat 20 people
● The average number of people in a party is four, and is normally distributed with a standard deviation (SD) of 2

- The inter-arrival time is exponentially distributed, with a mean of 6 minutes between arrivals
- On average, each party is at the table for 35 minutes, which is normally distributed with a standard deviation of 10 minutes.

Table S2.2 shows the cumulative probabilities for the distributions above.

Your employer has asked you to determine whether these parameters are realistic, using Monte Carlo simulation. Using the random numbers in Table S2.2, simulate the arrival and departure times for the first 25 parties arriving in an evening.

Table S2.2.   Cumulative probability distributions for example

Number in party (mean = 4, SD = 2)		Inter-arrival time ($\lambda = 0.10$)		Service time (mean = 35, SD = 10)	
Value	Cumulative probability	Value	Cumulative probability	Value	Cumulative probability
1	0.066807	0	0	20	0.066807
2	0.158655	1	0.095162582	22	0.096800549
3	0.308538	2	0.181269247	24	0.135666102
4	0.500000	3	0.259181779	26	0.184060092
5	0.691462	4	0.329679954	28	0.241963578
6	0.841345	5	0.39346934	30	0.308537533
7	0.933193	6	0.451188364	32	0.382088643
8	0.977250	7	0.503414696	34	0.460172104
9	0.993790	8	0.550671036	36	0.539827896
10	0.998650	9	0.59343034	38	0.617911357
		10	0.632120559	40	0.691462467
		11	0.667128916	42	0.758036422
		12	0.698805788	44	0.815939908
		13	0.727468207	46	0.864333898
		14	0.753403036	48	0.903199451
		15	0.77686984	50	0.933192771
		16	0.798103482	52	0.955434568
		17	0.817316476	54	0.971283507
		18	0.834701112	56	0.982135643
		19	0.850431381	58	0.989275919
		20	0.864664717	60	0.99379032

Shift scheduling

Pleased with your calculations, your employer has now asked you to use shift scheduling to determine how many wait staff the noodle bar will need to hire for its initial opening. The number of people per day has been calculated, but given the tight job market and full employment in the local area, the restaurant will only get staff by offering positions with a 5-day week, including two consecutive days off.

The following technique was described by Chase *et al.* (2000) for scheduling workers in this way.

Step 1. Determine the number of workers needed per day.

Day	M	Tu	W	Th	F	Sa	Su
Workers	8	10	7	9	12	12	6

Step 2. Copy the table in Step 1, and mark the two consecutive days with the lowest worker requirement (italicized in the table). This will give the first worker's schedule of days on and off. (Note that this might fall across Sunday and Monday, as in this example!). Then subtract 1 from each of the days that is not shaded.

Day	M	Tu	W	Th	F	Sa	Su
Worker 1	8	10	7	9	12	12	6
Worker 2	8	9	6	8	11	11	6

Again, choose the two consecutive days off for the second worker by identifying the two adjacent days with the lowest worker requirement. If there are two identical pairs, as in this example, choose the pair with the lowest adjacent requirement. If there is still a tie, choose the first pair.

Day	M	Tu	W	Th	F	Sa	Su
Worker 1	8	10	7	9	12	12	6
Worker 2	8	9	6	8	11	11	6
Worker 3	7	8	6	8	10	10	5

Keep repeating this procedure until all requirements have been filled.

Day	M	Tu	W	Th	F	Sa	Su
Worker 1	8	10	7	9	12	12	6
Worker 2	8	9	6	8	11	11	6
Worker 3	7	8	6	8	10	10	5
Worker 4	7	7	5	7	9	9	5
Worker 5	6	7	5	6	8	8	4
Worker 6	6	6	4	5	7	7	4
Worker 7	5	5	4	5	6	6	3
Worker 8	5	4	3	4	5	5	3
Worker 9	4	4	3	3	4	4	2
Worker 10	4	3	2	3	3	3	2
Worker 11	3	3	2	2	2	2	1
Worker 12	2	2	1	1	1	2	1
Worker 13	1	1	1	1	0	1	0
Worker 14	0	0	0	0	0	1	0

Thus, even though the maximum number of workers on any one day is 12, it will take 14 workers to cover the week under the 5 days on and 2 days off requirement. Note that the thirteenth worker scheduled is required for only Monday to Thursday, although the worker is hired to work 5 days, and the fourteenth worker is only required for 1 day! Perhaps worker 13 could be contracted to work on Saturday instead of Friday, to minimize the total workforce required.

SUMMARY

This chapter has introduced you to a structured process for analysing service operations, and to some common models and tools that are useful for analysing them. Normann's service management system model provides a high-level model for analysing service operations in terms of five service elements and the relationship between them. You can focus further on the service delivery element, through applying the transformation model, to understand how operations can help satisfy customers and clients more effectively. Finally, because you will find queues being used to match capacity and demand in so many types of service operations, the mathematical approach to analysing queuing was introduced.

Key terms

Arrival rate
Back office
Customer contact
Core services
Front office
Monte Carlo simulation
Multiple channel
Multiple phase
Queuing theory
Service blueprinting
Service guarantee
Service operations
Service package
Service *pokayoke*
Service rate
Service time
Shift scheduling
Simulation
Single channel
Single phase
Utilization

References

Chase, R. B., Acquilano, N. J. and Jacobs, F. R.(2000). *Operations Management for Competitive Advantage,* 9th edn. McGraw-Hill.

Heskett, J. L. (ed.) (1986). The multinational development of service industries. In *Managing in the Service Economy,* pp. 135–52. Harvard Business School Press.

Normann, R. (1991). *Service Management: Strategy and Leadership in Business,* 2nd edn. John Wiley & Sons.

Sasser, W. E., Olsen, R. P. and Wyckoff, D. D. (1978). *Management of Service Operations: Text, Cases and Readings.* Allyn & Bacon.

Shostack, G. L. (1984). Designing services that deliver. *Har. Bus. Rev.,* **Jan–Feb**, 133–9.

Further reading

Fitzsimmons, J. A. and Fitzsimmons, M. J. (2001). *Service Management: Operations, Strategy, and Information Technology*, 3rd edn (see especially Chapter 11). McGraw Hill.

Voss, C., Blackmon, K., Chase, R. *et al.* (1997). *Achieving World-Class Service*. Severn–Trent/London Business School.

Zeithaml, V. A. and Bitner, M. J. (2000). *Services Marketing: Integrating Customer Focus Across the Firm*, 2nd edn. McGraw Hill.

Sites of interest

http://www.wagamama.com/
http://www.yosushi.co.uk/

Index

ABC classification, 218–21
Acceptable quality level (AQL), 277–8
Acceptance sampling, 276–9
  sampling plans, 278–9
Activity-based accounting (ABC),
  312–13
Activity-on-arrow (AOA) diagrams,
  253–5
Activity-on-node (AON) diagrams, 255
Aggregate demand, 185
Aggregate planning, 210–11, 246
Agile manufacturing, 52, 53–4, 114,
  122–3
  versus mass customization, 123
Alliances:
  Japanese companies, 365
  world-class operations, 354–7
Amazon.com, 3, 5–6, 74, 318
American System of Manufacture
  (ASM), 22–3, 24, 271
Andersen Consulting, 3
Apple Computers, 38, 41, 55, 83, 234–5
Appraisal costs, 279
Arithmetic Integrated Moving Average
  (AriMA) models, 385
Arrival process, 418–19
Assets, 20
Assignment modelling, 398–403
Attributes, 276
Automation, 172
Automobile industry, 161–2
Averages, 181–2, *see also* Moving average
  technique

Back-room operations, 170
Balanced scorecard, 313–14
Batch production, 22–3, 106, 114,
  210
Bell Telephone Labs, 271
Benchmarking, 327–32
  objectives of, 329–30
  stages of benchmarking process,
    330–2
  types of, 329
Bi-variate data, 372–3
Bin systems, 218
Body Shop, 289–90
Botchit and Leggit, 99–100
Bottlenecks, 232–3
Bradford Health Trust, 329
Bridge model, 269
British Petroleum (BP), 155–6
British Standards Institute (BSI), 287
Buffer inventory, 212
Bullwhip effect, 192–3
Business process re-engineering
  (BPR), 325–7
  process mapping, 326–7

Café Aroma, 213
Calling population, 417–18
Capacity, 163–78
  definitions, 164–5
    actual capacity, 165
    design capacity, 164
    theoretical capacity, 164

Capacity (*cont.*)
  inputs to, 166–77
    acquiring inputs and distributing
      outputs, 177, 211
    facilities, 167–71
    technology, 171
    workforce, 171–7
  management in service operations,
    188–91
    demand management, 188–90
    supply management, 190–1
  management in supply operations,
    191–3
  measurement of, 165–6
  over-capacity, 162
  strategic capacity planning, 183–8
    chase strategies, 187
    demand management strategies,
      187–8
    level capacity strategies, 186
    long-range capacity planning, 185
    medium-range capacity planning,
      185–6
Capacity requirements planning (CRP),
  224
Carrefour, 104
Caterpillar, 40
Causal forecasting methods, 180, 182
Cellular layout, 117–19, 229
Certification, 286–8
Chain-based relatives, 398
Chase strategies, 187
Chief Executive Officer (CEO), 54
  role in managing operations, 59–62
Chrysler, 162–3, 356
Co-production, 58
Communications management, in
  projects, 244
Communications technology, 29
Compaq Corporation, 38, 83
Competition, 14, 49, 52
Computer-aided design (CAD), 89–90
Computer-aided manufacturing (CAM),
  89
Computer-integrated Manufacturing
  (CIM), 123
Computers, 29, *see also* Technology
Concurrent new product development
  (CNPD), 87–8

Conformity, 275, *see also* Quality
Consumer's risk, 277
Continuous improvement, 298–9,
  318–25
  fishbone diagram, 322–3
  five-why process, 324–5
  Pareto diagrams, 323
  PDCA cycle, 321–2
  world-class operations, 346–7
Continuous inventory systems, 216–17
  economic order quantity (EOQ)
    systems, 216–17
  fixed-order quantity systems, 216
Continuous production, 107–8, 113,
  210
Control, 183
Copyright, 94
Core competences, 19
Correlation techniques, 382–4
Costs:
  cost transparency, 141
  labour costs, 311
  management of, 20–1
  of inventory, 215–16
  of quality, 279–81
  overhead costs, 310
  project cost management, 244
  supply strategy, 141
Craft production, 22, 47, 112, 178, 270
Critical Chain Methods, 241
  project planning, 256–8
Critical Path Analysis (CPA), 241,
  254–5
Critical ratio (CR), 196
Cross-functional teams, 86–7
Customer attributes, 295
Customer complaints, 293
Customer contact, 16
Customer flows, 205–9
  queuing, 206–8, 416–26
  services as customer processing, 209
Customer satisfaction, 290
Customer-driven quality, 297
Customization, 78

Daewoo, 162
DaimlerChrysler, 162–3, 351, 356
Delegated sourcing strategy, 153–4

Dell Computers, 3, 30, 41, 55, 221
Delphi technique, 180, 182
Demand, 179
  aggregate demand, 185
  forecasting, 179–82
    causal methods, 180, 182
    qualitative methods, 180, 182
    time series methods, 180, 181–2
  management strategies, 187–8
    service operations, 188–90
  matching supply and demand, 182–97
    planning and control, 183–93
    scheduling, 193–7
Deming Prize, 293–4
Dependent variable, 378
Dependent-demand inventory, 221
Design capacity, 164
Design quality, 294–6
Design right law, 94
Direct labour costs, 311
Direct Line, 74
Direct workers, 171
Disney Corp., 80, 345
Double sampling plan, 278
Downsizing, 343–4
Du Pont, 241
Dyson, 81–2

Earliest due date (EDD), 195
Earliest event time (EET), 253
Early conflict resolution (ECR), 88
Economic order quantity (EOQ)
    systems, 216–17
Economies of scale, 103, 168–70
Economy, 309–10
Effectiveness measures, 141, 311
Efficiency measures, 140, 141, 310–11
Efficient Consumer Response (ECR),
    192
EMI, 75
Employees, 28
  involvement of, 298
  see also Human resource management;
    Workforce
Enterprise Resource Planning (ERP),
    123, 226, 316
Environment, 29
  environmental responsibility, 359–62

Ethics, 28
  world-class operations, 357–62
    environmental responsibility,
      359–62
    operations management and, 357–9
European Quality Award, 294
External demand, 179
External failure costs, 280, 281

Facilities:
  economies of scale, 168–70
  layout, 170–1
  location, 167–8
Farmhouse Cheesemakers' Cooperative,
    265–7
Federal Express, 58, 345
Finished-goods inventories, 212
Finite loading, 194
First come, first served (FCFS), 195
First Direct Bank, 67–8, 83, 293
First-mover advantage, 74
Fishbone diagram, 322–3
Five-why process, 324–5
Fixed time period systems, 217
Fixed-based relatives, 398
Fixed-order quantity systems, 216
Fixed-position layout, 114–15
Flexible manufacturing systems (FMS),
    110–11, 123
Flexible specialization, 52
Flows, see Operations flow management
Ford, 23–4, 86, 176, 350–1
Forecasting, 394–5
  demand, 179–82
    causal methods, 180, 182
    qualitative methods, 180, 182
    time series methods, 180, 181–2
  seasonal variation and, 391–4
    calculation of seasonal variation,
      391–3
    seasonally adjusted time series,
      393–4
Front-room operations, 170
Futurists, 182

Gantt chart, 196–7, 251–2
Gaps model, 290–2

General Motors, 23–4, 39, 123–4
Gillette, 78, 107
Globalization, 28

Hewlett Packard, 46, 121
Hollola Roll Finishing plant, 306–7
Honda, 38, 41, 320, 351–2
Hospitals, 203
House of quality matrix, 295, 296
Human resource management, 19–20
    downsizing, 343–4
    in world-class operations, 342–4
    project human resource management, 244
    see also Employees; Workforce
Hybrid cells, 117–19

IBM, 38, 349
Independent variable, 378
Independent-demand inventory, 221
Index numbers, 395–8
    definition of, 396–7
    index relatives, 397–8
        time series of relatives, 398
    notation, 397
Indirect workers, 171
Infinite loading, 194
Information flows, 210–11
Information technology, *see* Computers; Technology
Innovation, 20, 68, 69, 71
    Japanese companies, 365–6
    world-class operations, 347–53
    see also New product development (NPD)
Inspection:
    quality control, 276
    regression line calculation, 377
Intangibility, 16
Intellectual property, 94
Internal demand, 179
Internal failure costs, 280
Invention, 69
Inventory, 211–22
    costs of, 215–16
    location of, 212–14

management of, 215–22
    ABC classification, 218–21
    continuous inventory systems, 216–17
    independent- and dependent-demand inventory, 221–2
    periodic inventory systems, 217–18
    reasons for, 214–15
Investment, 48–9
Ishikawa diagram, 322

Japanese production systems, 24–5, 75, 272–3, 319–20, 363–6
    alliances, 365
    innovation, 365–6
    making best use of limited resources, 364
    manufacturing focus, 363–4
    recent trends, 366
    strategy, 364–5
Jobbing, 105, 113
Jobs, 173
Just-in-time (JIT) production, 24, 25, 50, 136, 227–32
    comparison with manufacturing resources planning (MRP), 231–2
    origins of, 227–8
    requirements of, 230–1

Kaizen, *see* Continuous improvement
Kanban production control, 229–30
Key Performance Indicators (PKI), 8
KeyLine, 208
Komatsu, 40

Labour costs, 311
Labour specialization, 173
Land Rover, 78
Lane Group, 290
Last arrived, first processed (LAFP), 195–6
Latest event time (LET), 253, 254
Layout, *see* Facilities; Processes
Leadership, quality and, 298
Lean production, 52, 135
    world-class operations and, 338–42
Lean supply management, 135

Learning curves, 176–7
Least slack time, 196
Least squares method, 377–82, 385–6
Lexus, 30
Lincoln Electric, 176
Line operations, 106–7, 113, 210
Linear functions, 374–6
    determining the gradient of a given
        line, 375–6
Linear regression, 182
Loading, 194
Longest processing time (LPT), 195
Lot tolerance percent defective (LTPD)
    level, 277–8
Lucent Technologies, 257

McDonald's, 3, 29, 207
Make-to-order, 213
Make-to-stock, 213
Malcolm Baldrige National Quality
    Award (MBNQA), 294
Manufacturing operations, 14–18
    capacity measurement, 165
    challenges for operations
        management, 30–2
    inventories, 212
    Japanese companies, 363–4
    materials flows, 209–10
    process design trends, 120–3
        agile manufacturing, 122–3
        mass customization, 121–2, 123
Manufacturing resource planning
    (MRP), 225–6
    comparison with JIT, 231–2
    limits of, 226–7
Manufacturing strategy, 47–57
    emergence of the strategic
        importance of operations, 49–51
    modern era, 52–5
    strategic resonance, 55–7
Manufacturing transformation, 9, 10
Manufacturing-based quality, 268
Market pull, 76
Market segment, 411–12
Market-led strategies, 45
Martin's Aeronautics, 273, 340
Mass customization, 52, 114, 121–2
    versus agile manufacturing, 123

Mass production, 24, 47–8, 49, 178, 353
Mass services, 111–12
Materials flows, 209–10
    management of, 210
    see also Inventory
Materials requirements planning systems
    (MRP), 222–4
Mazda, 110–11
Mergers and alliances, world-class
    operations, 354–7
Meta suppliers, 133
Method study, 172, 174–5
Microsoft, 171
Modular design, 96
Mongolian Wok, 59
Monte Carlo simulation, 422–4
Motorola, 74
Moving average technique, 181–2, 385,
    388–90
    centring a moving average series,
        389–90
Multi-skilling, 172, 229
Multi-variate data, 373, 376
Multiple sourcing, 152–3
Mumford's Machine Tools, 198–9
Mystery shopping, 293

National Patent Office, 94
New product development (NPD), 69–72
    best practice in, 85–94
        concurrent engineering, 87–8
        cross-functional teams, 86–7
        process integration, 88–90
        quality function deployment, 92–4
        strategic management of
            development projects, 90
        supplier involvement, 86
    importance of, 72–6
        failure factor, 75–6
        time-to-market, 74–5
    process of, 76–85
        developing the product concept,
            79–82
        developing the product design, 82–5
        filters, 78, 79
        testing and delivery, 85
    success measures, 73
    tools and techniques, 90–1

NHS Drop-in Centres, 203, 208
Nokia, 3
Non-profit organizations, capacity
    management, 166
Noodle bars, 406–7
Nordstrom's, 7–8
NUMMI plant, 173, 174

Oakmead Social Services office, 125–7
Obodex Computers Limited, 300–1
Operating characteristics curve (OC),
    278
Operational research techniques,
    398–403
Operations, 3–4, 21–2
  as an open system, 26–8
  definition, 5–6
  models of, 8–11
    manufacturing transformation, 9, 10
    service transformation, 9, 10
  strategic importance of, 49–51
  typology of, 13–18
  see also Manufacturing operations;
      Service operations
Operations flow management, 205–11
  computerized systems, 222–7
    enterprise resource planning
        (ERP), 226
    manufacturing resource planning
        (MRP), 225–7
    materials requirements planning
        systems (MRP), 222–4
  customer flows, 205–9
    queuing, 206–8
    services as customer processing, 209
  information flows, 210–11
  materials flows, 209–10
  theory of constraints, 232–4
  see also Inventory; Just-in-time
      production
Operations management, 6–7
  current issues, 26–8
    new scope of operations
        management, 26
    operations as an open system, 26–8
  environmental responsibility and,
      359–62
  ethics and, 357–9

history of, 21–6
new pressures on, 28–9
role of Chief Executive Officer
    (CEO), 59–62
Operations managers, 6
  new imperatives, 29
  responsibilities of, 19–21, 52–3, 100,
      203–4, 342
    assets, 20
    costs, 20–1
    human resources, 19–20
  role of, 11–13, 100
    strategic role, 46–7
Operations researchers, 120
Operations strategy, 101–2
Optimized Production Technology
    (OPT), 232–4
Orange, 80
Organizational complexity, 243
Organizational structure, 141–2
  supply strategy and, 142–3
Over-capacity, 162
Overhead costs, 310

P-chart, 285
Parallel sourcing, 154–5
Pareto principle, 218, 323
Parkway Theatre, Oakland, 187–8
Patents, 94
PDCA cycle, 320, 321–2, 330
Performance, 7, 8
  objectives, 29
  see also Continuous improvement;
      Radical performance
      improvement
Performance measurement, 307–18
  designing a performance
      measurement system, 314–16
  enlightened performance measures in
      practice, 316–18
  historical perspective, 309–11
    economy, 309–10
    effectiveness, 311
    efficiency, 310–11
  new approaches, 311–14
    activity-based accounting (ABC),
        312–13
    balanced scorecard, 313–14

service operations issues, 317
supply issues, 140–1, 317–18
Periodic inventory systems, 217–18
Phased Delivery Processes (PDP), 249
Pizza Hut, 293
Planning, 183–4, 210
    aggregate planning, 210–11
    project planning, *see* Project
        management
    strategic capacity planning, *see* Capacity
Platform products, 77–8
Policies, 7–8
Practices, 7–8
Pre-determined motion time studies
    (PMTS), 173
Prêt a Manger, 212–13
Prevention costs, 279
Price relative index, 397
Process control, 282–6
    control charts, 283–6
        attribute charts, 285–6
        for variables, 283–5
    process capability, 286
    statistical process control (SPC), 282,
        286
Process design, 101–3
Process intensive developments, 78
Process mapping, 326–7
Processes, 7, 25–6
    definition of, 6
    manufacturing process design trends,
        120–3
        agile manufacturing, 122–3
        mass customization, 121–2, 123
    physical layout, 103, 113–20
        fixed position layout, 114–15
        hybrid process/product cell,
            117–19
        process choice and, 113–14,
            119–20
        process layout, 115–16
        product layout, 116–17
    process integration, 88–90
    service processes, 111–12
    technology role in process design,
        123–4
    types of, 103–11
        batch, 22–3, 106, 114, 210
        continuous, 107–8, 113, 210

flexible manufacturing systems
    (FMS), 110–11, 123
    job, 105, 113
    line, 106–7, 113, 210
    project, 104–5, 113, 210, 239–40
Producer's risk, 277
Product layout, 116–17
Product moment correlation, 382
Product-based quality, 268
Products:
    life cycle, 69–71, 108–10
    platform products, 77–8
    see also New product development
        (NPD)
Professional services, 111, 114
Programme Evaluation and Review
    Technology (PERT), 241
Programme of work, 245–6
Project management, 241–2
    communications management,
        244
    cost management, 244
    designing the project process,
        245–7
    human resource management,
        244
    integration management, 244
    key project processes, 242–5
    procurement management, 244
    project planning, 246–58
        activity-on-arrow (AOA) diagrams,
            253–5
        activity-on-node (AON) diagrams,
            255
        critical chain project planning,
            256–8
        Gantt charts, 251–2
        overall plan, 247–8
        project planning software, 255–6,
            260
        stage-gate planning, 249–50
        work breakdown structure
            (WBS), 248–9
    risk management, 244
    scope management, 244
    time management, 244
Projects, 104–5, 113, 210, 239–40
    project complexity, 243–5
Prototypes, 85, 89

Public Private Finance (PPF), 134
Purchasing, 28, 131, 132–3
  definition, 132
  evolution to supply management,
    133–46
    economic factors, 135
    political factors, 134–5
    social/image changes, 135–6
    technology factors, 136
  see also Supply

Qualitative forecasting methods, 180,
  182
Quality, 231, 267–9
  cost of, 279–81
  definitions of, 267–9
  design quality, 294–6
  historical perspective, 270–5
    quality assurance, 271
    quality control, 270–1
    quality management, 272–3
    recent trends, 273–5
  quality at the source, 288
  quality management approaches,
    275–86
    acceptance sampling, 276–9
    inspection, 276
    process control, 282–6
  service quality, 288–93
    resolving problems, 292–3
    Servqual model, 290–2
  standards and certification, 286–8
  total quality management (TQM),
    296–300
  world-class operations, 344–7
  see also Performance measurement
Quality awards programmes, 293–4
Quality circles (QCs), 274, 319–20
Quality function deployment (QFD),
  92–4, 295
Quantity relative index, 398
Queuing, 205–8, 416–26
  importance of analysing queuing
    systems, 416–17
  mathematical analysis of, 417–22
    arrival process, 418–19
    calling population, 417–18
    queue configuration, 419–20

    queue discipline, 420
    service process, 420
  Monte Carlo simulation, 422–4
  number of queues versus number of
    servers, 207
  single-stage versus multiple stage
    queues, 208
Quicken, 83

Radical performance improvement,
  325–32
  benchmarking, 327–32
    objectives of, 329–30
    stages of, 330–2
    types of, 329
  business process re-engineering
    (BPR), 325–7
    process mapping, 326–7
RAND Corporation, 241
Range chart (R-chart), 285
Rank correlation, 382
Raw materials inventories, 212
Regression analysis, 376–82
  least squares method, 378–82, 385–6
  obtaining a regression line, 377–8
Relationships, in supply chains, 141
Renault, 162, 351
Resource constraints, 84
Resource management, 162, 203–4,
  308
  Japanese companies, 364
  manufacturing resource planning
    (MRP), 225–6
  see also Capacity; Operations flow
    management
Resource-based strategies, 45–6
Resource-to-order, 213
Reverse engineering, 95–6
Risk management, projects, 244
Rolls-Royce, 268
RS Components, 130–1

Sampling plans, 278–9
Scheduling, 193–7
  Gantt chart, 196–7
  project time management, 244
  shift scheduling, 425–6

Scientific management, 23, 173
Seasonal variation:
  calculation, 391–3
  seasonally adjusted time series,
    393–4
Sega, 4
Self-service, 54
Semi-averages technique, 377, 385,
  386–8
Sequencing, 194–6
Sequential sampling plan, 279
Service blueprinting, 414–16
Service factories, 112
Service fail-safing, 292–3
Service guarantees, 58, 292
Service operations, 14–19, 54
  analysis of, 414–22
    Monte Carlo simulation, 422–4
    queuing, 416–22
    service blueprinting, 414–16
    shift scheduling, 425–6
  capacity management, 188–91
    demand management, 188–90
    supply management, 190–1
  capacity measurement, 165–6
  challenges for operations
    management, 29–30
  customer processing, 209, see also
    Queuing
  definition of, 18
  importance of, 18–19
  management system analysis,
    410–13
    culture and philosophy, 411
    market segment, 411–12
    service concept, 412
    service delivery system, 412–13
    service image, 412
  materials flows, 209–10
  performance measures, 317
  service processes, 111–12
  strategies, 57–9
Service package, 413
Service quality, 288–93
  reliability, 286
  resolving problems, 292–3
  Servqual model, 290–2
Service recovery, 58, 292, 293
Service shops, 111

Service standards, 288
Service transformation, 9, 10
Servqual model, 290–2
Shell, 28
Shift scheduling, 425–6
Shortest processing time (SPT), 195
Simulation, 422
  Monte Carlo simulation, 422–4
Single sampling plan, 278
Single sourcing, 151–2
Sky TV, 3
Small-lot production, 230
Smith, Adam, 22
Social Services, 125–7
Sony, 3
Sourcing strategy, see Supply
Specialization of labour, 173
Specifications, 275–6
Staff, see Employees; Workforce
Stage-gate planning, 249–50
Standard time, 173
Standards, 286–8, 310
  environmental standards, 360–2
Statistical approaches, 372–94
  correlation techniques, 382–4
  linear functions, 374–6
  regression analysis, 376–82
  time series modelling, 384–91
Statistical process control (SPC), 282,
  286
Strategic operations, 52
Strategic positioning matrix, 147–8
Strategic resonance, 55–7
Strategic Transition model, 143–6
Strategy, 39–46
  elements of, 46–7
  Japanese companies, 364–5
  market-led versus resource-based
    strategies, 45–6
  new product development, 90
  operations strategy, 101–3
  origins of, 40–1
  project strategy, 245
  responsibility for, 43–4
  service operations strategy, 57–9
  strategy formulation, 41–3
  see also Manufacturing strategy
Subway sandwich shop, 213
Supersonic Transport project, 182

Suppliers:
capacity and capabilities of, 103
capacity management, 191–3
capacity measurement, 166
involvement in new product
development, 86
meta suppliers, 133
performance measurement, 317–18
Supplies, 212
Supply, 28, 132–6
as a strategic process, 137–40
definition, 132
management in service operations,
190–1
matching supply and demand, 182–97
planning and control, 183–93
scheduling, 193–7
position in supply chain, 14
project procurement management, 244
sourcing strategies, 146–55
delegated sourcing strategy, 153–4
multiple sourcing, 152–3
parallel sourcing, 154–5
positioning matrix, 147–8
single sourcing, 151–2
strategic supply wheel, 139–43
cost/benefit, 141
organizational structure, 141–3
performance measures, 140–1
relationship portfolio, 141
skills and competencies, 143
Transition model, 143–6
see also Purchasing; Supply chain
management
Supply chain management, 27–8, 131,
136–7
evolution from purchasing, 133–46
economic factors, 135
political factors, 134–5
social/image changes, 135–6
technology factors, 136
see also Supply
Swatch watches, 77–8
Sydney Olympic Games, 238–9
Sydney Opera House, 83

Tangibility, 16
Tasks, 173

Taylorism, 23
Technical constraints, 84
Technology, 53–4, 89–90
capacity and, 171
complexity, 243
purchasing and, 136
role in process design, 123–4
Technology push, 77
Tequila, 177
Theoretical capacity, 164
Theory of constraints, 232–4, 256
3M Corporation, 81, 82
Throughput management, see
Operations flow management
Time and work measurement, 172–3
Time series methods, 180, 181–2,
384–91
comparison of techniques, 391
forecasting, 394–5
method of least squares regression,
385–6
method of semi-averages, 386–8
moving average, 388–90
seasonally adjusted time series, 393–4
techniques for finding the trend, 385
time series of relatives, 398
Time-to-market, 74–5
Toronto Dominion Bank, 292
Total quality control, 273
Total Quality Management (TQM), 25,
136, 274, 296–300, 319
Toyota, 3, 34–5, 86–7, 88, 227–8,
319–20, 324–5, 352–3
Trademark registration, 94
Transcendent quality, 267–8
Transformation process, 8–11
Transition model, 143–6
Triumph Motorcycles, 38, 95–6

User-based quality, 268
Utzon, Jørn, 83

Valmet Corporation, 306
Value analysis, 295–6
Value engineering, 295–6
Value-based quality, 268
Variable measures, 276

Variables, 372–3, 378
Variances, 310–11
Variety of products, 13–14
Vendor assessment schemes, 140
Very Clever Software Company, 258–9
Volkswagen (VW), 71, 86
Volume, 13–14
Volvo Cars, 119–20

Wagamama, 408–9
West Country Farmhouse
    Cheesemakers' Cooperative, 265–7
Wok-Wok, 409–10
Work breakdown structure (WBS), 248–9
Work-in-progress (WIP) inventories, 212
Workforce, 171–3
  capacity measurement, 172–3
    image problem of work study,
        173–4
    learning curves, 176–7
    method study, 174–5
    work measurement, 175–6

shift scheduling, 425–6
see also Employees; Human resource
    management
World-class manufacturing (WCM), 136
World-class operations, 55, 337–66
  becoming world-class, 353–4
  ethical issues, 357–62
    environmental responsibility,
        359–62
    operations management and, 357–9
  human resource management role,
      342–4
  innovation role, 347–53
  lean production and, 338–42
  mergers and alliances, 354–7
  quality role, 344–7

X-chart, 284–5
Xerox, 328

Yamaha, 41
Yield management, 187–8
Yo! Sushi, 410